Global Environmental Politics

Dilemmas in World Politics
Series Editor: Jennifer Sterling-Folker, University of Connecticut

Why is it difficult to achieve the universal protection of human rights? How can democratization be achieved so that it is equitable and lasting? Why does agreement on global environmental protection seem so elusive? How does the concept of gender play a role in the shocking inequalities of women throughout the globe? Why do horrific events such genocide or ethnic conflicts recur or persist? These are the sorts of questions that confront policy makers and students of contemporary international politics alike. They are dilemmas because they are enduring problems in world affairs that are difficult to resolve.

These are the types of dilemmas at the heart of the Dilemmas in World Politics series. Each book in the Dilemmas in World Politics series addresses a challenge or problem in world politics that is topical, recurrent, and not easily solved. Each is structured to cover the historical and theoretical aspects of the dilemma, as well as the policy alternatives for and future direction of the problem. The books are designed as supplements to introductory and intermediate courses in international relations. The books in the Dilemmas in World Politics series encourage students to engage in informed discussion of current policy issues.

BOOKS IN THIS SERIES

SIXTH EDITION

Global Environmental Politics

PAMELA S. CHASEK

DAVID L. DOWNIE

JANET WELSH BROWN

WESTVIEW
PRESS

A MEMBER OF THE PERSEUS BOOKS GROUP

Westview Press was founded in 1975 in Boulder, Colorado, by notable publisher and intellectual Fred Praeger. Westview Press continues to publish scholarly titles and high-quality undergraduate- and graduate-level textbooks in core social science disciplines. With books developed, written, and edited with the needs of serious nonfiction readers, professors, and students in mind, Westview Press honors its long history of publishing books that matter.

Published by Westview Press,
A Member of the Perseus Books Group

Find us on the World Wide Web at www.westviewpress.com.

Every effort has been made to secure required permissions for all text, images, maps, and other art reprinted in this volume.

Westview Press books are available at special discounts for bulk purchases in the United States by corporations, institutions, and other organizations. For more information, please contact the Special Markets Department at the Perseus Books Group, 2300 Chestnut Street, Suite 200, Philadelphia, PA 19103, or call (800) 810-145, ext. 5000, or e-mail special.markets@perseusbooks.com.

Library of Congress Cataloging-in-Publication Data

Chasek, Pamela S., 1961–
  Global environmental politics / Pamela S. Chasek, David L. Downie,
Janet Welsh Brown. — Sixth edition.
      pages cm. — (Dilemmas in world politics)
  Includes bibliographical references.
  ISBN 978-0-8133-4896-4 (pbk.) — ISBN 978-0-8133-4897-1 (e-book)
  1. Environmental policy. I. Downie, David Leonard. II. Brown, Janet Welsh.
  III. Title.
  GE170.C46 2010
  363.7'056—dc23
                          2013002230

10 9 8 7 6 5 4 3 2

Contents

4   The Development of Environmental Regimes: Natural Resources, Species, and Habitats   175

5   Effective Environmental Regimes: Obstacles and Opportunities   237

6   Environmental Politics and Sustainable Development   283

7   The Future of Global Environmental Politics   321

Illustrations

Photographs

Boxes

Acknowledgments

This book has been made possible by the inspiration, encouragement, and assistance of our colleagues at Columbia University, Fairfield University, Manhattan College, the *Earth Negotiations Bulletin*, and the United Nations. We thank Gareth Porter and Janet Welsh Brown for initiating this book and then entrusting us to carry on. We also want to thank our editor, Anthony Wahl, and Westview Press for their support and positive attitude throughout this process.

In addition to all our colleagues who were thanked in earlier editions of this book, we thank Mary Brown, Scott MacKenzie, Colleen Reilly, and Sofia Trevino for their research assistance. We are grateful to the peer reviewers and users of previous editions who have provided their feedback and suggestions. Last, but certainly not least, David Downie thanks his family—Laura Whitman, William Downie, and Lindsey Downie—for making the good things in his life possible. Pamela Chasek thanks her family—Kimo, Sam, and Kai Goree—for all of their patience, support, and love.

—Pamela Chasek
David Downie

Acronyms

AOSIS	Alliance of Small Island States
APEC	Asia-Pacific Economic Cooperation
CBD	Convention on Biological Diversity
CDM	Clean Development Mechanism
CFCs	chlorofluorocarbons
CITES	Convention on International Trade in Endangered Species of Wild Fauna and Flora
CO$_2$	carbon dioxide
COFI	Committee on Fisheries (FAO)
COP	Conference of the Parties
CSD	Commission on Sustainable Development
CTE	Committee on Trade and Environment (WTO)
EC	European Community
EEZs	exclusive economic zones
ETMs	environmental trade measures
EU	European Union
FAO	Food and Agriculture Organization of the United Nations
FSC	Forest Stewardship Council
FTA	financial and technical assistance
G-77	Group of 77
GATT	General Agreement on Tariffs and Trade
GDP	gross domestic product
GEF	Global Environment Facility

GHGs	greenhouse gases
GM	Global Mechanism
GNI	gross national income
GNP	gross national product
HCFCs	hydrochlorofluorocarbons
HFCs	hydrofluorocarbons
HIPC	heavily indebted poor countries
IFCS	Intergovernmental Forum on Chemical Safety
IFF	Intergovernmental Forum on Forests
IGOs	intergovernmental organizations
IISD	International Institute for Sustainable Development
IMF	International Monetary Fund
INC	Intergovernmental Negotiating Committee
IOMC	Inter-Organization Programme for the Sound Management of Chemicals
IPCC	Intergovernmental Panel on Climate Change
IPEN	International POPs Elimination Network
IPF	Intergovernmental Panel on Forests
IPR	intellectual property rights
IUCN	International Union for the Conservation of Nature and Natural Resources/World Conservation Union
IUU	illegal, unreported, and unregulated
IWC	International Whaling Commission
LMOs	living modified organisms
MARPOL	International Convention for the Prevention of Pollution from Ships
MDGs	Millennium Development Goals
MEAs	multilateral environmental agreements

MMPA	Marine Mammal Protection Act
MOP	Meeting of the Parties
MSC	Marine Stewardship Council
NAFO	Northwest Atlantic Fisheries Organization
NEPAD	New Partnership for Africa's Development
NGOs	nongovernmental organizations
NIEO	New International Economic Order
OAS	Organization of American States
ODA	official development assistance
ODS	ozone-depleting substance(s)
OECD	Organization for Economic Cooperation and Development
PFOS	perfluorooctane sulfonate
PIC	prior informed consent
POPRC	Persistent Organic Pollutants Review Committee
POPs	persistent organic pollutants
SAICM	Strategic Approach to International Chemicals Management
TEDs	turtle excluder devices
TRAFFIC	Trade Records Analysis of Flora and Fauna in Commerce
UNCCD	United Nations Convention to Combat Desertification
UNCED	United Nations Conference on Environment and Development
UNCSD	United Nations Conference on Sustainable Development
UNCTAD	United Nations Conference on Trade and Development
UNDP	United Nations Development Programme
UNEP	United Nations Environment Programme
UNFCCC	United Nations Framework Convention on Climate Change
UNFF	United Nations Forum on Forests
UNGA	United Nations General Assembly

WHO	World Health Organization
WMO	World Meteorological Organization
WSSD	World Summit on Sustainable Development
WTO	World Trade Organization
WWF	World Wildlife Fund/Worldwide Fund for Nature

Chronology

1800   Atmospheric carbon dioxide (CO_2) and methane concentrations in the atmosphere hover around 270 to 290 parts per million (ppm) and 700 parts per billion (ppb), respectively. Most scientists today use these numbers as a pre–Industrial Revolution baseline for comparison.

1827   Jean-Baptiste Joseph Fourier, a French mathematician and physicist, publishes perhaps the first paper speculating on the existence of what we now call the *natural greenhouse effect*.

1859   John Tyndall, an Irish physicist, publishes results of laboratory experiments detailing the relative radiative forcing (greenhouse effect) of different gases in the atmosphere, including CO_2.

1872   Yellowstone National Park, the first national park in the United States, is created.

1896   Svante Arrhenius, a Swedish scientist, publishes an article that concludes that doubling the amount of CO_2 in the atmosphere would raise temperatures by 5 to 6 degrees Celsius.

1900 CO_2 concentration in the atmosphere reaches 295 ppm.

1902   The Convention for the Protection of Birds Useful to Agriculture is signed.

1903   The first international conservation NGO is formed: the Society for the Preservation of the Wild Fauna of the Empire.

1909   US president Theodore Roosevelt convenes the North American Conservation Conference in Washington, DC.

1911   The Treaty for the Preservation and Protection of Fur Seals is signed.

1913   The Commission for the International Protection of Nature is founded.

1933   The London Convention on the Preservation of Fauna and Flora in Their Natural State is signed.

1938   G. S. Callendar revisits Arrhenius's 1896 publication and argues that increases in CO_2 concentration could explain recent warming trends.

1940   The Convention on Nature Protection and Wildlife Preservation in the Western Hemisphere is signed.

1945   The United Nations is established.

1946   The International Convention for the Regulation of Whaling is signed; the International Whaling Commission (IWC) is created.

1947   The International Union for the Conservation of Nature (IUCN) is established, becoming the first international nongovernmental organization with a global outlook on environmental problems.

1949   The International Convention for the Northwest Atlantic Fisheries is signed.

1950   The World Meteorological Organization (WMO) is created.

—   The International Convention for the Protection of Birds is signed.

1952   A toxic mix of dense fog and sooty, black coal smoke kills at least four thousand people, and perhaps as many as twelve thousand, in the worst of London's "killer fogs."

1954   The International Convention for the Prevention of Pollution of the Sea by Oil is signed.

1956   The European Economic Community is established.

—   Roger Revelle and Charles David Keeling publish a paper on CO_2, showing the trend of increasing atmospheric concentrations over the past century.

1962   Rachel Carson publishes *Silent Spring*.

1963   The Agreement for the Protection of the Rhine Against Pollution is signed.

1967   The supertanker *Torrey Canyon* runs aground in the English Channel, causing a massive oil spill.

1969   The US Congress passes the National Environmental Policy Act (NEPA).

1971   The Ramsar Convention on Wetlands of International Importance is signed.

1972   The United Nations Conference on the Human Environment is convened in Stockholm.

—   The United Nations Environment Programme (UNEP) is created.

—   *The Limits to Growth* report is published.

— The Convention on the Prevention of Marine Pollution by Dumping of Wastes and Other Matter (London Convention) is signed.

— The Convention for the Conservation of Antarctic Seals is signed.

1973 The Convention on International Trade in Endangered Species of Wild Fauna and Flora (CITES) is signed.

— The International Convention for the Prevention of Pollution from Ships (MARPOL) is signed.

— The US Endangered Species Conservation Act becomes law.

1974 M. J. Molina and F. S. Rowland publish their theory that chlorofluorocarbons (CFCs) threaten the ozone layer.

— The World Population Conference is held in Bucharest, Romania.

1975 The UNEP Regional Seas Programme is created.

1976 The Convention for the Protection of the Mediterranean Sea against Pollution is signed.

— The UNEP International Register of Potentially Toxic Chemicals is established.

1977 The United Nations Conference on Desertification adopts the Plan of Action to Combat Desertification.

1979 The Convention on the Conservation of Migratory Species is signed.

— The First World Climate Conference, convened in Geneva by the World Meteorological Organization, UNEP, and the International Council for Science, warns of the danger of global warming.

1980 The Convention on the Conservation of Antarctic Marine Living Resources is signed.

— The World Conservation Strategy is launched by IUCN and UNEP.

— The *Global 2000 Report to the President* is published.

1982 Formal negotiations begin on protection of the ozone layer.

— IWC approves a three-year phaseout of commercial whaling.

1984 The International Tropical Timber Agreement (ITTA) is signed.

— The Union Carbide disaster occurs in Bhopal, India.

1985 The Vienna Convention for Protection of the Ozone Layer is signed.

— The Antarctic ozone-hole discovery is published in *Nature*.

— Canadian scientists discover abnormally high levels of persistent organic pollutants, or POPs, in some Inuit communities in northern Canada, revealing the global transport of toxic chemicals.

— Parties to the London Convention vote to ban all further dumping of low-level radioactive wastes in oceans until it is proven safe.

1987 The Montreal Protocol on Substances That Deplete the Ozone Layer is signed.

— The Report of the World Commission on Environment and Development (the Brundtland Report) is published as *Our Common Future*.

1988 The world's governments agree to establish the Intergovernmental Panel on Climate Change (IPCC).

1989 The Basel Convention on the Control of Transboundary Movements of Hazardous Wastes and Their Disposal is signed; the European Community reaches agreement with Africa, Caribbean, and Pacific states to ban hazardous waste exports to countries without the capacity to dispose of them safely.

— Sixty-seven governments attending the Ministerial Conference on Atmospheric Pollution and Climate Change call for stabilizing CO_2 emissions by 2000.

— CITES bans trade in African elephant ivory products.

1990 Parties to the Montreal Protocol significantly strengthen the Montreal Protocol and establish the Multilateral Fund.

— The IWC extends the ban on commercial whaling.

— The IPCC releases its First Assessment Report, concluding that the average global surface temperature has increased by 0.3 to 0.6 degrees Celsius since 1980.

1991 The Bamako Convention on the Ban of the Import into Africa and the Control of Transboundary Movement and Management of Hazardous Wastes within Africa is signed.

— The Global Environment Facility is established.

— The Protocol on Environmental Protection to the Antarctic Treaty is signed.

— The Volatile Organic Compounds Protocol to LRTAP is signed.

1992 The United Nations Conference on Environment and Development convenes in Rio de Janeiro.

— The United Nations Framework Convention on Climate Change is signed.

— The Convention on Biological Diversity is signed.

— The UN establishes the Commission on Sustainable Development.

1993 The United Nations Conference on Straddling and Highly Migratory Fish Stocks convenes.

1994 The United Nations Convention to Combat Desertification is signed.

— The General Agreement on Tariffs and Trade Uruguay Round concludes negotiations.

— The International Conference on Population and Development is held in Cairo.

— The Global Conference on the Sustainable Development of Small Island Developing States meets in Barbados.

1995 The World Conference on Social Development convenes in Copenhagen.

— The Agreement on the Conservation and Management of Straddling Fish Stocks and Highly Migratory Fish Stocks is signed.

— The World Trade Organization is established.

1996 The IPCC releases its Second Assessment Report, which concludes that there is a discernible human influence on the global climate.

1997 The UN General Assembly Special Session convenes to review the implementation of Agenda 21.

— CITES votes to reopen the ivory trade in Botswana, Namibia, and Zimbabwe.

— The Kyoto Protocol to the Framework Convention on Climate Change is signed.

1998 The Rotterdam Convention on the Prior Informed Consent Procedure for Certain Hazardous Chemicals and Pesticides in International Trade is signed.

1999 The Protocol on Liability and Compensation to the Basel Convention on the Control of Transboundary Movements and Hazardous Wastes and Their Disposal is adopted.

2000 The Cartagena Protocol on Biosafety is adopted by the Conference of the Parties to the Convention on Biological Diversity.

— The United Nations Forum on Forests is established.

— The Millennium Summit is held at the United Nations in New York.

2001   The Stockholm Convention on Persistent Organic Pollutants is signed.

—   The IPCC's Third Assessment Report concludes that the evidence of
       humanity's influence on the global climate is stronger than ever.

—   The Food and Agriculture Organization of the United Nations adopts the
       International Treaty on Plant Genetic Resources for Food and
       Agriculture.

2002   The World Summit on Sustainable Development is held in Johannesburg.

2003   The African Ministerial Conference on the Environment adopts the New
       Partnership for Africa's Development Environment Action Plan.

2004 CO_2 concentration in the atmosphere reaches an unprecedented 379 ppm.

2005   The Kyoto Protocol enters into force.

—   The Millennium Ecosystem Assessment is released; 1,300 experts from
       ninety-five countries provide scientific information concerning the
       consequences of ecosystem change for human well-being.

—   The European Union's Greenhouse Gas Emission Trading Scheme (EU
       ETS) begins operation as the world's first multicountry, multisector
       greenhouse-gas (GHG) emission trading scheme.

2006   The ITTA successor agreement (ITTA 2006) is adopted in Geneva.

—   UNEP adopts the Strategic Approach to International Chemicals
       Management.

—   The Stern Report makes a convincing economic case that the costs of
       inaction on climate change will be up to twenty times greater than the costs
       of measures required to address the issue today.

—   NASA reports that recovery of the ozone layer has begun as a result of
       reduced emissions of CFCs under the Montreal Protocol.

—   Review Conference of the Agreement for the Implementation of the
       Provisions of the United Nations Convention on the Law of the Sea
       (UNCLOS) relating to the Conservation and Management of Straddling
       Fish Stocks and Highly Migratory Fish Stocks (UN Fish Stocks Agreement)
       takes place in New York.

2007   The IPCC Fourth Assessment Report confirms that climate change is
       occurring, that the human contribution to this change is unequivocal, and
       that impacts are already apparent and will increase as temperatures rise.

—   The Nobel Committee awards the 2007 Nobel Peace Prize to the IPCC and
       former US vice president Albert Gore for their efforts to disseminate
       knowledge about climate change.

— The European Union announces its intention by 2020 to cut its GHG emissions by 20 percent from 1990 levels and require that 20 percent of total energy consumption come from renewable energies.

2009 The parties to the Stockholm Convention significantly expand the regime, limiting the production and use of nine additional toxic substances.

2010 Simultaneous Extraordinary Meetings of the Conferences of the Parties to the Basel, Rotterdam, and Stockholm conventions (ExCOPs) convene.

— The Resumed Review Conference of the Agreement for the Implementation of UNCLOS relating to the UN Fish Stocks Agreement convenes.

— The first session of the Intergovernmental Negotiating Committee to Prepare a Global Legally Binding Instrument on Mercury convenes in Stockholm.

— The Nagoya–Kuala Lumpur Supplementary Protocol on Liability and Redress to the Cartagena Protocol on Biosafety is adopted.

— The Nagoya Protocol on Access to Genetic Resources and the Fair and Equitable Sharing of Benefits Arising from Their Utilization is adopted.

2011 The International Renewable Energy Agency Assembly convenes for the first time.

— The UNFCCC creates the Ad Hoc Working Group on the Durban Platform for Enhanced Action to develop a protocol, another legal instrument, or an agreed outcome with legal force under the convention applicable to all parties.

2012 CO_2 levels in the atmosphere exceed 392 ppm, the highest for at least 650,000 years.

— The United Nations Conference on Sustainable Development is held in Rio de Janeiro.

— Governments agree to create a second commitment period for the Kyoto Protocol that will address GHG emissions during the period 2013–2020 and work toward a universal climate change agreement covering all countries from 2020, to be adopted by 2015.

2013 Countries reach agreement on a global treaty to limit mercury emissions.

1

The Emergence of
Global Environmental Politics

Until the 1980s, most governments regarded global environmental problems as minor issues, marginal both to their core national interests and to international politics in general. Then the situation changed. The rise of environmental movements in the industrialized countries and the appearance of well-publicized global environmental threats that could profoundly affect the welfare of all humankind—such as the depletion of the ozone layer, global climate change, and dangerous declines in the world's fisheries—awarded global environmental issues a much higher status in world politics. Today, environmental issues are viewed as internationally important both in their own right and because they affect other significant aspects of world politics, including economic development, international trade, humanitarian and social policy, and even international security.

Global concern about the environment developed in response to expanded scientific understanding of humanity's increasing impact on major components of the biosphere, such as the atmosphere, oceans, forests, soil cover, climate system, and a large number of animal and plant species. Many by-products of economic growth—such as the burning of fossil fuels, air and water pollution, release of ozone-destroying chemicals, production of toxic chemicals, increased use of natural resources, and decreasing forest cover—have put cumulative stresses on the physical environment that now threaten human health and economic well-being. The costs of these activities to future generations will be much higher in developing as well as highly industrialized countries than they are to the world's current population. The realization that environmental threats have serious socioeconomic and human costs and that unilateral actions by individual countries cannot solve them produced increased international cooperation aimed at halting or reversing environmental degradation.

This chapter provides an introduction to global environmental politics. It highlights key economic and environmental trends, introduces and defines important concepts, and traces some of the major intellectual currents and political developments that have contributed to the evolution of global environmental politics.

GLOBAL MACROTRENDS

Global demographic, economic, and environmental macrotrends describe key factors that drive global environmental politics. Indeed, the rise of global environmental politics can be understood only within the context of the major changes in the physical environment produced by the explosive growth in economic activity and population since World War II.

Humanity's potential stress on the environment is to some extent a function of three key factors: population, resource consumption, and waste production. One way to measure this impact is through an "ecological footprint," which measures humanity's demands on the biosphere by comparing humanity's consumption against the Earth's regenerative capacity, or biocapacity.[1] In other words, the ecological footprint measures the sum of all cropland, grazing land, forest, and fishing grounds required to produce the food, fiber, and timber we need and to absorb the wastes emitted. One influential study has found that humanity's annual demand on the natural world has exceeded what the Earth can renew in a year since the 1970s. This "ecological overshoot" has continued to grow and reached a 50 percent deficit in 2008. This means that it takes the Earth 1.5 years to regenerate the renewable resources that we use, and absorb the waste we produce, in that same year.[2]

Population Growth and Resource Consumption

Population growth affects the environment by increasing the demand for resources (including energy, water, food, and wood), the production of waste, and the emission of pollution. These relationships are not fixed, however, and most of the negative impacts on the environment and human health from pollution and resource extraction result from how we carry out certain activities rather than the growing population. Nevertheless, given the dominant economic and social patterns that have existed since the Industrial Revolution, the rapid growth of human population over the last one hundred years has significantly influenced the environment and will continue to do so throughout this century.

In 1900, global population stood at approximately 1.6 billion. Today it is more than 7 billion. It took fifty years for global population to go from 1.6 billion in 1900 to 2.5 billion in 1950. It then took only thirty-seven years for it to double, reaching 5 billion

FIGURE 1.1 **World Population Growth, 1950–2050 (projected)**

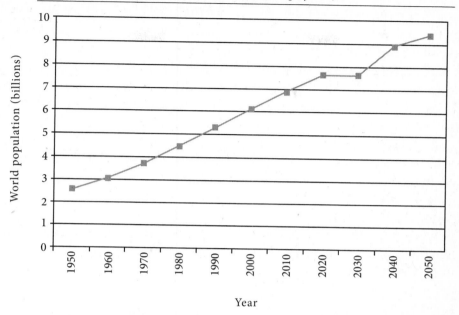

Source: United States Census Bureau, World Population Information, International Database, www.census.gov/population/international/data/worldpop/table_population.php.

in 1987. It passed the 6-billion mark only twelve years later, and reached 7 billion in late 2011. Global population is expected to surpass 9 billion by 2050 and 10 billion by 2100[3] (see Figure 1.1).

Projections of future population growth depend on fertility trends, which can be affected by economic development, education, widespread disease, and certain population-related policies. World population is currently growing at a rate of 1.2 percent annually. While significantly less than the peak growth rate of 2.04 percent from 1965 to 1970 and less than the rate of 1.46 percent from 1990 to 1995,[4] this still means a net addition of seventy-eight million people per year. Most of this growth will occur in developing countries, where environmental degradation, and its impact on human health, is already the greatest. Indeed, the United Nations Population Division estimates that between 2010 and 2050, nine countries will account for half of the world's projected population increase: India, Pakistan, Nigeria, Ethiopia, the United States, the Democratic Republic of Congo, Tanzania, China, and Bangladesh. The vast majority of children born each year, perhaps as many as 90 percent, live in developing countries.

Population increases have been accompanied by large increases in the consumption of natural resources, including fresh water, forests, topsoil, fish stocks, biodiversity, and fossil fuels. In addition, per capita consumption of natural resources has been rising much faster than population growth. For example, private consumption expenditures (the amount households spend on goods and services) increased more than fourfold from 1960 to 2000, even though the global population only doubled during this period.[5] This increase is positive in that it reflects growth in the standard of living for billions of people. At the same time, the aggregate human consumption of natural resources has largely passed sustainable rates.[6]

As more developing countries pursue the lifestyles of North America and Europe, the future will likely bring ever higher per capita rates of consumption unless resources are both consumed more efficiently and recycled more effectively. For example, the population of middle-income countries (including many of the world's emerging economies, like Brazil, China, India, Indonesia, Russia, and South Africa) has more than doubled since 1961, while the ecological footprint per person has increased by 65 percent.[7] The UN estimates that the global middle class will grow from 2 billion today to 4.9 billion by 2030, with consequentially large increases in demands for energy, food, water, and material goods.[8]

Despite large increases in the consuming class in Brazil, China, India, and other countries, the gulf in consumption levels within and between countries continues to draw attention. The 12 percent of the world's population that lives in North America and Western Europe accounts for 60 percent of private consumption spending, while the one-third living in South Asia and sub-Saharan Africa accounts for only 3.2 percent. The United States, with less than 5 percent of the global population, uses about 20 percent of the world's fossil fuel resources—coal, oil, and natural gas.[9] The United States has had more private cars than licensed drivers since the 1970s, and until the oil-price shock of 2008, gas-guzzling SUVs were among the best-selling vehicles. The average size of new, single-family houses in the United States has grown by nearly 40 percent since 1950,[10] despite a decrease in the average number of people per household, and larger houses consume more resources, both in their construction and during their operation.

At the other end of the spectrum, 1.4 billion people—one out of five—live on less than $1.25 a day, nearly 1 billion people lack access to safe drinking water, and 2.5 billion people live without basic sanitation.[11] Today, the world's richest countries use on average eleven times more energy than the poorest ones; the richest comprise only 18 percent of the world's population, but they use nearly half its energy[12] (see Figure 1.2). The average American consumes five times more energy than the average global citizen, four and half times more than the average Chinese, and twenty times more than the average Indian (and the vast majority of this energy still comes from burning fossil

FIGURE 1.2 Global Energy Use, 2010

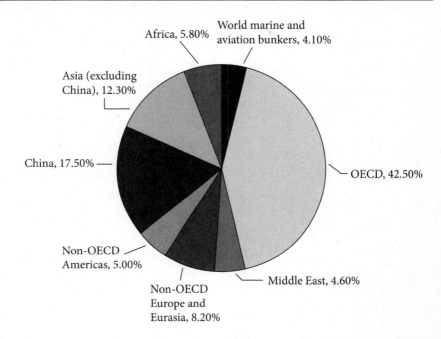

Source: International Energy Agency, *Key World Energy Statistics, 2012* (Paris: International Energy Agency, 2012).

fuels).[13] However, energy consumption in developing countries is increasing rapidly, driven by industrial expansion and infrastructure improvement, high population growth and urbanization, and rising incomes, which, in turn, enable families to purchase energy-consuming appliances and cars (see Figure 1.3). In 1980, China and India together accounted for less than 8 percent of the world's total energy consumption; in 2009 their share had grown to 23 percent.[14] In contrast, the US share of total world energy consumption contracted from 22 percent in 2005 to 20 percent in 2009.[15]

Natural Resources and Pollution

Population-growth and consumption patterns contribute to environmental degradation by increasing stress on both natural resources (such as fresh air and water, arable land, and fish stocks) and vital natural systems (such as the ozone layer and climate system). The increasing numbers of people and their needs for energy, food, transportation, and manufactured goods have far-reaching implications for climate change, pollution, and natural resources, especially agricultural land, forests, and fisheries.

FIGURE 1.3   **World Energy Consumption (quadrillion BTUs)**

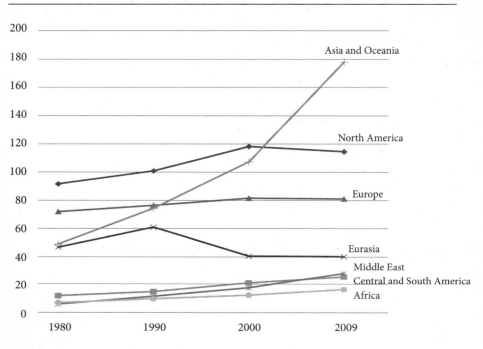

Source: Energy Information Administration, *International Energy Statistics* (Washington, DC: EIA, 2012), www.eia.gov/countries/.

Perhaps the largest aggregate impact that humans have on the biosphere is their carbon footprint (see Box 1.1), which has grown more than tenfold since 1960. The United States and China have the largest total national carbon footprints, with China emitting about 25 percent of global carbon emissions, followed by the United States with almost 20 percent. China has a much smaller per capita footprint than the United States (5.83 tonnes per person in 2009 versus 17.67 in the United States), but its population is more than four times as large. India's national footprint is the next largest, accounting for about 5 percent of global carbon emissions, but its per capita footprint of nearly 1.4 tonnes per person is even smaller than China's.[16]

If present trends in energy and fossil fuel consumption continue, energy-related emissions of CO_2 are projected to double from 21.5 billion metric tons in 1990 to 43.2 billion metric tons in 2035.[17] The decade 2000–2009 was the warmest decade for which observational records exist.[18] If present rates continue, global temperatures will rise by 3 degrees Celsius or more by the end of the century.[19]

More than two-thirds of the projected increase in emissions will come from developing countries, whose emissions are projected to be double that of industrialized

---

BOX 1.1   WHAT IS A CARBON FOOTPRINT?

A carbon footprint is a measure of the impact that activities have on climate change. Many daily activities cause emissions of greenhouse gases, including burning gasoline when driving, burning oil or gas for home heating, or using electricity generated from coal or natural gas. These types of emissions form the *primary footprint*: the sum of direct emissions of carbon dioxide from the burning of fossil fuels for energy consumption and transportation. More fuel-efficient cars have a smaller primary footprint, as do energy-efficient light bulbs in your home or office. The *secondary footprint* is the sum of indirect emissions of greenhouse gases during the lifecycle of products used by an individual or organization. For example, the greenhouse gases emitted during the production of plastic for water bottles, as well as the energy used to transport the water, contribute to the secondary carbon footprint. Products with more packaging will generally have a larger secondary footprint than products with a minimal amount of packaging.

Source: Maggie L. Walser, Stephen C. Nodvin, and Sidney Draggan, "Carbon Footprint," in *Encyclopedia of Earth*, ed. Cutler J. Cleveland (Washington, DC: Environmental Information Coalition, National Council for Science and the Environment, 2012), www.eoearth.org /article/Carbon_footprint.

---

countries by 2035[20] (see Figure 1.4). Developing countries will remain big users of coal, the most carbon-intensive of fuels. Power stations, cars, and trucks will be responsible for most of the increases in energy-related emissions. Since combating climate change requires stabilizing and then reducing greenhouse gas (GHG) emissions, many policy makers and scientists agree on the importance of avoiding, or at least reducing, emissions increases. Doing so is difficult given current population, energy, and consumption trends, but it may be possible through large increases in the use of renewable energy, further advances in energy efficiency, and a shift in consumption patterns toward inherently less energy- and resource-intensive goods and services.

The world's freshwater resources are under serious stress. Increased water consumption and rising population mean that about 80 percent of the world's population now lives in countries with high levels of threat to water security.[21] Agricultural water use accounts for about 75 percent of total global consumption, mainly through crop irrigation. Industrial use accounts for about 20 percent and domestic uses for 5 percent[22] (see Figure 1.5). By 2030, water use is expected to increase by 40 percent, and nearly 65 percent of all water withdrawals will be required for food production to meet the needs of the growing population.[23] Today, about 3.4 billion people live in regions with absolute water scarcity, and two out of three people in the world could be living under conditions of water stress.[24]

FIGURE 1.4   **World Energy-Related Carbon Dioxide Emissions, 1990–2035**

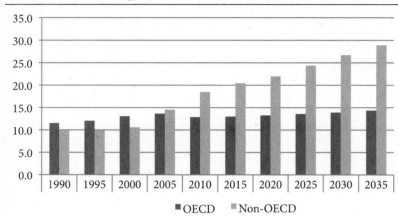

Source: US Energy Information Administration, *International Energy Outlook 2011* (Washington, DC: EIA, 2011), www.eia.gov/ieo/pdf/0484(2011).pdf.

The convergence of population growth, rising demand for lumber and fuelwood, and the conversion of forests to agriculture have also put increasing pressure on the world's forests, especially in developing countries. At the beginning of the twentieth century, the world contained about five billion hectares of forested area; now fewer than four billion hectares remain.[25] Deforestation, in turn, has contributed to the loss of biodiversity (the variety of living things), including the extinction of species and the loss of genetic diversity within species. Scientists began warning in the 1980s that the destruction of tropical forests, which hold an estimated 50 to 90 percent of all species, could result in the loss of one-fourth, or even one-half, of the earth's species within a few decades. Moreover, the earth's biodiversity is not confined to the tropical forests: Human actions have dramatically transformed virtually all of the earth's ecosystems. Despite the growing number of nature reserves, national parks, and other protected areas, a recent UNEP/IUCN report concluded that half of the world's richest biodiversity zones remain entirely unprotected.[26] The Millennium Ecosystem Assessment (see Box 1.2) estimated that between 10 and 50 percent of species are currently threatened with extinction, including 12 percent of bird species, 23 percent of mammals, and 25 percent of conifers (cone-bearing trees).[27]

Many of the world's major fisheries are overfished or on the verge of collapse. The declining global marine catch over the past few years, the increased percentage of over-exploited fish stocks, and the decreased proportion of non–fully exploited species provide strong evidence that the state of world marine fisheries is worsening.[28] Because the waters and biological resources of the high seas belong to no nation, it is not

FIGURE 1.5   Evolution of Global Water Use

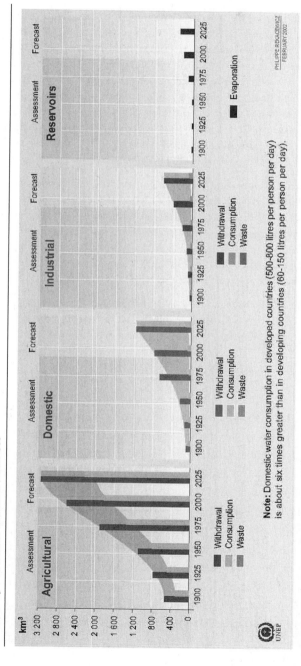

Source: Igor A. Shiklomanov, State Hydrological Institute (SHI, St. Petersburg) and United Nations Educational, Scientific, and Cultural Organization (UNESCO, Paris), 1999. Reprinted with permission from UNEP, *Vital Water Graphics: An Overview of the State of the World's Fresh and Marine Waters* (Nairobi: UNEP, 2002).

BOX 1.2   WHAT IS THE MILLENNIUM ECOSYSTEM ASSESSMENT?

The Millennium Ecosystem Assessment examined the health of the world's ecosystems and the consequences of ecosystem change for human well-being. Sponsored by the United Nations and other international organizations and initiated in 2001, the assessment involved the work of more than 1,360 experts worldwide who conducted comprehensive reviews of current knowledge, scientific literature, and field data. Their findings, contained in five technical volumes and six synthesis reports, provide a state-of-the-art scientific appraisal of the condition and trends in the world's ecosystems and the services they provide (such as clean water, food, forest products, flood control, and natural resources) and the options to restore, conserve, or enhance the sustainable use of ecosystems.

The core finding of the assessment, released in 2005, is that human actions are rapidly depleting Earth's natural resources and putting such strain on the environment that the ability of the planet's ecosystems to sustain future generations can no longer be taken for granted. At the same time, the assessment shows that with appropriate actions it is possible to reverse the degradation of many ecosystem services over the next fifty years, but the changes in policy and practice required are substantial and not currently under way.

Assessment reports and information on its findings, history, operation, participants, and use by scientists and policy makers can be found on the Millennium Ecosystem Assessment website: www.millenniumassessment.org.

surprising that overfishing has become a serious problem. According to the Food and Agriculture Organization of the United Nations (FAO), an estimated 87 percent of major marine fish stocks have been fully exploited or overexploited. The Atlantic Ocean and the Mediterranean and Black Seas contain stocks with the greatest need for recovery, followed by the Pacific Ocean, Northwest and Southeast Atlantic, Southeast Pacific, and Southern Oceans.[29] Staples such as tuna, swordfish, Atlantic salmon, and even cod could soon be on the endangered list. This would cripple the industries they support. In addition, inefficient fishing practices waste a high percentage of each year's catch; twenty million metric tons of bycatch (unintentionally caught fish, seabirds, sea turtles, marine mammals, and other ocean life) die every year when they are carelessly swept up and discarded by commercial fishing operations.[30]

Marine environments are also under siege from land-based sources of marine pollution, believed to account for nearly 80 percent of the total pollution of the oceans. The major land-based pollutants are synthetic organic compounds; excess sedimentation from mining, deforestation, or agriculture; biological contaminants in sewage;

and excessive nutrients from fertilizers and sewage. Large quantities of plastic and other debris can be found in the most remote places of the world's oceans. Plastic persists almost indefinitely in the environment and has a significant impact on marine and coastal biodiversity.[31]

Human impacts on wetlands are also increasing. Wetlands cover about thirteen million square kilometers of the earth.[32] Different types of wetlands serve as important sources of drinking water, natural sinks for carbon dioxide, fish nurseries, natural irrigation for agriculture, water cleansing systems, and protection against floods and storms. In the United States alone, wetlands provide approximately $23 billion worth of coastal area storm protection. Wetlands are also some of the most important biologically diverse areas in the world, providing essential habitats for many species. Despite an international treaty, the Ramsar Convention, dedicated to their protection, wetlands are increasingly filled in or otherwise destroyed to make way for buildings and farms or damaged by unsustainable water use and pollution. Fifty percent of the world's wetlands have been destroyed in the last hundred years. A 2012 report concluded: "There is an urgent need to put wetlands and water-related ecosystem services at the heart of water management in order to meet the social, economic and environmental needs of a global population predicted to reach 9 billion by 2050."[33]

Land degradation, water shortages, increasing demands for food, and other factors are combining to create negative feedbacks. Almost three out of five people in developing countries—some three billion—live in rural areas. But most of the land available to meet current and future food requirements is already in production. Further expansion will involve fragile and marginal lands. As land becomes increasingly scarce, farmers are forced to turn to intensive agriculture, including the use of dramatically higher levels of irrigation and chemicals. This, in turn, will contribute to soil erosion and salinization, deteriorating water quality, and desertification. Population growth and development are also converting forests into agricultural land and urban areas.

In addition, soaring food prices in recent years have increased the number of people vulnerable to starvation, severe hunger, and malnutrition. The World Bank estimated that food prices increased 140 percent from January 2002 to February 2008.[34] Agricultural prices in 2011 exceeded their 2008 peaks by 17 percent.[35] Reasons for the escalating prices include rising demand, changes in weather patterns possibly linked to climate change, the use of food crops for biofuels, and certain agriculture policies, including subsidies in developed countries.

Changing diets, economic growth, an expanding world population, and urbanization are combining to increase demand for food and raise prices. This includes the increasing demand for meat and fish among the growing number of middle-class consumers in China and India and other developing countries. While their consumption of such food is still far below that in Europe, North America, Australia, and New Zealand, the increase has led to a substantial growth in the demand for feed for animals and aquaculture fish. Because it takes many pounds of feed and water to produce a pound of animal meat, using grains as feed for animals removes a significant amount of resources and raises prices.[36] Food production costs have also increased, including the price of seeds partly because of patents and other intellectual property rights, as well as higher costs for fuel (for machinery and vehicles), fertilizers, pesticides, water, land, and labor.

Weather has had a major impact on food supply. In 2010 alone, a record number of nations (nineteen) set temperature records. Recent extreme weather events included a Russian heat wave, dry weather in Brazil, drought in some parts of the United States and historically strong storms in other parts, and flooding in Australia, Pakistan, and West Africa. Overall, weather variability, possibly resulting from climate change, is having a significant impact on international food prices.[37]

Another factor has been the large increase in biofuel production. Biofuels are liquid renewable fuels such as ethanol (an alcohol fermented from plant materials) and biodiesel (a fuel made from vegetable oils or animal fats) that can substitute for petroleum-based fuels. While potential future biofuels made from algae, seaweed, or plant waste would have significant economic and ecological benefits, the production of many current biofuels consumes significant amounts of pesticides, fertilizer, water, and energy; creates a large carbon footprint; and should not be considered environmentally benign.[38] In addition, manufacturing most of the biofuels currently in use shifts valuable resources (e.g., land, water, labor, capital) away from the production of food crops into the production of feedstock for biofuels. For example, in 2011, about 40 percent of US corn was used in the production of ethanol.[39] Because the United States is by far the world's largest producer and exporter of corn, this represented a diversion of about 15 percent of global corn production from food and feed to biofuel, increasing demand for corn and raising prices in global markets.[40] From 2006 to 2011 US ethanol expansion cost net corn-importing countries worldwide $11.6 billion in higher corn prices, with more than half of that cost, $6.6 billion, borne by developing countries.[41]

Environmental quality in urban areas continues to be a major problem and the situation could become far worse. In 2008, for the first time in history, the world's urban population equaled the rural population. Between 2011 and 2050, the population living in urban areas is projected to increase from 3.6 billion in 2011 to 6.3 billion in 2050. Thus, urban areas will likely absorb all the population growth expected over the next four decades while at the same time drawing in some of the rural population. Overall, the world is expected to be 67 percent urban in 2050[42] (see Figure 1.6).

While cities can provide significant economies of scale for environmentally friendly technology and practices, under current conditions in many parts of the

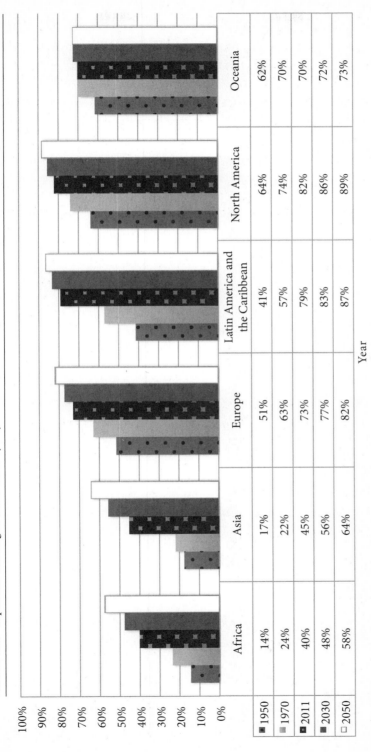

FIGURE 1.6 Population Residing in Urban Areas by Major Areas of the World, 1950, 1970, 2011, 2030, and 2050 (in percent)

	Africa	Asia	Europe	Latin America and the Caribbean	North America	Oceania
1950	14%	17%	51%	41%	64%	62%
1970	24%	22%	63%	57%	74%	70%
2011	40%	45%	73%	79%	82%	70%
2030	48%	56%	77%	83%	86%	72%
2050	58%	64%	82%	87%	89%	73%

Year

Source: United Nations Department of Economic and Social Affairs/Population Division, *World Urbanization Prospects: The 2011 Revision* (New York: United Nations, 2012), 12.

world, increasing urbanization implies heavier water and air pollution and higher rates of natural resource consumption. Air pollution in many major urban areas is already at harmful levels, responsible for more than one million deaths a year,[43] and air pollution in several megacities in Asia continues to worsen. Hundreds of millions living in poverty in urban areas lack consistent access to clean water or electricity. Municipal waste systems in many cities cannot keep pace with urban expansion.[44] The number of cities supporting at least ten million inhabitants is projected to rise from twenty-three in 2011 to thirty-seven in 2025[45] (see Table 1.1). Most of these large cities are located in developing countries. The current pace and scale of urbanization often strain the ca-

TABLE 1.1   **The World's Megacities, 2011**

RANK	URBAN AGGLOMERATION	POPULATION
1	Tokyo, Japan	37.2
2	Delhi, India	22.7
3	Mexico City, Mexico	20.4
4	New York–Newark, USA	20.4
5	Shanghai, China	20.2
6	São Paulo, Brazil	19.9
7	Mumbai, India	19.7
8	Beijing, China	15.6
9	Dhaka, Bangladesh	15.4
10	Calcutta, India	14.4
11	Karachi, Pakistan	13.9
12	Buenos Aires, Argentina	13.5
13	Los Angeles–Long Beach–Santa Ana, USA	13.4
14	Rio de Janeiro, Brazil	12.0
15	Manila, Philippines	11.9
16	Moscow, Russian Federation	11.6
17	Osaka-Kobe, Japan	11.5
18	Istanbul, Turkey	11.3
19	Lagos, Nigeria	11.2
20	Cairo, Egypt	11.2
21	Guangzhou, Guangdong, China	10.8
22	Shenzhen, China	10.6
23	Paris, France	10.6

Source: United Nations Department of Economic and Social Affairs/Population Division, *World Urbanization Prospects: The 2011 Revision* (New York: United Nations, 2012), 7.

pacity of local and national governments to provide even basic services to urban residents. While conditions have improved in some areas, the UN reports that more that more than 827.6 million were living in slums in 2010, up from 776.7 million in 2000.[46]

The trends described in this section are some of the most important forces that shape global environmental politics. They have resulted from the intense economic development, rapid population growth, inefficient production, and unsustainable resource consumption prevalent in many parts of the world. This is not to say that population growth and economic development are necessarily harmful. Indeed, most would argue they are not. Rather, it is the manner in which much of this economic development occurred, one characterized by high levels of resource consumption and pollution, which produced these troubling changes in the global environment. Thus, with these conditions as a backdrop, it is time to look at the issues and politics surrounding natural resources and the environment.

AN INTRODUCTION TO GLOBAL ENVIRONMENTAL POLITICS

Environmental problems do not respect national boundaries. Transboundary air pollution, the degradation of shared rivers, and the pollution of oceans and seas are just a few examples of the international dimensions of environmental problems. The cumulative impact that human beings have on the earth, together with an increased understanding of ecological processes, means that the environment cannot be viewed as a relatively stable background factor; indeed, the interactions between economic development and the complex, often fragile ecosystems on which that development depends have become major international political and economic issues.[47]

The sources, consequences, and actors involved in an environmental issue can be local, national, regional, or global. If the sources or consequences are global, or they transcend more than one international region, or the actors involved in creating or addressing the problem transcend more than one region, then we consider the activity and its consequences to be a global environmental issue.[48] The main actors in international environmental politics are states (national governments), international organizations, environmental nongovernmental organizations (NGOs), corporations and industry groups, scientific bodies, and important individuals (see Chapter 2).

Global environmental issues can be analyzed in many ways. From the economist's point of view, environmental problems represent negative "externalities"—the unintended consequences or side effects of one's actions that are borne by others. Externalities have always existed, but when the use of helpful, but polluting, technologies—such as coal, synthetic fertilizers, pesticides, herbicides, and plastics—expanded rapidly to keep pace with population growth and increased per capita consumption, they became critical.[49]

In this sense, the negative externalities that lead to environmental degradation are similar to the "tragedy of the commons." The ecologist Garrett Hardin observed that overgrazing unrestricted common lands, prior to their enclosure, was a metaphor for the overexploitation of the earth's common property: land, air, and water resources.[50] The root cause of overgrazing was the absence of a method for obliging herders to take into account the harmful effects that their own herds' grazing had on the other herders who shared the common land. One solution lay in assigning property rights so that owners could limit the use of the commons. Hardin recognized that air, water, and many other environmental resources, unlike the traditional commons, could not readily be fenced and parceled out to private owners who would be motivated to preserve them. Without sufficient knowledge or structures to restrain them, people (or states) will logically pursue their interest in utilizing the Earth's common resources until they are destroyed, resulting in the tragedy of the commons. How to address externalities and the damage they inflict on environmental resources that, by their very nature, no one can own is a central challenge in global environmental politics.

Oran Young, a political scientist, groups international environmental problems into four broad clusters: commons, shared natural resources, transboundary externalities, and linked issues.[51] Young describes the commons as the natural resources and vital life-support services that belong to all humankind rather than to any one country. These include Antarctica, the high seas, deep seabed minerals, the stratospheric ozone layer, the global climate system, and outer space. They may be geographically limited, as in Antarctica, or global in scope, such as the ozone layer and climate system. Shared natural resources are physical or biological systems that extend into or across the jurisdiction of two or more states. These include nonrenewable resources, such as pools of oil beneath the earth's surface; renewable resources, such as migratory species of animals; and complex ecosystems that transcend national boundaries, such as regional seas and river basins.

Transboundary externalities are activities that occur wholly within the jurisdiction of individual states but produce results affecting the environment or people in other states. Transboundary externalities include the consequences of environmental accidents, such as the 1986 explosion at the Chernobyl nuclear power plant in the former Soviet Union or the Baia Mare cyanide spill in 2000, when a retaining wall failed at a gold-processing plant in Romania, releasing cyanide and heavy metals into a river system, which killed fish and contaminated drinking waters in parts of Romania, Bulgaria, Hungary, and Serbia. Transboundary externalities can also include transnational air pollution or the loss of biological diversity, caused in part by the destruction of tropical forests, which leads to species extinction as well as reduced potential for developing new pharmaceuticals. Linked issues refer to cases where efforts to deal with environmental concerns have unintended consequences affecting other regimes, and vice versa. The most controversial issue of this type is the link between efforts to protect the environment and those to promote economic development within countries or trade between countries.

Different combinations of factors, including internal economic and political forces, foreign policy goals, and the impact of international organizations, NGOs, and corporations can influence a state's policy preferences on different environmental issues (see Chapter 2). Because the actual costs and risks of environmental degradation are never distributed equally among states, some governments are less motivated than others to participate in international efforts to reduce environmental threats. States often possess different views about what constitutes an equitable solution to a particular environmental problem. Yet, despite their disparate interests, in order to address most international environmental issues, states must strive for consensus, at least among those that significantly contribute to, and are significantly affected by, a given environmental problem.

Consequently, an important characteristic of global environmental politics is the significance of veto power. For every global environmental issue, there exists one or more states whose cooperation is so essential to a successful agreement for coping with the problem that it has the potential to block strong international action. When these states oppose an agreement or try to weaken it significantly, they become veto (or blocking) states and form veto coalitions.

The role of veto coalitions is central to the dynamics of bargaining and negotiation in global environmental politics. On the issue of a whaling moratorium, for example, four states, led by Japan, accounted for three-fourths of the whaling catch worldwide; they could therefore make or break a global regime to save the whales. Similarly, the major grain exporters (Argentina, Australia, Canada, Chile, the United States, and Uruguay) were in position to block the initial attempts to reach consensus on a biosafety protocol under the Convention on Biological Diversity for fear that the proposed provisions on trade in genetically modified crops were too stringent and would hamper grain exports (see Chapter 4).

Veto power is so important that powerful states are not free to impose a global environmental agreement on much less powerful states if the latter are strongly opposed to it and critical to the agreement's success. For example, industrialized countries could not pressure tropical-forest countries such as Brazil, Indonesia, and Malaysia to accept a binding agreement on the world's forests during the 1992 United Nations Conference on Environment and Development (UNCED) (see Chapter 4). Moreover, in global environmental negotiations, weaker states can use their veto

PHOTO 1.1   **Public opinion can play an important role in global environmental politics.**
Courtesy IISD/*Earth Negotiations Bulletin.*

power to demand compensation and other forms of favorable treatment. This occurred during the expansion of the ozone-layer regime, when India and China led a coalition of developing countries that successfully demanded a financial mechanism that would provide resources to assist them in meeting the higher costs of using new non–ozone-depleting chemicals (see Chapter 3). Nevertheless, although some developing states can prevent an agreement or bargain for special treatment on some environmental issues, in general the major economic powers wield greater leverage because of their larger role in global production and consumption and their ability to provide or deny funding for a particular regime.

A second and related characteristic of global environmental politics is that the political dynamics often reflect the roles of state actors in the production, use, or international trade of a particular product. The issue of international hazardous waste trading, for instance, is shaped by the relationship between industrialized countries that are exporting the waste and developing countries that are potential importers. Trade relations between tropical timber exporters and consuming nations are critical to the dynamics of tropical deforestation. Sometimes the trade patterns are so significant that they provide the producing/exporting countries or the importing countries with veto power.

A third characteristic of global environmental politics is that economic power can affect the positions of states and even the outcome of bargaining on international agreements in some circumstances, whereas military power is not particularly useful for influencing such outcomes. A country's ability to give or withhold economic benefits, such as access to markets or economic assistance, can persuade states dependent on those benefits to go along with that power's policy if the benefits are more important than the issue at stake in the negotiations. Thus, Japan and the Republic of Korea accepted international agreements on drift-net fishing and whaling because they feared loss of access to US markets. And Japan succeeded in ensuring the support of some small nonwhaling nations for its pro-whaling position by offering assistance to their fishing industries.

While states are the most important actors, a fourth characteristic of environmental politics is the importance in some cases of public opinion and nonprofit NGOs, especially national and international environmental NGOs. Environmental issues, like human rights issues, have mobilized the active political interest of large numbers of citizens in key countries, inducing shifts in policy that helped turn the tide for various environmental issues. Public opinion, channeled through electoral politics and NGOs into national negotiating positions, has influenced aspects of the global bargaining on whaling, endangered species, hazardous wastes, persistent organic pollutants (POPs), and ozone depletion. NGOs have also provided important input to global negotiations and been important parts of some implementation strategies. Public opinion and NGOs tend not to play comparable roles in security and economic negotiations. This situation may be changing, however, as indicated by the international initiatives to ban land mines and protests related to austerity measures imposed as part of multilateral economic agreements to reduce national debt burdens.

INTERNATIONAL REGIMES IN GLOBAL ENVIRONMENTAL POLITICS

Understanding global environmental politics requires understanding international regimes, a concept that scholars have defined in two very different ways. According to the first definition, a regime is a set of norms, rules, or decision-making procedures, whether implicit or explicit, that produces some convergence in the actors' expectations in a particular issue area. In this broad definition, the concept may be applied to a wide range of international arrangements, from the coordination of monetary relations to superpower security relations. This way of conceiving regimes has been strongly criticized for including arrangements that are merely patterned interactions, operational frameworks, and even methods to agree to disagree with no long-term predictability or stability.[52]

According to the second definition, the one used in this book, a regime is a system of principles, norms, rules, operating procedures, and institutions that actors create to regulate and coordinate action in a particular issue area of international relations. Principles are beliefs of fact, causation, and rectitude. Norms are standards of behavior. Rules are specific prescriptions or proscriptions for action. Operating procedures are prevailing practices for work within the regime, including methods for making and implementing collective choice. Institutions are mechanisms and organizations for implementing, operating, evaluating, and expanding the regime and its policy.[53]

Regimes are essentially international policy, regulatory, and administrative systems. Although states, as the dominant actors in the international system, are the primary and most important creators of international regimes, they are not the only actors involved in their creation or implementation. A regime usually centers on one or more formal international agreements, but key elements can also include the relevant actions of important international organizations, parts of other interrelated international agreements, and accepted norms of international behavior among actors active in the issue area (including governments, international organizations, NGOs, multinational corporations, and others). These elements together form the entire suite of principles, norms, rules, and procedures that govern and guide behavior on the particular issue.

Regimes of varying strength and effectiveness are found in most areas of international relations, including trade, money, environment, human rights, communications, travel, and even security. As a result, regimes receive a good deal of theoretical and empirical attention from scholars of international relations, and this represents an important development in the study of international cooperation—especially into how, why, and under what circumstances states attempt to cooperate or create international institutions and what factors influence the success of such attempts.[54]

One important line of progenitor theories is marked by concern for the impact and mitigation of structural anarchy, especially the difficulty of establishing international cooperation. (*Anarchy* in this usage does not mean chaos but the absence of hierarchy, specifically the lack of world government or other formal hierarchical structures to govern international politics.[55]) A second flows from scholars called "constitutionalists," who study treaties and the formal structure of international organizations, and from researchers employing the institutional process approach, which concentrates on examining how an organization's day-to-day practices, processes, and methods of operation influence outcomes.[56]

A third line of antecedents starts with the premise that despite structural anarchy, extensive common interests exist among states and their people and that scholars and statesmen must learn how these interests can be realized. Present in eighteenth-century enlightened optimism, nineteenth-century liberalism, and twentieth-century Wilsonian idealism, this view influenced in the 1970s a branch of legal and political scholarship concerned with world order and international law that argued that custom, patterned interaction, and the needs and wants of civilian populations are important sources of international law and require the respect of states.[57]

Functionalism represents a fourth important line of predecessors. Functionalism, often associated with the work of David Mitrany, argues that the scholarly and political focus of international cooperation must center not on formal interstate politics but rather on providing opportunities for technical (nonpolitical) cooperation among specialists and specialized organizations to solve common problems.[58] Functionalists argue that such technical cooperation can begin a process in which increasing interdependence and "spillover" (technical management in one area begetting technical management in another) will present opportunities for organizing more and more government functions internationally and technically rather than nationally and politically—a process that will slowly erode or bypass domestic regulators in favor of peaceful global institutions.

While attractively optimistic, functionalism proved inadequate to explain the totality of actions and outcomes in an international system in which politics is always a factor, states do not want to relinquish control, and technological determinism has not responded automatically to all (or even most) aspects of increasing interdependence. However, functionalist insights did influence several important theoretical approaches, including neofunctionalist integration theory, transnational relations theory, turbulent fields, complex interdependence, and regimes.[59]

Neofunctional integration theory critiqued and extended functionalism, arguing that gradual, regional integration is most important for understanding and creating effective international governance.[60] The approach added politics (including the importance of states and individual political figures) and regional encapsulation to functionalist strategies emphasizing spillover and managed incremental advancements. This approach also lost favor, particularly when Ernst Haas, formerly a leading proponent, argued that focusing exclusively on regional encapsulation had become inadequate for addressing new, "turbulent" issue areas of international relations characterized by different types of competing interests and high degrees of complexity and interdependence (which we now know include environmental issues). Haas argued that the interplay of knowledge, learning, and politics is critical to understanding and managing turbulent issue areas as well as the conduct and adaptability of international organizations created to address them.[61]

Research on transnational relations, which are nongovernmental interconnections and interactions across national boundaries, argued similarly that interdependence can fracture international politics into distinct issue areas and that states are neither the only important actors in international politics nor even totally "coherent" actors.[62] These insights culminated in "complex interdependence," proposed by Robert Keohane and Joseph Nye as an alternative to realism as a paradigm for understanding international relations.[63]

The study of regimes results from these lines of inquiry. If international relations are increasingly interdependent, influenced by new types of actors and interactions, and fractured into issue areas across which power and interests vary, then how actors choose to manage these issue areas—the regimes they create to manage them—becomes important to the conduct and study of international politics. Thus, regimes should be properly defined, examined, and explained.

John Ruggie is often credited with introducing the term *international regime* as a "set of mutual expectations, rules and regulations, plans, organizational energies and financial commitments, which have been accepted by a group of states."[64] Ernst Haas

PHOTO 1.2   **In multilateral negotiations, states believe they will be better off or no agreement will be reached.**
Courtesy IISD/*Earth Negotiations Bulletin.*

initially defined regimes as "collective arrangements among nations designed to create or more effectively use scientific and technical capabilities."[65] Robert Keohane and Joseph Nye first defined regimes instrumentally: "By creating or accepting procedures, rules or institutions for certain kinds of activity, governments regulate and control transnational and interstate relations. We refer to these governing arrangements as international regimes." In the same work, they defined a *regime* as a "network of rules, norms, and procedures that regulate behavior."[66] In 1983, a group of leading scholars working with Stephen Krasner attempted to standardize and extend regime study. Most definitions, including the one used in this volume, are variants of the definition they developed.[67]

States and other actors create regimes through multilateral negotiations. Negotiations take place when at least some states consider the status quo unacceptable or that negative consequences and high costs will occur if existing trends continue. Although reaching agreement on how to manage the problem is in a state's best interest, so is gaining as much as possible while giving up as little as possible. Nevertheless, the expected value of the outcome to each state, and hence the total value of the outcome, must be positive (or at least neutral), or else there would be no incentive to negotiate or to accept the outcome. In multilateral negotiations, states will not come to an agreement unless they believe they will be better off in some way than they would be with no agreement.[68]

Most regimes center on a binding agreement or legal instrument. For global environmental problems, the most common kind of legal instrument is a convention. A convention may contain all the binding obligations expected to be negotiated, or it may be followed by a more detailed legal instrument, often called a protocol, which elaborates more specific norms and rules. Since the members of most international regimes are states, regime rules apply to the actions of states. However, actors that engage in the activities addressed by regimes frequently include not only states and international organizations but also private entities, such as multinational corporations, banks, timber companies, and chemical companies. Thus, states participating in international regimes assume responsibility for ensuring that private entities within their jurisdiction comply with the norms and rules of the regime.[69]

If a convention is negotiated in anticipation that parties will negotiate one or more subsequent elaborating texts, it is called a *framework convention*. Framework conventions usually establish a set of general principles, norms, and goals for cooperation on the issue as well as how members of the regimes will meet and make decisions. The latter usually takes the form of a regular Conference of the Parties, an annual, biannual, or otherwise regularly scheduled gathering of all parties to the convention as well as interested observers (observers often include representatives from nonparty states, international organizations, NGOs, and industry groups). Framework conventions usually do not impose major binding obligations on the parties. A framework convention is then followed by the negotiation of one or more protocols, which spell out specific obligations on the overall issue in question or on narrower subissues.

A nonbinding agreement can form the centerpiece of a regime to the extent that it establishes norms that influence state behavior. This type of agreement is often referred to as soft law. Nonbinding agreements, codes of conduct, and guidelines for behavior exist for a number of global environmental problems, including land-based sources of marine pollution and sustainable forest management, with varying degrees of effectiveness. Some consider Agenda 21, the plan of action adopted at the 1992 Earth Summit, a soft-law "umbrella regime" for worldwide sustainable development because it defines goals and norms of behavior for a wide range of environmental and development issues. Although such nonbinding agreements can influence state behavior to some extent, regimes based on legal instruments are usually more effective. That is why some countries become dissatisfied with a given nonbinding code of conduct or other soft-law agreement and argue that it should be turned into a legally binding agreement.

Global Environmental Regimes

Today, regimes exist on a wide variety of global environmental issues from whale protection to climate change to hazardous wastes. Chapters 3 and 4 describe the development of, and challenges faced by, ten prominent regimes. As these cases demonstrate, global environmental regimes can vary significantly in their history, purpose, rules, strength, and effectiveness.

Environmental regimes change over time, often expanding and becoming stronger but sometimes weakening or changing in scope. The whaling regime, for example, grew out of the International Convention for the Regulation of Whaling (1946), which was originally intended as a regime for the regulation of commercial whaling but evolved into a ban on whaling in 1985 (see Chapter 4). The regime that seeks to control marine oil pollution began with the 1954 International Convention for the Prevention of Pollution of the Sea by Oil, which established rules only for ships within fifty miles (eighty kilometers) of the nearest coast, allowing for significant and deliberate oil spillage outside this area.[70] This ineffectiveness led some states in 1973 to create the International Convention for the Prevention of Pollution from Ships, also known as the MARPOL convention, which limits oil discharges at sea, prohibits them in certain sensitive zones, and sets minimum distances from land for the discharge of other pollutants. However, shipping interests in crucial maritime states opposed the MARPOL convention so strongly that it did not enter into force until a decade later. States also negotiated the Convention on the Prevention of Marine Pollution by Dumping of Wastes and Other Matter (London Convention, 1972), which prohibited the dumping of specific substances, including high-level radioactive wastes, and required permits for others. It was the first marine-pollution agreement to accept the right of coastal states to enforce prohibitions against pollution and became an important forum for negotiating further controls on ocean dumping.

In another example of regime evolution, until the 1970s virtually all wildlife conservation treaties lacked binding legal commitments and, perhaps consequentially, were ineffective in protecting migratory birds and other species. The first global convention on wildlife conservation that had strong legal commitments and an enforcement mechanism was the 1973 Convention on International Trade in Endangered Species of Wild Fauna and Flora (CITES; see Chapter 4). It set up a system of trade sanctions and a worldwide reporting network to curb the traffic in endangered species and thus, by eliminating the market, to reduce the incentive to capture, kill, or harvest endangered plants and animals. While effective in many instances, it also contains loopholes that allow states with interests in a particular species to opt out of the controls on it.

The regime that seeks to reduce hazardous waste, control its trade, and ensure its environmentally sound management and disposal began with negotiations initially aimed largely at preventing the movement (and sometimes outright dumping) of hazardous waste from rich countries, where it was produced, to poor countries. The regime's first and central agreement, the 1989 Basel Convention on the Control of Transboundary Movements of Hazardous Wastes and Their Disposal, does not prohibit the trade but establishes conditions for it (see Chapter 3). Dissatisfaction with this aspect of the agreement on the part of many developing countries, especially in Africa, resulted in the negotiation of an amendment that would ban waste exports. Subsequent negotiations have expanded the regime extensively, including developing detailed guidelines and norms for the management and disposal of hazardous wastes.

As noted above, many regimes are strengthened as efforts shift from creating an initial framework convention to negotiating and implementing specific protocols. For example, the regional regime controlling cross-border acid rain and air pollution in Europe began with the 1979 Convention on Long-Range Transboundary Air Pollution. This framework convention did not commit the signatories to specific emissions reductions. The regime was later strengthened considerably by the addition of eight protocols that financed the monitoring and evaluation of long-range air pollutants in Europe (1984); the reduction of sulfur emissions (1985 and 1994); the control of nitrogen oxides (1988); the control of emissions of volatile organic compounds (1991), heavy metals (1998), and POPs (1998); and the abatement of acidification and ground-level ozone (1999). The heavy metals and POPs agreements represented significant expansions of the core mandate established by the original convention.

The ozone regime also began with a framework convention (see Chapter 3). The 1985 Vienna Convention for the Protection of the Ozone Layer did not commit the parties to reducing ozone-depleting chemicals; in fact it did not even mention these substances by name. The Montreal Protocol (1987) represented the first real step toward protecting the ozone layer by requiring reductions in the use of certain chlorofluorocarbons (CFCs). Then, in the late 1980s and 1990s, significant advances in scientific understanding of the threat, the discovery of alternative chemicals, and the use of innovative regime rules allowed governments to reach a series of agreements that significantly strengthened the regime. The ozone regime now mandates the complete phaseout of CFCs and almost all other ozone-depleting substances (ODS), and the production of CFCs and several other ODS has been largely eliminated.

The agreement that created the climate regime, the 1992 Framework Convention on Climate Change (UNFCCC; see Chapter 3), also failed to impose binding targets and timetables for GHG emissions. It did call on industrialized countries to return emissions to 1990 levels but stated this as a nonbinding goal. With the adoption of the Kyoto Protocol in 1997, however, industrialized country parties agreed to reduce their collective emissions of six GHGs by at least 5 percent below 1990 levels by 2012.

Some treaties and regimes, like the 2001 Stockholm Convention on Persistent Organic Pollutants and the Montreal Protocol, have very clear, binding controls (see Chapter 3); others do not. The 1992 Convention on Biological Diversity (see Chapter 4), for example, does not obligate parties to measurable conservation objectives but instead requires the development of national strategies for the conservation of biodiversity. Similarly, the 1994 Convention to Combat Desertification (see Chapter 4), which established a regime to address land degradation in the drylands that results from the destruction of formerly productive lands' biological potential, calls for countries to draw up integrated national programs in consultation with local communities.

Some regimes, such as the ozone and CITES regimes, are considered successes. These regimes have not completely solved the environmental issues they address, and each contains loopholes, but the situation is far better than it was before they were created. However, many regimes have had only mixed successes at best. Nevertheless, negotiation of the central agreement and other aspects of the regime (such as the related activities of international organizations) provide greater opportunities for addressing the environmental issue in question than when no regime exists (either because negotiations failed or none were attempted).[71] Thus, while the biodiversity and climate regimes have not come close to solving those problems—in fact each problem continues to accelerate, with potentially disastrous results—the situation would be far worse, and the prospects for future improvements more remote, if the regimes did not exist.

Evidence for this conclusion exists in issues that have no extant regimes or for which initial attempts to create a regime have failed. For instance, several efforts to create some type of regime for the protection of coral reefs have failed to gain traction, and coral reefs continue to degrade rapidly around the world. Shark populations continue to fall, largely as a result of sharks killed as bycatch, to make shark-fin soup, and for use in commercial products, including cosmetics. Efforts to initiate binding global protections for most sharks have failed, although a broad conservation plan was agreed on in 2010 to protect several species under the auspices of the Convention on Migratory Species.[72] Many countries have laws protecting coastal mangroves, but many of these same countries also sanction their enclosure or even tear them down to create ponds for shrimp farms or for coastal development. Without an international regime leading all countries to adjust their behavior simultaneously, this situation is likely to continue, and mangroves (and the ecological and economic value they have) will continue to disappear.

Theoretical Approaches to International Regimes

Several major theoretical approaches have been used to explain how international regimes come into existence and why they change.[73] These include structural, game-theoretic, institutional-bargaining, and epistemic-community approaches. Each may help explain one or more international regimes, but none individually can account for all the regimes described and analyzed in this book.

The structural, or hegemonic-power, approach holds that the primary factor determining regime formation and change is the relative strength of the state actors involved in a particular issue and that "stronger states in the issue system will dominate the weaker ones and determine the rules of the game."[74] This approach suggests that strong international regimes are a function of a hegemonic state that can exercise leadership over weaker states and that the absence of such a hegemonic state is likely to frustrate regime formation.

The structural approach can be viewed in two ways, one stressing coercive power, the other focusing on "public goods." In the coercive-power variant, regimes are set up by hegemonic states that use their military and economic leverage over other states to bring them into regimes, as the United States did in setting up trade and monetary regimes immediately after World War II.[75] The second variant views the same postwar regimes as the result of a hegemonic power's adopting policies that create public goods, that is, benefits open to all states who want to participate, such as export markets in the United States and establishing the dollar as a stable currency for international payments.

However useful the structural approach has been to explain the creation of post–World War II economic systems, it cannot explain why global environmental regimes have been negotiated. In the 1970s and 1980s, the United States was not a military hegemon but part of a bipolar system with the Soviet Union. Beginning in the mid-1980s, the United States faced the rise of competing economic powers in Japan and Europe. Moreover, the European Union, whose member states negotiate on global environmental issues as a single bloc, became the economic equal of the United States in the late 1990s. Finally, the United States did not seek to create many of these environmental regimes. From 1981 to 1993 and from 2001 to 2009, both crucial periods in the creation and expansion of most global environmental regimes, the United States had presidents ideologically hostile toward international environmental regulation; consequently, the United States did not take many lead positions (as the theory argues a hegemonic state must do). Thus, the creation and expansion of these regimes depended on wide consensus among a number of states, not on imposition by the United States.[76]

Another approach to understanding regime creation is based on game theory and utilitarian models of bargaining. In game theory, bargaining scenarios are examined under different conditions with regard to the number of parties involved, the nature of the conflict (zero-sum or non–zero-sum), and the assumptions that the actors are rational (they will try to pursue outcomes favorable to them) and interconnected in some way—that is, they cannot pursue their own interests independently of the choices of other actors. This approach suggests that small groups of states, or coalitions, are more likely to succeed in negotiating an international regime than a large number because each player can more readily understand the bargaining strategies of the other players. Political scientist Fen Osler Hampson took this approach into account when he analyzed the process of regime creation as an effort by a small coalition of states to form a regime by exercising leadership over a much larger number of national actors.[77]

Nevertheless, for an environmental regime to succeed, it must include all states that have a large impact on the issue, including potential veto states. Veto states follow their own interests (as all states do), so a veto state in a small group will likely be as prone to opposition as it would be in a large group of states. And if veto states are left outside the small group, they will still be in a position to frustrate regime formation when the regime is enlarged, or they may simply refuse to join the regime, limiting the regime's success.

Another approach is the epistemic-communities model, which emphasizes the impact of international learning and transnational networks of experts and bureaucrats, primarily on the basis of scientific research into a given problem, as a factor influencing the evolution of regimes.[78] This approach, advanced initially to explain the creation of, and compliance with, the Mediterranean Action Plan, identifies intra-elite shifts within and outside governments as the critical factor in the convergence of state policies in support of a stronger regime. The shifts empowered technical and scientific specialists allied with officials of international organizations. These elites thus formed transnational epistemic communities, that is, communities of experts sharing common values and approaches to policy problems.

The importance of scientific evidence and expertise in the politics of many global environmental issues cannot be ignored. Indeed, a significant degree of scientific understanding and consensus has sometimes been a minimum condition for serious international action on an issue. The impetus for agreement in 1990 that the world should phase out CFCs completely came from incontrovertible scientific evidence that damage to the ozone layer was much greater than previously thought and that CFCs were largely responsible. The Kyoto Protocol was made possible, in part, by the Second Assessment Report of the Intergovernmental Panel on Climate Change, which found that the earth's temperature had increased and that there is a "discernible human influence" on climate.

However, while scientific elites have played supportive and enabling roles in certain environmental negotiations, on some issues they remained divided or even captured by particular government or private interests. And on other issues, such as the whaling ban, the hazardous waste trade, desertification, the Antarctic, and the ocean dumping of radioactive wastes, scientists have contributed little to regime formation or strengthening. In some of these cases, scientific elites were not particularly influential in policy making, while in others key actors explicitly rejected scientific findings as the basis for decision.[79]

The case studies presented in Chapters 3 and 4 also suggest that theoretical approaches based solely on a unitary actor model (one suggesting that state actors can be treated as though they are a single entity encompassing an internally consistent set of values and attitudes), ignoring the roles of domestic sociopolitical structures and processes, are likely to form poor bases for analyzing and predicting the outcomes of global environmental bargaining. Negotiating positions usually reflect domestic sociopolitical balances and may change dramatically because of a shift in those balances. For example, after Barack Obama was elected president, the United States dramatically shifted its stance from opposing to supporting global negotiations that would elaborate a regime to reduce mercury emissions. Although the structure of an issue in terms of economic interests may indicate which states are most likely to join a veto coalition, domestic political pressures and bargaining can tip the balance for or against regime creation or strengthening. A fully complete theoretical explanation for global environmental regime formation or change must incorporate the variable of state actors' domestic politics.

A nuanced analysis of regime formation and strengthening, therefore, should link international political dynamics with domestic politics and view the whole as a "two-level game." While representatives of countries are maneuvering the outcome of bargaining over regime issues, officials must also bargain with interest groups within their domestic political systems. Because the two processes often take place simultaneously, the arenas influence each other and become part of the negotiations at each level.[80]

A theoretical explanation for the formation of global environmental regimes must also leave room for the importance of the rules of the negotiating forum and the linkages between the negotiations on regimes and the wider relationships among the negotiating parties. The legal structure of the negotiating forum—the "rules of the game" regarding who may participate and how authoritative decisions are to be made— becomes particularly important when the negotiations take place within an already established treaty or organization.[81] The ozone and whaling cases illustrate how these rules can be crucial in determining the outcomes of the negotiations.

Economic and political ties among key state actors can also sway a veto state to compromise or defect. Particularly when the environmental regime under negotiation does not involve issues central to the economy of the states that could block agreement, the potential veto state's concern about how a veto would affect relations with states important for economic or political reasons sometimes makes possible the formation or strengthening of a regime.

PARADIGMS IN GLOBAL ENVIRONMENTAL POLITICS

Public policy and regimes are shaped not only by impersonal forces, such as science, technological innovation, and economic growth, but also by people's, governments', and institutions' perception of reality. In times of relative stability, public policies and systems of behavior tend to flow in accordance with dominant paradigms, or sets of beliefs, ideas, and values. A dominant paradigm is challenged when contradictions appear between its assumptions and observed reality. If these contradictions are not resolved, eventually it gives way to a new paradigm through a process known as a paradigm shift.[82]

Because economic and environmental policy are intertwined in many ways, the paradigm that has dominated public understanding of environmental management during the period of rapid global economic growth in the last two centuries has been essentially a system of beliefs about economics. It has been referred to as the *exclusionist paradigm* because it excludes human beings from the laws of nature. It has also been called *frontier economics*, suggesting the sense of unlimited resources characteristic of a society living on an open frontier.[83]

In capitalist societies, this paradigm has rested primarily on two assumptions of neoclassical economics: the free market will tend to maximize social welfare, and there exists an infinite supply of both natural resources and "sinks" for disposing of the wastes that accrue from exploiting those resources—provided that the free market is operating efficiently. Humans will not deplete a resource, according to this worldview, as long as technology is given free rein and prices are allowed to fluctuate enough to stimulate the search for substitutes; in this way, absolute scarcity can be postponed indefinitely into the future.[84] Waste disposal is viewed as a problem to be cleaned up after the fact—but not at the cost of interference with market decisions.[85] Because conventional economic theory is concerned with the allocation of scarce resources, and nature is not considered a constraining factor, this paradigm considers the environment largely irrelevant to economics. (Despite a different economic and political ideology, the former Soviet Union and other communist states also shared this assumption.) The traditional international legal principles of state sovereignty (including control over resources within a state's borders) and unrestricted access to the Earth's common resources, such as the oceans and their living resources, buttressed the exclusionist paradigm.

Rise of an Alternative Paradigm

In the 1960s, the dominant paradigm came under attack. The critique started in the United States and then spread to Europe and other regions. The 1962 publication of Rachel Carson's *Silent Spring* documenting the dangers to human health from synthetic pesticides marked the beginning of an explosion of popular literature about new threats to the environment, including radiation, lead, toxic wastes, and air and water pollution. The first mass movement for environmental protection, which focused on domestic issues including air and water pollution, developed in the United States in the late 1960s. Throughout this period, research and writing on environmental issues began to raise awareness that economic activity without concern for the environmental consequences carried high costs to society. Parallel changes in public concern about pollution also occurred in other industrialized countries. The burst of environmental concern in the United States led to the passage of a series of landmark pieces of legislation, including the National Environmental Policy Act of 1969, the 1970 Clean Air Act, the 1970 establishment of the US Environmental Protection Agency, and new rules to combat water pollution in 1972. These laws and those that built on them dramatically decreased air, water, and soil pollution in the United States. The National Environmental Policy Act also directed federal agencies to support international cooperation in "anticipating and preventing a decline in the quality of mankind's world environment."[86]

But the United States was not alone. The first global environmental conference in history, the United Nations Conference on the Human Environment, convened in Stockholm in 1972. The motto of the Stockholm Conference, "Only One Earth," was a revolutionary concept for its time. The 114 states attending the conference (Soviet bloc states boycotted the meeting because of Cold War disputes) approved a landmark declaration containing twenty-six broad principles on the management of the global environment along with an action plan containing 109 recommendations for international environmental cooperation. These recommendations included creating a new international organization, the United Nations Environment Programme (UNEP), to provide a focal point for environmental action and coordination of environmentally related activities within the UN system. In preparation for, or as a result of, Stockholm, environmental ministries and agencies were established in more than one hundred countries (most governments did not have such ministries before 1972). Stockholm also marked the beginning of the explosive increase in nongovernmental and intergovernmental organizations dedicated to environmental preservation, with an estimated hundred thousand such organizations formed in the subsequent twenty years.[87]

The rise of environmental consciousness in the 1960s and early 1970s attacked the dominant paradigm but did not produce a widely accepted set of alternative assumptions about physical and economic realities that could become a competing worldview. The essential assumptions of classical economics remained largely intact. Confronted with evidence that existing patterns of resource exploitation could cause irreversible damage, proponents of classical economics continued to maintain that such exploitation was still economically rational.[88]

Over time, however, an alternative paradigm challenging the assumptions of classical economics began to take shape. Two of the intellectual forerunners of this paradigm were the *Limits to Growth* study by the Club of Rome, published in 1972, and *Global 2000: The Report to the President*, released by the US Council on Environmental Quality and the Department of State in 1980.[89] Each study applied global-systems computer modeling to the projected interactions among population, economic growth, and natural resources and concluded that if current trends continued, many ecosystems and natural resources would become seriously and irreversibly degraded and that these environmental developments would then have serious and negative economic consequences. Because each study suggested that economic development and population growth were on a path that would eventually strain the earth's "carrying capacity" (the total amount of resource consumption that the earth's natural systems can support without undergoing degradation), the viewpoint underlying the studies was generally referred to as the *limits-to-growth perspective.*

Defenders of the dominant paradigm, among them Herman Kahn and Julian Simon, criticized these studies for projecting the depletion of nonrenewable resources without taking into account technological changes and market responses. These critics argued that overpopulation would not become a problem because people are the world's "ultimate resource," and they characterized the authors of studies as "no-growth elitists" who would freeze developing countries out of the benefits of economic growth. They argued that human ingenuity would enable humanity to leap over the alleged limits to growth through new and better technologies.[90] These arguments found a following among those concerned about economic growth. The development of an alternative paradigm was then set back in the early 1980s, when the Reagan administration in the United States and the Thatcher government in the United Kingdom embraced policies consistent with the exclusionist paradigm.

Despite these political developments, knowledge about ecological principles and their relationship to economic development continued to spread. A global community of practitioners and scholars began to emerge, allied in the belief that ecologically sound policies should replace policies based on the exclusionist paradigm.

By the mid-1980s, *sustainable development* had emerged as the catchphrase of the search for an alternative paradigm, and the term was heard with increasing frequency at conferences around the world.[91] An important milestone was the 1987 publication by the World Commission on Environment and Development of *Our Common Future* (better known as the Brundtland Report after the commission's chair, former Norwegian prime minister Gro Harlem Brundtland). The United Nations established the Brundtland Commission to examine the impact of environmental degradation and natural resource depletion on future economic and social development. The commission's report is considered a landmark in global environmental politics in part because it helped to define, legitimize, and popularize the concept of sustainable development. Drawing on and synthesizing the views and research of hundreds of people worldwide, it also codified some of the central beliefs of the emerging sustainable development paradigm.

The Brundtland Commission defined sustainable development as "development that meets the need of the present without compromising the ability of future generations to meet their own needs."[92] The central themes of its report criticized economic and social systems (and the dominant paradigm) for failing to reconcile those needs. It asserted that the earth's natural systems have finite capabilities and resources and that the continuation of existing economic policies carries the risk of irreversible damage to the natural systems on which all life depends.

The sustainable development paradigm emphasizes the need to redefine the term *development*. It posits that economic growth cannot continue at the expense of the Earth's natural capital (its stock of renewable and nonrenewable resources) and vital natural support systems such as the ozone layer, biodiversity, and a stable climate. Instead, the world economy must learn to live off the "interest" of the Earth's natural capital. That means reducing the amount of resources used per unit of gross national product (GNP), shifting from fossil fuels to renewable energy, and reusing and recycling rather than consuming and discarding resources. It implies a transition to sustainable systems of natural resource management, efforts to stabilize world population,[93] and a more measured approach to consumption.

The sustainable development paradigm holds that future generations have an equal right to use the Earth's resources—a concept known as intergenerational equity.[94] The approach also affirms the need for greater equity between and within nations. Highly industrialized countries such as the United States, which use a disproportionate share of the world's environmental resources, are seen as pursuing an unsustainable type of economic growth, as are societies in which grossly unequal distribution of land and other resources produces significantly negative impacts. To meet current and future needs, developing countries must meet the basic needs of the poor in ways that do not deplete the countries' natural resources, and industrialized countries must examine attitudes and actions regarding unnecessary and wasteful aspects of their material abundance.[95]

One of the main anomalies of the classical economic paradigm is its measure of macroeconomic growth, that is, GNP. Advocates of sustainable development note that GNP fails to reflect the real physical capability of an economy to provide material wealth in the future or to take into account the relative well-being of the society in general. Thus, a country could systematically deplete its natural resources, erode its soils, and pollute its waters without that loss of real wealth ever showing up in its income accounts. Moreover, the economic expense of trying to fix these problems would actually add to GNP.

In the second half of the 1980s, some economists began to study how to correct this anomaly in conventional accounting and to advocate for governments and international organizations to use alternatives to GNP—such as "real net national product," "sustainable social net national product," or "index of sustainable economic welfare"— which include changes in environmental resources as well as other indicators that measure human welfare.[96] Of particular importance is the annual United Nations Development Programme's (UNDP) *Human Development Report*, which uses "human indicators" to rate the quality of life in all countries by measures other than economic ones, including literacy, life expectancy, and respect for women's rights.[97] The Himalayan kingdom of Bhutan measures well-being not through GNP but through a Gross National Happiness Index that provides an overview of performance across nine domains: psychological well-being, time use, community vitality, cultural diversity, ecological resilience, living standard, health, education, and good governance.[98] The World Bank calculation of genuine savings helped to pioneer the inclusion of social and environmental aspects when assessing the wealth of nations.[99] The Organization for Economic Cooperation and Development's (OECD) Global Project on Measuring the Progress of Societies fosters the use of novel indicators in a participatory way.[100] The Environmental Sustainability Index ranks countries on twenty-one elements of sustainability covering natural resource endowments, past and present pollution levels, environmental-management efforts, and contributions to the protection of the global commons.[101] The EU and its member states have developed and use a broad range of social and environmental indicators, often regrouped in sets of sustainable development indicators. The EU also promotes and supports the use of internationally recognized indicators in neighboring countries and developing countries.[102]

The use of these and related approaches reflects an increasing awareness that free markets alone often fail to ensure the sustainable use of natural resources. Because the market usually does not address externalities effectively, the approach argues that prices should reflect the real costs to society of producing and consuming a given resource or emitting pollution that harms people or the environment. Conventional free market economic policies, however, systematically underprice or ignore natural resources.[103] Public policies that do not correct for market failure thus encourage overconsumption and more rapid depletion of renewable resources and the degradation of environmental services (i.e., the conserving or restorative functions of nature; for example, the conversion of carbon dioxide to oxygen by plants and the cleansing of water by wetlands). Adjusting the markets to send such price signals and exchanging income taxes for green taxes are means of implementing the "polluter pays" principle, endorsed by the 1992 Rio Declaration on Environment and Development (see Chapter 6). Placing an upper limit on consumption is another method.[104]

PHOTO 1.3   UN Conference on Environment and Development, Rio, 1992. NGO
representatives join hundreds of thousands who signed the Earth Pledge leading up to the Earth
Summit.
Photo by Charles V. Barber, World Resources Institute.

The alternative paradigm gained significant credibility through the Earth Summit
in June 1992. The conference, which drew the participation of 110 heads of state, nearly
10,000 official delegates from 150 countries, and thousands of NGO representatives,
was a monumental effort by the international community to reach consensus on principles and a long-term work plan for global sustainable development. Conceptually,
its explicit focus on integrating environmental and development policies represented
a major step forward from the Stockholm Conference on the Human Environment
twenty years earlier.

The major output of the Earth Summit was a nonbinding agreement called Agenda
21 (referring to the twenty-first century), a global compendium of possible actions for
creating more sustainable societies. A 294-page document, Agenda 21 addresses every
major environmental issue, international policies affecting environment and development, and the full range of domestic social and economic policies. UNCED also
produced two nonbinding sets of principles—the Rio Declaration on Environment
and Development and the Statement of Forest Principles—that helped create norms

and expectations.[105] Two major global treaties, the UNFCCC and Convention on Biological Diversity, were negotiated independently of the UNCED process but on parallel tracks and opened for signature at the Earth Summit. They are often called the
Rio Conventions.

Negotiations on Agenda 21 acted as a bellwether for the state of international consensus on the full range of issues affecting the long-term sustainability of human society, including domestic social and economic policies, international economic
relations, and cooperation on global commons issues. Questions concerning financial
resources, technology transfer (the transfer of scientific and technological knowledge,
patents, or equipment, usually from the most industrialized nations to the developing
ones), education, and capacity building for implementing Agenda 21 and global environmental agreements formed the core of the compact reached at Rio and remain
central issues today. The agreement reached in Rio essentially held that developing
countries would try to put into practice more environmentally sound development
policies if the industrialized countries agreed to provide the necessary support, that
is, "new and additional" financial resources, technology transfer on concessional and
preferential terms, and assistance with capacity building, education, and training. Yet,
twenty years later, few countries have lived up to their Rio commitments or completely
embraced the sustainable development paradigm.

Paradigm Shift?

Within many powerful institutions in the United States, China, India, and other
countries, elements of the exclusionist paradigm still tend to dominate policy. Many
corporations, government ministries dealing with trade and finance, leaders of particular political parties, and some officials at the World Bank and other multilateral
institutions have been slow to change. Interest groups dominated by certain industries locked into old paradigms continue to determine many national political agendas, while the globalization of industry, finance, technology, and information has
gradually eroded certain aspects of the powers held by national authorities.[106]

Has the sustainable development paradigm failed? Delegates and observers asked
themselves this question as they gathered in Johannesburg, South Africa, in September
2002 at the World Summit on Sustainable Development (WSSD) to review the implementation of Agenda 21 and the other agreements adopted at the Earth Summit. The
mixed results from the meeting, which included expressions of concern regarding the
limited implementation of the UNCED agreements and new action plans but few
meaningful commitments, produced no definitive answer.

During and since the WSSD, some have argued that the sustainable development
paradigm has not failed but that its ascendancy has stalled because of the rise of a vari-
ation of the exclusionist paradigm: globalization.[107] Globalization became identified

with a number of trends, including a greater international movement of commodities, money, information, and people, as well as the development of technology, organizations, legal systems, and infrastructures to allow this movement. Economic globalization means globe-spanning economic relationships. The interrelationships of markets, finance, goods and services, and the networks created by transnational corporations are particularly important manifestations.

Observers see globalization as different from the sustainable development paradigm. They argue that globalization policies advocate the liberalization of international markets, reducing trade and other national economic barriers, minimizing regulations on the market (especially in highly regulated developing countries), and granting rights to corporations to invest in any country of their choice without restraints or conditions. According to this view, governments should not interfere with the free play of the market, and social or developmental concerns (for instance, obtaining grants from developed countries to aid developing countries) should be downgraded.[108]

Actions by powerful countries supported the ascendancy of the globalization paradigm. Former UNDP administrator James Gustave Speth argued that some US policy makers saw globalization as supplanting the need for international assistance and even the sustainable development paradigm. "Trade, not aid" became a Washington mantra during the George W. Bush administration. Moreover, even among those US policy makers favorable to environmental and development objectives, the priority given to the trade and globalization agenda tended to occupy the available political space and crowd out sustainable development concerns.[109] The same argument could be made about key policies in China, India, and Russia, among other large countries.

Speth and others also argued that the eclipse of some UNCED commitments resulted from more than the ascendancy of the globalization paradigm. At UNCED, governments expected the post–Cold War period to bring a peace dividend of financial and political resources that could then be applied to promoting environmental and development objectives. Instead, by the WSSD in 2002, the United States and others had become enmeshed in a series of military and peacekeeping engagements, including the war on terrorism triggered by the September 11, 2001, terrorist attacks, which consumed much of their available time, energy, and money.[110]

As governments started preparing for the most recent global environmental summit, the United Nations Conference on Sustainable Development (UNCSD or Rio+20), held in Rio de Janeiro in June 2012, the concerns were the same, but the language had changed. The UNCSD was charged with securing renewed political commitment for sustainable development, assessing progress and implementation gaps in meeting previously agreed commitments, and addressing new and emerging challenges. In addition, the UN General Assembly called for the conference to focus on two themes: (1) a green economy in the context of sustainable development and poverty eradication and (2) the institutional framework for sustainable development. Discussions surrounding the green economy, which, according to one prominent definition, results in improved human well-being and social equity while significantly reducing environmental risks and ecological scarcities, became increasingly prominent during the preparatory meetings leading up to Rio+20.[111] In its simplest expression, a green economy can be thought of as one that is low carbon, resource efficient, and socially inclusive. In a green economy, growth in income and employment is driven by public and private investments in economically productive activities that also reduce carbon emissions and pollution, enhance energy and resource efficiency, and prevent the loss of biodiversity and ecosystem services.[112]

During the last few years, the idea of a green economy has entered the mainstream of policy discourse. Traction for the green economy concept has been aided by technological developments in key industries, disillusionment with the prevailing paradigm, and unease produced by the financial and economic crisis of 2008. These and other factors combined to create new interest in models and practices through which material wealth is produced without exacerbating environmental risks, resource scarcities, and social disparities.[113]

Much of the research and policy work on a green economy has placed emphasis on internalizing environmental externalities in prices to send the right signals to producers and consumers—that is to "get the prices right." Other discussions focus on the importance of government actions that assist research, development, and deployment of new technologies in key sectors; finance infrastructure investments; provide supportive policy environments for green investments by the private sector; and ensure that green economy policies support employment and income generation for the poor.[114] Other discussions point toward the need for greater awareness within the private sector regarding the opportunities represented by the green economy and the importance of responding to government policy reforms and price signals through higher levels of financing and investment.[115]

Supporters of the green economy paradigm, like the sustainable development paradigm, believe it offers a way to reconcile the competing economic aspirations of rich and poor countries in a world that faces climate change, pollution, and ecological scarcity. A green economy can meet this challenge, they argue, by offering a development path that reduces carbon dependency, promotes resource and energy efficiency, and lessens environmental degradation. As economic growth and investments become less dependent on liquidating environmental assets and sacrificing environmental quality, both rich and poor countries can attain more sustainable economic development.[116]

During the Rio+20 process, however, the green economy paradigm met with resistance from many developing countries. Bolivia summed up the opposition, asserting that no single development model—whatever its color—should be imposed and that the rights of developing states to pursue their own development paths must be upheld.[117] Martin Khor, executive director of the South Centre, argued that embracing the green economy model posed risks for developing countries because:

- The green economy is defined in a one-dimensional manner and promoted in a purely "environmental" manner, without considering fully the development and equity dimensions.
- A "one size fits all" approach is taken, treating all countries in the same manner. This would lead to failures either for environment, for development, or for both. The levels and stages of development of countries must be fully considered.
- The green economy is inappropriately used for trade protectionist purposes. In particular, rich countries may use this to justify unilateral trade measures against the products of developing countries.
- The green economy is used as new conditionality on developing countries for aid, loans, and debt rescheduling or debt relief.[118]

These issues shaped the debate leading up to Rio+20. The final document adopted at the conference articulated the challenges in moving to an alternative economic paradigm:

> We affirm that there are different approaches, visions, models and tools available to each country, in accordance with its national circumstances and priorities, to achieve sustainable development in its three dimensions which is our overarching goal. In this regard, we consider green economy in the context of sustainable development and poverty eradication as one of the important tools available for achieving sustainable development and that it could provide options for policymaking but should not be a rigid set of rules. We emphasize that it should contribute to eradicating poverty as well as sustained economic growth, enhancing social inclusion, improving human welfare and creating opportunities for employment and decent work for all, while maintaining the healthy functioning of the Earth's ecosystems.[119]

Will the exclusionist, globalization, sustainable development, or green economy paradigm dominate future political and economic perspectives? Will policy continue to reflect elements of all these approaches? Some argue that a future paradigm shift will not result from changing economic or political interests but rather require a "revolution of social consciousness and values."[120] Paul Raskin, for example, believes a new sustainability paradigm is possible, but it will "happen only if key sectors of world society come to understand the nature and the gravity of the challenge, and seize the opportunity to revise their agendas."[121] Governments and, more importantly, people do not necessarily change entrenched behaviors when they become aware of the seriousness of a potential threat. Such behavior change sometimes requires a broader societal shift. Although globalization remains a powerful force, some signs point to sustainable development having a chance of becoming fully "mainstreamed" in certain economic and political circles. The EU, for example, has formally recognized the need to change unsustainable consumption and production patterns and move toward a more integrated approach to policy making.[122] Political rhetoric often exceeds actual policy changes in this area, but some European and other governments (e.g., Costa Rica) do appear committed to achieving economic growth that is truly sustainable through relying increasingly on alternative energy, eliminating many toxic chemicals, improving energy efficiency, and adopting the precautionary principle to guide decision making on environment and human health issues.

Environmental Change as a Security Issue

Two other possible paradigms have emerged that influence global environmental politics. The first holds that environmental degradation and resource depletion can affect national security. The central idea is that environmental degradation and resource scarcity act as threat multipliers that augment other conditions known to cause violence between opposing groups within a state or even between states. As argued by Thomas Homer-Dixon, who helped to pioneer our understanding of this issue, resource scarcity, ecosystem collapse, and other environmental problems can act as tectonic stresses, exacerbating existing political, social, or economic instability to the point that armed conflict occurs.[123] Environmental degradation can help cause or increase the impact of other problems known to contribute to violence within or between states, such as resource disputes, refugee movements, poverty, hunger, and weak governments.

Changing climate conditions contributed to the devastating ethnic conflict in Darfur, Sudan.[124] The government and several rebel groups had opposed each other for years, reflecting the long-standing animosity that existed between elements of the Afro-Arab ethnic groups that dominate in the North and the non-Arab farming ethnic groups in the South as well as the territorial ambitions of particular actors. Over time, severe changes in rainfall patterns, increasing drought, and deteriorating soils caused many farmers to block off the remaining fertile land, fearing that shared use by the herders would ruin it. Many Arab herders were angry that they were not receiving their share of the land, leading to violent clashes, which were then used by some political leaders as excuses to widen the conflict. Environmental factors did not cause the violence, but they pushed other factors, including poverty, increasing ethnic and political divisions, and the territorial ambitions of certain groups, past the tipping point into widespread, systematic violence.

In North America, the collapse of fisheries in northwestern Mexico contributed to the decision by some fishermen to become involved in drug smuggling and other crimes.[125] Similarly, overfishing and illegal fishing off the coast of Somalia contributed to the increase in piracy. Large criminal enterprises, many of which pose threats to local security, are responsible for 50–90 percent of illegal logging around the world.[126] In Haiti, massive deforestation (less than 2 percent of the nation remains forested) led to severely eroded hillsides, massive soil erosion and runoff, and declining water quality. This exacerbated the already difficult situation for rural farmers trying to work the country's mountainous terrain. Soil runoff from the mountains also polluted many of the nation's already overfished coastal areas, nearly eliminating fishing as a source of income. With no means to make a living in rural areas, the vast majority of Haitians moved to city slums, most living without clean water or proper sanitation, producing conditions that worsened the impact of the massive earthquake in 2010, which killed more than three hundred thousand and left at least one million Haitians homeless.

US and European political, military, and intelligence communities have accepted certain aspects of the emerging paradigm that environmental degradation can lead to security concerns.[127] Of particular concern is climate change, which could produce huge numbers of refugees from flooded coastal areas, increase water and food scarcity, spread disease, and weaken economies in parts of the world that are already vulnerable, unstable, prone to extremism, or that suffer significant cultural, ethnic, or economic divisions. Africa, for example, while "least responsible for greenhouse gas emissions, is almost universally seen as the continent most at risk of climate-induced conflict—a function of the continent's reliance on climate-dependent sectors (such as rain-fed agriculture) and its history of resource, ethnic and political conflict."[128] Similarly, with conditions in the Middle East already volatile, "climate change threatens to reduce the availability of scarce water resources, increase food insecurity, hinder economic growth and lead to large-scale population movements."[129]

Environmental degradation and the mismanagement of natural resources can fuel conflict between and within states and contribute to poverty and state failure. On the flip side, war and other security issues can affect the environment. Military spending absorbs government finances and policy attention that might otherwise be dedicated to environmental protection. Military operations, even in peacetime, consume large quantities of natural resources. Armed conflict itself produces habitat destruction, overexploitation of natural resources, and pollution. Civil wars in Africa, Asia, and Latin America have destroyed many hectares of forests and wetlands.

Armed conflict also has an impact on states' and regions' abilities to guard protected areas and enforce conservation regulations.[130] This is particularly true during civil war or in very weak states, where the breakdown of the rule of law, increased availability of weapons, and disrupted economic and agricultural production all affect environmental protection. In the Congo, for example, armed conflict since 1994 has had a severe impact on many nature reserves, including some designated as World Heritage sites. Governments, international organizations, and NGOs have faced huge obstacles as a result of the "proliferation of arms and ammunition; displaced people, military, and dissidents; a general breakdown of law and order; uncontrolled exploitation of natural, mineral and land resources by various interest groups; and the increased use of wild areas as refuges and for subsistence."[131] Antipoaching patrols ceased in many areas for different periods, and increased poaching, harvesting game for food, and habitat destruction seriously affected wildlife populations in some parks. Drug traffickers, either on their own or in alliance with rebel groups, sometimes prevent the enforcement of wildlife conservation, habitat protection, or deforestation laws in parts of Bolivia, Colombia, Mexico, and Peru by essentially controlling access to certain areas or bribing or intimidating inspectors and other officials.[132]

The environment and security paradigm replaces traditional analyses that assume that environmental degradation is irrelevant to a state's national security interests. This does not imply that the environment is more important than traditional security calculations, but it does argue that an analysis of factors that can negatively affect a state's security must include environmental degradation and resource mismanagement (much as the sustainable development paradigm argues that serious environmental degradation can negatively affect a state's economy). It is not clear, however, that increased awareness of this relationship will lead to new types of actions by developing-country or donor-country governments to ward off resource collapse in vulnerable parts of Africa, Asia, Latin America, and the Caribbean. Nor is it clear that recognition of the serious regional and even global security problems potentially posed by climate change will lead to increased efforts to reduce GHG emissions.

The Precautionary Principle: A New Paradigm for Environmental Policy?

The exclusionist paradigm implies that economic policy calculations need not factor in resource scarcity and environmental degradation. If resource scarcity begins to occur, the market will respond by raising prices, which will reduce demand and spur the search for substitutes, thereby averting a crisis. Similarly, there is no need to consider or take steps to avoid environmental problems before they occur, as these can be remedied after the fact if the market demands it.

Unfortunately, while these deductions make sense from a purely market perspective, they fail to account accurately for the physical limitations of the earth's biological and physical systems. It is true that prices will rise, and incentives will exist to develop substitutes when scarcity becomes an issue, but for some environmental problems, these market forces will occur too late. Certain environmental impacts cannot be remedied once they occur, at least not on timescales relevant to human economic and political systems. If the ozone layer thins significantly, a rainforest gets destroyed, a coral reef dies, the climate system shifts to a different equilibrium, a species becomes extinct, or a human life is shortened by air, water, or toxic pollution, these changes will last, if not forever, then at least for a very, very long time.

In other cases, operating under the exclusionist paradigm simply represents a poor economic decision because the impacts of the environmental degradation caused by some types of pollution might cost far more than economic benefits accrued from emitting it. Deforestation in Haiti and some other areas is an example. For the country as a whole, the economic benefits of using the wood or cleared land are far fewer than the economic costs associated with the harm caused to fisheries, farming, and fresh-water resources resulting from the severe erosion and runoff from hills and mountains that no longer have trees to hold the soil in place. In other cases, such as climate change or ozone depletion, the economic costs associated with the worst consequences of the problem are higher than the cost of taking steps to prevent them from occurring.

Those holding this position argue that in many situations, the best policy—from an environmental, human health, and economic point of view (and perhaps an ethical one as well)—is to avoid producing certain serious environmental problems in the first place. The difficulty, of course, is that the complexity of many environmental issues prevents clear calculations of an activity's environmental costs, while its economic benefits are usually quite clear. Thus, the lack of scientific certainty regarding the range, extent, and cost of environmental impacts from particular activities or products can prevent effective policy in the face of strong lobbying by economic interests.

The precautionary principle attempts to resolve this dilemma and provide guidance in the development of national and international environmental policy in the face of scientific uncertainty. The most widely used definition of the precautionary principle was set forth by governments in 1992 at the Earth Summit in Principle 15 of the Rio Declaration: "Where there are threats of serious or irreversible damage, lack of full scientific certainty shall not be used as a reason for postponing cost-effective measures to prevent environmental degradation."[133]

Those supporting the use of the precautionary principle argue that it leads to several main policy-relevant ideas:[134]

- the importance and efficacy of taking preventative action, even in the face of uncertainty, when the lack of action might produce essentially irreversible, unwanted impacts on the environment or human health;

- the need to shift the burden of proof from those seeking to protect human health and the environment to those supporting a particular activity or product. Rather than forcing others to prove something is definitely harmful, which has traditionally been the case, now proponents of, for example, using a particular chemical would show it is not harmful;
- the need to keep science and rational arguments central to decision making involving health and environmental issues with the understanding that complete scientific certainty or unanimity regarding future harm is not required to make policy designed to protect the environment or human health from irreversible damage; and
- the importance of asking why we should risk irreversible or very serious harm for a particular product or activity.[135]

Several important global environmental statements and treaty regimes contain elements of the precautionary principle either explicitly or implicitly.[136] For example, the Ministerial Declaration from the Second International Conference on the Protection of the North Sea (1987) states, "In order to protect the North Sea from possibly damaging effects of the most dangerous substances, a precautionary approach is necessary which may require action to control inputs of such substances even before a causal link has been established by absolutely clear scientific evidence."[137] The Montreal Protocol on Substances That Deplete the Ozone Layer (1987) also endorsed the concept of precautionary policy, stating that parties to the agreement are "determined to protect the ozone layer by taking precautionary measures to control equally total global emissions of substances that deplete it."[138]

The climate regime includes the concept of precaution as one of its central principles. Article 3 of the UNFCCC (1992) states,

> In their actions to achieve the objective of the Convention and to implement its provisions, the Parties shall be guided, *inter alia*, by the following: . . .
>
> The parties should take precautionary measures to anticipate, prevent, or minimize the causes of climate change and mitigate its adverse effects. Where there are threats of serious or irreversible damage, lack of full scientific certainty should not be used as a reason for postponing such measures.[139]

The 2000 Cartagena Protocol on Biosafety expressly allows parties to ban imports of genetically modified organisms, even where there is a "lack of scientific certainty due to insufficient relevant scientific information and knowledge" concerning health or environmental impacts.[140] The 2001 Stockholm Convention on Persistent Organic Pollutants defines the objective of the regime: "Mindful of the precautionary approach as set forth in Principle 15 of the Rio Declaration on Environment and Development, the objective of this Convention is to protect human health and the environment from persistent organic pollutants."[141] In addition, the treaty states that "precaution" should be used when considering additional substances to add to the control measures and that the lack of scientific certainty regarding the precise levels of a substance's toxicity or propensity for long-range transport and bioaccumulation shall not be grounds for failing to consider controlling it under the regime.

Local and national laws in a number of countries have also incorporated the principle. Most important is the EU announcement in 2000 stating that the precautionary principle will guide EU policy decisions on environmental and human health issues and is also a "a full-fledged and general principle of international law."[142]

Even though there is increasing reference to the precautionary principle in international politics, arguments exist that it should not be accepted as a principle of international law (on par with universally accepted principles such as sovereignty). Some argue that shifting the burden of proof means that decisions will not be based on scientific certainty but rather on "emotional and irrational" factors.[143] Others argue that precautionary actions will cost too much, harming companies and hindering economic development.[144] Some argue that it is essentially impossible to prove that anything in all situations is totally safe.[145] Some believe that too many different definitions and interpretations of the principle exist to make it a clearly defined principle of international law. By one count, at least fourteen different definitions, formulations, and uses of the precautionary principle exist in international policy.[146] Others note that its acceptance by international legal bodies as a guiding point of international law is not universal.[147] For example, during the George W. Bush administration, the United States argued during several international negotiations that the precautionary principle was not an accepted principle of international law that bound states to certain norms. Under this interpretation, references to precaution in treaties that the United States signed or ratified related only to the particular activity under discussion—not a general international legal principle applicable across all countries and issues.[148]

Other analysts, legal scholars, and policy makers dismiss these arguments. They believe that inclusion of the precautionary principle (or its key elements under another name) in so many international treaties, its status within the EU, and its emergence in local and national laws in countries around the world prove that "the precautionary principle has evolved from being a 'soft law' 'aspirational' goal to its present status as an authoritative norm recognized by governments and international organizations as a firm guide to activities affecting the environment."[149]

Clearly the precautionary principle has become a part of many international environmental policies, having found its way into an increasing number of global regimes, influenced international decision making, and been more and more accepted in debates on national policies in multiple countries. Yet if the precautionary principle is a new dominant paradigm, why don't we see greater levels of international commitments with regard to climate change, biodiversity, forests, and fisheries?

Perhaps there is no real dominant paradigm. It appears that multiple paradigms exist today and compete for primacy. Elements of the exclusionist paradigm still influence some global, national, local, and corporate policies, but so, too, do elements of the sustainable development paradigm and the precautionary principle.

At the same time, the totality of the evidence supports the thesis that we could be in a time of paradigm transition: from exclusionist premises to sustainable development and precaution. But the future is far from clear. As economies, populations, cities, energy production, and resource demands continue to grow, the paradigms that influence current and future policy debates could go a long way toward determining what the world will look like.

CONCLUSION

Global environmental politics involve actions by, and interactions among, states and nonstate actors that transcend a given region and that affect the environment and natural resources of multiple regions or the entire planet. The emergence of environmental issues in world politics reflects growing awareness of the cumulative stresses that human activities have on the Earth's resources and life-support systems.

Much of global environmental politics focuses on efforts to negotiate and implement multilateral agreements or other mechanisms for cooperation to protect the environment and natural resources. Some of these agreements stand at the center of global environmental regimes of varying effectiveness that seek to govern or guide specific state behaviors regarding the environmental problem in question.

Legitimate differences in economic, political, and environmental interests make achieving unanimity among states responsible for, or directly affected by, an environmental problem a political and diplomatic challenge. One or more states often have the ability to block or weaken a multilateral agreement, and finding ways to overcome such blockage is a major concern. For a regime to form, veto states must be persuaded to abandon their opposition or at least to accept a compromise.

Other obstacles stem from socioeconomic paradigms that justify essentially unlimited exploitation of nature and discount the impact of pollution and deteriorating ecosystems on economic and social well-being. Despite the weakening of these paradigms and widespread recognition of an alternative sustainable development paradigm, the rise of globalization and the resilience of aspects of the traditional paradigms have complicated the shift to potential new models centered around a green economy, incorporation of the precautionary principle, and global sustainable development.

Subsequent chapters in this book explore these and other key issues in global environmental politics. Chapter 2 examines the main actors in global environmental politics. States are the most important actors because they negotiate international legal instruments, create global environmental regimes, and adopt economic, trade, and regulatory policies that directly and indirectly affect the environment. At the same time, nonstate actors also play major roles. International organizations, treaty secretariats, NGOs, and multinational corporations help set the global environmental agenda, initiate and influence the process of regime formation, and carry out actions that directly affect the global environment.

Chapters 3 and 4 look at the development of ten important global environmental regimes: ozone depletion, hazardous wastes, toxic chemicals, climate change, biodiversity, whaling, trade in endangered species, fisheries, desertification, and forests. Each issue is analyzed with a focus on what occurred during different stages in the development of the regime and the role of veto coalitions and other major causal factors.

Chapter 5 looks at obstacles to creating, implementing, and complying with environmental regimes and the means of effective implementation. The first two sections examine factors that make it difficult to create regimes with strong control measures and for states to implement them. The third section outlines methods to improve regime implementation, compliance, and effectiveness. The final section discusses options for increasing the financing available to help implement global environmental regimes. Because inadequate financial and technical resources and counterproductive economic incentives inhibit the ability of many countries to implement or expand environmental regimes, financial issues have been at the center of global environmental policy debates for many years and will continue to be for the foreseeable future.

Chapter 6 explains how the evolution of global environmental politics cannot be understood completely outside the context of the North-South relationship and the other two pillars of sustainable development: economic and social development. Chapter 7 concludes our discussion with some thoughts on the past, present, and future of global environmental politics.

2

Actors in the Environmental Arena

States are the most important actors in global environmental politics. States adopt the broad economic, regulatory, trade, and development policies that affect the environment. They decide which issues receive formal consideration by the international community directly (through advocacy for international action on a particular issue) and indirectly (through membership in the governing councils of international organizations). States negotiate the international legal instruments that create and implement global environmental regimes. Donor states influence the effectiveness of these regimes and other environmental policies through aid programs and donations to implementation programs and multilateral banks.

But nonstate actors also exert significant and increasing influence on global environmental politics. Intergovernmental organizations (IGOs) help to set the global environmental agenda, initiate and mediate the process of regime formation, and cooperate with developing countries on projects and programs directly affecting the environment. Treaty secretariats influence agenda setting and financing issues that affect global environmental regimes. Nongovernmental organizations (NGOs) also participate in setting the agenda, influencing negotiations on regime formation and shaping the environmental policies of donor agencies toward developing countries. Multinational corporations influence bargaining over regime creation and carry out actions that directly affect the global environment. This chapter examines the roles that these actors play in global environmental politics.

NATION-STATE ACTORS: ROLES AND INTERESTS

Perhaps the most important actions by state actors in global environmental politics concern the creation, implementation, and expansion of international environmental regimes. In regime negotiations, a state may play one of four roles: lead state,

49

supporting state, swing state, or veto (or blocking) state. A lead state has a strong commitment to effective international action on the issue, moves the negotiation process forward by proposing its own formula as the basis for an agreement, and attempts to win the support of other state actors.

A supporting state speaks in favor of a lead state's proposal in negotiations. As the price for its acceptance of an agreement, a swing state demands a concession to its interests but not one that would significantly weaken the regime. A veto or blocking state either opposes a proposed environmental regime outright or tries to weaken it to the point that it cannot be effective.

States sometimes change roles. Canada shifted from a swing state in the climate negotiations under the liberal government of Paul Martin to a veto state under the conservative government of Stephen Harper. Sometimes states play different roles for strategic reasons, such as shifting from a swing to a veto role because threatening a veto is sometimes the best means of enhancing bargaining leverage. For example, during the critical second Meeting of the Parties to the Montreal Protocol in London in June 1990, India and China refused to join an agreement that would bind them to phase out chlorofluorocarbons (CFCs) in 2010 until the industrialized countries agreed to provide significant financial assistance to developing countries to assist them in their transition to less harmful, but equally productive, chemicals and more advanced technology.

There may be more than one lead state on a given issue. For example, Canada and Sweden both played lead roles in initiating action resulting in negotiations on persistent organic pollutants (POPs). Sometimes a state steps forward to advance a policy that puts it clearly in the lead for a particular period, as Germany did with the climate-change issue in 1990 and Canada did with the fisheries issue in 1992. As issues go through several stages, the role of lead state may shift from one state or combination of states to another. In the negotiation of the Vienna Convention for the Protection of the Ozone Layer in 1985, Finland and Sweden took the lead by submitting their own draft convention and heavily influencing the draft put before the conference. In 1986, the United States stepped into the lead role by proposing a gradual 95 percent reduction in CFCs, and by 1990 several industrialized countries had become the lead states by working for a CFC phaseout before 2000. In the early 1990s, the European Union (EU) emerged as the lead state in negotiations to phase out other ozone-depleting chemicals such as methyl bromide and hydrochlorofluorocarbons (HCFCs).

Lead states use a wide range of methods for influencing other state actors on a global environmental issue. A lead state may:

- fund, produce, and/or call attention to research that defines the problem and demonstrates its urgency, as when Canadian research revealed long-range dangers posed by POPs, and when US-based research revealed a threat to the earth's protective ozone layer;

- seek to influence public opinion in target states, as Canada did when it supplied US tourists with pamphlets on the acidification of its forests and waters and instructed its Washington, DC, embassy to cooperate with like-minded US environmental organizations;
- use its diplomatic clout to encourage an international organization to identify the issue as a priority, as when the United States and Canada persuaded the Organization for Economic Cooperation and Development (OECD) to take up the issue of protecting the ozone layer and phasing out CFCs, and when the African countries persuaded the United Nations to begin negotiations on a treaty to combat desertification;
- rely on the worldwide network of NGOs to support its position in other countries and at international conferences, as the Alliance of Small Island States (AOSIS) did in its proposal to place quantitative limits on greenhouse gas (GHG) emissions in the Kyoto Protocol negotiations;
- make a diplomatic démarche to a state that is threatening a veto role, as the United States did with Japan on African elephant ivory; or
- pledge to commit financial or technical resources to the problem, such as the positive incentives that industrialized countries accepted in the Montreal Protocol and Stockholm Convention, and so gain significant developing-country participation.

Although scientific-technological capabilities and economic power cannot ensure that a lead state will prevail on an environmental issue, they constitute valuable assets for helping to create a regime. When a big power like the United States takes a lead role through scientific research, unilateral action, and diplomatic initiative, as it did on the issue of ozone protection, it helps to sway states that do not otherwise have clearly defined interests in the issue.

States play different roles in different issues. A lead state on one issue may be a potential veto state on another. Whether a state plays a lead, supporting, swing, or veto role in regard to a particular global environmental issue depends primarily on domestic political factors and the relative costs and benefits of the proposed regime. Another variable, which has been important in some issues, is the anticipation of international political consequences, including increased international prestige or damage to the country's global image.

Domestic Political Factors

A state's definition of its interests with regard to a particular global environmental issue and its consequential choice of role depend largely on domestic economic and political interests and ideological currents. Whether a government opposes, supports, or leads on an issue depends first on the relative strength and influence of powerful economic and bureaucratic forces and domestic environmental constituencies. Ideological factors related to broader domestic political themes can also play prominent roles in the definition of interests.

Domestic economic interests are particularly prominent in promoting veto roles. When the Liberal Democratic Party dominated Japanese politics, for example, major trading companies generally received government support for their interests in whaling because of their close ties to the party.[1] Norway's fishing industry, which claims to have suffered declining fish catches because of the international protection of whales, has prevailed on its government to defend Norwegian whaling before the international community. The United States has been a swing or veto state on climate-change and chemical-related issues because of pressure from domestic oil, gas, automobile, and chemicals manufacturers.

A state's position on a global environmental issue sometimes reflects the interests of dominant socioeconomic elites. Indonesia, for example, allocates control over a large proportion of its forest resources to a relatively small elite of concessionaires. According to data from the Indonesian Ministry of Forest's Production Forest Utilization Quarterly Report in 2011, seven conglomerates in Indonesia control more than nine million hectares of land, including large forest concessions that will likely be exempt from any moratorium on forest clearing established under the country's Reducing Emissions from Deforestation and Degradation (REDD) program.[2] The extent of holdings could complicate Indonesia's efforts to reduce emissions from logging and plantation development.[3]

Government bureaucracies with institutional interests that could be negatively affected by global action on a particular environmental issue often attempt to influence the adoption of swing or blocking roles. During the negotiation of the Montreal Protocol in the mid-1980s, officials in the US Departments of Commerce, Interior, and Agriculture, together with the Office of Management and Budget, the Office of Science and Technology Policy, and some members of the White House staff, began to reopen basic questions about the scientific evidence and the possible damage to the US economy from imposing additional CFC controls, but they were overruled.[4]

Taking a lead role on a global environmental issue becomes far more likely if there is little or no domestic opposition. The United States could easily take the lead role on the issue of whaling, for example, because the US whaling industry had already been eliminated. Similarly, the absence of significant bureaucratic or business interest in opposing a ban on imports of African elephant ivory products made it easy for the United States to assume a lead role on that issue.

The existence of a strong environmental movement can be a decisive factor in a state's definition of its interest on an issue, especially if it is a potential swing vote in parliamentary elections. The sudden emergence of West German and French bids for leadership roles on certain environmental issues in 1989 reflected in large part the upsurge of public support for strong environmental protection policies in Europe. The German Green Party had already won 8.2 percent of the vote in the 1984 European Parliament elections, and by 1985 the Greens, backed by popular environmental sentiment, were a strong force in the German parliament.[5] Before the 1989 European Parliament election, polls indicated a new surge in environmentalist sentiment in Germany and France. As a result, in early 1989 both countries became part of a lead coalition of states proposing negotiations on a framework convention on climate change to stabilize carbon dioxide (CO_2) emissions.

But a strong environmental movement does not guarantee that a state actor will play a lead or supporting role on a particular issue. US environmental organizations are among the largest and best organized in the world, but they have been unable to sway US policy regarding climate change or ratification of the Biodiversity, Basel, Rotterdam, or Stockholm conventions. Powerful interests that oppose US participation in these treaties and an environmental movement that has been unable to influence the outcomes of congressional or presidential elections are responsible for this failure.

Conversely, the absence of a strong environmental movement makes it more likely that a state will play a swing or blocking role on an international environmental issue. For example, Japanese NGOs are relatively underdeveloped in comparison with those in North America and Europe, and the Japanese political system makes it difficult for interest groups without high-level political links to influence policy. The Japanese government therefore felt little or no domestic pressure to support regimes on African elephants, whaling, and drift-net fishing. In contrast, US wildlife NGOs placed a great deal of domestic pressure on the US government to take strong positions on these issues.

A final domestic political factor that can shape a country's definition of its interest in an environmental regime is the ideology or belief system of the policy maker. Although the United States had exported very little of its hazardous waste, the George H. W. Bush administration led the veto coalition against a ban on hazardous waste exports to developing countries because of its hostility to regulatory intervention in national and international markets. The first Bush administration also vetoed a proposal for industrialized states to set targets for per capita energy use because officials saw this as unwarranted state interference in consumer preferences.[6]

Comparative Costs and Benefits of Environmental Regimes

A second group of variables that shape the definition of national interest in a global environmental issue includes the potential risks and costs of an environmental threat as well as the costs and benefits associated with the proposed regime.[7] Exceptional

PHOTO 2.1   Canada pushed for strong action on POPs after the discovery that the chemicals tend to bioaccumulate in the Arctic food chain and disproportionately affect Inuit communities in northern Canada.
Courtesy IISD/*Earth Negotiations Bulletin.*

vulnerability to the consequences of environmental problems has driven countries to support, or even take the lead on, strong global action. Thirty-two small island states especially vulnerable to sea-level rise because of global warming formed AOSIS in November 1990 to speak with a single, more influential voice in the climate negotiations and to become the strongest proponent of international action to reduce GHG emissions.

Sweden and Norway, which led the fight for the Convention on Long-Range Transboundary Air Pollution, have been the major recipients of sulfur dioxide from other European countries, and their lakes and soils are also acid sensitive. The damage from acid rain therefore appeared earlier and was more serious in those Nordic countries than in the United Kingdom or Germany. Similarly, Canada pushed for strong action on POPs after the discovery that the chemicals tend to bioaccumulate in the Arctic food chain and disproportionately affect Inuit communities in northern Canada.

The costs of compliance with a given global environmental regime may differ dramatically from one country to another, and such differences have sometimes shaped the roles played by states in regime negotiations. The negotiation of the Montreal Protocol provides several examples of states whose roles were linked with economic interests. Former United Nations Environment Programme (UNEP) executive director Mostafa Tolba is reported to have observed, "The difficulties in negotiating the Montreal Protocol had nothing to do with whether the environment was damaged or not. . . . It was all who was going to get the edge over whom."[8] Because of an earlier unilateral ban on aerosols using ozone-depleting chemicals, the United States was ahead of members of the European Community (EC) and Japan in finding substitutes for CFCs in aerosol cans; it therefore joined Canada and the Nordic states in supporting such a ban. The EC and Japan rejected a ban on CFC aerosols in the early 1980s in part because they did not yet have technological alternatives. The Soviet Union, fearful that it would be unable to develop new technologies to replace CFCs, resisted the idea of significant CFC cuts until 1987. China and India, which were minor producers at the time but already gearing up for major production increases, also feared that the transition to ozone-safe chemicals would be too costly without noncommercial access to alternative technologies. Moreover, India's chemical industry planned to export half its projected CFC production to the Middle East and Asia.

The anticipated economic costs of compliance were the underlying issue during the negotiations that resulted in the Kyoto Protocol to the United Nations Framework Convention on Climate Change (UNFCCC). Achieving reductions in GHG emissions is easier and/or cheaper for some countries than others. For example, EU states are generally net importers of fossil fuels and have learned how to reduce energy use without compromising economic growth. Because the EU states saw that their cost of compliance would be comparatively low, they were able to play a lead role in the negotiation of the Kyoto Protocol.

International Political and Diplomatic Considerations

States also consider potential benefits or costs to broader international interests when considering whether to assume a lead or veto role on a particular global environmental issue. A state may hope to gain international prestige by assuming a lead role, or it may decide against a veto role to avoid international opprobrium or damage to its relations with countries for which the environmental issue is of significantly greater concern.

Concern for national prestige—a state's reputation or status in the international community—was once confined to the issue area of international security. Beginning in the early 1990s, a few states began to regard leadership on the global environment as a means of enhancing their international status. In 1994, then EU environment commissioner Yannis Paleokrassas hailed the prospect of a region-wide carbon tax, which would give the EU a lead role in climate change and result in "the resumption of world environmental and fiscal leadership by the European Union," suggesting that the EU would gain a new kind of international prestige.[9]

At the 1992 Earth Summit, the United States tarnished its image in the eyes of many observers because it stood alone in rejecting the Convention on Biological Diversity (CBD). Germany and Japan, among other countries, shared US unhappiness concerning some provisions in the CBD but shunned a veto role for fear of damaging their prestige. A George H. W. Bush administration official later charged that Germany and Japan had departed from the US position in part to demonstrate their new status as emerging, independent world powers.[10]

A state's concern about how a veto role might affect its image sometimes focuses on a particular country or group of countries. For international trade in hazardous wastes, for example, the decision by France and the United Kingdom in 1989 to alter their position and not play a veto role stemmed in part from a broader national interest in maintaining close ties with former colonies in Africa. Japan chose not to block efforts to ban trade in African elephant ivory in 1989 largely because it feared damage to its relations with its most important trading partners, the United States and Europe. Canada ratified the Kyoto Protocol in 2002 in part to protect its "environmentally progressive international image."[11] However, Canada withdrew from Kyoto in 2011, when the conservative government of Steven Harper, no longer concerned about its international image, objected to the estimated cost of compliance.[12]

Subnational Actors

National governments, despite their assertion of exclusive rights to act in international relations, are no longer the only governmental actors in global environmental politics. In recent years, cities, states, and provinces have shown increased interest in adopting their own environmental and energy policies, and these could have a major impact on global environmental problems, especially climate change. Although municipal and state governments are unlikely to usurp national government functions in regime strengthening, they may reinforce and supplement efforts by national governments. Large cities are major producers of GHGs in part because of their heavy consumption of energy, the biggest source of CO_2 emissions. With this in mind, in May 2005 a bipartisan group of 132 US mayors, frustrated by the George W. Bush administration's refusal to ratify the Kyoto Protocol, pledged that their cities would try to meet Kyoto's US target: a 7 percent reduction in GHG emissions from 1990 levels by 2014. The cities ranged from liberal centers such as Los Angeles, California, to strongholds of conservatism such as Hurst, Texas. By 2012 more than 1,054 mayors, representing a total population of over eighty-eight million had signed onto the Mayors Climate Protection Agreement.[13]

In some cities, GHG reduction policies are well under way. Seattle's municipal power utility, Seattle City Light, was the first in the nation to become carbon neutral in 2005, with no net GHG emissions. City Light programs also avoided the release of

PHOTO 2.2   New York City mayor Michael Bloomberg, speaking at the Bali Climate Change Conference in 2007 with London's deputy mayor, Nicky Gavron, is one of the mayors who signed the Mayors Climate Protection Agreement.
Courtesy IISD/*Earth Negotiations Bulletin.*

more than 663,000 metric tons of carbon dioxide into the atmosphere in 2011—the equivalent of taking 146,000 cars off the road for a year.[14] In November 2007, the New York City Council passed a law with the goal of reducing citywide GHG emissions by 30 percent below 2005 levels by 2030. The law also requires the city to reduce the carbon footprint of municipal operations much more quickly: by 30 percent by 2017.[15]

There has also been action to reduce GHG emissions at the US state level. By the end of 2012, thirty-seven states plus the District of Columbia had renewable portfolio standards in place. Renewable portfolio standards are policies that require electricity providers to obtain a minimum percentage of their power from non–fossil-fuel energy resources (such as solar, wind, geothermal, biomass, and hydropower) by a certain date. Together, these states account for two-thirds of the electricity sales in the United States. For example, California requires electric utilities to have 33 percent of their retail sales derived from eligible renewable energy resources by 2020; New York originally enacted a renewables target of 25 percent of state electricity consumption by 2013, but expanded this in January 2010 to 30 percent by 2015; and Illinois and Minnesota will derive 25 percent by 2025.[16]

Nine Northeast and Mid-Atlantic states have agreed to limit GHG emissions through a cooperative effort called the Regional Greenhouse Gas Initiative (RGGI). Connecticut, Delaware, Maine, Maryland, Massachusetts, New Hampshire, New York, Rhode Island, and Vermont will require a 10 percent reduction in GHG emissions from power plants by 2018. Governor Chris Christie of New Jersey pulled his state out of RGGI in 2011. The Regional Greenhouse Gas Initiative is the first mandatory, market-based CO_2 emissions-reduction program in the United States. The first auction of CO_2 allowances was held in September 2008, and the first compliance period for each state's linked CO_2 budget trading program began January 1, 2009. The RGGI auctions emission allowances on a regular basis and as of 2012 had generated more than $1 billion for renewable energy programs.[17]

The United States is not the only country in which activities are taking place at the state and provincial levels. In May 2008, Australia's most populous state, New South Wales, announced that all government operations, including state-run schools, hospitals, and police stations, would be carbon neutral by 2020.[18] In British Columbia, Canada, the Greenhouse Gas Reductions Target Act set a target of reducing GHG emissions by at least 33 percent below 2007 levels by 2020 and included the long-term target of an 80 percent reduction below 2007 levels by 2050. Another Canadian province, Quebec, is planning to work with the state of California to establish a cap-and-trade system to reduce GHG gas emissions.[19] Several large cities in the developing world have begun working with foundations, NGOs, international organizations, and major corporations to reduce their energy use and GHG emissions through energy-efficiency projects and retrofitting old buildings (many of which yield savings for the city government through reduced energy and other operational costs).[20]

INTERGOVERNMENTAL ORGANIZATIONS

The influence of IGOs on global environmental politics has greatly increased since 1972 (see Box 2.1). IGOs are formed by member states either for multiple purposes—for instance, the United Nations and various regional associations such as the Organization of American States (OAS)—or for more specific purposes, examples of which include the Food and Agriculture Organization (FAO) and the World Health Organization (WHO), both specialized agencies of the United Nations. IGOs range in size and resources from the World Bank, which has a staff of more than 10,000 and lends billions of dollars annually, to UNEP, with its annual budget for the 2012–2013 biennium of $474 million and a professional staff of 589.

Although ultimately accountable to governing bodies made up of representatives of their member states, IGO staff can take initiatives and influence outcomes on global issues. The professional skills of these bureaucrats can be an important factor in environmental negotiations. IGO bureaucracies have widely varying degrees of independence. Senior staff at UNEP and the FAO must take their cues from their governing councils in setting agendas, sponsoring negotiations, and implementing development and environment programs. Governing councils comprise all or large subsets of the governments that participate in the IGO. They usually meet every one to three years to provide formal guidance to the IGO. At the World Bank, which depends on major donor countries for its funds, the staff nevertheless has wide discretion in planning and executing projects.

An IGO may influence the outcomes of global environmental issues in several ways:[21]

- It may help determine which issues the international community will address through its influence on the agenda for global action.
- It may convene and influence negotiations on global environmental regimes.
- It may provide independent and authoritative information on a global environmental issue.
- It may develop norms or codes of conduct (soft law) to guide action in particular environmental issue areas.
- It may influence states' environmental and development policies on issues not under international negotiation but relevant to global environmental politics.
- It may affect the implementation of global environmental policies through the provision of funds.

BOX 2.1   PROMINENT INTERGOVERNMENTAL ORGANIZATIONS IN GLOBAL ENVIRONMENTAL POLITICS

Many intergovernmental organizations (IGOs) play important roles in different aspects of global environmental politics. These include but are not limited to:

African Development Bank (AfDB)
Asian Development Bank (ADB)
UN Food and Agriculture Organization (FAO)
Global Environment Facility (GEF)
Inter-American Development Bank (IDB)
International Monetary Fund (IMF)
International Maritime Organization (IMO)
Intergovernmental Panel on Climate Change (IPCC)
International Tropical Timber Organization (ITTO)
Organization for Economic Cooperation and Development (OECD)
Organization of the Petroleum Exporting Countries (OPEC)
United Nations Development Programme (UNDP)
United Nations Environment Programme (UNEP)
United Nations Population Fund (UNFPA)
United Nations Human Settlements Programme (UN-HABITAT)
World Bank
World Health Organization (WHO)
World Meteorological Organization (WMO)
World Trade Organization (WTO)

No IGO influences global environmental politics by performing all these functions. IGOs tend to specialize in one or more political functions, although one may indirectly influence another.

Setting Agendas and Influencing Regime Formation

In the past, UNEP dominated the agenda-setting function of global environmental politics because of its mandate to catalyze and coordinate environmental activities and to serve as a focal point for such activities within the UN system (see Box 2.2). Through decisions by its governing council, UNEP identifies critical global environmental threats requiring international cooperation. In 1976, for example, the UNEP Governing Council chose ozone depletion as one of five priority problems, and consequently UNEP convened a meeting of experts in Washington, DC, which adopted the World Plan of Action on the Ozone Layer in 1977—five years before negotiations on a global agreement began.

UNEP played a similar role in initiating negotiations on climate change. Along with the World Meteorological Organization (WMO), UNEP sponsors the Intergovernmental Panel on Climate Change (IPCC) to study scientific and policy issues in preparation for negotiations on a global convention on climate change. UNEP convened international negotiations on many of the major environmental conventions of the past two decades: the Vienna Convention for the Protection of the Ozone Layer (1985), the Montreal Protocol on Substances that Deplete the Ozone Layer (1987), the Basel Convention on the Control of Transboundary Movements of Hazardous Wastes and Their Disposal (1989), the Convention on Biological Diversity (1992), the Stockholm Convention on Persistent Organic Pollutants (2001), and the Minamata Convention on mercury (2013). With the FAO, UNEP convened the negotiations that resulted in the 1998 Rotterdam Convention on the Prior Informed Consent Procedure for Certain Hazardous Chemicals and Pesticides in international trade.

UNEP also has sought to shape the global environmental agenda by monitoring and assessing the state of the environment and disseminating that information to governments and NGOs. Since its founding in 1972, UNEP has acted as the secretariat for the UN's system-wide Earthwatch program and has established:

- the Global Environmental Monitoring System/Water Programme to provide authoritative, scientifically sound information on the state and trends of global inland water quality;
- the Global Resource Information Database, a global network of environmental data centers facilitating the generation and dissemination of key environmental information;
- the UNEP World Conservation Monitoring Centre, as the world biodiversity information and assessment center.

BOX 2.2   WHAT IS UNEP?

The United Nations Environment Programme (UNEP) is the lead United Nations organization on environmental issues. It was founded as a result of the United Nations Conference on the Human Environment in June 1972, and its original mandate was to promote, catalyze, and coordinate the development of environmental policy within the UN system and internationally. UNEP's current mission is "to provide leadership and encourage partnership in caring for the environment by inspiring, informing, and enabling nations and peoples to improve their quality of life without compromising that of future generations."

UNEP assists the development and implementation of international environmental policy, helps to monitor and raise awareness of environmental issues, assists developing countries in implementing environmentally sound policies, promotes environmental science and information and how they can work in conjunction with policy, seeks to coordinate United Nations environmental activities, and encourages sustainable development at the local, national, regional, and global levels.

UNEP's headquarters is in Nairobi, Kenya, and it maintains offices and units in several other countries (such as the UNEP Chemicals office in Geneva that houses the secretariats for the Basel, Rotterdam, and Stockholm conventions). UNEP has a relatively small staff and budget compared to many UN organizations. This reflects its original mandate to act as a catalyst and coordinator rather than an on-the-ground manager of large programs like UNDP, UNICEF, and WHO. Nevertheless, UNEP has had notable successes, particularly in assisting the development, implementation, administration, and expansion of global environmental regimes.

For updated information on UNEP, including current focal areas, see www.unep.org.

UNEP has also undertaken a number of global assessments, including five Global Environmental Outlook assessments (since 1995), seven ozone assessments (since 1998), the Global Biodiversity Assessment (1995), the Cultural and Spiritual Values of Biodiversity Assessment (1999), the Global Marine Assessment (2001), the Global Mercury Assessment (2002), the Global International Waters Assessment (2003), the Millennium Ecosystem Assessment (2005), the Global International Waters

Assessment (2006), and the International Assessment of Agricultural Knowledge, Science and Technology for Development (2008).

Former UNEP executive director Mostafa Tolba influenced environmental diplomacy through direct participation in the negotiations. In informal talks with the chiefs of EC delegations during the negotiations on the Montreal Protocol, he lobbied hard for a phaseout of CFCs.[22] At the London Conference of the Parties (COP) in 1990, he convened informal meetings with twenty-five environment ministers to work out a compromise on the contentious issue of linking protocol obligations with financial assistance and technology transfer. He also urged a compromise to bridge the gap between US and Western European timetables for a CFC phaseout (see Chapter 3). At the final session of the negotiations on the CBD, Tolba took over when there appeared to be gridlock on key issues regarding the financing mechanism, and he virtually forced the acceptance of a compromise text (see Chapter 4).

Tolba sometimes openly championed the developing countries against the highly industrialized countries. During the final round of negotiations that created the Basel Convention, for instance, he fought for a ban on shipping hazardous wastes to or from noncontracting parties and for a requirement that exporters check disposal sites at their own expense. But Tolba and the developing countries lost on both issues because they were opposed by the waste-exporting states (see Chapter 3).

Tolba's retirement and replacement with a new executive director, Elizabeth Dowdeswell, reduced UNEP's role in agenda setting for most of the 1990s. While UNEP has had its share of successes during this period, it struggled to keep pace with the dramatic changes in international environmental policy making. Chronic financial problems, the absence of a clear focus and mission for the institution, challenges associated with its location in Nairobi, and management difficulties all contributed to the erosion of UNEP's participation in the international environmental policy-making process.[23]

In February 1998, Klaus Töpfer was appointed UNEP's executive director, a position he held until 2006. In a demonstration of renewed faith in the organization, its leadership, and its work program, donor pledges to UNEP's Environment Fund increased. During Töpfer's tenure, UNEP developed the Global Earth Observation System of Systems to achieve comprehensive, coordinated, and sustained earth observations and so improve integrated environmental assessment; developed the Strategic Approach for International Chemicals Management; improved the scientific base of UNEP; and created the Global Ministerial Environment Forum to keep under review the state of the global environment, to assess environmental challenges continuously, to identify new and emerging issues, and to set assessment priorities.[24]

Achim Steiner became UNEP's fifth executive director in 2006. In 2007, UNEP adopted a new medium-term strategy[25] that further streamlined its operations to

PHOTO 2.3   **UNEP, under Executive Director Achim Steiner, has played an agenda-setting role
for international action on mercury pollution.**
Courtesy IISD/*Earth Negotiations Bulletin.*

focus and continue to set the agendas on six crosscutting thematic priorities: climate
change, disasters and conflicts, ecosystem management, environmental governance,
harmful substances and hazardous waste, and resource efficiency (sustainable consumption and production). UNEP also embarked on negotiations for a global agreement on mercury.

The UN Commission on Sustainable Development (CSD) also had opportunities
to play an agenda-setting role in global environmental politics during its twenty-year
history. The CSD was responsible for reviewing progress in the implementation of
Agenda 21 and the Rio Declaration on Environment and Development, as well as providing policy guidance to follow up the Johannesburg Plan of Implementation. It was
the high-level forum for sustainable development within the UN system. No other
UN institution examined head-on the linkages between the environmental, social,
economic, and political arenas on a global scale. The commission generated greater
concern for some issues on the international sustainable development agenda. By creating the Intergovernmental Panel on Forests and, subsequently, the Intergovernmental Forum on Forests, the CSD successfully focused the forest issue and created more
understanding that forests are owned by someone and provide a livelihood for many
people (see Chapter 4). Freshwater resources and energy are two issues that did not
receive much attention in 1992 and gained more prominence under the CSD's agenda

and, through that, at the 2002 World Summit on Sustainable Development. Similarly, the CSD's discussions on sustainable production and consumption patterns, sustainability indicators, and the need for technology transfer, education, and capacity building in developing countries have raised the profiles of these issues.

On oceans, at CSD-7 in 1999, delegates stressed the importance of finding ways and means to enhance the annual debate on oceans and the law of the sea. A CSD recommendation to the UNGA resulted in the establishment of the United Nations Open-Ended Informal Consultative Process on Oceans and the Law of the Sea, which has taken place annually since 2000 to improve deliberations on developments in oceanic affairs and strengthen international cooperation on ocean-related issues.[26]

For twenty years, however, the CSD struggled with moving beyond abstract debate to true agenda setting. The commission increasingly was seen as dysfunctional, as it was unable to reach agreement on how to move forward on energy, sustainable consumption and production, chemicals, wastes, and other key sustainable development issues. As a result, the 2012 United Nations Conference on Sustainable Development agreed to replace the CSD with a new intergovernmental, high-level political forum (see Chapter 7).[27]

Providing Independent and Authoritative Information

IGOs can also influence global environmental politics by providing independent and authoritative scientific information to states, other IGOs, the public, and the press. By their very nature, many environmental problems do not lend themselves to precision. The causes and long-term effects of particular environmental problems are not always clear. In very few cases are all scientific issues completely understood and their future implications projected with confidence before negotiations begin. Many environmental problems are so complex scientifically, with so many different parameters, interrelations, and correlations that cannot easily be stated as precise causal relationships, that the substance of what is being negotiated, what is an appropriate trade-off, what is a reasonable fallback position, and what are effective outcomes can be difficult to define for many years.[28] At the same time, the probable environmental consequences could be catastrophic. Therefore, states are left in the unenviable position of having to elaborate policies on issues rife with uncertainties.

The scientific community has always played a role in intergovernmental environmental treaty negotiations, going back to some of the earliest negotiations on oceans. As environmental issues, like climate change, have become more technical, and as scientific uncertainty about possible long-term effects has grown, policy makers rely on scientists to present the facts and projections, which often set the stage for treaty negotiations. As a result, international networks of cooperating scientists and scientific institutions have become actors in global environmental policy. Huge teams of scientists can review each other's work, perform integrated assessments, and generate ideas that far exceed the aggregation of each individual's particular knowledge.[29]

One of the first international bodies of scientists to provide independent and authoritative information to international negotiators was the Ozone Trends Panel. While not an official IGO, as it was organized by NASA, it was a sixteen-month comprehensive scientific exercise involving more than one hundred scientists from ten countries. Released in March 1988, the report of the Ozone Trends Panel made headlines around the world: ozone-layer depletion was no longer a theory; it was substantiated by hard scientific evidence, and CFCs and halons were implicated beyond a reasonable doubt. Thus the state of the science had fundamentally changed, bringing pressure for a complete phaseout of CFCs and a strengthening of the Montreal Protocol. Further scientific evidence in the subsequent five years led to the complete phaseout of CFCs and halons, along with phaseouts and reductions in the use of a number of other ozone-depleting chemicals as the ozone regime was strengthened.[30]

The best-known example of an IGO providing authoritative scientific information is the IPCC. Established by the WMO and UNEP in 1988, the IPCC is charged with providing independent scientific advice on the complex issue of climate change. The panel was asked to prepare, based on available scientific information, a report on all aspects relevant to climate change and its impacts and to formulate realistic response strategies. The first assessment report of the IPCC, released in 1990, served as the basis for negotiating the UNFCCC. Since then, the IPCC has released three additional comprehensive assessment reports (1995, 2001, and 2007), as well as other reports on specific topics, and has involved the work of thousands of scientists from around the world. Its work has been so essential that in 2007, the IPCC and former US vice president Al Gore were jointly awarded the Nobel Peace Prize for their efforts to build up and disseminate greater knowledge about human-made climate change and to lay the foundations for the measures needed to counteract such change.

There have been several attempts to use the IPCC model to create scientific bodies to serve other conventions. The Millennium Ecosystem Assessment, called for by UN Secretary-General Kofi Annan, examined the consequences of ecosystem change for human well-being and the scientific basis for action needed to enhance the conservation and sustainable use of those systems and their contribution to human well-being. The assessment was coordinated by UNEP and overseen by representatives of different conventions (the Convention on Biological Diversity, Convention to Combat Desertification, Ramsar Convention on Wetlands, and Convention on Migratory Species) as well as national governments, UN agencies, civil society representatives, and the private sector. More than 1,300 scientists and other experts from ninety-five countries were involved in its work between 2001 and 2005. Like the IPCC, the Millennium

Ecosystem Assessment evaluated an immense array of scientific literature, government and IGO reports, and field data, and ultimately published five technical volumes.[31]

To follow up on the Millennium Ecosystem Assessment, after five years of international negotiations, in April 2012 more than ninety governments agreed to officially establish the Intergovernmental Science-Policy Platform on Biodiversity and Ecosystem Services (IPBES). When it begins work in 2014, it will provide scientifically sound and relevant information to support more informed decisions on how biodiversity and ecosystem services are conserved and used around the world. It will serve as an interface between the scientific community and policy makers that aims to build capacity for and strengthen the use of science in policy making.[32]

Developing Nonbinding Norms and Codes of Conduct

International organizations also influence global environmental politics by facilitating the development of common norms or rules of conduct that do not have binding legal effect on the participating states. A variety of creative nontreaty measures, often called "soft law," have been developed to influence state behavior on environmental issues. Soft-law measures include codes of conduct, declarations of principle, global action plans, and other international agreements that create new norms and expectations without the binding status of treaties.[33]

These nonbinding agreements are negotiated by groups of experts representing their governments, usually through processes convened by intergovernmental organizations. Most UN agencies have contributed to this process, but UNEP has done the most to promote it. Concerning the management of hazardous waste, for instance, a UNEP ad hoc working group of experts helped draft guidelines in 1984. In 1987, the same process produced guidelines and principles aimed at making the worldwide pesticide trade more responsive to the threats these substances pose to the environment and human health. Other examples include the 1980 International Programme on Chemical Safety and the 1985 Action Plan for Biosphere Reserves, each of which has become the recognized standard in its field.

Since 1963, the Joint FAO/WHO Food Standards Programme (via the Codex Alimentarius Commission) has developed food standards, guidelines, and codes of practice aimed at protecting the health of consumers and ensuring fair trade. The FAO has drafted guidelines on the environmental criteria for the registration of pesticides (1985) and the International Code of Conduct on the Distribution and Use of Pesticides (1986).

The 1995 FAO Code of Conduct for Responsible Fisheries sets out principles and international standards of behavior for responsible practices with a view to ensuring the effective conservation, management, and development of living aquatic resources. It builds on thirty years of FAO work on the issue (see Box 2.3). The FAO Committee on Fisheries (COFI), consisting of FAO member states, was established in 1965 as a subsidiary body of the FAO Council and has remained the primary global forum for the consideration of major issues related to fisheries and aquaculture policy. Until the late 1980s, COFI focused on problems of coastal states in the development of their fisheries, especially after they acquired two-hundred-mile coastal fishing zones in the 1970s. But when the pressures of overfishing on global fish stocks became increasingly difficult to ignore, COFI and the FAO Secretariat began pushing more aggressively for new international norms for sustainable fisheries.

The FAO Secretariat has helped mobilize international support for more sustainable fisheries management by collecting and analyzing data on global fish catch, issuing

BOX 2.3   WHAT IS THE FAO?

The Food and Agriculture Organization of the United Nations (FAO) leads international efforts to defeat hunger, advance agricultural productivity, and ensure food safety. It serves both developed and developing countries, acting as a neutral forum where nations meet to discuss issues, negotiate agreements, and create programs. The FAO also serves as a source of knowledge and information, helping developing countries modernize and improve agriculture, forestry, and fisheries practices and ensure good nutrition for all. FAO work currently focuses on food security, natural resource management, forestry and fisheries, early warning of food emergencies, disaster recovery, food safety, bio-energy, and other issues. Since its founding in 1945, the FAO has paid special attention to developing rural areas, home to 70 percent of the world's poor and hungry people.

Today, the FAO has 191 member states, two associate members, and one member organization, the European Union. Its headquarters are in Rome, and it has an extensive set of regional, subregional, and country offices. The FAO works in partnership with institutions of all kinds: United Nations agencies, national governments, private foundations, large NGOs, grassroots organizations, companies, professional associations, and others. Some partnerships operate at the national level or in the field; others are regional or global in nature. In 2010–2011, the FAO implemented programs and projects with a total value of $1,707 million. More information on the FAO can be found at www.fao.org.

annual reviews on the state of the world's fisheries, and organizing technical workshops. These efforts helped to focus government and NGO attention on such issues as excess fishing capacity and fisheries subsidies. In 1991, COFI recommended that the FAO should develop the concept of responsible fisheries in the form of a code of conduct, and the FAO Secretariat convened negotiations, which resulted in the adoption of the 1995 Code of Conduct for Responsible Fisheries. The code of conduct is the most comprehensive set of international norms for sustainable fisheries management that currently exists, and despite not being legally binding, it has influenced state and producer practices.

Soft-law agreements are often a good way to avoid the lengthy process of negotiating, signing, and ratifying binding agreements. They do not require enforcement mechanisms and can sometimes depend on the adherence of networks of bureaucrats who share similar views of the problem. But when soft-law regimes are adopted because key parties are unwilling to go beyond nonbinding guidelines, then the agreed-on norms are not usually particularly stringent, and state compliance is likely to be uneven at best. The 1985 Code of Conduct on the Distribution and Use of Pesticides and the 1985 Cairo guidelines on international hazardous waste trade are examples of this pattern.

Soft law may be turned into binding international law in two ways: principles included in a soft-law agreement may become so widely regarded as the appropriate norms for a problem that they are ultimately absorbed into treaty law, or political pressures may arise from those dissatisfied with spotty adherence to soft-law norms that they successfully advocate for international negotiations to turn a nonbinding agreement into a binding one.

Influencing National Development Policies

IGOs affect global environmental politics by influencing the environmental and development policies of individual states outside the context of regime negotiations. National policy decisions on how to manage forests, generate and use energy, increase agricultural production, allocate government resources, regulate pollution, and manage other economic, development, and environment issues determine how sustainable the country will be and the impact it will have on global environmental issues. IGOs can influence such policies, and thus the sustainability of societies, in several ways:

- They provide financing for development projects, as well as advice and technical assistance that help shape the country's development strategy.
- They provide financing for environment-protection projects.
- They provide financing, technical assistance, training, and capacity building to create or improve government agencies.

- They undertake research aimed at persuading state officials to adopt certain policies.
- They provide targeted information to government officials, NGOs, the private sector, and the public.
- They focus normative pressure on states regarding sustainable development policy issues.

The FAO, for example, is the world's principal repository of global fishery statistics. The FAO compiles, collates, analyzes, and integrates fishery and aquaculture data and information, creating a range of information products that are relevant, timely and easily available to users (in print and electronically). In agriculture, FAO helps

---

BOX 2.4   WHAT IS UNDP?

The United Nations Development Programme (UNDP) is the UN global development organization. Headquartered in New York, UNDP has offices in 177 countries and territories, which work with national governments, IGOs, NGOs, and others to implement programs and build developing countries' capacity to address local, national, and global development challenges. In each country office, the UNDP resident representative also normally serves as the resident coordinator of development activities for the United Nations system as a whole. Through such coordination, UNDP seeks to ensure effective use of UN and international aid resources.

UNDP's networks also help to implement, link, and coordinate efforts to achieve the Millennium Development Goals (MDGs), including the overarching goal of cutting poverty in half by 2015. To accomplish the MDGs and encourage global development, UNDP focuses on helping countries build and share solutions to the challenges of poverty reduction, crisis prevention and recovery, environment and energy, HIV/AIDS, and democratic governance. UNDP's annual *Human Development Report* contains updated global and national statistics while also focusing attention on key development issues. UNDP is among the largest UN agencies. The UNDP administrator is the third highest ranking member of the United Nations after the United Nations secretary-general and deputy secretary-general.

For more on UNDP, see www.undp.org. For the *Human Development Report*, see hdr.undp.org/en.

farmers to diversify food production, protect plant and animal health, market their products, and conserve natural resources. The FAO provides capacity building to farmers in integrated pest management to reduce reliance on chemical pesticides. The FAO also provides technical assistance and advice to help countries develop and improve national forest programs, plan and carry out forest activities, and implement effective forest legislation. More than 120 countries have benefited from the FAO's forestry guidance over the last twenty years.[34]

The United Nations Development Programme (UNDP), with a budget of more than $5 billion annually, a staff exceeding ten thousand worldwide, and liaison offices in 177 countries, is a large source of multilateral grant-development assistance (see Box 2.4). Since the adoption of the Millennium Development Goals in 2000, UNDP has concentrated on coordinating global and national efforts to achieve them, including the overarching goal of cutting poverty in half by 2015. Its focus is helping countries build and share solutions to the challenges of democratic governance, poverty reduction, crisis prevention and recovery, environment and energy, and HIV/AIDS. UNDP also helps developing countries attract and use aid effectively.

In the area of environment and energy, UNDP works to strengthen national capacity to manage the environment in a sustainable manner to advance poverty reduction efforts. UNDP supports developing countries to mainstream environment and energy issues into development planning; mobilize finance for improved environmental management; address increasing threats from climate change; and build local capacity to better manage the environment and deliver services, especially water and energy.[35]

UNDP is also one of the three implementing agencies of the Global Environment Facility (GEF; see Box 2.5) and is the lead UN agency in building the capacity of developing-country governments for sustainable development activities. UNDP also assists in building capacity for good governance, popular participation, private-sector and public-sector development, and growth with equity, all of which are necessary in promoting sustainable human development.

IGOs may influence state policy by focusing normative pressures on states regarding the environment and sustainable development, even when no formal international agreement exists on the norm.[36] UNDP has gone the furthest of any UN agency in this regard, calling for the allocation of resources for human development (health, population, and education) by donor countries and developing-country governments, at particular levels, as a norm in the context of what it calls "sustainable human development." Through its annual *Human Development Report*, which ranks nations according to their provision of these social services, UNDP pressures developing countries into devoting more of their budgets to these social sectors.

BOX 2.5 WHAT IS THE GEF?

GEF

The Global Environment Facility (GEF) is the largest international funder of projects that address global environmental issues. It provides grants to developing countries and countries with economies in transition for projects in six focal areas: biodiversity, climate change, international waters, land degradation, the ozone layer, and persistent organic pollutants. The GEF is also the designated financial mechanism for four global environmental agreements: Convention on Biological Diversity (CBD), Convention to Combat Desertification (UNCCD), United Nations Framework Convention on Climate Change (UNFCCC), and Stockholm Convention on Persistent Organic Pollutants (POPs). For each of these conventions, the GEF assists eligible countries in meeting their regime obligations under rules and guidance provided by the conventions and their conferences of parties. The GEF is also associated with other regimes, including several global and regional agreements that address transboundary water systems and the Montreal Protocol on Substances that Deplete the Ozone Layer.

Since its creation in 1991, the GEF has provided more than $11.5 billion in grants and leveraged more than $57 billion in cofinancing for over 3,215 projects in more than 165 countries. Through its Small Grants Programme, the GEF has also made more than 16,030 small grants directly to civil society and community-based organizations, totaling $653.2 million. Governments agreed to restructure the GEF, originally a pilot program of the World Bank, in 1994 and moved it out of the World Bank system. The decision to make the GEF an independent institution was designed in part to enhance the involvement of developing countries in the decision-making process and in the implementation of the projects. Since 1994, the World Bank has served as the trustee of the GEF trust fund and provided administrative services. Many other international organizations—including UNDP, UNEP, FAO, and several regional development banks—as well as NGOs and other actors, work with national governments to implement GEF-funded projects.

The GEF secretariat handles the organization's day-to-day operations. Based in Washington, DC, it reports directly to the GEF Council and GEF Assembly. The GEF Council is the main governing body, functioning as an independent board of directors with primary responsibility for developing, adopting, and evaluating GEF programs. Composed of representatives from 16 developing countries, 14 developed countries, and 2 countries with transitional economies, the council meets twice each year. All decisions are by consensus. The GEF Assembly includes representatives from all 182 member countries. It meets every three to four years and is responsible for reviewing and evaluating the GEF's general policies, operation, and membership. The assembly also considers and approves proposed amendments to the GEF Instrument, the document that established the GEF and sets the rules by which the GEF operates.

For more information on the GEF, see www.gefweb.org.

TREATY SECRETARIATS

Treaty secretariats are a specific type of IGO established by an international treaty to manage the day-to-day operation of the treaty regime.[37] Their staffs consist of international civil servants tasked with pursuing the treaty's objectives. Most treaty secretariats are established initially to administer the process of negotiating the treaty and convening follow-up meetings, but their role usually shifts after the treaty's adoption and entry into force to facilitating regime operations and helping parties implement their commitments. Despite common core functions, secretariats vary considerably in their size, funding, additional responsibilities, degree of activism, and linkages to other secretariats and treaties.

Secretariats are located in disparate parts of the world, have varying levels of autonomy, and focus on separate, but interrelated, environmental problems. The CBD Secretariat is located in Montreal, Canada; UNCCD and the UNFCCC are in Bonn, Germany; the Convention on International Trade in Endangered Species of Wild Fauna and Flora (CITES) and the Basel, Rotterdam, and Stockholm conventions are in Geneva, Switzerland; and the Ozone Secretariat is in Nairobi, Kenya. Some secretariats, like the Convention on Migratory Species Secretariat (Bonn), serve more than one convention. Some of the larger secretariats, like the UNFCCC Secretariat, have well over one hundred professional members, while the Secretariat of the Ramsar Convention on Wetlands (Gland, Switzerland) has sixteen. Several secretariats, such as those for the ozone, biodiversity, and chemicals regimes, are part of UNEP. Some, like the Climate Secretariat, are administered by the UN Secretariat or other UN agencies.

Treaty secretariats have a number of core tasks that include:

- arranging and servicing meetings of the Conference of the Parties (COP) and all subsidiary bodies;
- preparing and transmitting reports based on information received from the COP and subsidiary bodies;
- preparing reports on secretariat implementation activities for the COP;
- ensuring coordination with relevant international bodies and NGOs;
- liaising and communicating with relevant authorities, nonparties, and international organizations;
- compiling and analyzing scientific, economic, and social data and information;
- monitoring adherence to treaty obligations;
- giving guidance and advice to parties; and
- providing expert technical advice to parties.[38]

Increasingly, treaty secretariats are also involved in raising funds for treaty implementation and awareness-raising activities and to provide training, capacity building,
and technical assistance to developing countries. Secretariats can also create synergies
by coordinating and cooperating with other secretariats. The need for close cooperation is obvious: integrated ecosystems are addressed by fragmented international management. For example, the success of the UNFCCC is directly conditioned by at least
ten other international treaties, while the CBD intersects with dozens of international
conventions.[39]

Treaty secretariats may influence the treatment of global environmental issues in
ways that are quite similar to the international organizations discussed earlier in this
chapter. A secretariat's level of influence depends largely on its mandate, its funding,
and the professional and personal commitment of the staff. Essentially, however, treaty
secretariats have two overarching areas of impact:

1. Treaty secretariats can influence the behavior of actors by changing their knowledge
   and belief systems.
2. Treaty secretariats can influence political processes through the creation, support, and
   shaping of norm-building processes for issue-specific international cooperation.[40]

Treaty Secretariats as Knowledge Brokers

Environmental treaty secretariats embody the institutional memory of the regime
they serve. A secretariat provides continuity for negotiations that stretch through
numerous sessions over a period of years (including both the negotiation and the
implementation of the treaty), during which there may be considerable turnover
among government negotiators.[41] More specifically, they possess expert knowledge
of various categories: technical and scientific knowledge on the problem, administrative and procedural knowledge (which they will often generate themselves), and
the diplomatic knowledge that is paramount to deal with the complex interlinkages
characteristic of international regimes, particularly in the environmental field.[42]

As knowledge brokers, secretariats are in a position to manage and even control
the horizontal flow of information between national governments and the vertical flow
of information between international organizations, national governments, and local
stakeholders. This information can take the form of syntheses of scientific findings, such
as the Ozone Secretariat's reports on the impact that HCFCs (chemicals controlled
under the Montreal Protocol) have on climate change. Even though many secretariats
do not have the means or the mandate for actual scientific research, they have the ability to collect and disseminate scientific knowledge. For example, the CBD Secretariat

maintains close links with the scientific community through international scientific cooperative programs, such as DIVERSITAS, and the participation of staff members in relevant scientific symposia. The secretariat gathers scientific information on the different natural science issues of biodiversity conservation in the various ecosystems as well as on administrative, social, legal, and economic aspects of the problems, for instance, of access and benefit sharing. This knowledge is processed and made available through preparatory documents, the secretariat's website, periodic reports, a newsletter, and a comprehensive handbook.[43]

Knowledge and information management is another key role for treaty secretariats. The COP, its subsidiary bodies, national policy makers, NGO and corporate stakeholders, and other interested actors, such as the media, scientists, and members of civil society, draw on and interpret the information and documentation compiled and disseminated by the secretariat in their analytical, political, and scientific assessments and the related discourses.[44] The frequency of visits to and downloads from its website highlights the usefulness of the Climate Secretariat's role in information management. Website usage grew from 309,657 visits in 1999 to nearly 10 million in 2012. In 2012 alone, 3.8 terabytes (38,000 gigabytes) of information were downloaded.[45] The website contains information about the regime and ongoing negotiations, progress in implementation of the UNFCCC and the Kyoto Protocol, official documents, and background data and other information on climate change.

Secretariats can also act as knowledge brokers by convening expert panels and academic assessments, which can help to raise concern among external actors to the level needed to have an impact on political activity. For example, the UNFCCC Secretariat holds numerous workshops on scientific and technical topics related to the convention's mandate. It also promotes the use of side events during meetings of the COP or the subsidiary bodies in which scientists and other nongovernmental experts share information with policy makers and with each other.

Treaty Secretariats and the Political Process

Treaty secretariats can influence political processes through the creation, support, and shaping of norm-building processes for issue-specific international cooperation, such as the advance informed-agreement provisions in the Biosafety Protocol and the prior informed consent (PIC) procedure under the Rotterdam Convention. They can initiate conferences to follow up on treaties or to introduce relevant new topics to the parties. They are usually in charge of administering negotiations on the implementation or expansion of the regime. In this case, secretariat staff can exercise considerable influence "even when they are not key players during the negotiation stage."[46] For example, the Biodiversity Secretariat demonstrated a balanced and continuous effort to facilitate dialogues and negotiations on both the issues of biosafety and access to genetic resources and the fair and equitable sharing of benefits arising from their use, which contributed to the successful adoption of the Cartagena and Nagoya Protocols.

Secretariats can also influence the political process through capacity building. While secretariats are not funding agencies or responsible for providing resources for on-the-ground activities, some do play enabling roles for capacity building at the national and local levels. For example, a secretariat provides basic informational materials on its convention and its sociopolitical implications, such as those developed by the UNCCD Secretariat. The Ozone Secretariat produces training materials for customs agents. The CITES Secretariat provides training materials for wildlife enforcement offi-

PHOTO 2.4   Ozzy Ozone was developed by UNEP under the Multilateral Fund to help educate children on how to protect themselves from the sun's harmful UV rays and to give practical tips on how to enjoy the sun safely and how to help save the earth's ozone layer. Courtesy IISD/*Earth Negotiations Bulletin.*

cers. The Rotterdam Convention Secretariat provides a training manual to explain the convention and its obligations to those responsible for the export of chemicals. Some secretariats provide booklets and games that explain the issues to children (e.g., "The Ozone Story," the Ozzy Ozone game, and the UNESCO/UNCCD teachers' kit on desertification).

Some secretariats and the chief administrators stick closely to their administrative and facilitative roles, performing only those tasks specifically assigned to them. Others, while also performing the normal administrative and facilitative roles, are more proactive. They seek to push the agenda, looking for new initiatives and trying to get governments to support and implement them.[47] Secretariats in the latter category benefit from skillful and charismatic leadership. UNEP executive director Mostafa Tolba did this in the early years of the ozone regime—inviting, cajoling, and pressuring somewhat reluctant or disinterested governments to come back to the bargaining table to expand the regime, initiating ideas and advancing concerns that might have otherwise been overlooked and pushing negotiators toward compromise solutions on difficult issues.[48] He played a similar role during negotiations that created the Basel Convention on the Control of Transboundary Movements of Hazardous Wastes and Their Disposal.

More often than not, however, the secretariat's role in the negotiations is less overt and more facilitative—the important but often unrecognized, and sometimes pivotal, role of promoting a smooth process, which can be crucial in steering negotiations toward a successful outcome.[49] For example, the Climate Secretariat tends not to generate and broker analytical knowledge on climate change and related economic or regulatory policies; instead it mainly processes and administers factual information. In other words, the secretariat does not exert influence on the parties about whether a particular decision or action is politically desirable and should be taken in order to mitigate or adapt to climate change. Rather, it influences how things are done once parties have agreed that measures have to be taken.[50]

Nevertheless, it is important to note that treaty secretariats sometimes become more active players in global environmental politics than some governments and other actors may prefer. When secretariats move beyond fulfilling their basic functions and begin influencing global discourse through knowledge management, advancing the institutionalization or expansion of a convention, or proactively assisting in capacity building, they become stakeholders in their own right. Government officials occasionally upbraid secretariat officials for moving beyond a purely facilitative role, arguing that secretariats should not influence policy development.[51] At other times they are praised for acting in pursuit of the stated goals of the regime. Thus, in many respects, determining the most effective or legitimate role for a secretariat within a given issue area remains an open question.[52]

MULTILATERAL FINANCIAL INSTITUTIONS

In terms of direct impact on the development and environmental policies of developing states, some of the most powerful IGOs are the multilateral financial institutions, including the World Bank (see Box 2.6), the International Monetary Fund (IMF), and the regional development banks, because of the amount of financial resources that they transfer to developing countries every year in support of particular development strategies and economic policies. Within these IGOs, donor countries are the dominant players, and voting is weighted according to the size of a country's contributions. The United States has the most power in the World Bank and the Inter-American Development Bank. Japan has the most power in the Asian Development Bank.

Environmental activists have viewed the World Bank's influence on the policies of its borrowers as contributing to unsustainable development. Historically, the bank was driven by the need to lend large amounts of money each year; by a bias toward large-scale, capital-intensive, and centralized projects; and by its practice of assessing proj-

---

BOX 2.6   WHAT IS THE WORLD BANK?

The World Bank is the largest source of international financial and development assistance to developing countries. It is not a bank in the conventional sense but a group of development institutions owned by 188 member countries. Together they provide low-interest loans, interest-free credits, and grants to developing countries for a wide array of purposes that include investments in education, health, public administration, infrastructure, financial and private-sector development, agriculture, and environmental and natural resource management.

The World Bank consists of a number of different institutions. The first, the International Bank for Reconstruction and Development (IBRD), was created by the United States and its allies in 1944 to facilitate post–World War II reconstruction. Over the years it was joined by four other institutions—the International Development Association (IDA), International Finance Corporation, Multilateral Guarantee Agency, and International Center for the Settlement of Investment Disputes—and their collective mandate changed to worldwide poverty alleviation and economic development.

Source: The World Bank website, www.worldbank.org.

---

ects according to a quantifiable rate of return (how the loan contributes to conventional gross national product calculations), while it discounted longer-term, unquantifiable social and environmental costs and benefits. In the 1970s and 1980s, the World Bank supported schemes to colonize rain forests in Brazil and Indonesia, cattle-ranching projects in Central and South America, dams on the Narmada River in India, tobacco projects in Africa that contributed to accelerated deforestation, and a cattle-development project in Botswana that contributed to desertification.[53]

In response to persistent, well-orchestrated pressure from NGOs, criticism by some prominent members of the US Congress, and calls for it to become part of the solution to global environmental problems rather than a contributor, the World Bank began a process of evolution in the mid-1980s toward greater sensitivity to the environmental implications of its lending. These reforms included mandatory environmental assessment procedures and the public disclosure of these assessments in advance of project approval. In addition, the bank's board of executive directors mandated a series of sector-specific policies to guide World Bank investment in such areas as forestry and energy, including a ban on financing logging in primary tropical forests.[54]

Along with these policy reform efforts, the World Bank pursued structural changes and investment strategies intended to demonstrate its commitment to environmentally sustainable development. A separate environmental unit created in the 1980s evolved into a vice presidency for environmentally and socially sustainable development in the 1990s. The bank recruited staff with technical environmental credentials. By the mid-1990s, the bank had developed a portfolio of environment-sector projects, ranging from support for national environmental agencies to investments in national parks.[55] Many continued to criticize the bank, however, saying that its environmental reforms were merely efforts to deflect outside criticism and that no major changes had occurred in the bank's overall performance. Critics pointed to the bank's support for an oil pipeline project in West Africa, despite the opposition of most internal environmental specialists, as an example of how lending imperatives tied to traditional models of economic growth continued to outweigh environmental considerations.[56]

In response to continued criticism, in 2001 the bank adopted a new strategy titled *Making Sustainable Commitments: An Environment Strategy for the World Bank*. The strategy noted the need for mainstreaming "the environment into investments, programs, sector strategies, and policy dialogue."[57] The strategy placed the environment within the institution's poverty reduction mission and highlighted three objectives: improving the quality of life, enhancing the quality of growth, and protecting the regional and global commons. The strategy also enunciated an institutional commitment to facilitate partnerships between the public and private sectors, as well as with civil society; to address environmentally sensitive issues; and to promote better environmental management at both the country and the global levels.[58]

In 2004, Frances Seymour from the World Resources Institute noted that the World Bank had still not succeeded in mainstreaming sustainability into its operations. She stated that this resulted from three factors: bank staff continued to view environmental issues as purely based on compliance, staff did not see environmental issues as integral to their operations, and those affected by bank projects remained underrepresented.[59]

In 2008, the Independent Evaluation Group (IEG) of the World Bank echoed some of these concerns. Its report found that the World Bank had positively influenced how countries set their environmental priorities and how private firms address internal environmental management but had been less effective helping countries actually address these priorities, in part because of the scale and complexity of the problems involved and varying interest in receiving bank support. Mainstreaming had progressed over the previous five years but had not been fully implemented, and shortfalls had also occurred in priority setting, compliance, and helping public- and private-sector clients achieve sustainable results.[60] The IEG recommended that the bank remedy internal constraints, including poor knowledge, inadequate capacity, and insufficient coordi-nation concerning environmental challenges.[61]

In June 2012 the World Bank released a new environment strategy for 2012 to 2022 aimed at supporting countries to pursue sustainable development.[62] The strategy iden-tifies seven priority areas for the World Bank's engagement in environment projects: wealth accounting and ecosystem valuation, protection of oceans, pollution manage-ment, low-emission development, adaptation, disaster risk management, and small island states' resilience. Among other things, the strategy recognizes the growing role of the private sector in addressing sustainability concerns and the need to ensure that global markets promote sustainable development.

Environmental NGOs, including Friends of the Earth, expressed skepticism, warn-ing that the strategy may be relying too much on private-sector interventions and mar-ket mechanisms. They argued that greater private-sector involvement in a project could lead to decreased capacity to monitor social and environmental impact. The Sierra Club noted that there was a lack of operational details in the strategy and that it, instead, focused on rhetoric and broad goals.[63]

Others praised the strategy, noting that the current economic model, driven by un-sustainable patterns of growth and consumption, is putting too much pressure on an already threatened environment.[64] It is also worth noting that World Bank commit-ments addressing environment and natural resource management have grown from $1.5 billion or 8.4 percent of World Bank lending in 2001 to $6.3 billion or 14.3 percent in 2011.[65]

The IMF (see Box 2.7) was slower than the World Bank and regional banks to ac-knowledge the need to take environmental considerations explicitly into account in its lending operations. It defined its role as limited to helping countries achieve a bal-ance of payments and pay off their international debts. Only in 1991 did the IMF ex-ecutive board consider for the first time the extent to which the IMF should "address environmental issues." It decided that the IMF should avoid policies that might harm the environment but that it should not conduct research or build up its own expertise on the possible environmental consequences of its policies.[66] In 1996, the IMF and the World Bank put in place a joint initiative for heavily indebted poor countries that aimed to reduce the debt-service burden of eligible countries to sustainable levels and help them exit from the debt-rescheduling process. In turn these countries must adopt and pursue strong and sustained programs of adjustment and reform. This initiative is supposed to help eliminate external debt as an impediment to achieving sustainable development.[67]

Because the World Bank addresses environmental issues and supports an extensive work program on environmental and other sectoral issues, the executive board of the IMF decided early that the IMF should not duplicate the bank's work in this area.

BOX 2.7   WHAT IS THE IMF?

The International Monetary Fund (IMF) works to foster global growth and economic stability. It provides policy advice and financing to countries in economic
difficulties and also works with developing nations to help them achieve macroeconomic stability and reduce poverty. Founded in 1944 and headquartered in
Washington, DC, the IMF is a specialized agency of the United Nations but has its
own charter, governing structure, and finances. The highest decision-making body
of the IMF, the board of governors, consists of one governor and one alternate governor for each of its 188 member countries. Voting power among the governors is
distributed based on the size of each country's share of the global economy. Thus,
the United States, Japan, and EU countries wield primary influence. In November
2012, for example, Angola had 0.12 percent of the board's voting power, while the
United States had 17.69 percent.

 The work of the IMF focuses on three main areas: economic surveillance, lending,
and technical assistance. Surveillance refers to the monitoring of economic and
financial developments and the provision of policy advice, aimed especially at crisis prevention. The IMF also lends to countries with balance of payments difficulties, providing temporary financing and supporting policies aimed at correcting
the underlying problems. It also provides loans to low-income countries aimed especially at poverty reduction. Finally, the IMF provides countries with technical
assistance and training in its areas of expertise. In recent years, the IMF has employed elements of its surveillance and technical assistance work to help develop
standards and codes of good practice as part of international efforts to strengthen
the global financial system. Financing for IMF activities comes mainly from the
money that countries pay as their capital subscription when they become members. The size of these payments also varies by the size of their economy.

Sources: International Monetary Fund, "IMF Members' Quotas and Voting Power, and IMF
Board of Governors," www.imf.org/external/np/sec/memdir/members.aspx, accessed November 3, 2012. For general information on the IMF, see www.imf.org.

The IMF also believes that its mandate and expertise constrain its ability to address
environmental issues to specific types of work. The IMF's involvement in environmental policy is thus limited to areas that have a serious and perceptible impact on a
country's macroeconomic outlook. The IMF's climate-change activities focus on providing advice to member countries when climate change can have a significant impact

on economic and financial stability, including the appropriate tax level and base; the possible role of complementary policies, such as clean technology research and development; the balance between carbon and other taxes in the government's budget; and the treatment of forestry and other nonenergy emissions. For example, in 2011 the IMF, in collaboration with the World Bank and others, undertook a study for the Group of 20 (or G-20: finance ministers and central bank governors from nineteen countries and the EU) on the effectiveness and revenue potential of a wide range of fiscal options for climate finance, including potential charges for international aviation and maritime emissions, carbon taxes, and other fiscal instruments.[68]

The IMF also assists countries with environmental tax policy for pollution and management of renewable resources, such as forests. Even in these respects, the IMF sometimes runs into obstacles. At times, a member country does not have a national environmental action plan or a stated national strategy to protect the environment. Even where they do exist, such plans or strategies are sometimes not specific enough to allow the IMF staff to consider their macroeconomic implications. Sometimes, the authorities themselves are not fully committed to environmental objectives because of pressure from one or more interest groups or because these objectives conflict with short-run economic growth or with some other objective of the country's policy makers. Thus, the IMF argues, it can integrate environment into its policy dialogue only to the extent that member countries allow it to do so.[69]

REGIONAL AND OTHER MULTILATERAL ORGANIZATIONS

Regional and other multilateral organizations play an increasing role in environmental politics. Some, such as the regional fisheries management organizations, are specific functional groups that have taken on environmental responsibilities out of necessity. Others have broad political and economic agendas that now also include environmental issues. Still others have been specifically established to address environmental concerns.

The European Union is the only regional organization whose decisions obligate its members. In the 1950s, six European countries decided to pool their economic resources and set up a system of joint decision making on economic issues. To do so, they formed several organizations, of which the European Economic Community was the most important (the name was eventually shortened to the European Community).[70] The group grew in size, and the 1992 Maastricht Treaty introduced new forms of cooperation between the then twelve members on issues such as defense, justice, and home affairs, including the environment. By adding this intergovernmental cooperation to the existing "community" system, the Maastricht Treaty created the European Union. The EU is unique in that its now twenty-seven member states have set up common institutions to which they delegate some of their sovereignty so that decisions on specific matters, including agriculture, fisheries, and trade, can be made at the European level. Both individual EU member states and the EC itself, as a "regional economic integration organization," can ratify and join global environmental agreements.[71] During regime negotiations, EU states negotiate as a single entity, giving their negotiating positions considerable importance.

Collective environmental action by EU states began in 1972 (then as the EC) with the first in a series of action plans. During the first four action plans, the community adopted more than two hundred pieces of legislation, chiefly concerned with limiting pollution by introducing minimum standards, including for waste management and air and water pollution. The sixth action program for the environment set out EU priorities up to 2010 on climate change, nature and biodiversity, environment and health, and the management of natural resources and waste.

In 2010, the EU adopted Europe 2020, a ten-year growth strategy that focuses on smart growth (developing an economy based on knowledge and innovation), sustainable growth (promoting a more resource-efficient, greener, and more competitive economy), and inclusive growth (fostering a high-employment economy delivering social and territorial cohesion). The strategy sets goals in the areas of employment, innovation, education, poverty reduction, and climate/energy. EU targets for sustainable growth include:

- reducing GHG emissions by 20 percent compared to 1990 levels by 2020. The EU is prepared to go further and reduce by 30 percent if other developed countries make similar commitments and developing countries contribute according to their abilities, as part of a comprehensive global agreement;
- increasing the share of renewables in final energy consumption to 20 percent; and
- moving toward a 20 percent increase in energy efficiency.[72]

The Organization of American States (OAS), one of the oldest regional organizations, was the first to hold a presidential summit specifically focused on the environment when it convened the Summit of the Americas on Sustainable Development in Bolivia in December 1996. The Department of Sustainable Development is the principal technical arm of the OAS General Secretariat that supports OAS member states in the design and implementation of policies, programs, and projects oriented to integrate environmental priorities with poverty alleviation, and socioeconomic development goals, including integrated water management, energy and climate-change mitigation, risk management and climate-change adaptation, biodiversity and sustainable land management, and environmental law.

The fifth Summit of the Americas in Port of Spain, Trinidad and Tobago, in 2009 focused on environmental sustainability, reaffirming the region's commitment to sustainable development and recognizing the adverse impacts of climate change on the region and the need to reduce GHG emissions. Member states also agreed to collaborate on the sustainable management of forests, including efforts for reducing deforestation; the sustainable management of protected areas and World Heritage Sites; protecting endangered and migratory species; combating illegal international trafficking of biodiversity; promoting the exchange of scientific knowledge on biodiversity, such as through the Inter-American Biodiversity Information Network; recognizing and sharing the benefits arising from access to and use of genetic resources and associated traditional knowledge; and promoting the conservation of marine resources and the protection of marine ecosystems.[73]

The African Union, which evolved out of the Organization of African Unity, includes the promotion of sustainable development as one of its official objectives. At its inaugural summit in mid-2001, the African Union adopted the New Partnership for Africa's Development (NEPAD) as a blueprint for the continent's future development. NEPAD's primary objectives are eradicating poverty in Africa, placing African countries on a path of sustainable growth and development, and halting the continent's marginalization in the globalization process. NEPAD recognizes the need to protect the environment not only for Africa's benefit but also for the many natural resources of global importance the continent holds, including a wide range of flora and fauna, paleoanthropological resources, and immense forests that act as carbon sinks. These resources could be degraded without support from the international community. Implicit in NEPAD's approach is the need for the developed world to support Africa's sustainable development for the sake of both Africans and the wider global community.

In 2003, the African Union adopted the NEPAD Environmental Action Plan. The plan is organized into clusters of program and project activities to be implemented over a ten-year period. Areas of emphasis include land degradation, drought, and desertification; wetlands; invasive species; marine and coastal resources; cross-border conservation of natural resources; and climate change.[74]

Asia-Pacific Economic Cooperation (APEC) was formed in 1989 in response to the growing interdependence among Asia-Pacific economies. Its work includes consideration of three categories of environmental issues: air, atmospheric, and water pollution, especially those related to energy production and use; resource degradation; and demographic shifts, including rural out-migration, food security, and urbanization. At their November 1998 meeting in Kuala Lumpur, Malaysia, APEC economic leaders reiterated their "commitment to advance sustainable development across the entire spectrum of [their] workplan including cleaner production, protection of the marine environment and sustainable cities."[75]

APEC held its first ocean-related ministerial meeting in South Korea in 2002, with the theme, "Toward the Sustainability of Marine and Coastal Resources." During the meeting, ministers discussed sustainable fisheries, ocean science and technology, marine environmental protection, and integrated coastal management and adopted the Seoul Oceans Declaration. In September 2007, APEC leaders adopted a Declaration on Climate Change, Energy Security, and Clean Development, which supported a post-2012 international climate-change arrangement that "strengthens, broadens and deepens the current arrangements and leads to reduced global emissions of greenhouse gases."[76]

In 2011, twenty-one APEC leaders expressed commitment to green growth at their nineteenth summit in Honolulu. The declaration approved at the meeting called for phasing out inefficient fossil-fuel subsidies, promoting energy efficiency, incorporating low-emissions strategies into economic growth plans, working to prohibit trade in illegally harvested forest products, and undertaking additional activities to combat illegal logging and associated trade.[77]

The Group of 77 (G-77), which functions as the "negotiating arm of the developing countries" within the UN system, is an important international entity in environmental politics.[78] The G-77 was established in 1964 by 77 developing countries at the end of the first session of the United Nations Conference on Trade and Development. Although its membership has grown to more than 130 countries, the original name was retained because of its historic significance. China, which has the status of associate member, also plays an influential role in the G-77. As the largest Third World coalition in the United Nations, the G-77 provides the means for developing countries to articulate and promote their collective interests, enhance joint negotiating capacity in the UN system, and promote economic and technical cooperation among developing countries.[79] Since the early 1990s, as more developing countries have become involved in the negotiation of multilateral environmental agreements, the G-77 has played key roles in these negotiations.

The OECD is also an actor on the international environmental stage. The OECD's thirty-four current members include all the major industrialized countries plus Chile, Mexico, South Korea, and Turkey. The OECD has played a key role in promoting sustainable consumption and production within its member states and provides a great deal of background information and support on such issues as climate change, trade and environment issues, and transport and the environment.

States have created regional organizations explicitly to address environmental issues. One such organization is the Pacific Regional Environment Programme (SPREP).[80] Created in 1982, SPREP has developed a framework for environmentally sound planning and management suited to the Pacific island region. In order to improve and protect the environment, SPREP's action program aims to build national capacity in environmental and resource management. SPREP also provides capacity building, training, and support for member states to improve their ability to represent their interests in international negotiations and UN global conferences.

The African Ministerial Conference on the Environment is a permanent forum in which African ministers of the environment discuss mainly matters of relevance to the environment of the continent. It was established in 1985, when African ministers met in Egypt and adopted the Cairo Programme for African Cooperation. The conference is convened every second year.

The Central American Commission on Environment and Development was established in 1989 to enable improved regional cooperation on environment and development issues. Since then, the commission has adopted different regional agreements on the conservation of biological diversity, climate change, transboundary movements of hazardous wastes, the management and conservation of forest ecosystems, sustainable development in oceans and coastal areas, and access to genetic resources.[81]

NONGOVERNMENTAL ORGANIZATIONS

The emergence of the global environment as a major issue in world politics coincided with the emergence of NGOs as important actors in environmental politics.[82] Although business organizations are often included in the UN definition of an NGO, we use the term here to denote an independent, nonprofit organization not beholden to a government or a profit-making organization.

NGO influence on global environmental politics stems from three principal factors. First, NGOs often possess expert knowledge and innovative thinking about global environmental issues acquired from years of focused specialization on the issues under negotiation. Second, NGOs are acknowledged to be dedicated to goals that transcend narrow national or sectoral interests. Third, NGOs often represent substantial constituencies within their own countries and thus can command attention from policy makers because of their potential ability to mobilize these people to influence policies and even tight elections.

In the industrialized countries, most NGOs active in global environmental politics fall into one of three categories: organizations affiliated with international NGOs (INGOs)—that is, NGOs with branches in more than one country; large national organizations focused primarily on domestic environmental issues; and think tanks, or research institutes, whose influence comes primarily from publishing studies and proposals for action.

Some INGOs are loose federations of national affiliates; others have a more centralized structure. Friends of the Earth International, based in Amsterdam, is a confederation of seventy-six national independent affiliates, half of which are in developing
countries. At an annual meeting, delegates democratically set priorities and select five
or more campaigns on which to cooperate. Greenpeace is one of the largest INGOs;
it has offices in forty countries and more than 2.8 million financial supporters and
members.[83] Its international activities are tightly organized by a well-staffed headquarters (also in Amsterdam) and guided by issues and strategies determined at an
annual meeting.

WWF (formerly known as the World Wildlife Fund and the World Wide Fund for
Nature) is the world's largest and one of the most experienced independent conservation organizations. Headquartered in Switzerland, WWF has five million members
worldwide and works in one hundred countries. WWF's mission is the conservation
of nature and the preservation of biodiversity and healthy ecological systems through
the protection of natural areas and wild plants and animals, sustainable use of renewable resources, more efficient energy use, and reducing pollution. It also works on
crosscutting sustainability issues, including climate change, toxics, trade and investment (e.g., WTO rules), indigenous and traditional peoples (e.g., intellectual property
rights), the impacts of tourism, and what WWF sees as the root causes of biodiversity
loss: poverty, migration, macroeconomic policies, and poor enforcement of environmental legislation.

The European Environmental Bureau, organized in 1974, is now a confederation
of more than 140 environmental citizen organizations based in EU member states.
The bureau seeks to help improve EU environmental policies and sustainable development policies by effectively integrating environmental objectives in horizontal and
sectoral policies of the EU and ensuring compliance with effective strategies to realize
these objectives.

The second category of NGOs includes the big US environmental organizations,
almost all of which have international programs. Some, such as the Sierra Club, the
National Audubon Society, and the National Wildlife Federation, were formed in
the late nineteenth and early twentieth centuries around conservation issues. Others,
including the Environmental Defense Fund and the Natural Resources Defense Council, arose in the early 1970s in an attempt to use legal, economic, and regulatory processes to affect national policy, with an initial focus on air and water pollution. Along
with Friends of the Earth USA, they have come to play effective roles in related international issues, particularly in the negotiations on climate and ozone and efforts to
reshape the policies of the multilateral development banks. Other organizations with
more specific agendas have also become more internationally active on their issues;
among these are Defenders of Wildlife and the Humane Society.

Environmental think tanks, normally funded by private donations or contracts, rely primarily on their technical expertise and research programs to influence global environmental policy. Prominent examples include the World Resources Institute, which publishes well-respected reports on the global environment and policy studies on specific issues. Publications from the Worldwatch Institute have often identified new problems and suggested alternative approaches to international issues. The International Institute for Environment and Development in London drew early attention to the connection between the environment and poverty in developing countries. In a few countries, government-funded but nevertheless independent institutes seek to influence both the policies of their own governments and international negotiations. The International Institute for Sustainable Development (IISD) of Canada and the Stockholm Environment Institute of Sweden have played such roles. These organizations all collaborate with colleagues in other countries.

Unlike the environmental NGOs of the North, environmentalism in developing countries grew out of what some of its founders saw as a "lopsided, iniquitous and environmentally destructive process of development" and is often interlinked with questions of human rights, ethnicity, and distributive justice.[84] Southern NGOs have tended to stress land use, forest management, fishing rights, and the redistribution of power over natural resources.[85] They also tend to be more critical of consumerism and uncontrolled economic development than their colleagues in the North. But there are many exceptions, such as the Chilean and Argentinean NGOs interested in the ozone layer and the NGOs in low-lying coastal areas or small islands that are concerned about climate change. Developing-country NGOs have often become involved in international policy issues through opposition to multilateral bank projects and government policies that displace villages or threaten forests, and they have tended to regard multinational corporations as enemies of the environment. Critical of their governments on most domestic policies, NGO members committed to environmental protection have often been harassed, subjected to political repression, and jailed. In some countries, however, they have acquired political legitimacy and a measure of influence on national environmental-policy issues.

India, which is symbolic of a number of developing countries, has an environmental movement whose origins date back to the Chipko movement, which started in the Garhwal Himalaya in April 1973. Between 1973 and 1980, more than a dozen instances were recorded in which men, women, and children threatened to hug forest trees rather than allow them to be logged for export. Unlike environmentalists in the North, however, the Indian activists were not interested in saving the trees but in using the forest for agricultural and household requirements.[86]

The Chipko movement was the forerunner of, and the direct inspiration for, a series of popular movements in defense of community rights to natural resources, some of which continue to this day. Some of these struggles revolved around forests; in other instances, around the control and use of pasture lands, minerals, or fisheries. Most of these conflicts have pitted rich against poor: logging companies against hill villagers, dam builders against forest tribal communities, multinational corporations deploying trawlers against traditional fisherfolk in small boats.[87]

Some of the most important aspects of Brazil's environmental movement can be traced to the 1980s, when rubber tappers organized to resist destruction of the forests that supported them and that they had tended for decades. In 1989, after a cattle rancher murdered Chico Mendes, a key leader of the rubber tappers, popular support grew, and the Brazilian government began to take more meaningful action. The country set aside "extractive reserves" to protect forests where tapping and other sustainable extraction could continue.

In Sarawak, Malaysia, loggers cleared 2.8 million hectares, or 30 percent, of the forest between 1963 and 1985. Many of the timber licenses issued by the Sarawak government covered the customary land of the natives who depend on the forests for food and shelter—indeed, for their very survival. Beginning in early 1987, natives started erecting blockades across timber roads in a desperate attempt to stop the logging.[88] Logging protests and blockades continue in Malaysia, with aggressive deforestation activities producing serious disputes like those that occurred in 2011 and 2012.[89]

The Green Belt Movement, based in Kenya, is an influential grassroots NGO that focuses on conservation, community development, and capacity building. Founded in 1977 by the late Wangari Maathai (under the auspices of the National Council of Women of Kenya), it aims to create a society of people who consciously work for the continued improvement of their environment and for a greener, cleaner Kenya. Programs include tree planting, biodiversity conservation, civic and environmental education, advocacy and networking, food security, and capacity building for women and girls. In 2004, Maathai received the Nobel Peace Prize for her efforts with the Green Belt Movement—the first Nobel Peace Prize given to an environmentalist.[90]

Many environmental and development battles continue to be fought at the community level in developing countries, but some NGOs and coalitions in those countries also tackle a broader range of environmental and development issues. The Third World Network, for example, is an independent nonprofit international network of organizations and individuals involved in issues relating to development, the Third World, and North-South issues. Its mission is to bring about a greater articulation of the needs and rights of peoples in the Third World, a fair distribution of world resources, and forms of development that are ecologically sustainable and fulfill human needs. To this end, the Third World Network conducts research into economic, social, and environmental issues pertaining to the South; publishes books and magazines; organizes and participates in seminars; and represents southern interests and perspectives at international fora such as UN conferences and processes. Headquartered in Penang, Malaysia, the Third World Network also has regional offices in Goa, India, and Geneva, Switzerland.[91]

The Center for Science and Environment in India seeks to increase public awareness of scientific, technological, environmental, and development issues and to search for solutions that people and communities can implement themselves. It works on a wide range of issues in India, including air and water pollution, human health, climate change, and monitoring the environmental performance of Indian industry. Like the Third World Network, it is also involved at the global level and represents southern interests and perspectives at international fora.[92]

Developing-country NGOs often form national-level coalitions, such as the Indonesian Forum for Environment, which unites over four hundred environmental organizations countrywide. Indigenous minorities in nine Amazon basin countries have organized national-level coalitions, which, in turn, have formed a coordinating body (called COICA, for its Spanish name) to lobby for a voice in all Amazon development projects affecting them. More broadly, recognition of indigenous groups at the Rio Earth Summit, including in Chapter 26 of Agenda 21, combined with their highly visible participation in subsequent global conferences and the work of the CBD, have boosted the rights of indigenous peoples and provided them with a way to influence international environmental negotiations.

International coalitions of NGOs working on a specific environmental issue have also become a means of increasing NGO influence. The Antarctic and Southern Oceans Coalition brings together over thirty organizations working to ensure that the Antarctic continent, its surrounding islands, and the great Southern Ocean survive as the world's last unspoiled wilderness. The Climate Action Network, formed in 1989, has more than seven hundred member organizations in ninety countries that work to promote government and individual action to limit human-induced climate change.

Relations between northern and southern NGOs are not always smooth. There has long been a rift within the Climate Action Network between northern and southern NGOs regarding the balance of climate responsibility and associated commitments under the Kyoto Protocol. There was a similar division in the discussions of a forest treaty. In this matter, also, the southern NGOs' position tended to parallel that of their governments. A southern resentment of northern NGOs sometimes persists, especially at the big international conferences, at which the better-prepared, better-financed US and European NGOs are heavily represented.

Despite potential tensions, however, there have been many instances of close North-South NGO cooperation. One example is the Pesticide Action Network, a network of more than six hundred NGOs, institutions, and individuals in more than ninety countries working to replace hazardous pesticides with ecologically sound alternatives. Five

PHOTO 2.5   The International POPs Elimination Network mobilized grassroots support for a global treaty to eliminate POPs.
Courtesy IISD/*Earth Negotiations Bulletin.*

autonomous regional centers coordinate its projects and campaigns. The Pesticide Action Network and partner groups from around the world have been working together to lobby for the phaseout of POPs during the negotiation and implementation of the Stockholm Convention on Persistent Organic Pollutants, and they provide technical and financial assistance to help developing countries eliminate POPs (see Chapter 3).

Another successful coalition of North-South NGOs has been the International POPs Elimination Network (IPEN), which works for the global elimination of POPs on an expedited, yet socially equitable, basis. Founded by a small number of NGOs, IPEN was formally launched in June 1998 during the first session of formal negotiations on creating a global treaty to control and/or eliminate POPs. Throughout the five negotiating sessions, IPEN grew to become a coalition of more than seven hundred public health, environmental, consumer, and other NGOs in over one hundred countries. The network worked to mobilize grassroots support for a global treaty to eliminate POPs. It also leveraged the resources and created a forum for NGOs and activists from around the world to participate in the negotiations. IPEN coordinated NGO conferences and workshops at each of the five negotiating sessions and continues to be active in the regime, including efforts to add additional POPs to the convention.[93]

One of the most important organizations through which NGOs influence environmental politics is the International Union for the Conservation of Nature and Natural Resources (IUCN), which brings together more than 1,200 member organizations in 160 countries, including more than two hundred governments and nine hundred NGOs, and some eleven thousand scientists and experts in a unique worldwide partnership. Governed by a general assembly of delegates from its member organizations that meets every three years, the IUCN has had a major influence on global agreements on wildlife conservation. Although member government organizations, which often embrace only broad consensus positions, tend to limit the group's actions, IUCN has been successful in drafting environmental treaties and assisting in monitoring their implementation.

Influencing Environmental Regime Formation

NGOs can attempt to influence the development, expansion, and implementation of international regimes in various ways, such as:

- raising public awareness about particular issues and conducting education campaigns;
- influencing the global environmental agenda by defining a new issue or redefining an old one;
- lobbying governments to accept a more advanced position on an issue;
- proposing draft text to be included in conventions in advance of negotiations;
- lobbying and participating in international negotiations;
- generating press attention;
- supporting ratification and implementation of an environmental treaty by the government in their host country;
- bringing lawsuits to compel national action on an issue;
- organizing consumer boycotts to pressure international corporations;
- providing reporting services;
- assisting implementation of the regime, particularly in developing countries; and
- monitoring the implementation of conventions and reporting to the secretariat and/or the parties.

One example of an NGO influencing the global environmental agenda is the role played by WWF and Conservation International in creating the demand for banning commerce in African elephant ivory. In particular, the groups published a detailed report on the problem, circulating it to the parties to CITES, and engaged in public education campaigns.

Pressing for changes in the policy of a major actor is sometimes the best way for NGOs to influence an international regime. In efforts to protect the ozone layer, during the late 1970s the US Clean Air Coalition, a group of national environmental organizations, successfully lobbied for a domestic ban on aerosols and the regulation of CFCs. Because they lobbied for a total phaseout of CFCs before negotiations on the Montreal Protocol began, they contributed to US international leadership on this issue. Similarly, three US NGOs working with pro-treaty biotechnology firms were a major influence in the Clinton administration's decision to reverse the Bush administration's position and sign the Biodiversity Convention (although the United States still has not ratified it).[94]

Greenpeace's monitoring of and reporting on the toxic waste trade was a key factor in encouraging a coalition of countries to push for a complete ban on North-South waste trade under the Basel Convention. The Inuit Circumpolar Conference, an NGO representing 150,000 Inuit of Alaska, Canada, Greenland, and Chukotka (Russia), participated in negotiations that produced the Stockholm Convention on Persistent Organic Pollutants, and their stories concerning the dangers that toxic chemicals pose for the future of their people put a human face on the need to eliminate POPs.

Although effective consumer boycotts are rare in international environmental politics (they are more common on local and national issues), an NGO-organized boycott of Icelandic products, including protests of fast-food and supermarket chains that sold fish caught by Iceland's fishing fleet, because of Iceland's pro-whaling stand, contributed to a temporary two-year halt to that country's whaling.[95] Other notable NGO-led boycotts include Mitsubishi making concessions on forest policy following a campaign spearheaded by Rainforest Action Network and Shell agreeing to dispose of its offshore Brent Spar oil platform on land (rather than dumping it at sea as originally planned).[96]

NGOs can influence international regimes in a more specialized way by writing potential text for inclusion in a convention or amendment and circulating it in advance of the negotiations in the hope that it will be formally supported and submitted by a national delegation. In exceptional cases, this strategy can even include developing an entire draft convention. Few NGOs have the staff resources to devote to such a task, and only IUCN has succeeded in having draft conventions used as the basis for negotiations. The Convention Concerning the Protection of the World Cultural and Natural Heritage, signed in 1972 in Paris, was based on a draft produced by IUCN. CITES, signed in 1973, was the result of an IUCN initiative that went through three drafts over nearly a decade.[97]

NGOs have become especially active and well organized in lobbying at international negotiations. The COPs to most environmental conventions permit NGO observers, enabling NGOs to be actively involved in the proceedings. Certain NGOs specialize in the meetings of particular conventions and over the years have acquired a high level of technical and legal expertise. The Humane Society of the United States has been lobbying at meetings of the International Whaling Commission (IWC) since 1973, and Greenpeace has been active in the COP to the London Convention since the early 1980s. The Climate Action Network was extremely active during the negotiation of the UNFCCC and the Kyoto Protocol, and it has also participated in the negotiations to strengthen the climate regime. The Pesticide Action Network and IPEN have been active in lobbying at negotiations for the Stockholm Convention on POPs.

NGOs also influence international conferences by providing scientific and technical information and new arguments to delegations already sympathetic to their objectives.

In the process leading up to the whaling moratorium, NGOs supplied factual information on violations of the whaling convention as well as scientific information not otherwise available to the delegations.[98] In some circumstances, NGOs have a particularly strong influence on a key delegation's positions, an example being the 1991–1992 biodiversity negotiations when WWF-Australia and other NGOs were consulted on major issues in the convention before the Australian delegation adopted positions.[99] The Foundation for International Environmental Law and Development has assisted the Alliance of Small Island States (AOSIS) within the context of the climate-change negotiations, providing AOSIS with advice and legal expertise, enabling the alliance to wield greater influence in the climate negotiations.[100] Greenpeace provided a great deal of technical support to African and other developing countries that supported a ban on the dumping of hazardous wastes in developing countries during the negotiation of the Basel Convention.

NGOs can also provide useful reporting services during these conferences. Since 1972, NGOs at selected UN-sponsored environmental conferences have published *ECO*, which provides a combination of news stories and commentary. The *Earth Negotiations Bulletin*, published by IISD, has provided objective reports of many different environment and development negotiations since 1992.[101] Countries cannot easily or effectively report about ongoing negotiations on their own. Were a government to attempt to provide such information, the reports would be derided as biased. If the United Nations or a formal secretariat published daily reports, they would have the status of official documents, and member governments would have difficulty agreeing on their content, style, and tone. However, because the NGO community, including impartial research institutions like IISD, is already providing the information, governments and international organizations have little incentive to step in.[102]

NGOs can sometimes assist governments in implementing the provisions of environmental regimes. This can include offering assistance in drafting national legislation, providing technical and scientific assistance on relevant issues, and brokering the provision of essential financial support. NGOs can also influence regime formation by monitoring compliance with an agreement once it goes into effect. Investigation and reporting by NGOs can put pressure on parties that are violating provisions of an agreement. They can demonstrate the need for a more effective enforcement mechanism (or for creation of a mechanism where none exists) or help build support for further elaboration or strengthening of the existing regime rules.

This NGO function has been especially important with regard to the CITES and whaling regimes. The international Trade Records Analysis of Flora and Fauna in Commerce (TRAFFIC), a joint wildlife-trade monitoring program of WWF and IUCN, plays a vital role in supplementing the CITES Secretariat in monitoring the compliance of various countries with CITES bans on trade in endangered species.[103]

PHOTO 2.6   The *Earth Negotiations Bulletin*, published by IISD, has provided real-time reports
of many different environment and development negotiations since 1992.
Courtesy IISD/*Earth Negotiations Bulletin.*

Climate networks in the United States and the EU have produced detailed reviews of
countries' national climate action plans. Greenpeace's aggressive reporting of hazardous wastes dumped in violation of the Basel Convention helped build support for
a full ban on international shipping of such wastes to non-OECD countries.

BUSINESS AND INDUSTRY

Private business firms, especially multinational corporations, are important and interested actors in global environmental politics. Their core activities, although often
essential, consume resources and produce pollution, and environmental regulations
can directly affect their economic interests. Corporations also have significant assets
for influencing global environmental politics. They have good access to decision
makers in most governments and international organizations and can deploy impressive technical expertise on the issues in which they are interested. They have
national and international industrial associations that represent their interests in
policy issues, as well as significant financial and technical resources important to
developing solutions.

Corporations often oppose national and international policies that they believe will impose significant costs on them or otherwise reduce expected profits. Indeed, at times corporations have worked to weaken global environmental regimes, including ozone protection, climate change, whaling, hazardous wastes, chemicals, and fisheries. Corporations sometimes support an international agreement if it will create weaker regulations on their activities than those that they expect to be imposed domestically.

At the same time, however, corporate interests vary across companies and sectors, and some corporations have supported creating strong national and international environmental policy. When faced with existing strong domestic regulations on an activity with a global environmental dimension, corporations tend to support international agreements that will impose similar standards on competitors abroad. For example, on fisheries-management issues, US and Japanese fishing industries are more strictly regulated on various issues of high-seas fishing, particularly quotas on bluefin tuna and other highly migratory species, than other Asian fishing states (Republic of Korea, China, Taiwan, and Indonesia); their respective fishing industries therefore pushed the United States and Japan to take strong positions on regulation of high-seas fishing capacity in FAO negotiations in 1998.

A particular industry's interests regarding a proposed global environmental regime are often far from monolithic. On ozone, climate change, biodiversity, and fisheries, industries have been divided either along national lines or among industry sectors or subsectors. On climate, European-based energy firms have traditionally been more willing to see such agreements as business opportunities because they have had experience in using greater energy efficiency to become more profitable, whereas many US-based firms, which until recently had far less experience, have been more resistant to such plans.

But even the energy industry is not united on the issue of climate change. Royal Dutch Shell and BP have decided to seek a seat at the table rather than remain in opposition, joining the Business Environmental Leadership Council, and reduced their GHG emissions. Royal Dutch Shell's emissions in 2009 were 35 percent lower than in 1990, and BP's emissions in 2010 were 10 percent lower than in 1990.[104] A number of utilities across the United States are moving to increase the production of electricity from solar and wind technologies. US automobile manufacturers have also noted opportunities for future markets by investing in hybrid and other technologies that reduce CO_2 emissions.

When companies see a positive stake in a global environmental agreement, they can dilute the influence of other companies that seek to weaken it. In 1992, the Industrial Biotechnology Association opposed the Biodiversity Convention because it feared the provisions on intellectual property rights would legally condone existing violations of those rights.[105] But the issue was not a high priority for most of the industry, and two of its leading member corporations, Merck and Genentech, believed the convention would benefit them by encouraging developing countries to negotiate agreements with companies for access to genetic resources. After those companies joined environmentalists in calling for the United States to sign the convention in 1993, the Industrial Biotechnology Association came out in favor of signing it.[106]

Similarly, when US industries interested in promoting alternatives to fossil fuels began lobbying at UNFCCC meetings in 1994, they reduced the influence of pro–fossil fuel industries, which had previously monopolized industry views on the issue. Similarly, because insurance companies are concerned about the increased hurricane and storm damage that climate change may cause, they are proactive in supporting targets and timetables for GHG emissions reductions. The insurance industry has tried to raise awareness among corporations regarding the dangers of climate change, including by conducting research projects on its negative economic consequences as well as the future impacts of storms and floods.[107]

Influence on Regime Formation

Business and industry affect global environmental regimes by influencing regime formation and by undertaking business activities that either weaken a regime or contribute to its effectiveness. To influence the formation of regimes, corporations attempt to:

- shape the definition of the issue under negotiation in a manner favorable to their interests;
- fund and distribute targeted research and other information supportive of their interests;
- initiate advertising campaigns to influence public opinion;
- persuade individual governments to adopt a particular position on a regime being negotiated by lobbying it in its capital; and
- lobby delegations to the negotiating conference on the regime.

Corporations had great success during the issue-definition phase associated with creation of the International Convention for the Prevention of Pollution of the Sea by Oil (1954). The major oil companies and global shipping interests (most of which the oil companies owned directly or indirectly) were the only actors with the technical expertise to make detailed proposals on maritime oil pollution. The technical papers submitted by the International Chamber of Shipping, comprising thirty national associations of shipowners, and the Oil Companies International Marine Forum, representing the interests of major oil companies, defined the terms of the discussion[108] and ensured that the convention would be compatible with oil and shipping interests—and quite ineffective in preventing oil pollution of the oceans. That degree of success in defining an issue is unlikely to recur in the future because governments and NGOs now have more expertise on issues being negotiated; furthermore, NGOs are better organized and more aggressive.

In most global environmental issues, corporations have relied on their domestic political clout to ensure that governments do not adopt strong policies adversely affecting their interests. The domestic US industry most strongly opposed to a ban on hazardous waste trade, the secondary-metals industry, helped persuade US officials to block such a ban in the negotiation of the Basel Convention. And on ozone depletion, Japan agreed to a phaseout of CFCs only after some of its largest electronic firms agreed they could eliminate their use.

For many years, industry lobbying in the United States succeeded in reducing the executive branch's flexibility in climate-change negotiations. Some of the most powerful trade associations launched the Global Climate Information Project in 1997. Through a multimillion-dollar print and television advertising campaign, the project cast doubt on the desirability of emissions controls in the Kyoto Protocol, then entering the final stages of negotiation, by arguing that such controls would raise taxes on gasoline, heating oil, and consumer goods and reduce the competitiveness of American businesses. An alliance of business and labor succeeded in persuading the US Senate to vote 95–0 for a resolution stating that the United States should not participate in a climate treaty that would require US GHG reductions without similar commitments from developing countries or that would result in serious harm to the US economy.[109]

Industry associations have been actively involved in influencing negotiations in several other global environmental regimes. Sometimes, industries with particular technical expertise or relatively unchallenged influence over the issue have been part of a key country's delegation. For example, the Japanese commissioner to the IWC has generally been the president of the Japanese Whaling Association.[110] US and Canadian food manufacturers have participated on US delegations to the FAO's Codex Alimentarius Commission, which sets international food standards.[111] The Israeli delegation to some ozone-layer negotiations included officials from a methyl bromide manufacturer during key negotiations on expanding controls on the chemical.[112] The Global Climate Coalition, an industry group, worked closely with the delegations from the United States and Saudi Arabia during the negotiation of the UNFCCC.

Like NGOs, representatives of corporate interests lobby negotiations by providing information and analysis to the delegations most sympathetic to their cause. During the climate-change negotiations, for example, coal and oil interests actively advised the US, Russian, and Saudi delegations on how to weaken the regime.[113] Industry groups had a particularly strong presence at the negotiating sessions for the

Cartagena Protocol on Biosafety. Their interest in participating in the negotiations grew during the talks: eight industry groups were represented at the first round of negotiations in 1996, and twenty such groups from many different countries were present at the final meetings in 1999.[114] Individual corporations, among them Monsanto, DuPont, and Syngenta (formerly Novartis and Zeneca), also sent their own representatives to many of the meetings.

Corporations may facilitate or delay, strengthen or weaken global environmental regimes by actions that directly affect the environment. They may take these actions unilaterally or based on agreements reached with their respective governments. Such actions can be crucial to a government's ability to commit itself to a regime-strengthening policy. The climate and ozone regimes are particularly sensitive to the willingness of corporations in key countries to take actions that will allow the international community to go beyond the existing agreement.

With regard to ozone protection, the US chemical industry delayed movement toward an international regime for regulating ozone-depleting CFCs in the early 1980s, in part by reducing their own research efforts on CFC substitutes.[115] Later, after developing effective substitutes, DuPont gave impetus to an accelerated timetable for a CFC phaseout by unilaterally pledging to phase out their production of CFCs ahead of the schedule already agreed to by the Montreal Protocol parties. In 1989, Nissan and Toyota pledged to eliminate CFCs from their cars and manufacturing processes as early as the mid-1990s. In 1992, Ford Motor Company pledged to eliminate 90 percent of CFC use from its manufacturing processes worldwide by the end of that year and to eliminate all CFCs from its air conditioners and manufacturing by the end of 1994.

Early in the climate-change negotiations, the Japanese auto industry, which accounts for 20 percent of Japan's CO_2 emissions, adopted a goal of improving fuel efficiency by 8.5 percent above its 1990 level by 2000, encouraging the Japanese government to make a commitment to stabilize national CO_2 emissions at 1990 levels by 2000.[116] More recently, numerous corporations around the world have pledged to reduce their GHG emissions and to improve their environmental accounting.[117]

Industry and Nonregime Issues

Corporations have their greatest political influence on a global environmental issue when there are no negotiations on a formal, binding international regime governing the issue. Under those circumstances, they are able to use their economic and political clout with individual governments and international organizations to protect particular economic activities that damage the environment.

For example, in the past, the agrochemical industry enjoyed strong influence on the FAO's Plant Protection Service, which was responsible for the organization's pesticide activities. The industry's international trade association even had a joint program with the FAO to promote pesticide use worldwide until the 1970s.[118] This influence was instrumental in carrying out the industry's main strategy for avoiding binding international restrictions on its sales of pesticides in developing countries. Instead of binding rules, the FAO drafted a voluntary "code of conduct" on pesticide distribution and use between 1982 and 1985 in close consultation with the industry.

In 1991, at the request of UNCED secretary-general Maurice Strong, Swiss industrialist Stephan Schmidheiny enlisted a group of forty-eight chief executive officers of corporations from all over the world to set up the Business Council for Sustainable Development to support the objectives of the Earth Summit. The business council issued a declaration calling for changes in consumption patterns and for the prices of goods to reflect environmental costs of production, use, recycling, and disposal.[119] In January 1995, the business council and the World Industry Council for the Environment, an initiative of the International Chamber of Commerce, merged into what is today a coalition of two hundred international companies united by a shared commitment to sustainable development via the three pillars of economic growth, ecological balance, and social progress. Drawing members from thirty-five countries and more than twenty major industrial sectors, the resulting World Business Council for Sustainable Development addresses a range of issues, including corporate social responsibility, access to clean water, capacity building, sustainable livelihoods, harmonizing international trade law with multilateral environmental agreements, and developing public-private partnerships in key areas of sustainable development, including energy and climate.[120]

CONCLUSION

State and nonstate actors play key roles in the creation and implementation of national and international environmental policy. State actors play the primary roles in determining the outcomes of issues at stake in global environmental politics, but nonstate actors—IGOs, NGOs, corporations, and treaty secretariats—influence the policies of individual state actors toward global environmental issues as well as the international negotiation process itself. Whether a state adopts the role of lead state, supporting state, swing state, or veto state on a particular issue depends primarily on domestic political factors and on the relative costs and benefits of the proposed regime. But international political-diplomatic consequences can also affect the choice of role.

IGOs, especially UNEP, WMO, and FAO, have played important roles in regime formation by helping to set the international agenda and by sponsoring and shaping negotiations on global environmental regimes and soft-law norms. The Bretton Woods institutions (World Bank and IMF) and certain UN agencies, particularly UNDP and FAO, influence state development strategies through financing and technical assistance. IGOs also seek to exert influence on state policy through research and advocacy of specific norms at the global level. Treaty secretariats, a subset of IGOs, can influence the behavior of political actors by acting as knowledge brokers and through the creation, support, and shaping of intergovernmental negotiations and cooperation.

NGOs influence the environmental regimes by defining issues, swaying the policy of a key government, lobbying negotiating conferences, providing information and reporting services, proposing convention text, and monitoring the implementation of agreements. They have also sought to change the policies and structure of major international institutions, such as the World Bank and the WTO, with varying degrees of success. They have been more successful when the target institution depends on funding from a key state that the NGOs can influence and less successful when the institution is relatively independent or has no tradition of permitting NGO participation in its processes.

Corporations also influence regime creation and expansion. Business and industry groups utilize technical expertise, privileged access to certain government ministries, and political clout with legislative bodies in attempts to veto or weaken—or in some situations strengthen—particular aspects of a regime. They can also directly affect the ability of the international community to meet regime goals by their own actions. They are able to maximize their political effectiveness in shaping the outcome of a global environmental issue when they can avert negotiations on a binding regime altogether.

3

The Development of Environmental Regimes: Chemicals, Wastes, and Climate Change

The development of global environmental regimes generally involves five inter-related processes or stages: agenda setting and issue definition, fact finding, bargaining on regime creation, regime implementation, and regime review and strengthening. The sequencing of these stages and the length of time each takes can vary greatly. The stages are also not always distinct; the issue-definition stage often overlaps with the fact-finding stage, which may, in turn, overlap with the bargaining stage; the implementation stage continues during the regime-review stage. Nevertheless, examining negotiations through these stages provides a framework that reduces some of the complexities of multilateral negotiations to a more manageable level for understanding and analysis.

Agenda setting and issue definition involve bringing the issue to the attention of the international community and identifying the scope and magnitude of the environmental threat, its primary causes, and the type of international action required to address the issue. An issue may be placed on the global environmental agenda by one or more state actors, by an international organization (usually at the suggestion of one or more member states), or by a nongovernmental organization (NGO). The actors that introduce and define the issue often publicize new scientific evidence or theories, as they did for ozone depletion, fisheries, and toxic chemicals. Issue definition may also involve identifying a different approach to international action on a problem, as it did for whaling, desertification, hazardous waste, and trade in endangered species.

Fact finding involves studying the science, economics, policy, and ethics surrounding the issue. This is done both to improve understanding of the issue and to build

101

international consensus on the nature of the problem and the most appropriate international actions to address it. Fact-finding efforts in different issue areas vary from well developed to nonexistent. Sometimes an intergovernmental organization can bring key actors together in an attempt to establish a baseline of facts on which they can agree, as the United Nations Environment Programme (UNEP) did in building support for negotiations on persistent organic pollutants (POPs). Sometimes states create a scientific body to review existing information and develop comprehensive consensus reports, as governments did when they created the Intergovernmental Panel on Climate Change (IPCC) prior to the start of global negotiations. When successful fact finding and consensus building do not occur before negotiations begin, scientific facts are more likely to be challenged by states opposed to international action. This occurred early in international discussions regarding the ozone layer. However, fact-finding efforts can be agreed to later in the process, even after negotiations begin, potentially resulting in greater consensus regarding the science and possible policy approaches (something that also occurred in the development of the ozone regime). At the same time, debates concerning key scientific and related facts can sometimes continue for years, even after a regime has been created, as we see in some aspects of the whaling regime.

The regime-creation stage involves bargaining among nation states (with other actors sometimes playing important roles) on the goals and content of global policy to address the issue. The fact-finding stage often shades into this bargaining stage. Meetings ostensibly devoted to establishing the scope and seriousness of the problem may also include attempts to delineate or discuss policy options.

The nature of global environmental politics means that regime proponents face difficult questions during the bargaining process. To be truly effective, a regime to mitigate a global danger such as ozone depletion or climate change must eventually have the participation of all states that contribute significantly to the problem. However, at some point, negotiators must determine whether to go ahead with a less than optimal number of signatories or to accommodate veto-state demands. These can be difficult decisions. Can the regime successfully address the problem without the participation of particular nations? Will the agreement be successful if it has universal support but is weakened by compromises with veto states?[1]

The outcome of the bargaining process depends in part on the bargaining leverage and cohesion of the veto coalition. Veto states can prevent the creation of a strong international regime by refusing to participate in it, or they can weaken it severely by insisting on concessions. In certain cases, an agreement may form without key members of the veto coalition and thus remain relatively ineffective, as in the Kyoto Protocol. In other cases, as happened with forests, a regime cannot be created. In some cases, as in the ozone regime, a effective regime can form or be strengthened through a difficult compromise between veto and lead states or when veto states change their position after receiving a particular concession, in response to new scientific information, as a result of changes in their internal politics, or in response to new technological developments and economic incentives.

Successful regime building does not end with the signing or ratification of a global environmental convention. Once established, a regime must be implemented by states and other actors. Most regimes also contain provisions for parties to review and, if they choose, to augment its effectiveness. In the regime review and strengthening stage, which exists in parallel with regime implementation, parties negotiate if and how to make the central provisions clearer or more stringent, how to improve implementation, and/or how to expand the scope of the regime. Regime strengthening may occur because new scientific evidence becomes available, because political shifts take place in one or more major states, because new technologies make addressing the environmental issue less expensive, or because the existing regime is ineffective in bringing about meaningful actions to reduce the threat.

The process of regime review and strengthening takes place within the processes mandated by the regime's central convention. The most important elements usually involve formal agreement by the convention's Conference of the Parties (COP) to strengthen or expand binding rules, normative codes of conduct, or regime procedures. This type of regime strengthening may take one of three forms:

1. The COP can adopt a new treaty, usually called a protocol, which establishes new, concrete commitments or targets. Examples of this convention-protocol approach include when parties to the 1985 Vienna Convention for the Protection of the Ozone Layer adopted the 1987 Montreal Protocol and the parties to the 1992 United Nations Framework Convention on Climate Change (UNFCCC) adopted the 1997 Kyoto Protocol. Parties to the 1979 Convention on Long-Range Transboundary Air Pollution, a regional treaty covering the Northern Hemisphere, have adopted eight protocols that identify specific measures to cut particular types and sources of pollution.
2. The COP can formally amend the original convention or a subsequent protocol. Examples include expanding the lists of chemicals controlled in the ozone and POPs regimes, "uplisting" species like the African elephant in the Convention on International Trade in Endangered Species of Wild Fauna and Flora (CITES), and establishing a moratorium on commercial whaling by the International Whaling Commission (IWC).
3. In some treaties, the COP can make decisions requiring important new actions by the parties without amending the convention or creating a new protocol, as in tightening the phaseout schedules in the Montreal Protocol, adding to the list of chemicals covered in the prior informed consent regime under the Rotterdam Convention, and adding persistent organic pollutants to the Stockholm Convention.

In the first type of regime expansion, interested states create a new treaty to strengthen a regime that began with a framework convention. As noted in Chapter 1, a framework convention does not establish detailed, binding commitments, such as targets or timetables for national actions, usually because negotiators could not reach agreement on such measures. Rather, framework conventions typically acknowledge the importance of the issue, mandate further study and information sharing, encourage or require the development of national or regional plans to address the threat, and create a conference of the parties for further consideration of the issue.

This two-stage approach allows the international community to establish the institutional and legal framework for future work even when agreement does not exist on the specific actions to be taken. However, the convention-protocol approach has been criticized for taking too much time. For example, it took more than six years to negotiate the UNFCCC and the Kyoto Protocol, and it took more than seven years for the protocol to enter into force. Yet the two-stage approach is often a negotiating necessity. The weaker framework convention is chosen not as a preferred option by lead states but because it represents the limit of what veto states will accept.

Protocols to a framework convention are an entirely new treaty and must be ratified by a certain number of signatories to enter into force.[2] Thus, only countries that "opt in" via formal ratification are bound by the terms of the new protocol.

In the second type of regime strengthening, a COP formally amends the treaty, changing or adding provisions in the main text or binding annex. Regime strengthening by formal amendment normally requires reaching decisions by consensus, with all parties agreeing, or if that is not possible, some treaties allow for approval by supermajority vote (usually two-thirds or three-fourths of those present and voting).[3] In most cases, states must then formally ratify the amendment, in a manner similar to the original treaty; states that choose not to ratify the amendment are not bound by it.

In a few regimes, however, certain amendments do not require formal ratification to become binding commitments; although in most of these treaties, parties have a period of time during which they can opt out if they do not wish to be bound by the amendment. For example, CITES and the IWC allow amendment by two-thirds and three-fourths majorities, respectively, but both have opt-out provisions for amendments. The Stockholm Convention allows each party to choose (at the time it joins the regime) if it will be immediately bound when additional toxic chemicals are added to the regime via future amendments or if it wants to preserve its right to opt in each time controls are placed on a new chemical by formally ratifying the amendment. These types of opt-out and opt-in arrangements allow changes to take effect, at least for some parties, without long ratification delays, but if they are not designed or managed effectively, they risk creating confusing situations in which many different parties are subject to many different sets of rules.

In the third type of regime strengthening, some treaties allow the COP to mandate new or stronger actions without a formal amendment or protocol procedure. These mechanisms exist to allow parties to change regime terms or technical details rapidly in response to new information. Many regimes allow the COP to make binding decisions on matters related to regime implementation, operation, or other issues provided that the decisions do not alter the text of the treaty. In most cases these decisions are reached by consensus (albeit sometimes with some states not perfectly happy), but many regimes allow for supermajority votes if consensus cannot be reached.

Some regimes go even further, allowing COP decisions to alter particular types of binding control measures. For example, the Montreal Protocol allows the Meeting of the Parties to adjust the targets and timetables for chemicals already controlled by the regime. Such decisions should be reached by consensus, but if all efforts at consensus fail, the treaty allows voting approval by a supermajority, although no vote has ever been held in the ozone regime. New ozone-depleting chemicals can be added to the protocol only by formal amendments, which require ratification. However, once a chemical is listed in the treaty, this innovative "adjustment mechanism" allows parties to strengthen the protocol's controls rapidly in response to new scientific information and technological developments. The Basel Convention allows "substantive decisions" to be made by a two-thirds majority of those present and voting, without any opt-out provision for those who oppose it. The Stockholm Convention provides for the COP to change certain technical annexes and other aspects of the convention without requiring formal ratification by parties (although changes to other aspects of the convention require either formal amendments with ratifications or, as noted above, opt-in or opt-out provisions).

In this chapter and Chapter 4, we analyze ten different environmental regimes. This chapter discusses the ozone, toxic chemicals, hazardous waste, and climate regimes. These regimes all seek to prevent the production, use, emission, and/or improper management of specific substances that endanger the environment and human health. As such, they can all be considered pollution-control regimes, which feature specific rules to limit particular substances from entering the environment. Chapter 4 shifts the discussion to regimes that address shared natural resources: physical or biological systems that extend into or across the jurisdictions of two or more states. In that chapter, we examine the biodiversity, whaling, endangered species, ocean fisheries, desertification, and forests regimes.

These ten regimes span a wide range of issues, actors, interests, political circumstances, and effectiveness. For each case, we outline the environmental issue, delineate key stages in the regime's development, and discuss the role of lead and veto coalitions in shaping the outcomes of bargaining. Their respective content, development, and impact reveal important similarities and differences in regime politics and help us understand why states sometimes agree to cooperate on global environmental issues despite divergent interests.

OZONE DEPLETION

Ozone is a pungent, slightly bluish gas composed of three oxygen atoms (O_3). Ninety percent of naturally occurring ozone resides in the stratosphere, the portion of the atmosphere ten to fifty kilometers (six to thirty miles) above the earth.[4] Commonly called the "ozone layer," stratospheric ozone helps to shield the earth from ultraviolet radiation (UV). Even though only about three of every ten million molecules in the atmosphere are ozone, the ozone layer absorbs all of the deadly UV-C radiation and most of the harmful UV-B radiation emitted by the sun. Therefore, destruction of the ozone layer would be catastrophic and significant depletion would be very harmful. Increased UV radiation would cause many more skin cancers and eye cataracts, weaken immune systems, reduce crop yields, harm or kill single-cell organisms, damage aquatic ecosystems, and speed the deterioration of certain plastics and other human-made materials, among other serious impacts.[5]

In the 1970s, scientists discovered that certain human-made chemicals, called chlorofluorocarbons (CFCs), posed a serious threat to stratospheric ozone.[6] CFCs release chlorine atoms into the stratosphere that act as a catalyst in the destruction of ozone molecules. Created in the 1920s to replace flammable and noxious refrigerants, CFCs are inert, nonflammable, nontoxic, colorless, odorless, and wonderfully adaptable to a wide variety of profitable uses. By the mid-1970s, CFCs had become the chemical of choice for coolants in air conditioning and refrigerating systems, propellants in aerosol sprays, solvents in the cleaning of electronic components, and the blowing agent for the manufacture of flexible and rigid foam. Scientists later discovered that other chemicals were also ozone-depleting substances (ODS), including halons (a very effective and otherwise safe fire suppressant), carbon tetrachloride, methyl chloroform, and methyl bromide. Each of these substances can release ozone-destroying chlorine or bromine atoms into the stratosphere, which then destroy ozone molecules.[7]

The economic importance of these chemicals, especially CFCs, made international controls very difficult to establish.[8] The absence of firm scientific consensus on the nature and seriousness of the problem, a strenuous antiregulatory campaign by corporations producing or using CFCs, concerns for the cost of unilateral regulation, worries on the part of developing countries that restricting access to CFCs would slow economic development, and opposition by the then European Community (EC) prevented effective action for many years.

The definition and agenda-setting stage of the ozone-depletion issue began in 1977 and continued until the early 1980s. The fact-finding process also lasted many years, because scientific estimates of potential depletion fluctuated widely from the late 1970s to the late 1980s, and no evidence had yet emerged in nature confirming the theory and laboratory findings. Indeed, when the bargaining process formally began in 1982, the exact nature of the threat was unclear even to proponents of international action.[9]

The United States, which at that time accounted for more than 40 percent of world-wide CFC production, took a lead role in the negotiations in part because it had already banned CFC use in aerosol spray cans, which accounted for a large percentage of total use at that time, and wanted other states to follow suit, and in part because of concern among key actors in the State Department, Environmental Protection Agency (EPA), and Congress.[10] However, for an international ozone-protection policy to succeed, it was essential that all states producing and consuming CFCs join the regime. Thus, the EC, which opposed controls, constituted a potential veto coalition because its member states also accounted for more than 40 percent of global CFC production (exporting a third of that to developing countries). West Germany supported CFC controls, but the EC position was effectively controlled by the other large producing countries—France, Italy, and the United Kingdom—which doubted the science, wanted to preserve their industries' overseas markets, and wished to avoid the costs of adopting substitutes. Japan, also a major producer and user of CFCs, supported this position.

Large developing countries, including Brazil, China, India, and Indonesia, formed another potential veto coalition. Their bargaining leverage stemmed from their potential to produce very large quantities of CFCs in the future—production that, if it occurred, would eviscerate the effectiveness of any regime.[11] While most developing countries did not play an active role early in the regime's development, they eventually used this leverage to secure a delayed control schedule and precedent-setting provisions on financial and technical assistance.

Although negotiations began with an explicit understanding that only a framework convention would be discussed, in 1983, the lead states (the United States, Canada, and the Nordic states) proposed adding binding restrictions on CFC production to the potential treaty. The veto coalition, led by the EC, steadfastly rejected negotiations on such regulations. Thus, the ozone regime's first agreement, the 1985 Vienna Convention for the Protection of the Ozone Layer, affirmed the importance of protecting the ozone layer and included provisions on monitoring, research, and data exchanges but imposed no specific obligations to reduce the production or use of CFCs. Indeed, the convention did not even mention CFCs by name. However, because of a late-stage lead-state initiative, the negotiators agreed to resume talks if further evidence emerged supporting the potential threat.[12]

Only weeks after nations signed the Vienna Convention, British scientists published the first reports about the Antarctic ozone hole.[13] Although the hole had been forming annually for several years, the possibility of its existence fell so far outside the bounds of existing theory that computers monitoring satellite data on stratospheric ozone had reportedly ignored its presence as a data error.[14] Publication of its existence galvanized proponents of CFC controls, who argued that the hole justified negotiations to strengthen the nascent regime (despite the lack of firm evidence linking the hole to CFCs until 1989).[15] Thus, faced with domestic and international pressure, the veto states returned to the bargaining table in early 1986. These negotiations concluded in September 1987 with agreement on the Montreal Protocol.

During these negotiations, the lead states—a coalition that now included Canada, Finland, Norway, Sweden, Switzerland, and the United States—initially advocated a freeze, followed by a 95 percent reduction, in production of CFCs over a period of ten to fourteen years. The industrialized-country veto coalition—the EC, Japan, and the Soviet Union—eventually proposed placing a cap on production capacity at current levels. Lead states argued that a capacity cap would actually allow for an increase in real CFC production because many manufacturers outside the United States already possessed significant excess production capacity. Thus, even if a cap was imposed, European producers could increase their actual output of CFC production while maintaining their current capacity, gaining economic benefits from the regime. Lead states responded with a series of counterproposals before eventually proposing a 50 percent cut as a final offer during the last stages of the negotiations. After stating for months that it could not accept more than a 20 percent reduction, the EC relented and accepted the compromise proposal in the final days of the last round of negotiations in Montreal.

The 1987 Montreal Protocol on Substances That Deplete the Ozone Layer mandated that industrialized countries freeze and then reduce their production and use of the five most widely used CFCs by 50 percent by 2000. Halon production would be frozen on the same terms. Developing countries were given ten extra years to meet each obligation, allowing them to increase their use of CFCs before taking on commitments. Instrumentally, this "grace period" helped gain agreement from a potential developing-country veto coalition, which argued they deserved access to these important chemicals. Substantively, creating the two control schedules was recognition that industrialized countries had emitted almost all the CFCs in the atmosphere to that point and that developing countries needed access to these important and now inexpensive chemicals to aid their economic development. As such, the grace period reflects the principle of common but differentiated responsibilities, which has since become a mainstay of international environmental politics. The principle states that all countries have a common responsibility to address global environmental issues but that some countries have special responsibilities to act first or take special actions because of their large contribution to the problem or their access to greater financial and technological resources to address it.

The protocol also included important provisions establishing scientific and technological assessment panels to provide parties with independent and authoritative information, requiring parties to report on their ODS production and use, banning trade in CFCs and halons with countries that did not ratify the agreement, creating provisions for reviewing the effectiveness of the regime, and strengthening controls through amendments and "adjustments." The innovative provision for adjustments allows parties to strengthen controls on chemicals already controlled under the protocol by a decision of the Meeting of the Parties (MOP). The MOP meets annually and is the supreme decision-making body of the regime, composed of all countries that have ratified the protocol. Unlike formal amendments, adjustments do not require ratification by countries but instead became binding on all parties immediately after adoption.

The ten-year evolution of the EC position from rejecting all discussion of control measures to proposing a production cap to accepting a compromise 50 percent reduction target reflected several factors: disunity within the EC (Belgium, Denmark, the Netherlands, and West Germany supported CFC regulations), the personal role played by UNEP executive director Mostafa Tolba, diplomatic pressures by the United States, pressure from European NGOs, and reluctance by the EC to be seen as the culprit should negotiations fail. The evolution of the lead-state position from seeking a near 95 percent cut to accepting a 50 percent cut reflected the need to include the Europeans in the protocol. Understanding that a regime without countries responsible for 40 percent of global production could not succeed, lead states concluded that it was better to compromise at 50 percent cuts (even though these carried far higher adjustment costs for the lead states, as they had already taken most of the lost-cost reduction measures, while the Europeans had done almost nothing) in the hope that these could be strengthened in the future, rather than to create a regime without the EC.

The 1987 Montreal Protocol is widely considered a historic achievement in global environmental politics. Six factors stand out.

- It was the first treaty to address a truly global environmental threat.
- The protocol required significant cuts in the production and use of several very important chemicals, central to economic activity in key industries.
- The final agreement was reached in the absence of clear scientific proof concerning the problem, making it perhaps the first prominent example of application of the precautionary principle in a global environmental treaty (even if that precise term does not appear in the treaty).

- Key architectural elements of the protocol, including the control measures, reporting requirements, assessment panels, differentiated responsibilities for developing countries, and review procedures influenced aspects of later environmental treaties.
- The protocol contained clear and effective mechanisms for expanding the treaty in response to new information through both formal amendments to add new chemicals and adjustments to strengthen existing controls.
- The protocol proved over time to be a significant success (see below), something that cannot be said for several other global environmental agreements.

At the same time, it is also important to note that the original Montreal Protocol (before its significant expansion in the 1990s) addressed only five CFCs and three halons (ignoring, at least for the time being, other known ODS); required that these chemicals be reduced, not eliminated; neglected to require that CFC alternatives not damage the ozone layer; included no provisions for independent monitoring of ODS production and use; and contained no real provisions for providing financial and technical assistance to developing countries to help them implement the regime. Thus, while hailing the initial protocol as a great success, some of those most worried about the problem doubted the new agreement would be sufficient to truly safeguard the ozone layer over the long term.[16]

Regime Strengthening

Within months of the Montreal accord, in late 1987, scientists announced that their initial studies suggested that CFCs were likely responsible for creation of the ozone hole, which continued to grow larger every year, although natural processes peculiar to Antarctica contributed to its severity. Studies during the next two years solidly confirmed these findings. In March 1988, satellite data revealed that stratospheric ozone above the heavily populated Northern Hemisphere had also begun to thin.[17] In 1989 the regime's Scientific Assessment Panel concluded that the world's scientific community had reached broad agreement that CFCs were indeed depleting stratospheric ozone.[18]

This period also saw significant changes in the economic interests of key actors. After strenuously objecting to national and international CFC controls in the 1970s and most of the 1980s, in 1988 DuPont announced that it would soon be able to produce CFC substitutes. DuPont was followed by other large chemical companies, including several in Europe. Now that they could make substitutes, the major CFC manufacturers changed their position. They no longer opposed a CFC phaseout but lobbied instead for an extended transition period and against controls on their new alternatives, particularly hydrochlorofluorocarbons (HCFCs), a class of CFC substitutes that deplete ozone but at a significantly reduced rate. In response to these scientific and economic changes, and to increased pressure from domestic environmental lobbies, the EC abruptly shifted roles.[19]

By June 1990, when the second Meeting of the Parties to the Montreal Protocol (MOP-2) convened in London, EC states had assumed a lead role in the difficult negotiations that significantly strengthened the ozone regime. The resulting agreement, the 1990 London Amendment and Adjustment, was historic in its own right, requiring that parties completely phase out the production and use of the original eight CFCs and halons, carbon tetrachloride, and all other CFCs and halons by the year 2000 and methyl chloroform by 2005 (see Box 3.1).[20]

Because the long-term success of the ozone regime also depended on getting large developing countries to participate, a second historic achievement in London was the creation of the Multilateral Fund for the Implementation of the Montreal Protocol. The first such fund established under an environmental agreement (it also influenced the creation of the Global Environment Facility), the Multilateral Fund assists developing countries and "countries with economies in transition" in implementing the protocol.[21] The fund addressed demands by many developing countries, most importantly China and India, which had refused to join the regime until it included specific provisions for financial assistance, especially with regard to gaining access to the new alternatives to CFCs. The Multilateral Fund meets the incremental costs to developing countries of implementing the control measures of the protocol and also finances the development of national plans, capacity building, technical assistance, information sharing, training, and operation of the fund's secretariat. The incremental costs in this case are the extra expense of producing or using ODS alternatives.

The Multilateral Fund is replenished every three years and administered by an executive committee made up of seven donor and seven recipient countries. Replenishment levels are negotiated by the MOP. The total budget for the 2012–2014 triennium is $440 million.[22] Since its establishment, the fund has disbursed over $2.8 billion to support more than 6,800 projects in 145 countries and is widely considered a key ingredient in the success of the ozone regime. The existence and effectiveness of the fund has made it easier, both politically and economically, for many developing countries to accept a series of agreements to accelerate ODS phaseout schedules. The fund gave them confidence that financial assistance would be available to assist them in implementing the new controls.[23]

Parties strengthened the regime again in 1992 at MOP-4 in Copenhagen. Once again, they acted in response to increasing evidence of accelerating ozone-layer depletion as well as significant progress in the deployment of CFC substitutes. The 1992 Copenhagen Amendment and Adjustment accelerated the existing phaseout schedule and added controls on methyl bromide, a toxic fumigant used in agriculture and once the second most widely used insecticide in the world by volume. Parties also agreed to

BOX 3.1 CHEMICALS CONTROLLED BY THE MONTREAL PROTOCOL

- *Chlorofluorocarbons* (CFCs): Inert, long-lived, nontoxic, noncorrosive, non-flammable, and extremely versatile chemicals used in refrigeration and air conditioning systems, in spray cans as aerosol propellants, to make flexible and rigid foams (e.g., seat cushions and Styrofoam), in solvents, and in many other applications. The five most widely used CFCs formulations were controlled under the original 1987 Montreal Protocol. The remainder were regulated under the 1990 London Amendment.
- *Halons*: Primarily in fire extinguishing systems and first controlled under the 1987 Montreal Protocol.
- *Carbon tetrachloride*: Used primarily as a solvent or cleaning agent but also in fire extinguishers and as an industrial chemical, including in the creation of refrigerants. First controlled under the 1990 London Amendment.
- *Methyl chloroform*: Also used as a solvent. First controlled under the 1990 London Amendment.
- *Hydrochlorofluorocarbons* (HCFCs): Originally developed in the 1950s for air conditioning but not widely used until reformulations were introduced in 1989 as replacements for CFCs. While much less destructive than CFCs, HCFCs also contribute to ozone depletion. First controlled under the 1992 Copenhagen Amendment.
- *Methyl bromide*: A powerfully toxic pesticide and insecticide used in agriculture, especially for high-value crops; fumigating structures to kill pests, especially termites; and quarantine treatment of shipping containers and agricultural commodities awaiting export. First controlled under the 1992 Copenhagen Amendment.
- *Hydrobromofluorocarbons*: Not widely used but added to the protocol under the 1992 Copenhagen Amendment to prevent new uses.
- *Bromochloromethane*: A new ODS that some companies sought to introduce to the market in 1998 but added to the protocol in the 1999 Beijing Amendment for immediate phaseout to prevent its use.

Source: Although widely available, information is this section expands and updates a United Nations Environment Programme, "Backgrounder: Basic Facts and Data on the Science and Politics of Ozone Protection," press release, September 18, 2008, ozone.unep.org/Events/ozone_day_2008/press_backgrounder.pdf.

phase out HCFCs by 2030 (with all but 0.5 percent being eliminated by 2020[24]), since unlimited growth of HCFCs would have eventually become just as harmful to the ozone layer as the CFCs they replaced.[25] Additionally, MOP-4 established the Implementation Committee, which examines cases of possible noncompliance and makes recommendations to the MOP aimed at securing compliance.[26] The Copenhagen adjustment also included creation of "essential use exemptions" that allow a party to propose continued use of certain ODS for specific purposes beyond the final phaseout date if it believes that no alternatives are available. The MOP must then formally approve the uses and amounts proposed by the party. While providing a loophole, the inclusion of exemptions was a way to overcome the lowest common denominator problem (see Chapter 5) and appease potential veto states from blocking the introduction of faster phaseout dates.

By the conclusion of the 1992 negotiations, the EU and United States had largely reversed the roles they played during the 1970s and 1980s. In 1993 this switch became even clearer when the EU led the first in a series of attempts to accelerate HCFC controls. Opposing them was a veto coalition that included the United States (the key lead state in the 1970s and 1980s), Australia, China, and India, which argued that further restrictions on HCFCs would not reduce damage to the ozone layer enough to justify the extra economic costs. They also argued that such measures would punish firms that had made significant and good-faith investments in HCFC technologies, preventing them from recouping their investment; increase the use of hydrofluorocarbons (HFCs), which while not ozone depleting are very potent greenhouse gases (GHGs) and manufactured in several European companies; and detract attention and resources from other measures that would have a greater impact on protecting the ozone layer.

A similar division developed with respect to methyl bromide. Since the early 1990s, NGOs had called for a rapid phaseout of methyl bromide because of its threat to both human health (as a toxic pesticide) and the ozone layer (as an ODS). Many industrialized countries, including the United States and the EU, had taken steps domestically to limit, and in some cases phase out, methyl bromide and supported regulating it under the protocol. However, the United States successfully championed a significant loophole in the ozone regime that allows parties to continue using methyl bromide for "critical agricultural uses" even after its official phaseout date. This procedure gives the requesting country significant latitude in defining what constitutes a critical use— far more than in the essential-use exemption process for CFCs and halons. The United States led the push for this new loophole in response to intense domestic lobbying from influential agricultural interests, particularly in California. The EU and other lead states on the methyl bromide issue reluctantly accepted this new exemption as the best way forward given the opposition of a potential veto coalition.[27]

PHOTO 3.1   **Anti–methyl bromide picket signs outside of the first Extraordinary Meeting of the Parties to the Montreal Protocol in Montreal in March 2004.**
Courtesy IISD/*Earth Negotiations Bulletin.*

This strategy proved correct when the 1997 Montreal Amendment and Adjustment accelerated the phaseout of methyl bromide. The new agreement required industrialized countries to phase out methyl bromide by 2005 and developing countries by 2015. Developing countries had previously committed only to a freeze by 2002 (see Table 3.1). Potential veto states within the developing-country coalition accepted the new requirements in part because the agreement included language that they would be eligible to receive assistance earmarked for methyl bromide projects from the Multilateral Fund and because, like the United States, they knew that if necessary, they could exercise the exemption for "critical agricultural uses." The 1997 agreement (reached at MOP-9) also addressed the issue of illegal trade in CFCs, creating new licensing systems for CFC imports and exports and for regular information exchanges between parties. Over the years, the restrictions on new CFCs had created a black market for these chemicals, and the new rules sought to make it more difficult to sneak them across borders under false pretenses.

At MOP-11, held in Beijing in 1999, the EU finally secured US agreement to strengthen controls on HCFCs, albeit modestly. The 1990 Beijing Amendment and Adjustment added bromochloromethane (a newly developed ODS) to the regime, eliminating its production by 2002. Parties also agreed to mandatory reporting on the use of methyl bromide for quarantine and preshipment applications. The use of methyl bromide to clean shipping containers as part of quarantine and preshipment procedures is another large (but less controversial) exempted use of the pesticide, but parties (after a push by lead states) agreed that requiring reports on the amounts used would provide information useful to discouraging unnecessary or excessive applications and the unapproved diversion of methyl bromide to other uses. These steps show both the impact of exemptions, as loopholes that allow extended use of a controlled substance, and the potential importance of tightening certain technical details, such as reporting, which sometimes can serve to reduce the use of a substance through means other than direct regulations.

TABLE 3.1 Montreal Protocol Chemical Phaseout Schedules

CHEMICALS	DEVELOPED COUNTRIES	DEVELOPING COUNTRIES
Chlorofluorocarbons (CFCs)	Phase out by 1996	Phase out by 2010
Halons	Phase out by 1994	Phase out by 2010
Carbon tetrachloride	Phase out by 1996	Phase out by 2010
Methyl chloroform	Phase out by 1996	Freeze by 2003 at average 1998–2000 levels, reduce by 30 percent by 2005 and 70 percent by 2010, and phase out by 2015
Hydrobromofluorocarbons (HBFCs)	Phase out by 1996	Phase out by 1996
Hydrochlorofluorocarbons (HCFCs)	Reduce by 35 percent by 2004, 75 percent by 2010, 90 percent by 2015, and phase out by 2020, allowing 0.5 percent for servicing purposes during the period 2020 to 2030	Freeze by 2013 at the average 2009–2010 levels; reduce by 10 percent by 2015, 35 percent by 2020, 67.5 percent by 2025; phase out by 2030, allowing for an annual average of 2.5 percent for servicing purposes during the period 2030 to 2040.
Methyl bromide (CH$_3$Br)	Phase out by 2005	Freeze by 2002 at average 1995–1998 levels, reduce by 20 percent by 2005, and phase out by 2015
Bromochloromethane (BCM)	Phase out by 2002	Phase out by 2002

Note: Exemptions exist for continuing production and consumption of small amounts for "essential uses" for some ODS after the phaseout date and larger exemptions exist for critical agricultural, quarantine, and preshipment uses of methyl bromide.

Source: Although widely available, information here expands on a similar list in Ozone Secretariat, "Basic Facts and Data on the Science and Politics of Ozone Protection," UNEP, September 18, 2008, http://ozone.unep.org/Events/ozone_day_2008/press_backgrounder.pdf.

In September 2007, parties marked the twentieth anniversary of the protocol by returning to Montreal for the nineteenth MOP and strengthening the ozone regime. In a surprising development, the 2007 Montreal Adjustment moved the phaseout of HCFC production and consumption forward by a full decade and augmented the interim cuts. This agreement, heralded worldwide in environmental policy circles, represented an important accomplishment for addressing both ozone depletion and climate change (as noted, HCFCs are powerful GHGs). It was also the most significant strengthening of the ODS controls in a decade and revealed new attitudes on the part of former veto and swing states, with the United States suddenly switching to a lead position on accelerating the HCFC phaseout, emphasizing the positive climate aspects of the move. In an example of the political interlinkages that often arise in environmental politics, in addition to protecting the ozone layer, the United States apparently wanted a climate victory in the ozone negotiations to buttress its image and negotiating position in the parallel climate-change talks.

China, the biggest producer of HCFCs, and with India a longtime opponent of accelerating the HCFC phaseout in developing countries, shifted from veto to swing states. China is the world's leading manufacturer of air conditioners that use HCFC-22 as a refrigerant. After initially blocking the agreement, China eventually agreed to the new requirements in exchange for political commitments that the next replenishment of the Multilateral Fund would include substantially more funding for HCFC alternatives. Australia, India, Russia, and other former veto or swing states also relented and chose not to block the agreement. Despite their concerns about the feasibility and cost of speeding HCFC elimination, they eventually accepted lead-state arguments in support of the new HCFC controls. The potential veto states also did not want the blame for scuttling a deal on the protocol's anniversary.[28] As noted by an observer at the talks, "An agreement on HCFCs was therefore timely and served several interests. Many developing country delegates saw new policy commitments on HCFCs as a way to ensure continued availability of funding. . . . Industrialized countries saw an agreement on accelerated phaseout of HCFCs as an easy win for climate, [and one that included] action by both developed and developing countries."[29]

The 2007 Montreal Adjustment marked the last major strengthening of ODS regulations to date. However, subsequent MOPs continued to review, develop, and expand the regime in other ways. As noted above, every three years parties negotiate the replenishment level for the Multilateral Fund. The MOP also reviews work by the Multilateral Fund annually, outlining priorities and adjusting policy as needed. Each year parties also review essential-use nominations, and these have declined significantly over the last decade. Parties have attempted to reduce use of the critical-use exemption for methyl bromide. Additionally, the Montreal Protocol became the first regime to hold paperless meetings, when the 2008 MOP replaced the huge number of official

PHOTO 3.2   The Montreal Protocol Meeting of the Parties in 2008 in Doha, Qatar, became the first global environmental negotiation to replace the avalanche of official documents with electronic versions.
Courtesy IISD/*Earth Negotiations Bulletin.*

documents produced and copied prior to and during a global environmental meeting with electronic versions, establishing a precedent that other regimes began to follow.[30]

Despite this impressive history, the most significant recent effort to expand and strengthen the regime has not been successful. "The two most widely used substitutes for CFCs—HCFCs and HFCs—are also potent greenhouse gases, as are some byproducts created during their production. HCFCs are addressed under the Montreal Protocol and their climate impact, while significant, will decline and eventually be eliminated if countries fulfill their obligations (something that is not guaranteed). HFCs are not ODS, however, and thus do not naturally fall under the purview of the Montreal Protocol."[31] A coalition of lead states, which includes many small island developing countries, Canada, Mexico, Morocco, and the United States, have repeatedly proposed amending the protocol and placing controls on HFCs. Supported by the EU, Norway, Switzerland, and others, they argue that parties to the Montreal Protocol have a responsibility to address HFCs, as these substances might not exist were it not for the treaty's controls on CFCs. Such an amendment would also allow developing countries to receive support from the Multilateral Fund to reduce HFC use and emissions. Lead states made these arguments again during the twenty-fourth MOP in 2012, but their proposals were blocked once more by a coalition of veto states, led by India, Iran, and Saudi Arabia with support from China and others. These states argue that the Montreal Protocol cannot legally address chemicals that do not directly affect the ozone layer; HFCs are needed for economic development, especially as HCFCs are phased out; implementing controls on HFCs would take resources away from eliminating HCFCs and methyl bromide; and addressing non-ODS climate issues under the ozone regime complicates the climate negotiations and represents a way for industrialized countries to delay further commitments in the climate regime.[32] Lead states have stated they intend to push for HFC controls again at future COPs.

The Ozone Regime Today

The ozone regime is widely considered the most successful global environmental regime. The protocol currently mandates the elimination of ninety-six chemicals (see Table 3.1), although as noted, exemptions exist for continuing production and consumption of small amounts of "essential uses" for some CFCs and halons after the phaseout date and larger exemptions exist for critical agricultural and quarantine and preshipment uses of methyl bromide. The ozone regime has eliminated nearly all production and use of new CFCs, halons, carbon tetrachloride, and methyl chloroform.[33] Despite the exemptions (and perhaps even because of them, as exemptions help keep potential veto states in the regime), methyl bromide production has declined drastically. HCFC reductions are proceeding in rough accordance with the control schedule. As a result, the atmospheric abundance of all major ODS except HCFCs is declining, as is the amount of chlorine and bromine in the stratosphere, and ozone depletion has largely stabilized.[34] "Because Argentina, Brazil, China, the EU, India, Indonesia, and Thailand, among many other countries, did not take meaningful action to reduce CFCs and other ODS until they joined the Montreal Protocol, and because key ODS alternatives were invented or commercialized in response to controls established by the Protocol, these declines [in ODS production and use] must be attributed to the impact of the ozone regime."[35]

The Ozone Secretariat calculates that without the Montreal Protocol, global CFC consumption would have reached about three million tons in 2010 and eight million tons by 2060, resulting in as much as 50 percent depletion of the ozone layer by 2035.[36] By preventing the increases in UV radiation that would have occurred from this depletion, studies indicate that the Montreal Protocol prevented tens of millions of cases of fatal skin cancer and many more millions of nonfatal skin cancer and eye cataracts, as well as significant damage to plants and ecosystems, including many food crops, and very negative impacts on aquatic organisms.[37]

Because most ODS are potent GHGs, the ozone regime has also delivered substantial climate benefits. Just the reductions in CFC and halon emissions prior to 2000 prevented the equivalent of approximately 25 billion tons of carbon dioxide (CO_2)

emissions—or several times as much as the initial targets of the Kyoto Protocol.[38] Looking forward, the 2007 agreement to speed the phaseout of HCFCs will eliminate about 7 to 9 metric tons of HCFCs, equal to the CO_2 produced by one hundred million cars.[39] Overall, the Montreal Protocol is estimated to have averted GHG emissions equal to more than 135 billion tons of carbon dioxide.[40]

Despite its many successes, stratospheric ozone levels in general terms remain lower than before CFCs starting attacking them, and the Antarctic ozone hole remained near its worst levels as late as 2011.[41] The regime is on pace to reverse this, but doing so requires completing the phaseout of CFCs in all developing countries, including essential-use exemptions for metered-dose inhalers; implementing and funding the complete transition away from HCFCs; and ensuring that HCFCs are not replaced by substances with high global-warming potential or other harmful environmental impacts. Parties must also eliminate methyl bromide, which remains an important and contentious challenge despite reductions in the use of critical-use exemptions. Parties must also deploy substitutes for the few remaining exempted uses of halons, eliminate illegal trade in ODS, prevent the commercial development of new ODS, and continue to provide funding to assist some developing countries in meeting these challenges. Each task includes a different set of hurdles, and success is not guaranteed.

Another critical challenge is effectively managing ODS currently contained in wastes and implementing and funding ODS destruction. "Every kilogram of ODS produced since the 1920s but not yet vented to the atmosphere lies trapped somewhere waiting to escape. Many millions of tons of CFCs remain in old or discarded refrigerators, air-conditioners, insulating foam, and dozens of other products and wastes, collectively known as 'ODS Banks.' A hundred thousand tons of ODSs enter the waste stream every year. Eventually, all the ODSs contained in these banks that we do not capture and recycle or destroy will reach the atmosphere."[42] Currently, ODS leakage from banks represents the largest threat to the ozone layer when one factors the ozone-depleting properties of each chemical.[43] Many developing countries lack the regulatory infrastructure, financial resources, expertise, and equipment to manage or destroy ODS banks in an environmentally sound manner, especially given the immense volume of older refrigerators and air conditioners in use around the world or already in the waste stream. "Addressing ODS banks will require difficult choices regarding resource allocation. Failing to act could lead to unnecessary emissions, while focusing too many resources on ODS banks might preclude effective action in other important areas."[44]

Explaining the Ozone Regime

Four sets of large-scale causal factors shaped development of global ozone policy: the necessity of accommodating veto states, advancing scientific knowledge and increasing consensus about that knowledge, changing patterns of economic interests among the major actors, and the extant development of the regime:[45]

1. As with other regimes discussed in this volume, one major factor affecting the development, timing, and content of the ozone regime was that all countries with significant existing or potential ODS consumption had to be included in the regime for it to succeed. This required lead states to compromise with veto states during key stages of the regime's development.[46]

2. Advancing scientific knowledge led to discovery of the threat, galvanized epistemic networks and certain policy makers, changed public opinion, undercut arguments by control opponents, and, at different times, significantly enhanced prospects for strengthening the regime.[47]

3. The economic interests of the major actors, including lead and veto states, influenced development of the ozone regime in several different ways. Not surprisingly, economic interests tied to CFCs and other ODS often prevented stronger controls. Yet, during several crucial periods, the development of effective ODS substitutes altered economic interests, helping parties strengthen the regime, most significantly in 1990 and 1992. In addition, the creation of the Multilateral Fund changed the calculations of many developing countries, turning veto and swing states to regime supporters.[48]

4. Regime design matters.[49] The existence and framework of the Vienna Convention allowed governments to press forward far more quickly and effectively on a binding protocol. Provisions of the protocol allowed governments to strengthen it far more rapidly than would have been possible otherwise. In particular, the requirements to review the effectiveness of the control measures, the mandates for comprehensive scientific and technical assessments, the ability for parties to "adjust" existing controls through MOP decisions, and the generally effective operation of the Multilateral Fund, all created significant opportunities for strengthening the regime relatively quickly in response to new developments.[50]

The history of global ozone policy illustrates the role that veto coalitions can play in weakening regime rules, how states sometimes shift roles, and the potential impact on global environmental policy of changing domestic politics, advancing scientific knowledge, technological innovations, changing economic interests, and particular sets of regime rules. The impact of these factors can vary significantly over time and from case to case, however, and the future is far from certain. Nevertheless, if countries fully implement all the requirements in the ozone regime (still an "if"), then the ozone layer over most of the earth could fully recover around 2050, with the more extensive depletion above Antarctica recovering later this century.

HAZARDOUS WASTE

Hazardous wastes are discarded materials that can damage human health or the environment. This includes wastes that consist of or contain heavy metals, toxic chemicals, infectious medical wastes, and corrosive, flammable, explosive, or radioactive substances. Estimates vary, but several billion tons of hazardous wastes are generated each year, although the precise figure is unknown.[51] Industrialized countries generate the vast majority of this waste, but quantities are increasing rapidly in certain developing countries. Most hazardous waste remains in the country in which it was produced, but some is shipped across international boundaries for a variety of reasons. Most of this movement is between Organization for Economic Cooperation and Development (OECD) countries, but an increasing amount of waste, especially electronic waste (e-waste), gets exported to developing countries.

In the 1970s and 1980s, laws regulating hazardous waste disposal grew in OECD countries, and many individual firms began to seek cheaper sites for their disposal.[52] As a consequence, North-South hazardous waste shipments began to increase significantly. Developing countries or firms within them, particularly the poorer states in Africa, Central America, South Asia, and the Caribbean, were tempted by offers of substantial revenues for accepting wastes but lacked the technology or administrative capacity to dispose of them safely. Some of this trade was legal, but much was not, with the wastes entering countries covertly as a result of bribes to corrupt officials or labeled as something else. In some cases, businesses interested in recycling products containing hazardous materials (such as the ship-breaking industry in South Asia or parts of the e-waste industry) circumvented import rules or ignored or obstructed domestic environmental and human-health regulations.

During this period several notorious cases of illegal dumping also occurred. In one, the cargo ship *Khian Sea* went to sea in 1986 in search of a disposal site for fourteen thousand tons of incinerator ash containing high levels of lead, cadmium, and other heavy metals. The ash came from incinerators in Philadelphia. It had previously gone to New Jersey, but New Jersey refused to accept any more after 1984. The ship spent almost two years at sea, looking for a place that would accept its cargo, during which it changed its name twice. In January 1988, it dumped four thousand tons of ash in Haiti; it dumped the remaining ten thousand tons in November at different spots in the Atlantic and Indian oceans.

The issue-definition stage began in 1984 and 1985, when a UNEP working group of legal and technical experts developed a set of voluntary guidelines on the management and disposal of hazardous wastes (the Cairo Guidelines). The guidelines specified prior notification of the receiving state of an export, consent by the receiving state prior to export, and verification by the exporting state that the receiving state has requirements for disposal at least as stringent as those of the exporting state.

These soft-law guidelines did not satisfy some key actors, however, most notably African states that received the bulk of illegal hazardous waste exports. Some of these states characterized trade in hazardous waste as a form of exploitation of poor and weak states by rich countries and businesses and sought to define the issue as a problem requiring an outright ban rather than soft-law guidelines or regulations allowing some shipments. This characterization drew support from NGOs and some officials in industrialized states, particularly in Europe. Parliamentarians from the EC later joined with representatives of sixty-eight developing states from Africa, the Caribbean, and the Pacific in calling for the banning of international trade in wastes. Developing countries also called for industrialized countries to create internal laws prohibiting waste exports to developing countries.

The bargaining stage began in 1987, when UNEP, at the request of governments comprising UNEP's Governing Council, organized formal negotiations to control international trade in hazardous wastes. During the next eighteen months, major differences emerged between African lead states and industrialized countries that were swing and veto states. African states wanted a total ban on such waste exports and export-state liability when illegal traffic did occur, in part because many developing countries did not possess the administrative, financial, or technical ability to enforce a ban on their own. Waste-exporting states wanted a convention that would permit the trade, providing that importing countries were notified and agreed to accept it—something known as a prior informed consent regime.

The final round of negotiations took place in March 1989 in Basel, Switzerland, where the veto coalition, led by the United States, took advantage of the fact that some poor countries wished to continue accepting wastes. At the time, the United States exported only about 1 percent of its hazardous wastes (although this was a large amount by weight), mostly to Canada and Mexico, but it led the veto coalition largely because of an ideological position that rejected limitations on its right to export and practical concerns regarding implementing the proposed treaty. The veto coalition gave the ban supporters a choice: accept an informed consent regime, or get no treaty. The Organization of African Unity proposed language to ban waste exports to countries that lacked the same level of facilities and technology as the exporting nations and to require inspection of disposal sites by UN inspectors, but many industrialized countries rejected these proposals.[53]

The 1989 Basel Convention on Control of Transboundary Movements of Hazardous Wastes and Their Disposal prohibited the export of hazardous wastes to countries with less advanced storage and disposal facilities unless the importing state had detailed information on the waste shipment and gave prior written consent.[54] Agreements between signatory and nonsignatory states were permitted, although they needed to conform to the terms of the convention. Critics charged that the convention did not go further than the existing regulations in most industrialized countries— regulations that had already failed to curb legal or illegal waste traffic. They also noted that the convention lacked precision on key definitions, such as "environmentally sound" and even "hazardous wastes," and contained no liability provisions to deter illegal dumping or provide cleanup costs.[55]

International Waste Policy Outside the Basel Convention

In April 1989, soon after the formal adoption of the Basel Convention and three years before it entered into force, thirty mostly industrialized countries (not including the United States) pledged to dispose of most of their wastes at home and to ban the export of hazardous wastes to countries that lacked the legal and technological capacity to handle them.[56] Later in 1989, the EC reached agreement, after extended negotiations, to ban waste shipments from its countries to sixty-eight former European colonies in Africa, the Caribbean, and the Pacific. The EC had sought an exception for exports to countries with "adequate technical capacity," but developing countries insisted on a total ban.[57]

In 1991, twelve African states signed the Bamako Convention on the Ban of the Import into Africa and the Control of Transboundary Movement and Management of Hazardous Wastes within Africa.[58] In 1992, Costa Rica, El Salvador, Guatemala, Honduras, Nicaragua, and Panama adopted the Regional Convention on the Transboundary Movement of Hazardous Wastes. In 1995, South Pacific governments, Britain, and France signed the Waigani Convention banning the importation of hazardous and radioactive wastes into more than a dozen South Pacific countries. These regional agreements, combined with other unilateral and multilateral policies, initially created stronger hazardous waste mechanisms outside the Basel Convention than within it.

The Ban Amendment

In May 1992, after receiving ratification from the required twenty countries (Article 35), the Basel Convention entered into force, three years after negotiations concluded. It was a weak regime, with limited binding rules and without ratification by any of the major waste-exporting states that composed the victorious veto coalition during the negotiations. In less than two years, however, growing demands for stronger action helped lead states strengthen the regime.

By early 1994, more than one hundred countries had passed domestic legislation banning the import of hazardous wastes, although not all of them had the administrative capacity to do so unilaterally.[59] This development shows an important potential consequence of a global environmental regime: the strengthening of relevant domestic law. Some of the credit must also go to Greenpeace, which published and publicized a report documenting one thousand cases of illegal toxic waste exports.[60] Even the United States, although not a party to the regime, signaled it would support a ban on hazardous waste exports if the ban exempted scrap metal, glass, textiles, and paper, which are widely traded for recycling.[61]

Building on these developments, at the Basel Convention's second COP (COP-2), a broad coalition pressed for adopting a complete ban on hazardous waste exports from OECD countries to non-OECD countries, including those exported for recycling.[62] They argued that shipments of recyclables often were not for recycling but for dumping and that the OECD countries would never reduce their creation of wastes as long as they could ship some to developing countries.

The Group of 77 (G-77), the lead coalition, called for the proposed ban to go into effect immediately. Denmark called for it to begin in 1995. Australia, Canada, Germany, Japan, the Netherlands, the United Kingdom, and the United States countered that any ban should exempt recyclables. China and the former socialist states of Central and Eastern Europe came out in favor of the G-77 proposal. Greenpeace, demonstrating the impact that NGOs can have within certain regimes at certain times, also made an important contribution by releasing a seven-year study of more than fifty recycling operations in non-OECD countries that provided concrete evidence of widespread dumping of hazardous wastes falsely labeled and shipped as "recyclables" as well as many other shipments of recyclables that had not been recycled at all but just dumped in developing countries.[63]

Despite intensive lobbying by waste exporting countries, particularly in support of allowing bilateral agreements on hazardous waste exports for recycling, the G-77 remained firm, agreeing to negotiate only on the timetable for implementing a ban. Confronted with non-OECD unity, the veto coalition began to divide, with some withdrawing their opposition. The veto coalition was also weakened because several of its members, including the United States, had not ratified the Basel Convention and, as nonparties, remained technically outside the decision-making process. They could speak in opposition to the ban, but their views did not officially count as opposing a consensus decision, and they could not vote if matters came to that. When debate ended, COP-2 approved the ban. Countries opposed to the ban obtained nothing more than a delay in its full implementation.

One year later, at COP-3, parties significantly strengthened the decision by adopting the ban as a formal amendment to the convention (COP-2 approved the ban in a far less legally binding form). The Ban Amendment prohibits export of hazardous wastes for final disposal or recycling from countries listed in Annex VII of the convention (which currently includes all the industrialized-country parties) to non-Annex VII countries. The Ban Amendment does not prevent a developing country from receiving hazardous wastes from an industrialized country because they can do so by joining Annex VII. In 2011, after years of debate regarding the status of the amendment and legal requirements for its formal ratification, parties agreed that the Ban Amendment requires ratification by three-quarters of the parties that were parties at the time of its adoption for the amendment to enter into force.[64] As of March 2013, the Ban Amendment had not entered into force.

A central reason inhibiting ratification of the Ban Amendment is its prohibition on exports of wastes intended for recovery and recycling. Many industrialized countries, as well as an increasing number of developing ones (including China and India), have significant economic interests in maintaining the trade in wastes for recycling—including ships, electronics, scrap metal, glass, cardboard, paper, and some chemicals. As a result, not only has the Ban Amendment not entered into force, but the total amount of waste shipments rose sharply during the first decade of the convention's existence, especially among wastes intended for recycling. While recycling in theory is environmentally benign, this activity in certain industries in many developing countries releases air and water pollutants, toxic chemicals, and heavy metals into local environments and the workers.

Another issue involves definitions, including which wastes are defined as "hazardous" for the purposes of recycling and recovery and thus covered within the scope of the convention. To remedy this situation, the COP authorized technical working groups to draw up lists of banned and exempted wastes. COP-4 approved the first of these lists; in doing so, it diffused industry arguments that nobody knew what the ban was banning. Supporters of the Ban Amendment hoped that the new lists would speed its ratification and implementation. While this did not occur, many countries that have not ratified the Ban Amendment still support the lists, as they provide greater clarity to other elements of the convention.

COP-9 in 2008 included a renewed effort to move the Ban Amendment forward.[65] At the end of the meeting, in the absence of a substantive agreement, the president of the COP issued a "president's statement" urging parties to cooperate on a series of steps that would achieve the ban's core objective—to protect vulnerable populations from the environmental and health threats posed by hazardous wastes—which all parties supported. The steps included improving national capacities to monitor and trace shipments of hazardous wastes and to monitor, detect, and control illegal traffic; establishing criteria for classifying materials as hazardous in relation to the ban; and requiring a prior informed consent (PIC) procedure and use of precise customs codes.[66] The president's statement received support from many parties as the first opportunity for productive discussion on the underlying intent of the Ban Amendment in many years. Switzerland and Indonesia offered to initiate a follow-up process to enhance prospects for more substantive and productive discussion at future COPs.

Acting as conduits between the lead and veto states, the Indonesian and Swiss initiative yielded agreement on a number of issues that enhance prospects that the Ban Amendment will receive sufficient ratifications or that its central purpose will be more widely implemented through other mechanisms, perhaps including additional controls on unwanted shipments of hazardous wastes. To this end, at COP-10, parties agreed to decisions that provided further legal clarity to the status and purpose of the amendment, addressed illegal traffic, and provided more assistance to developing countries to address challenges some face prohibiting the import of hazardous wastes.

Regime Strengthening

Stalemate on the Ban Amendment did not prevent efforts to strength the regime in other ways, albeit not always successfully. For example, in December 1999, COP-5 adopted the Basel Protocol on Liability and Compensation, which addressed developing countries' concerns that they lack sufficient funds and technologies to prevent or cope with the consequences of illegal dumping or accidental spills. The protocol establishes provisions for determining liability and compensation for damage resulting from the legal or illegal transnational movement of hazardous wastes. Thirteen years later, however, the liability protocol has not received the ratifications necessary for it to enter into force.[67]

Concerns that the Basel Convention was having little practical effect led to a decision by COP-6 in 2002 to establish a prioritized action plan for implementing the convention through 2010. The plan emphasized the need to address the environmentally sound management of priority waste streams such as lead-acid batteries, PCBs, used oil, electronics, and obsolete pesticides. Subsequent COPs took additional action to support implementing the plan, especially in developing countries.

COP-6 also streamlined the institutional architecture of the convention, created a compliance mechanism to review and assist implementation (modeled somewhat on the procedure in the Montreal Protocol), and confirmed the role of the Basel Convention Regional Centers to facilitate implementation in developing countries through building capacity, educating the public, collecting data, reporting, promoting environmentally sound waste management, easing the transfer of cleaner production technologies, and helping to train customs officials. There are now fifteen such centers located in different parts of Africa, Asia, Eastern Europe, and Latin America. Additional centers may be created in the future.[68]

In 2006, an egregious incident of hazardous waste dumping in Côte d'Ivoire served to highlight the original purpose of the convention and the dangers associated with hazardous waste. An old chemical tanker carrying more than four hundred metric tons of heavily contaminated wash water (water used to clean its holds) sailed to Nigeria to deliver a different cargo and then docked in Abidjan, a port city of five million people and the economic capital of Côte d'Ivoire. Under the cover of night, the contaminated wastewater was transferred to tanker trucks belonging to a local company, which then dumped it at sixteen different open-air sites around the city, many near water supplies or fields growing food. At least fifteen people died, thousands were hospitalized, and over a hundred thousand sought medical treatment, overwhelming local hospitals. Many fishing, vegetable, and small livestock activities were halted, associated businesses closed, and workers were laid off. Protests erupted over suspicions of (unproven) government corruption in the scandal.[69] The incident highlighted the absence of effective tracking systems for the transboundary movement of hazardous waste and the concern that these shipments, both legal and illegal, might be producing more environmental damage than recognized.

Continuing the effort to strengthen the regime by prioritizing certain activities, in 2008 COP-9 established a process to review the extant implementation and effectiveness of the convention and the drafting of a new strategic plan. During the COP, many parties called the current "Strategic Plan to 2010" a success in providing guidance to parties, the secretariat, regional centers, IGOs, NGOs, and corporations regarding the regime's priorities, where to focus efforts, and how to allocate limited resources. Nevertheless, some delegates noted that many activities outlined in the plan had not been carried out because of inadequate financial resources; thus, the success of a new plan would depend on the provision of sufficient financial and technical assistance both to the Basel Convention regional centers and to developing countries to assist them in implementing the convention.[70]

To address these concerns, as well as similar arguments in other forums, in 2009 UNEP initiated the Consultative Process on Financing Options for Chemicals and Wastes. "Ideally, this process will enable Parties to the [Basel, Rotterdam, and Stockholm] conventions to streamline and link funding for related chemicals and wastes projects, thereby increasing the efficiency and availability of funds to support developing country implementation."[71] The results to date have been inconclusive. The Consultative Process has produced a policy paper, "but concrete action has yet to be taken to decide whether and how it might be implemented."[72]

In 2011, COP-10 adopted an updated strategic framework for 2012 to 2021 that, for the first time, includes specific goals and performance indicators to measure progress in implementing the Basel Convention. Many delegates "said this was long overdue, stressing that without concrete goals and indicators, it is very difficult to measure progress" and that the new system "will increase transparency and accountability around implementation."[73] However, developing countries again expressed concerns regarding the lack of adequate financial and technical resources. In their view, the outcome of the UNEP Consultative Process on Financing for Chemicals and Wastes, efforts to strengthen the Basel Convention Regional Centers, and the provision of assistance to implement the guidelines on the environmentally sound management of wastes and the steps to stop illegal traffic would largely determine the extent to which the new strategic framework is implemented in many countries.[74]

Technical Guidelines, E-Wastes, and Partnerships

The practical impact of the Basel Convention has been strengthened significantly through the development and updating of technical guidelines designed to assist industry and governments manage hazardous waste in an environmentally sound manner. Guidelines are now in place for more than twenty different types of hazardous wastes, including waste oil, biomedical and health-care wastes, persistent organic pollutants (POPs), individual chemicals such as PCBs, obsolete ships, and mobile phones.

The development of technical guidelines provides an example of effective regime strengthening even in an area where few new binding rules have been created. The guidelines related to chemicals, pesticides, and some other substances also contribute to implementing the new international emphasis on addressing the environmentally sound management of the entire life cycle of hazardous substances: production, use, emission, waste management, and disposal. This approach has been emphasized within the Strategic Approach to International Chemicals Management (SAICM) initiative, the Consultative Process on Financing for Chemicals and Wastes, and the synergies initiative.

SAICM is a broad initiative created by governments in 2006 that sets out a policy framework for the global, sound management of chemicals throughout their entire life cycle so that, by 2020, chemicals are produced and used in ways that minimize significant adverse effects to human health and the environment.[75] SAICM involves a range of stakeholders involved in different aspects of chemicals production, use, and disposal, including civil society, industry, national and local governments, and intergovernmental agencies.

The synergies initiative seeks to implement more effective global policy on hazardous chemicals and wastes by getting the Basel, Rotterdam, and Stockholm conventions, their secretariats, and their subsidiary bodies to coordinate and combine certain administration and implementation activities.[76] Supporters believe this will substantially improve the efficiency and effectiveness of all three conventions, enhance information exchange, direct more resources to implementation activities, and yield other benefits, including "advantageous synergies unavailable if the three processes remain entirely distinct."[77] Basel COP-8 and subsequent COPs of the Rotterdam and Stockholm conventions created an ad hoc joint working group to prepare recommendations on enhanced cooperation and coordination. Basel COP-9 was the first to address the recommendations, and after some debate the parties agreed to adopt them, as did the Rotterdam and Stockholm COPs. Since then, the three conventions have held coordinated COPs; begun to establish joint secretariat services with regard to information management, public awareness, budget cycles, and common administrative functions; initiated cooperative use of regional centers; and begun work to synchronize reporting requirements and coordinate other activities.

As part of the effort to improve the environmentally sound management of hazardous wastes, and in recognition of a growing problem, parties initiated serious discussions of electronic wastes, or e-wastes, at COP-8 in 2006.[78] E-wastes include discarded, broken, or obsolete electronic devices, including computers, printers, monitors, televisions, phones, and CD, DVD, and MP3 players, as well as their parts and components. Globally, e-waste generation is growing by about 40 million tonnes a year.[79] Much of this equipment contains hazardous materials, including heavy metals such as lead, cadmium, and beryllium and a variety of toxic chemicals, including certain flame retardants. Processing e-waste, particularly in developing countries, can yield important resources but can also cause serious pollution and health problems if proper care is not taken to protect workers and prevent release of the pollutants into the environment via direct dumping, poorly designed and operated landfills, open-pit burning, or incinerator exhaust and ashes.[80] Some parties supported using the Basel Convention to seek reductions in the amount of e-waste produced by requiring effective recovering and recycling programs that would prevent the items from entering the waste stream or being shipped to developing countries, where they are broken apart and harvested for materials (some EU states have such life-cycle requirements on various items). COP-8 reached consensus on a formal declaration regarding the importance of addressing e-wastes, outlined measures that parties could take domestically, and agreed that parties would work collectively in the future to address the issue.[81]

Two years later, at COP-9 in 2008, parties began this process.[82] Among other decisions, COP-9 adopted five technical guidelines and an overall guidance document for the environmentally sound management of used and end-of-life mobile phones. The guidelines address design considerations relevant to reducing hazardous waste, the collection, refurbishment, and recycling of used and end-of-life mobile phones, the transboundary movement of collected phones, and the management of hazardous waste from end-of-life mobile phones. The guidelines built on the Mobile Phone Partnership, launched in 2002, in which mobile phone manufacturers and service providers partnered with the Basel Convention to develop and promote the environmentally sound management of end-of-life mobile phones.

COP-9 also established the Partnership for Action on Computer Equipment patterned after the mobile-phone process. The computer equipment partnership will

PHOTO 3.3   **A Chinese child sits among a pile of wires and e-waste. Children can often be found dismantling e-waste containing many hazardous chemicals known to be potentially very damaging to children's health.**
© Greenpeace/Natalie Behring.

promote dialogue among governments, industry, NGOs, and academic experts; develop technical guidelines and a certification program for environmentally sound repair, refurbishment, and recycling of computer equipment and components; offer expert advice and participation in relevant initiatives; and work with the Basel Convention and parties to promote effective action.[83] While some expressed concern that involving companies would weaken these efforts, others believed that the concerns for market image, financial interests, and technical expertise of many computer and electronic companies could form the basis for productive partnerships on computers and other e-waste similar to the mobile-phone experience (which some had viewed as a kind of experiment).

Moving Forward

The current global regime for managing hazardous waste and controlling its international movement is far different from the original weak regime created in 1989. The expanded Basel Convention has helped to eliminate some of the worst forms of toxic-waste dumping, improved the management of hazardous wastes, and established frameworks, guidelines, and partnerships that could portend more improvements in the future. The evolution of the Basel Convention shows how veto power can dissipate over time when faced with a strong coalition that includes developing countries and some key OECD countries. The information, publicity, and political pressure generated by several NGOs, especially Greenpeace and the Basel Action Network, also played an important role. Once the hazardous waste trade issue became a political symbol uniting developing countries, it overcame the leverage of waste exporters that had weakened the regime in 1989. And once the regime branched out toward selected efforts to help reduce the creation of certain wastes and improve the management of all wastes, it expanded its network of supporters and increased its relevance.

Yet the hazardous waste regime faces many challenges. While many promising policy initiatives and economic incentives have emerged to promote more effective recycling of some of this waste, several of the central goals of the regime—to reduce the amount of waste produced, limit its movement, and induce its environmentally sound management—have become more difficult to achieve. Indeed, both the production and the transboundary movement of hazardous waste continue to grow. This trend is difficult to address given the increasing industrialization of many developing countries. For example, a recent study predicts that by 2020 e-waste in India from discarded computers will be 5 times higher than its level in 2007 and 2 to 4 times higher in China and South Africa; e-waste from televisions will be 1.3 to 2 times higher in China and India; and e-waste from mobile phones will be 7 times higher in China and 18 times higher in India.[84]

In addition, the Ban Amendment and Liability Protocol have not received sufficient ratifications to enter into force, and the United States still has not ratified the Basel Convention itself. Long-standing issues, such as the export of hazardous wastes for recycling, and newer issues, such as e-waste, the dismantling of ships, and the synergies initiative, all require significant attention. Finally, parties must continue to grapple with the challenge of securing sufficient funding to support key regime priorities. Delegates have told observers that efforts spent creating and revising the technical guidelines matter little to a developing country that lacks the financial resources or cadres of technically trained personnel to administer and enforce them.[85] As the Basel Convention approaches its twenty-fifth anniversary, addressing these challenges will determine the long-term impact of the hazardous waste regime.

TOXIC CHEMICALS

The systematic development and use of chemicals for commercial purposes began after World War II. Of the millions of chemical substances known in industry and scientific research, tens of thousands have been produced for regular use in the industrial, agriculture, and service sectors. Since the 1960s, more than 100,000 chemicals have been registered for commercial use in the EU alone,[86] and around the world more than 248,000 different chemical products are commercially available.[87] A major center of economic activity, the global chemicals industry engages in over $3 trillion of business annually.[88] Most of this activity remains in industrialized countries, but production and use of all types of chemicals are rising rapidly in developing countries.[89] Indeed, China leads the world in combined chemical purchases and sales.[90]

Many chemicals enter the market and become widely used before systematic assessments are made,[91] and detailed analyses of the potential impacts on human health and the environment exist for only a small number of these substances.[92] Not all chemicals are hazardous, of course, but toxic chemicals are produced or used in virtually every country in the world. Toxic chemicals include poisons, carcinogens, teratogens (affecting offspring), mutagens (affecting genes), irritants, narcotics, and chemicals with dermatological effects. Toxics are released into the environment through the normal use of certain products (e.g., pesticides and fertilizers), industrial and manufacturing practices that involve or produce hazardous chemicals, leakage from wastes, mismanagement, accidents, and intentional dumping. Once they have been dispersed into the environment, the complete cleanup of many toxic chemicals is difficult, sometimes impossible, and their harmful effects can continue for many years.

The issue-definition phase for toxic chemicals began in the 1960s, when concern started to grow about potentially negative impacts from pesticides and other chemicals. Instrumental in this process were both groundbreaking publications, especially Rachel Carson's *Silent Spring*, and high-profile accidents, such as the 1968 tragedy in Kyushu, Japan, in which 1,300 people were poisoned after eating rice contaminated with high levels of PCBs.[93] In the late 1960s and early 1970s, new risk assessments led some industrialized countries to adopt domestic regulations on a relatively small set of hazardous chemicals. The United States, for example, banned DDT in 1972 and initiated controls on PCBs in 1976.[94] During this period, the OECD became one of the first international organizations to address toxic chemicals, focusing on information exchange and improving scientific understanding and policy measures within its members.

Stimulated in part by discussion on hazardous chemicals at the 1972 United Nations Conference on the Human Environment in Stockholm,[95] governments adopted several multilateral agreements in the 1970s and early 1980s to help protect oceans, regional seas, and rivers from dumping and pollution.[96] In 1976, UNEP created the International Register of Potentially Toxic Chemicals to gather, process, and distribute information on hazardous chemicals. The United Nations Food and Agriculture Organization (FAO) and UNEP led development of both the 1985 International Code of Conduct for the Distribution and Use of Pesticides and the 1987 London Guidelines for the Exchange of Information on Chemicals in International Trade. Unfortunately, many developing countries lacked the regulatory infrastructure that would enable them to use the information made available through these initiatives.[97]

In 1989, amendments to the FAO Code of Conduct and the UNEP London Guidelines created a voluntary prior informed consent (PIC) procedure to help countries, especially developing countries, learn about chemicals that had been banned or severely restricted in other countries so that they could make informed decisions before they allowed them as imports. Although the voluntary PIC system was seen as a victory for NGOs, which had long called for its adoption, and for developing countries, because they hoped it would assist them in identifying and regulating such imports, many of its supporters also believed that a voluntary system would eventually prove insufficient.[98]

The fact-finding stage, in general terms, began during the formal preparations for the 1992 Earth Summit in Rio during which governments agreed to devote an entire chapter in Agenda 21 to chemicals. Among other actions, Agenda 21 called on states to create a mandatory PIC procedure and to improve coordination among the many national agencies and international organizations working on chemicals and related issues. To this end, governments created the Intergovernmental Forum on Chemical Safety (IFCS) in 1994 to address coordination among governments and the Inter-Organization Programme for the Sound Management of Chemicals (IOMC) in 1995 to address coordination among international organizations.[99] The fact-finding process continued in these bodies.

Governments then asked UNEP and the FAO to convene global negotiations with the goal of adopting a binding PIC procedure. The result was the 1998 Rotterdam Convention on the Prior Informed Consent Procedure for Certain Hazardous Chemicals and Pesticides in International Trade, which mandates that parties export certain toxic chemicals only with the informed consent of the importing party.[100]

During this period, concern began to grow regarding a particular set of toxic chemicals known as persistent organic pollutants, or POPs. Scientists and policy makers usually define POPs as possessing four key characteristics: toxicity, persistence, bioaccumulation, and long-range environmental transport. Some believed that international action might be warranted to limit their production and use.

POPs are toxic. While extensive variations occur across substances, species, and exposures, the observed or suspected impacts of POPs on wildlife and humans include reproductive disorders, birth defects, cancers, developmental impairment, damage to central and peripheral nervous systems, immune system impairment, and endocrine disruption.[101] POPs are also stable and persistent compounds that resist photolytic, chemical, and biological degradation. This means that once released into the environment, most POPs remain toxic for years before breaking down.

POPs also bioaccumulate. Once ingested, they are readily absorbed by, and remain in, the fatty tissue of living organisms. Over time, POPs concentrations can build up in animals and people, potentially reaching ten thousand times the background levels found in the surrounding environment. Fish, birds, mammals, and humans can absorb high concentrations of POPs quickly if they eat multiple organisms in which POPs have already accumulated. Mammals, including humans, can then pass these chemicals to their offspring through breast milk.

Finally, POPs engage in long-range transport across national borders and can be found in ecosystems, waterways, animals, and people thousands of kilometers from the nearest location of their production, use, or release. POPs travel through air currents, waterways, migrating animals, food chains, and a process known as the "grasshopper effect," in which POPs released in one part of the world can, through a repeated process of evaporation and deposit, be transported through the atmosphere to regions far away from the original source (see Figure 3.1).

In the 1980s and 1990s, Canada and Sweden played lead roles in the issue-definition and fact-finding phases by both supporting POPs research and putting POPs on the agenda of several international forums. Much of this work had been initiated after sci-

FIGURE 3.1   Migration of Persistent Organic Pollutants

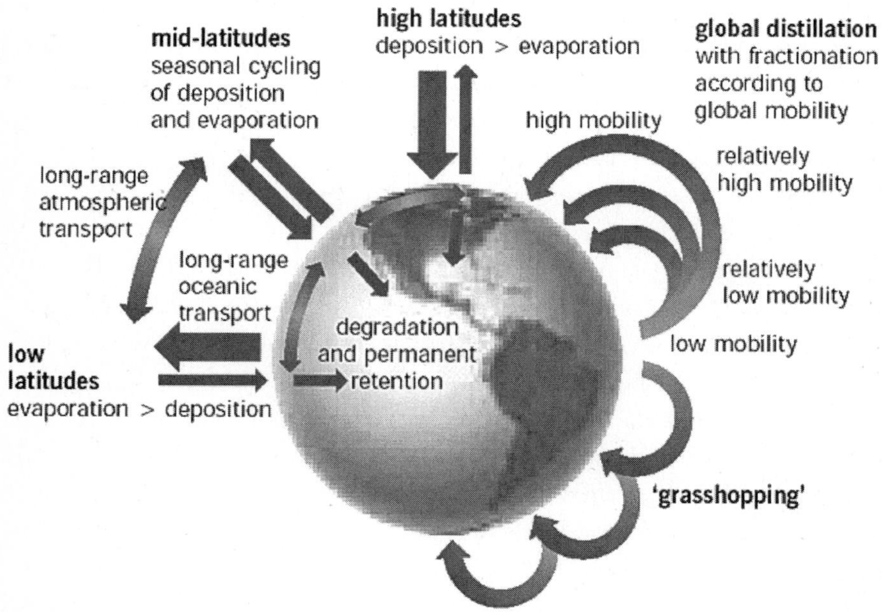

Source: GEO-3: Global Environment Outlook, UNEP, www.unep.org/Geo/geo3/english/fig212.htm.

entific studies found very high levels of certain POPs in the Arctic, including in wildlife and even in the breast milk of Inuit women in northern Canada, thousands of miles from the nearest source of emissions.[102] These findings and subsequent studies added a normative component to the issue-definition phase because POPs were now seen as a threat to the food chain, and thus the cultural survival, of the Inuit.[103]

The issue-definition phase reached a turning point in May 1995, when UNEP's Governing Council called for an international assessment of twelve POPs known as the "dirty dozen": the pesticides aldrin, chlordane, dieldrin, DDT, endrin, furans, heptachlor, mirex, and toxaphene; the industrial chemicals PCBs and hexachlorobenzene (which is also a pesticide); and two unintentionally produced substances, dioxins and furans, which are created when certain substances burn or through particular industrial activities. UNEP acted in response to growing scientific data regarding the transnational movement and toxicity of POPs, increasing evidence of POPs in various food chains, and the cumulative political efforts of the lead states, NGOs, and representatives of the Inuit and other indigenous peoples whose traditional food sources were becoming contaminated by POPs. Other initiatives also contributed to the process. For example, in November 1995 the Intergovernmental Conference to Adopt a Global Programme of Action for Protection of the Marine Environment from Land-Based Activities (GPA) called for talks on a legally binding treaty targeting the dirty dozen. This shows the potentially important impact that calling for action in multiple venues can have on initiating or advancing the fact-finding or negotiation stages.

In response to UNEP's call, the IOMC established a UNEP/IFCS ad hoc working group on POPs to proceed with fact finding. In June 1996, the working group concluded that scientific evidence supported international action to reduce the risks posed by POPs. In February 1997, governments comprising the UNEP Governing Council endorsed this conclusion and authorized formal negotiations aimed at creating a global POPs treaty.

The fact-finding process continued in eight regional workshops on POPs that UNEP and the IFCS convened in preparation for the negotiations. More than 138 countries participated in the workshops, which greatly increased awareness of POPs issues, particularly in developing countries and countries with economies in transition. Preparations also included convening preliminary meetings and studying previous negotiating processes on chemicals and specific aspects of the Rotterdam PIC Convention, the Aarhus POPs Protocol to the Convention on Long-Range Transboundary Air Pollution, the Montreal Protocol, and other initiatives to see what lessons could be learned.[104]

The bargaining stage officially began in June 1998 and lasted three years. Individual sessions included five official weeklong meetings of the Intergovernmental Negotiating Committee (INC), the main negotiating body; two meetings of the Criteria Expert

Group, which focused on developing procedures for identifying and adding new chemicals to the treaty; a weeklong negotiation (officially called a consultation) and other meetings and communications focused exclusively on financial and technical assistance; numerous formal contact groups; and countless intersessional communications and informal consultations.[105]

During the negotiations, the EU, Canada, NGOs, and representatives of northern indigenous peoples played the lead role in support of a strong regime. Indeed, the POPs negotiations were notable for the prominent role given to the Inuit and other northern indigenous peoples to speak to delegates and the press concerning the threats that POPs posed to their health and their cultural heritage of subsistence hunting and fishing.

Countries playing veto roles shifted according to the specific issue in question. Interestingly, no governments opposed creating controls on the dirty dozen. The issue-definition and fact-finding phases, combined with other efforts that took place before the negotiations, produced a ringing endorsement at INC-1 of the need for global regulations. This consensus also reflected a general acceptance of the science regarding POPs and the relatively modest adjustment costs given that industrialized countries had already established significant controls on the dirty dozen.

The EU and NGOs also supported creating controls on chemicals beyond the dirty dozen (as was done in the regional Aarhus POPs Protocol). The opposing veto coalition included many developing countries, the United States, and Japan, with support from companies that made or used the chemicals in question. African countries and health-related NGOs strongly opposed the elimination of DDT because its use was essential for battling mosquitoes that spread malaria (malaria kills nearly one million people a year),[106] a position that quickly gained near-universal support.

Although agreement existed on the need to phase out the rest of the dirty dozen, Australia, Brazil, China, India, Indonesia, the United States, and other countries stated that they needed individual exemptions for specific uses of certain chemicals, at least for a short period. For example, Russia, the United States, and other countries noted that because PCBs were once widely used in electrical transformers and other equipment, and even though new equipment using PCBs was no longer produced, hundreds of thousands of tons of PCBs were still in use in existing equipment around the world. Australia and China supported the continued use of mirex to control termites, including in telephones, in remote areas. Botswana and China supported continued use of chlordane to protect wooden dams and certain other structures from insects. Other parties argued they would need small amounts of aldrin for use as an insecticide during the transition to alternatives.

To address these concerns and overcome potential veto-state positions on individual POPs, negotiators agreed on the concepts of "acceptable purposes" and "specific

PHOTO 3.4 **WWF protesters outside the POPs negotiations in Bonn, Germany, in March 2002.** Courtesy IISD/*Earth Negotiations Bulletin.*

exemptions," although a variety of views existed on which chemicals or uses deserved such exemptions and how they should be administered. This followed, in general terms, what had occurred a decade earlier during expansion of the ozone regime: when parties strengthened that regime by agreeing to eliminate CFCs and halons, and later methyl bromide, they included allowances for various types of exemptions to address the specific concerns of potential veto states.

Going into the negotiation stage, governments knew they would need to create provisions for providing financial and technical assistance to developing countries to help them implement the regime as well as a mechanism for adding new chemicals to strengthen the agreement.[107] Industrialized and developing countries disagreed strongly on the mechanism for providing financial assistance. Countries also disagreed about possible procedures for adding new chemicals, if the treaty should include a noncompliance procedure, and institutional links to other treaties. Resolving these and other issues required difficult and detailed negotiations.

The resulting 2001 Stockholm Convention on Persistent Organic Pollutants seeks to protect human health and the environment by eliminating or reducing the production, use, trade, and emission of POPs. The treaty divides POPs into three categories, according to their source and the type of control measures placed on them. Substances slated for elimination are addressed in Article 3 and listed in Annex A. Substances whose production and use will be severely limited, like DDT, are addressed in Article 3 and listed in Annex B. POPs produced inadvertently, as unintentional by-products of other activities, are addressed in Article 5 and listed in Annex C. Since the complete elimination of Annex C substances is often technically impossible, parties agree to take specific steps to "minimize and where feasible eliminate" their emission by seeking to apply the relevant "best available techniques" (BAT) and "best environmental practices" (BEP), including those spelled out in annexes to the convention.

To ensure an effective phaseout process, parties must also ban the import or export of all POPs controlled under the convention (except for narrowly defined purposes or environmentally sound disposal); promote the use of the best available technologies and practices for reducing emissions and managing POP wastes; and take steps to prevent the development and commercial introduction of new POPs. Parties must also develop national implementation plans; report on the production, import, and export of the controlled POPs; and review the effectiveness of the convention at regular intervals.

Because the original treaty focused on the dirty dozen, the convention mandates that all parties eliminate the production and use of aldrin, chlordane, dieldrin, endrin, heptachlor, hexachlorobenzene, mirex, PCBs, and toxaphene; restrict the production and use of DDT to what is needed for disease-vector control and when there are no suitable and affordable alternatives;[108] and minimize the release of dioxins and furans into the environment.

In addition to the broad health-related exemption granted for DDT, the treaty includes a specific exemption for PCBs that allows countries to maintain existing equipment containing PCBs until 2025. The convention also allows any party to produce and use certain POPs for delineated "acceptable purposes." The convention also created a category of "country-specific exemptions" that permit specific parties to continue using small amounts of specific POPs for specific purposes for specific amounts of time. Each party when ratifying the treaty must indicate which country-specific exemptions it will claim (e.g., using mirex for termite control). The exemption then lasts for five years, no questions asked. After that, an extension for another five years must be specifically granted by the COP.

As seen in the ozone case, an important factor in the long-term effectiveness of an environmental regime is the process it contains for increasing the scope and strength of its environmental protections in response to new information or technological developments. The Stockholm Convention established specific scientifically based criteria and a step-by-step procedure for identifying, evaluating, and adding chemicals to the treaty (Article 8 and Annexes D, E, and F). This critical feature, which sought to ensure the convention's relevance beyond the dirty dozen, took a long time to develop. During negotiations, the EU advocated a process emphasizing the precautionary principle and allowing for the addition of chemicals relatively easily and quickly. The United States, Japan, Australia, and others wanted more sovereign control and a more regimented mechanism that required explicit risk analyses and clear evidence of existing harm before the COP could add a chemical.[109]

The process agreed on represents a working compromise between these views, incorporating elements of precaution, risk analysis according to set criteria, use of experts, flexibility, and sovereign control by the parties (see Figure 3.2).[110] Under the treaty, any party may nominate a chemical for evaluation. A POPs Review Committee (POPRC), made up of thirty-one experts nominated by parties, then works on behalf (and under the oversight) of the COP to examine the nominated chemical in detail. The POPRC first determines whether the substance can be considered a POP under the terms of the treaty by examining if its toxicity, persistence, bioaccumulation, and potential for long-range environmental transport meet the specific criteria set out in the convention. If a substance meets the POPs criteria, the committee then drafts a risk profile to evaluate if future emissions of the substance would produce significant adverse environmental or human-health impacts. If the POPRC determines it would, the committee develops a risk-management evaluation that assesses the relevant costs and benefits of international controls. Finally, based on these analyses, the POPRC decides to recommend, or not to recommend, that the COP consider controlling the substance under the convention. In carrying out these interrelated tasks, the POPRC is instructed to employ the specific scientific criteria for identifying and evaluating candidate POPs (as set out in Annex D of the convention); to follow specific information requirements for developing a risk profile for candidate POPs (Annex E); to consider socioeconomic impacts of controlling a POP in developing the risk-management evaluation (Annex F); and to include a strong perspective of precaution. Each stage (criteria, risk profile, risk-management evaluation) typically takes one year, but some chemicals may progress more slowly if the POPRC requires additional time to gather and review relevant information.

As demanded by the EU, precaution informs the process in such a way that the absence of strict scientific certainty does not prevent the COP from controlling a potentially hazardous substance.[111] At the same time, sovereign control is preserved, as demanded by the United States and other countries. Parties must nominate a POP to begin the process. All parties can submit comments and suggest changes to the POPRC outputs before they become final. The COP, which meets every two years, reviews the POPRC's recommendation, considers socioeconomic issues associated with potential listing, and holds final decision-making authority regarding controls and exemptions. Thus, the convention seeks to create a clear demarcation between science and politics. The POPRC creates a science-based foundation for considering action, and governments that comprise the COP make the final policy decision.[112]

As noted above, to organize the control measures, and to make the addition of chemicals more orderly, the convention establishes three annexes that group substances by

140

FIGURE 3.2   Process for Adding New Chemicals to the Stockholm Convention

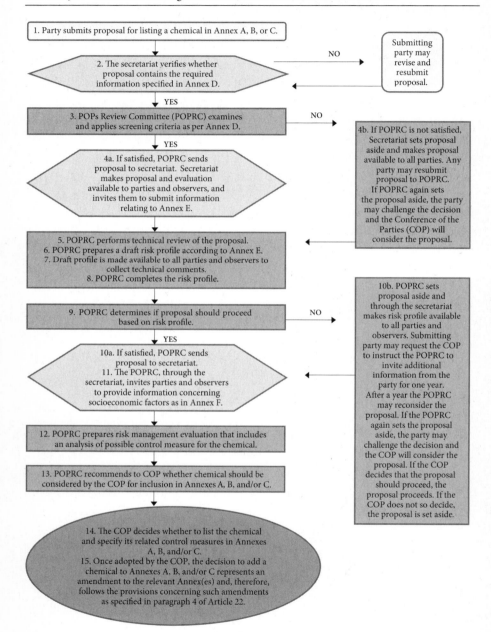

the type of restrictions placed on them. New chemicals slated for elimination go into Annex A, those to be restricted go into Annex B, and unintentionally produced substances go into Annex C. This means that adding chemicals requires amending only the relevant annex, not the main body of the convention. However, states could not agree if additions to the annexes should be immediately binding on all parties or subject to formal ratification (amendments to the main text require ratification). In a compromise, they created what are referred to as opt-in and opt-out provisions. Countries that ratify the treaty can choose to be an opt-in party, which means they are not required to address a chemical added to an annex unless they formally ratify the change; otherwise the addition automatically applies to them (the so-called opt-out provision). While potentially confusing,[113] the entire package makes it easier to add chemicals and speeds the implementation of the new controls.

Another critical feature of the convention is the financial mechanism that assists developing countries and countries with economies in transition in meeting their treaty obligations. Under the convention, industrialized countries must provide new financial resources, albeit at unspecified levels, and promote the transfer of technical assistance. Although nearly all negotiators acknowledged the importance of providing financial and technical assistance, very different views existed regarding the proper level and delivery mechanisms. Developing countries strongly supported creating a new stand-alone financial institution patterned after that developed under the Montreal Protocol. They opposed designating the Global Environment Facility (GEF) as the financial mechanism because of concerns about the GEF's willingness to address POPs as a priority area and to follow direction from the Stockholm Convention COP on POPs-related issues. The G-77 also insisted that all financial and technical assistance be new and additional to current programs so that POPs-related activities did not mean less financial and technical assistance in other areas. Donor countries strongly supported using the GEF, stating that doing so would reduce administrative costs, provide parties with important expertise, and produce synergies, as new financial and technical assistance programs could be bundled and augmented with existing programs in other forums, such as the Rotterdam and Basel conventions.

In the final compromise, the GEF was provisionally designated as the main financial mechanism, as it is in the climate and biodiversity regimes. The COP reviews the GEF's performance on a regular basis and has the option of making a final decision to use or exclude the GEF. Industrialized countries agreed to provide new and additional financial resources for POPs, and the COP gives instructions to, and receives reports from, the GEF with regard to its role in the financial mechanism.

In response to the concerns expressed during the negotiations, the GEF created a dedicated chemicals focal area and POPs program. Since 2001, the GEF has allocated more than $500 million to POPs projects in more than 135 countries. The GEF has also leveraged more than $700 million of additional funding—primarily from governments but also from the private sector, international organizations, foundations, and NGOs—to support POPs projects.[114]

The Stockholm Convention entered into force in 2004. It currently has 179 parties.[115] Most countries and all the major producers and users of toxic chemicals have ratified the convention except for Israel, Malaysia, and the United States. Although the George W. Bush administration supported the treaty and intended to push for its ratification by the Senate, the terrorist attacks on September 11, 2001, put the White House on a war footing, allowing a few opponents in the Senate to block consideration of the treaty out of concern for how the regime might expand.[116] Yet this may have been a tactical error: as a nonparty, the United States may speak at the COPs, but its voice does not count in actual decision making, and it cannot vote during POPRC meetings. As a major donor to the GEF, a major trade partner, and a large producer, consumer, and regulator of chemicals, the US voice at the negotiations is respected.[117] However, while the United States can effectively support lead coalitions, it cannot act as a veto state on issues relating to regime expansion.

Regime Expansion: Adding New Chemicals

The regime-strengthening process began almost as soon as the convention was signed. In May 2005, COP-1 adopted important decisions on the budget, the financial mechanism, and operation of the POPRC, among other issues necessary for the regime to operate.[118] Six months later, the POPRC held its first meeting. The committee addressed several operational issues, such as developing procedures for handling confidential information and delineating procedures for the participation of additional experts. POPRC-1 then began considering the first five chemicals proposed by parties for possible inclusion in the convention:

- chlordecone, once widely used as an agricultural pesticide (nominated by the EU);
- hexabromobiphenyl, an industrial chemical used as a flame retardant, mainly in the 1970s (nominated by the EU);
- lindane, a broad-spectrum insecticide for treating seeds, soils, plants, animals, and people whose production had decreased in recent years, although a few countries still produced and used it (nominated by Mexico);
- pentabromodiphenyl ethers, used in PCB products and as a fungicide, flame retardant, and chemical intermediate and also produced unintentionally during combustion and as an impurity in certain solvents and pesticides (nominated by Norway); and
- PFOS (perfluorooctane sulfonic acid, its salts, and perfluorooctane sulfonyl fluoride), which was still produced and widely used in several countries and found in electric

and electronic parts, firefighting foam, photo imaging, hydraulic fluids, and textiles (nominated by Sweden).

In 2006, POPRC-2 adopted risk profiles for the five substances considered at its first meeting. Following a positive review by COP-3 on the progress of its work, in 2007 POPRC-3 approved risk-management evaluations for five chemicals and formally recommended that COP-4 (scheduled for 2009) consider adding these substances to the convention. This process was subsequently repeated for five additional chemicals, including endosulfan, which POPRC recommended for listing only after significant debate and strong opposition from India.

This work by the POPRC set the stage for debates and final decisions by the COP. Anticipation was high prior to COP-4 in 2009, as participants and observers wondered if parties would be able to reach agreement to expand the regime. During the debate, the state that had nominated the POP acted as the lead state on that substance, with support from different parties depending on the substance (in some instances parties work together as a coalition but choose a particular party to make the formal nomination for political reasons).[119] The EU, Norway, Switzerland, and several other countries strongly supported listing all nine substances. Veto states varied depending on which countries opposed listing the chemical (a significant issue at COP-4 only in the case of PFOS) or insisted on specific exemptions or certain acceptable purposes. Veto states were empowered to the extent that they were willing to prevent consensus on listing a chemical unless certain exemptions were allowed; if they could credibly claim they would not ratify an amendment (in theory this only works for countries that produce or use sufficient quantities of a substance to threaten the effectiveness of the controls); or if they were willing to withhold support on an unrelated issue if their position was not adopted.

An important issue for some chemicals was the annex in which they would be placed. Lead states usually pushed for inclusion of chemicals in Annex A, which mandates elimination. Some states pushed for one or two chemicals to be placed in Annex B, which establishes restrictions but no near-term elimination. Parties also disagreed on the category of potential exemptions that should be applied to a chemical. Lead states argued that only specific, time-limited exemptions be allowed. Other states supported the more lenient "acceptable purpose" category, which allows larger and less controlled levels of exempted use. Finally, many of the most contentious listing issues were interrelated from a bargaining standpoint. For example, a veto state could offer to relent on listing or acceptable purposes for one chemical in exchange for the creation of more special exemptions for another substance or compromise on issues related to financial and technical assistance.

In the end COP-4 added nine chemicals to the convention, with certain exemptions and acceptable purposes included for five. This significantly strengthened the regime only five years after the treaty entered into force. Two years later, COP-5 added endosulfan, a pesticide still widely used in India, after significant debate and acceptance of several specific exemptions and acceptable purposes (see Box 3.2).

The nominations of new chemicals by parties and subsequent action by the POPRC and the COP proved that the procedures for adding new substances work. It also confirmed that lead states, particularly countries within the EU, intended to nominate and support consideration of additional chemicals in accordance with the precautionary principle. Indeed, five additional chemicals, four nominated by the EU and one by Norway, are currently under review.[120]

At the same time, potential obstacles were revealed. As noted by participants and observers, POPRC-4 "marked a shift in the work of the Committee from considering what are commonly referred to as 'dead' chemicals to those 'live' chemicals that are still in use in many parts of the world."[121] By creating the POPRC, the Stockholm Convention attempted to separate the scientific and technical consideration of nominated POPs, which are the purview of the POPRC, from the economic and political concerns of parties, which are discussed by the COP. In essence, the POPRC addresses whether the convention can control a substance. Then the COP decides if it should. The lines can blur, however, because the convention asks the POPRC to include certain socioeconomic considerations in the risk-management evaluation phase. This was not an important issue on most of the substances that the POPRC considered at its first meetings, but the shift to evaluating toxic chemicals still in widespread production and use presents a new challenge. At POPRC-4 and -5, some participants took positions that appeared to reflect their home country's economic and political views as much as a technical evaluation of the POP's toxicity, persistence, bioaccumulation, long-range environmental transport, and consequential risks to human health and the environment. This produced some strong exchanges during these POPRC meetings and even some contentious votes.[122]

Ultimately, parties did decide to list PFOS and, more importantly, endosulfan. At the time of its listing, endosulfan was still used as a pesticide in some countries, particularly India. The Indian government tried to prevent its addition to the control measures. The final COP decision to list endosulfan (albeit with exemptions won by India) led to domestic pressure within India (from both environmentalists and manufacturers of alternatives) to eliminate the production and use of this pesticide. Although several chemicals currently under review in POPRC present even more challenging tests of the regime's ability to reach agreement to control live substances, the endosulfan case suggests that these challenges are surmountable and that the Stockholm Convention can also "play an important agenda-setting role that can help influence domestic decision-making even in the presence of particular economic interests."[123]

Financial and Technical Assistance

While the convention established general mandates, it also required the COP to take action to implement and strengthen the provisions on financial and technical assistance. COP-1 and -2 took a number of important procedural steps, but the discussions revealed that the split between donor and recipient countries present during

---

BOX 3.2   POPs CONTROLLED UNDER
THE STOCKHOLM CONVENTION

THE DIRTY DOZEN: POPS CONTROLLED UNDER THE ORIGINAL CONVENTION

- Pesticides: aldrin, chlordane, DDT, dieldrin, endrin, heptachlor, mirex, toxaphene
- Industrial chemicals: PCBs, hexachlorobenzene (also a pesticide)
- By-products: dioxins, furans

POPS ADDED TO THE CONVENTION

- Pesticides: chlordecone, endosulfane, hexabromobiphenyl, hexachlorocyclo-hexane, lindane, pentachlorobenzene (also an industrial chemical)
- Industrial chemicals: hexabromobiphenyl, PFOS, tetrabromodiphenyl ether, pentabromodiphenyl ether
- By-products: several of the chemicals above are also sometimes produced as by-products

POPS LISTED IN ANNEX A: ELIMINATION

(Some POPs are listed in more than one Annex.)

- aldrin, chlordane, chlordecone, DDT, dieldrin, endrin, heptachlor, hexabro-mobiphenyl, hexachlorobenzene, hexachlorocyclohexane, lindane, mirex, pen-tachlorobenzene, tetrabromodiphenyl ether/pentabromodiphenyl ether, toxaphene

POPS LISTED IN ANNEX B: RESTRICTED

- DDT; PFOS

POPS LISTED IN ANNEX C: MINIMIZE AND WHERE FEASIBLE ELIMINATE

- dioxins, furans, hexachlorobenzene, hexachlorocyclohexane, PCBs, pentachlorobenzene

the convention's negotiation had not dissipated. By COP-4 in Geneva in May 2009, the suite of intersecting issues on financial resources and technical assistance had become complex.[124] Among other issues, the parties needed to review reports on the operations and extant effectiveness of the financial mechanism, particularly the GEF; decide if the regime should keep the GEF as the principal entity of the financial mechanism; if so, provide updated guidance to the GEF regarding how the COP wanted it to operate in supporting the convention; review needs-assessment reports on the potential costs for developing countries to implement the regime; make decisions in response to this information, including preferences for POPs-related funding levels in the next round of negotiations on replenishing the GEF; and select regional centers through which capacity building and technical assistance would flow.

Further complicating matters, the bargaining strategies of many participants caused these and other issues to become interlinked. This is not uncommon during global environmental negotiations, but it forced delegates to search for a complex package deal that almost prevented decisions on issues on which there was no disagreement. For example, many developing countries would not allow a decision on the listing of additional chemicals until a satisfactory resolution was reached on the package of financial and technical assistance issues. The EU attempted to include noncompliance as part of the overall compromise package. China, India, and others essentially refused to consider a package that included a noncompliance procedure. Some countries dug in their heels on issues relating to certain chemicals in an attempt to get movement on other chemicals or on an unrelated issue.

In the end, these linkages produced a stalemate that almost derailed the meeting. Finally, after 4:00 AM on Saturday (the meeting was supposed to end at 6:00 PM on Friday), long after the interpreters had left the building, a final compromise allowed the COP to adopt a package of decisions that added nine new chemicals and reaffirmed the GEF as the principal entity for the financial mechanism.[125] COP-4 also called on donors to take the funding-needs assessment of developing countries, as revealed in their national implementation plans, and the listing of new chemicals in the convention into full consideration during the fifth replenishment of the GEF. It requested that the GEF continue its efforts, called for by previous COPs, to streamline the processes for applying for and receiving financial assistance.

One year later, in May 2010, global negotiations for the GEF-5 replenishment concluded, with thirty-five donors agreeing to provide the GEF with $4.34 billion to support GEF activities from July 1, 2010, to June 30, 2014, a 54 percent increase above the 2006–2010 GEF-4 level. Of the total replenishment, $425 million was dedicated to the chemicals focal area.[126] The GEF reported that its Stockholm Convention–related funding during GEF-5 will focus on reducing POPs releases, "in particular PCB phase out and disposal, and removal and disposal of obsolete pesticides . . . [and]

making headway on the reduction of releases of unintentionally produced dioxins and furans from industrial and non-industrial sources. Pilot interventions to address the newly added POPs will be also supported and funds will still be provided to eligible countries to review and update their National Implementation Plans."[127]

COP-5 in 2011 reviewed the work of the GEF and if it was fulfilling the terms of the agreement it had signed with COP to act as the main financial mechanism for the regime. The COP agreed to continue the GEF's role and finalized terms of reference for a study that will inform the next official review of the financial mechanism. Parties have also endorsed creation of Stockholm Convention regional and subregional centers in Algeria, Brazil, China, Czech Republic, Iran, India, Kenya, Kuwait, Mexico, Panama, Russia, Senegal, South Africa, Spain, and Uruguay. These centers, some of which also act as Basel Convention Regional Centers, are intended to serve as official nodes for capacity building, transfer of technology, and technical assistance.

While significant progress has been made by the GEF and the COP in developing mechanisms for providing financial and technical assistance, concerns remain that not enough funds are begin earmarked for POPs projects and that too little of the allocated money is actually spent to reduce emissions of POPs. Going forward, the COP will continue to review the GEF, regional centers, and other international organizations regarding their impact and cost-effectiveness. At the same time, political preferences of the donors for the GEF, and of many developing countries for the centers, may leave the current architecture unchanged for many years.

Creating Networks

In 2009, COP-4 endorsed establishment of a global DDT partnership, the Global Alliance. This network of stakeholders—including doctors, health agencies, international organizations, NGOs, national governments, corporations, and scientists—works to develop and deploy more effective and cost-efficient alternative products, methods, and strategies to control malaria than the use of DDT. COP-4 also created the PCB Elimination Network to strengthen efforts to phase out equipment containing PCBs. Members include experts from multiple treaty secretariats, international organizations, governments, NGOs, research institutions, and industry. The network exchanges information, evaluates PCB use, supports pilot programs in developing countries, promotes improved techniques for managing PCBs, and develops recommendations for further action.

The DDT Global Alliance and PCB Elimination Network Global Alliance both seek to identify gaps in existing initiatives, improve coordination among relevant actors, catalyze new action, and take advantage of the global scale of the Stockholm Convention for awareness-raising and information-sharing. The networks, which might not exist without the convention, demonstrate how regimes can enhance the impact of their formal regulations by developing "initiatives that coordinate and support multi-sector action among governments, corporations, non-governmental organizations (NGOs) and other stakeholders to achieve common goals."[128]

Synergies

For several years, the EU, Switzerland, and others have played lead roles in various regimes pushing the concept of creating formal coordination among the three main chemical and waste conventions to achieve synergies and reduce costs. As noted above, in 2005 and 2006 the Basel, Rotterdam, and Stockholm COPs established a joint working group on synergies to examine the issue, develop background materials, and draft recommendations. Although this process was far from complete, by the time of POPs COP-3 in 2007, the joint working group had clarified key concepts, purposes, and potential outcomes of the process, helping to transform the "concept of synergies from a nebulous norm into a series of practical actions, such as adopting a streamlined reporting system, that parties see as being beneficial."[129] At COP-3, parties to the Stockholm Convention strongly supported the initiative—unlike at previous COPs, where developing countries expressed significant concern that the process would divert attention and resources away from technical assistance. The final proposal of the ad hoc working group, submitted in 2008, was considered first, by virtue of the calendar, by the Basel and Rotterdam COPs prior to POPs COP-4 in May 2009. COP-4 then issued the final approval needed to begin the groundbreaking initiative.

In February 2010, parties convened simultaneous Conferences of the Parties to the Basel, Rotterdam, and Stockholm conventions (Ex-COP). The Ex-COP adopted a single omnibus decision on synergies that outlined the intention to offer joint services, organize joint activities, synchronize budget cycles, conduct joint audits, coordinate or combine many managerial functions, coordinate review arrangements, develop joint clearinghouse and other information and communications activities, and establish a new executive secretary to oversee the secretariats of all three conventions. In 2011, POPs COP-5 confirmed this decision and formally addressed practical budgeting and other issues designed to enhance this process.

In April and May 2013, the three conventions held their COPs on successive days as well as an Ex-COP in a busy two-week period in Geneva and reviewed and advanced the synergies agenda. Certain operational elements within the three convention secretariats and regional centers have already started to merge, especially within the joint secretariat location in Geneva. The secretariat has stated that this has already yielded financial savings associated with administration and meeting costs but the larger challenge of effectively integrating programs to improve the environmentally sound management of chemicals and wastes will be the true test.[130]

Effective implementation of the synergies initiative will likely enhance the effectiveness of the conventions, promote cost-savings at the national and secretariat level, and allow more resources and attention to shift toward implementation. Indeed, if effective, elements of the synergies initiative could help to address several obstacles to effective environmental policy, which will be discussed further in Chapter 5, including poorly designed, uncoordinated, or contradictory regimes; overburdened national bureaucracies; and inadequate resources.

Noncompliance Procedures

Creating effective noncompliance procedures has proven a difficult task for most environmental regimes. The Montreal Protocol is one of the very few regimes possessing a working procedure for examining potential cases of state noncompliance. Article 17 of the Stockholm Convention states that the COP will develop "mechanisms for determining noncompliance with the provisions of this Convention and for the treatment of Parties found to be in noncompliance." The EU has attached significant importance to developing a robust noncompliance procedure and played a strong lead role on the issue. Several industrialized countries, such as Switzerland, support this position. Other industrialized countries and some developing countries attach less importance to the issue, acting as potential swing states. Another group of developing countries, often led by China and India, constitute a powerful veto coalition. They link implementation and effectiveness to the provision of financial resources and argue that a noncompliance procedure can only be developed after such assistance has been provided. They emphasize that any procedure related to compliance should not be punitive but assistance oriented and focus on identifying obstacles to effective compliance in a given party so that additional assistance can be targeted effectively.

Attempts to resolve these differences during negotiation of the convention failed, leading to the compromise language in Article 17, which, unlike nearly all the other parts of the convention requiring action by the COP, carried no deadline. COP-1 created an open-ended working group on noncompliance to allow delegates the opportunity to consider the issue in detail. However, discussions at each succeeding COP have yielded little substantive progress (and sometimes generated heated debates) beyond a preliminary draft text covered with square brackets and alternative formulations supported by different groups. (Square brackets are used to indicate portions of a draft document on which parties do not agree.) While parties seem to agree that the noncompliance mechanism for the POPs regime should be facilitative rather than punitive, differences remain on other fundamental issues, including the ultimate objective and underlying principles of the noncompliance procedure, how to initiate action on potential cases of noncompliance (some countries reject giving either the secretariat or other parties the authority to initiate the procedure), whether the provision of specific levels of financial and technical assistance can be evaluated under the noncompliance mechanism, and the composition and decision-making processes for the compliance committee.

Opinions vary widely among parties and outside experts regarding the proper purpose, most efficacious design, and even the necessity of a noncompliance procedure. If the deadlock continues, observers will watch to see if it negatively affects discussion on other matters, such as listing new chemicals. Alternatively, if parties find a compromise, will resolution of the noncompliance mechanism positively impact discussions on other issues?

Successes and Challenges

The global regime for toxic chemicals has expanded significantly since governments adopted the Stockholm Convention in 2001. Nearly 180 countries have ratified the convention. Ten new chemicals have been added. Production, use, and emissions of controlled POPs have likely declined, as has the use of specific-exemptions for the original dirty dozen. The POPRC continues to evaluate candidate POPs nominated by parties. The GEF created a dedicated chemicals focal area, earmarked a specific level of funds for chemicals projects, and helped to mobilize more than $700 million in additional cofinancing. Regional centers have been selected to serve as nodes for capacity building and technical assistance. Technical guidelines have been developed to help measure and reduce dioxin and furan emissions as well as emissions from POPs waste. Global networks have been created to speed deployment of alternatives to DDT and the phaseout of PCBs. Awareness regarding the production, use, and impacts of toxic chemicals has increased within many national governments. The synergies initiative has produced some initial cost-savings and augmented productive coordination within the Basel, Rotterdam, and Stockholm conventions.

At the same time, and like all the other regimes discussed in this book, the Stockholm Convention faces significant challenges. Perhaps the most important is continuing to address "live" chemicals. The regime has taken the first, difficult steps in this direction in the debates on PFOS and endosulfan. However, many more POPs exist, and concern is rising over a new class of endocrine disruptors that may affect humans at low doses over long periods and might be found in some brands of everyday products, including plastics, pesticides, and detergents.[131] Two related challenges are attracting ratifications from the few large producers and consumers of toxic chemicals that are not yet parties and working to ensure that the opt-in/opt-out structure does not create situations in which key countries remain outside the regime with regard to individual POPs.[132]

Exemptions represent another challenge. Acceptable purpose and country-specific exemptions might be political necessities that overcome the lowest-common-denominator problem by establishing asymmetrical controls, but they can weaken the impact of listing a particular chemical, especially if the country in question both produces and consumes the substance. Although countries have retired most exemptions for the original dirty dozen, some of the chemicals added to the convention carry larger lists of acceptable purposes and country-specific exemptions. For the regime to be effective over the long term, the COP must prevent parties from renewing these exemptions and reduce acceptable uses, especially if there is evidence of nontoxic alternative substances or practices. This could represent a significant challenge, however, if parties "find it difficult to stand in opposition to renewal of another's exemption if they themselves are hoping to find support for continuing an exemption."[133]

Another challenge, common to all environmental regimes, is the need for more financial and technical resources to assist some developing countries' transition away from the use of toxic chemicals and to improve the management of those that remain. While donor countries and the GEF have significantly increased assistance, further regime strengthening will require the availability and proper application of sufficient financial and technical assistance for some states and some substances.

Finally, the synergies initiative presents an important challenge and opportunity. Establishing effective, institutionalized coordination, collaboration, and selective consolidation among the Stockholm, Rotterdam, and Basel conventions will not be easy, but it is a necessary step toward establishing environmentally sound, implementable controls on all aspects of their life cycle. Many parties recognize the need for a comprehensive approach, and this has been called for by several international forums, including the 2002 World Summit on Sustainable Development, the 2012 Rio+20 Conference, the UNEP Governing Council, the Intergovernmental Forum on Chemical Safety, and SAICM. The greater efficiencies and productive synergies of closer collaboration and even merging appropriate aspects of the conventions and their secretariats can raise their collective profiles, augment more successful and less costly implementation, and provide more opportunities for regime expansion in the future. The synergies initiative has advanced considerably, and the results of the coordinated meeting of the three COPs in 2013 and the follow-up activities in 2014 and 2015 could reveal a great deal regarding the long-term impact of this process.

CLIMATE CHANGE

The release of heat-trapping GHGs from human activities, including the burning of fossil fuels and deforestation, is intensifying the natural greenhouse effect and warming the planet. Relatively small amounts of warming can cause surprisingly large changes in climate. Anthropogenic warming is already being observed and will increase as GHGs increase.[134]

The resulting climate change will produce a host of potentially harmful impacts. These include increased incidence of drought and floods, expanded ranges for certain crop-eating pests and tropical diseases (such as malaria), sea level rise, significantly higher extinction rates, disruption of global and regional weather patterns, ocean acidification, and potentially very serious damage to regional freshwater resources, food production, coral reefs, mountain ecosystems, and even the Amazon basin. Some of these impacts are already being observed.[135] Significantly reducing the amount of GHGs released from human activity will reduce, or mitigate, the extent of future impacts.

Climate change is the prototype of a global commons issue. The Earth's climate system affects all nations, and broad international cooperation is required to mitigate global warming. Developing an effective regime to mitigate climate change has been complicated by the multiple sources of GHG emissions; by scientific uncertainties regarding the precise scope and timing of future impacts; and by dependence on global climate modeling, which is not yet an exact science. Perhaps most important, however, is that energy remains central to every nation's economy; the policy changes required to reduce GHG emissions raise difficult questions about who should bear the short-term economic costs and how to allocate the potential long-term benefits. Even to stabilize the amount of CO_2 in the atmosphere (which would not reduce the warming caused by emissions already in the atmosphere) would require cutting current emissions by roughly one-half or more. That would necessitate major increases in energy efficiency and conservation and a switch from coal and oil to natural gas and renewable sources, all of which would affect powerful economic and political interests.

GHG emissions from the burning of fossil fuels account for roughly 80 percent of total world GHG emissions. Deforestation and methane emissions contribute most of the rest. Fossil fuel burning has increased atmospheric concentrations of CO_2 by nearly 24 percent since 1959 (see Figure 3.3). The top twenty emitters of CO_2, led by China (25 percent) and the United States (16 percent), account for about 77 percent of the world's emissions (see Table 3.2 and Figure 3.4). Preliminary data for February 2013 show highest-ever recorded levels of CO_2.[136]

Scientists have long known that the buildup of CO_2 in the atmosphere can cause climate change. The first scientific article suggesting that atmospheric temperatures will rise as atmospheric CO_2 concentrations increase was published in 1896.[137] A research article in 1938 argued that carbon dioxide levels were climbing and might be responsible for raising global temperatures.[138] However, the process of issue definition did not really begin until the mid-1980s. The World Meteorological Organization (WMO) and UNEP took the first major step by organizing a 1985 conference in Vil-

FIGURE 3.3   Atmospheric Concentration of Carbon Dioxide at Mauna Loa, Hawaii, 1959–2011

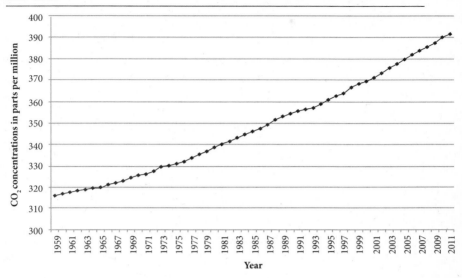

Source: Carbon Dioxide Information Analysis Center, cdiac.ornl.gov.

lach, Austria, that produced a scientific consensus statement that global warming was a serious possibility.[139] In 1986, WMO, NASA, and several other agencies issued a three-volume report concluding that climate change was already taking place at a relatively rapid rate. The unusually hot summer of 1988 accelerated media and congressional attention in the United States and even thrust the climate issue into the presidential campaign.[140]

The fact-finding process coincided with the issue-definition stage. In 1988 WMO and UNEP, at the request of member states, organized the Intergovernmental Panel on Climate Change (IPCC) in an attempt to establish a common factual basis for negotiations that would focus on policy options.[141] The First Assessment Report of the IPCC—approved by the participating states after long, grueling negotiations in August 1990—affirmed that global warming is a serious threat. The report predicted that if states continue to pursue "business as usual," the global average surface temperature would rise at a rate unprecedented in human history. However, despite the success of the first IPCC report in establishing a stronger scientific consensus on climate change, it failed to establish consensus on the economics of the problem—one of the key points of contention during subsequent negotiations.

Formal negotiations for a climate convention began in February 1991 under the auspices of the Intergovernmental Negotiating Committee for a Framework Convention

TABLE 3.2   Top Twenty Countries by Total CO_2 Emissions from Fossil-Fuel Combustion, 2010 (in 1,000 metric tons of carbon)

COUNTRY	1990 EMISSIONS	2010 EMISSIONS	PERCENT CHANGE, 1990–2010	2010 PER CAPITA EMISSIONS
China	658,554	2,247,534	241%	1.68
United States	1,326,725	1,497,865	13%	4.84
India	188,344	564,474	200%	0.47
Russia	565,901	460,551	–19%	3.25
Japan	319,704	310,481	–3%	2.44
Germany	276,425	207,966	–25%	2.55
Iran	61,954	156,730	153%	2.09
Korea	65,901	153,580	133%	3.14
Canada	122,739	141,402	15%	4.15
Saudi Arabia	58,646	134,653	130%	4.61
United Kingdom	156,481	134,498	–14%	2.16
Indonesia	41,032	129,970	217%	0.55
Mexico	104,907	127,127	21%	1.15
South Africa	90,963	123,229	35%	2.47
Brazil	56,966	114,419	101%	0.59
Italy	115,925	111,252	–4%	1.84
Australia	79,943	99,685	25%	4.45
France	108,576	98,879	–9%	1.57
Poland	100,020	84,541	–15%	2.21
Thailand	26,134	81,614	212%	1.20
Total top 20	4,525,840	6,980,450	54%	2.37
Global total	6,144,000	9,138,791	49%	1.30

Sources: Tom Boden and T. J. Blasing, "Record High 2010 Global Carbon Dioxide Emissions from Fossil-Fuel Combustion and Cement Manufacture," Carbon Dioxide Information Analysis Center, Oak Ridge National Laboratory, 2012, cdiac.ornl.gov/trends/emis/prelim_2009_2010 _estimates.html; Tom Boden, Gregg Marland, and Robert J. Andres, "National CO_2 Emissions from Fossil-Fuel Burning, Cement Manufacture and Gas Flaring: 1758–2006," Carbon Dioxide Information Analysis Center, Oak Ridge National Laboratory, 2009, cdiac.ornl.gov/trends/emis/tre_tp20.html.

FIGURE 3.4   Global CO$_2$ Emissions from Fossil-Fuel Burning, 2010

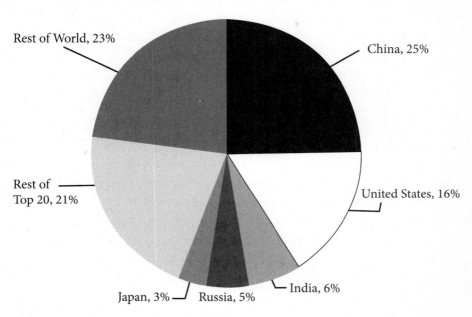

Source: Tom Boden and T. J. Blasing, "Record High 2010 Global Carbon Dioxide Emissions from Fossil-Fuel Combustion and Cement Manufacture," Carbon Dioxide Information Analysis Center, Oak Ridge National Laboratory, 2012, cdiac.ornl.gov/trends/emis/prelim_2009_2010 _estimates.html.

on Climate Change, which had been created by the United Nations General Assembly. In the beginning, the "energy culture" of states generally determined whether a state would join a lead-state or veto-state coalition with regard to GHG emissions targets and timetables. Three groups of states were initially distinguished:[142]

- *States with few indigenous fossil-fuel resources and relatively dependent on imported energy; thus they have learned to maintain high living standards while reducing their use of fossil fuels:* This group included Japan and many European Community (EC) states, including Denmark, Finland, France, Italy, the Netherlands, and Sweden.
- *States with large supplies of cheap energy resources and a culture of highly inefficient energy use:* This group included Brazil, China, India, Mexico, Russia, and the United States.
- *States highly dependent on fossil-fuel exports for income:* This group included the Arab oil states, Australia, Norway, and, initially, the United Kingdom.

The initial coalition of lead states (Finland, the Netherlands, Norway, and Sweden) squared off with the United States, as leader of the veto coalition, first on whether to hold global negotiations on climate change and then on whether the negotiations should seek to produce a protocol containing specific obligations on emissions. The lead states wanted to negotiate a framework convention in parallel with negotiations for a protocol limiting emissions, to be completed no later than a year after the convention. The United States insisted on holding talks only on a framework convention, with no parallel negotiations on protocols, arguing that regulating carbon releases would require major changes in fossil-fuel consumption and, consequently, lifestyles and the industrial structure. In October 1990, Japan broke ranks with the United States on the issue by committing itself to stabilizing its GHG emissions at 1990 levels by 2000. That left the United States and the Soviet Union alone among industrialized countries rejecting a target and timetable for controlling GHG emissions.[143]

The EC became the key lead state in the negotiations by virtue of its previous announced commitment to lower its joint CO_2 emissions to 1990 levels by 2000. Australia, Austria, Denmark, Germany, Japan, the Netherlands, and New Zealand also committed themselves to reducing their emissions by 2000 or 2005.

Had binding commitments for controlling GHG emissions been included in the text, developing countries' agreement would have been crucial. The large, rapidly industrializing countries (Brazil, China, and India) already accounted for 21 percent of global emissions in 1989 (about the same as the United States), and as their economies grew, their emissions levels would certainly rise. Because they viewed fossil fuels as a vital component of their success as potential industrial powers, they formed a potential veto coalition.[144]

The negotiating session in February 1992 ended without resolution of the issue of a stabilization target and timetable. British, Dutch, German, and other EC member governments sent officials to Washington in an unsuccessful effort to persuade the United States to go along with a binding commitment to stabilize emissions at 1990 levels by 2000. Then, during the April 1992 session, President George H. W. Bush personally called Prime Minister Helmut Kohl of Germany and asked him to drop his government's demand for the stabilization commitment in return for Bush's participation in the upcoming Earth Summit. Bush announced his decision to attend the Rio conference only after the final draft text of the convention was completed without reference to binding commitments to controlling GHGs.[145]

In June 1992, 154 countries signed the United Nations Framework Convention on Climate Change (UNFCCC) at the Earth Summit in Rio. The convention requires Annex I parties (40 industrialized countries including the EC states, Japan, Russia, and the United States) to take steps aimed at reducing their GHG emissions in 2000 to "earlier levels"—a phrase interpreted by the EC to mean 1990 levels—but does not commit governments to hold emissions to a specific level by a certain date. Nor does it address emissions-reduction targets after 2000. But the text does provide for regular review of the "adequacy" of the commitments.

The UNFCCC entered into force in March 1994, after ratification by the minimum-necessary 50 states.[146] Today, 195 countries are parties, including the United States. While the veto power exercised by the United States and, to a lesser extent, Russia prevented inclusion of binding targets and timetables in the UNFCCC, it could not prevent efforts to begin negotiations on a binding protocol. The EC issued a statement upon signing the convention calling for an early start on negotiation of an agreement with binding targets and timetables. Germany joined with an international network of NGOs and the Alliance of Small Island States (AOSIS) to press for a significant strengthening of the regime.

Kyoto Protocol

The first COP to the UNFCCC convened in Berlin in March 1995. In addition to its work on initiating implementation of the UNFCCC, the COP agreed to negotiate, by the end of 1997, quantitative limits on GHG emissions beyond 2000. The COP created a new subsidiary body, the Ad Hoc Group on the Berlin Mandate, to conduct the negotiations (COPs often place large and potentially divisive issues into separate subsidiary bodies that can meet more frequently). However, the COP could not agree if the new limits on GHG emissions should represent real reductions from current levels, as opposed to simply reduced levels of future emissions, or which countries would be subject to the new commitments. The EU supported a commitment of substantial reductions, but the JUSCANZ group (Japan, the United States, Canada, Australia, and New Zealand), which constituted a new veto coalition, opposed negotiations for reduced emissions. The ad hoc group met eight times between August 1995 and December 1997.

AOSIS played a lead role by submitting the first draft of the protocol. The EU maintained its lead-state role by tabling a proposal to reduce emissions of the three main GHGs (carbon dioxide, methane, and nitrous oxide) from 1990 levels by at least 7.5 percent by 2005 and by 15 percent by 2010. The EU proposal would allow some EU member countries, such as Germany, to undertake deeper emissions reductions and poorer EU states to accept lower targets, provided the overall EU reduction reached 7.5 percent. In sharp contrast, the United States proposed stabilizing emissions of six GHGs (including three whose impacts were less quantifiable) at 1990 levels by 2008–2010 for all Annex I parties.

The United States also proposed allowing countries to meet their targets through emissions trading with other parties. Countries able to exceed their emissions-reduction requirements would be able sell those excess reductions, or credits, to a country that was having trouble meeting its targets. In theory, this would allow countries with relatively inexpensive options to make more reductions while allowing countries that only had very expensive options to do less. If the system worked, it would encourage greater technological innovation (as some countries sought to sell credits for profit) while allowing the world as a whole to achieve the same GHG reductions at a lower cost.

The EU did not oppose the concept of emissions trading but objected to the US proposal because it established few conditions for how the trading would occur. The EU and many developing countries were particularly concerned that the US proposal would assign emissions reductions to Russia and former Soviet bloc states in Central and Eastern Europe. These emissions were referred to as "hot air" because these countries' emission levels were already down more than 30 percent from 1990 as a result of the closure of so many obsolescent plants following the collapse of communism and the ongoing restructuring of their economies. Because emissions-reduction and trading levels would be pegged to 1990 levels, these countries would be able to sell emissions-reduction credits for emissions that no longer existed (hot air). This would allow parties buying the hot air to meet their reduction targets on paper but without actually reducing GHG emissions. Some developing countries also objected because countries purchasing credits would be able to delay serious efforts to transition away from fossil fuels. Other parties argued the proposed protocol should allow parties to fulfill only a certain percentage of their required reductions through trading.

Australia introduced another important issue: differentiation. It argued that because its economy depended far more heavily on exports of fossil fuels (coal) than the average Annex I party, it should not have to reduce its emissions as much as other countries. The demand for differentiation became another way for the veto coalition to seek to reduce its costs for complying with a possible targets-and-timetables agreement by allowing some states to justify lower targets.

As parties gathered for COP-3 in Kyoto in 1997 (the planned deadline for adopting a protocol), differences between lead and veto states had grown even further. The United States, which had previously supported equal reductions for all industrialized-country parties, endorsed the concept of differentiation to accommodate the greater economic burdens that equal reductions would impose on certain states. The US delegation also took the position that it could not accept any emissions reductions unless large developing countries also agreed to binding emission reductions—a condition mandated by a unanimous vote in the US Senate. This proposal was unacceptable to developing countries. New Zealand similarly demanded that developing countries specify by 2002 how much they would slow their emissions over the subsequent twelve years.

Following a week and a half of intense negotiations, delegates finally adopted the Kyoto Protocol.[147] The protocol requires industrialized-country parties to reduce their collective emissions of six GHGs (carbon dioxide, methane, nitrous oxide, HFCs, perfluorocarbons, and sulfur hexafluoride) by at least 5.2 percent below their 1990 levels between 2008 and 2012. Countries had different requirements within this collective mandate, ranging from a 10 percent increase for Iceland (which already had very low emissions because of its reliance on geothermal and hydroelectric power) to 8 percent reductions for the EU and most of the countries in Eastern Europe. Switzerland and Canada had 8 and 6 percent reductions, respectively. Russia and New Zealand only had to freeze emissions. Australia could increase emissions by 8 percent. The United States agreed to a 7 percent reduction but won a concession that the three newer GHGs (hydrofluorocarbons, perfluorocarbons, and sulphur hexafluoride) would be calculated from a 1995, rather than a 1990, baseline. The different national requirements did not reflect a specific formula based on objective criteria but rather the result of bargaining, in particular between veto states and the EU. The presence of so many different requirements made the overall target less ambitious and was the first in a number of developments that limited the protocol's impact.

The US proposal for a formal commitment by developing countries to control and eventually reduce their emissions was dropped after China, India, and other developing-country parties attacked it, making clear that they constituted a broad and firm veto coalition on the issue and would not compromise. Arguing for the importance of upholding the principle of common but differentiated responsibilities, these delegations even rejected an opt-in position that would have provided for voluntary adoption of an emissions target by non–Annex I states.

To reduce the costs of achieving its emissions targets, the Kyoto Protocol allows countries to use three "flexibility mechanisms": the Clean Development Mechanism (CDM), joint implementation, and emissions trading.[148] Although many argued that the environmental integrity of the protocol and inequity among member states represented potential weaknesses in the flexibility mechanisms, proponents successfully argued that they were necessary to achieve consensus to lower emissions below 1990 levels.

The CDM allows developed countries to finance or invest in projects that avoid GHG emissions in developing countries and receive credits that they may apply toward meeting mandatory limits on their own emissions. Joint implementation is similar, but instead of involving cooperation between developed and developing countries, it promotes collaboration between industrialized countries and countries with economies in transition (the former Soviet bloc). For example, a joint implementation project could involve German support for replacing an aging coal-fired plant in Romania with a more efficient energy source. CDM and joint implementation projects must result in emissions reductions greater than would have otherwise occurred, and all governments involved must approve them for the credits to be valid. The third Kyoto mechanism is emissions trading, whereby an Annex I party with excess emissions credits sells its credits to another Annex I party unable to meet its commitments. Developing countries had initially opposed that provision but finally agreed in order to avoid a complete collapse of the negotiations.

Provisions in the Kyoto Protocol stated that it could enter into force only after ratification by fifty-five parties, including enough Annex I countries that their collective emissions represented at least 55 percent of the CO_2 emissions from Annex I countries in 1990. Designed to ensure that the protocol would have a meaningful impact if it entered into force, the requirement also provided bargaining leverage for industrialized countries, which could withhold ratification in exchange for compromises on particular uses. Thus, while most developing countries and small island states ratified immediately, many Annex I parties signaled their intention to use subsequent COP meetings to address remaining concerns and negotiate more favorable terms before they ratified.

Not until COP-7, held four years later in Morocco, did delegates finally reach agreement on ways to operationalize the Kyoto Protocol. The leverage enjoyed by a veto coalition of Annex I countries known as the Umbrella Group (Australia, Canada, Iceland, Japan, New Zealand, Norway, Ukraine, Russia, and sometimes the United States), which had not yet ratified the protocol but were needed to allow it to enter into force, allowed them to push the EU and developing countries (which negotiated on these issues as a bloc through the Group of 77) to accept a weaker compliance system, more favorable terms for using the flexibility mechanisms, greater state sovereignty with respect to regime operations, and minimized requirements for providing information on carbon sinks. These terms reduced the costs to veto states of meeting the reductions targets, as they could now use the flexibility mechanisms more and reduce their domestic emissions less.[149]

Despite the progress made on elaborating the implementation details of the Kyoto Protocol, however, the question remained: Would the protocol ever enter into force? Many believed it would not after President George W. Bush announced in March 2001 that he would not seek US ratification of the agreement: "I oppose the Kyoto Protocol because it exempts 80 percent of the world, including major population centers such as China and India, from compliance, and would cause serious harm to the U.S. economy," he wrote, also citing what he called "the incomplete state of scientific knowledge of the causes of, and solutions to, global warming."[150] Although the protocol could enter into force without the United States, it would need the ratification of at least all members of the EU, as well as Canada, Japan, and the Russian Federation.

By mid-2004, Russia had become the focus of attention. With more than 120 countries having ratified already—including more than 30 Annex I parties representing 44 percent of that group's 1990 emissions, the 55 percent was now tantalizingly close, even without US involvement. If Russia, which represented 17.4 percent of 1990 emissions, signed on, the treaty would have more than enough support to push it over the top.

Interestingly, most observers believed that Russia would gain economically from ratifying the protocol because the emissions trading provisions would enable it to sell credits for emissions that had already been eliminated when the fall of communism eliminated government support for many inefficient heavy industries. Russia might also receive financial aid for preserving and expanding its Siberian forests for use as carbon sinks. While these factors played a role, in the end it was Russia's desire for admission into the World Trade Organization that provided the final incentive. The EU had told Moscow that it would support Russia's admission only after it ratified Kyoto.[151] On November 18, 2004, Russia ratified the protocol, which then entered into force on February 16, 2005 (the protocol, like most treaties, specifies a ninety-day delay between the final ratification required and the actual entry into force). As of March 2013, 191 countries and the European Union had ratified the Kyoto Protocol. The United States is the only industrialized country that has not ratified; Canada formally withdrew from the protocol in December 2011.

Post-Kyoto Commitments

Yet even before the Kyoto Protocol entered into force, significant attention had already turned to the question of what would happen when the first commitment period ended in 2012. Article 3.9 of the protocol provides for commitments for subsequent periods for Annex I parties. Neither the precise nature nor the duration of such commitments is specified. Many believed that negotiations on a successor regime to the Kyoto Protocol's first commitment period would have to begin in 2008 to avoid a gap between the first commitment period and subsequent commitment periods (many believed a gap between commitment periods would create counterproductive uncertainty and complications for countries and industry). Negotiations on a successor agreement were expected to take at least two years, and the new agreement's entry into force could take at least another two years. Yet achieving consensus on the nature of such an agreement—including its goals and requirements, burden sharing, inclusion of developing countries, and means to ensure participation by both the United States, among the world's largest per capita emitters of GHGs, and China, the world's largest total GHG emitter—would not be easy. The first challenge, however, was to reach an agreement to begin formal negotiations and achieve consensus on the terms of reference for the negotiating process. Parties set a deadline to provide incentive for achieving this preliminary step: the December 2007 Climate Change Conference in Bali, Indonesia.

To facilitate the deliberations, two parallel processes were established in 2005 (at UNFCCC COP-11 and Kyoto Protocol MOP-1 in Montreal; as related agreements

PHOTO 3.5   **Climate-change negotiations in Bali were often so crowded that delegates sat on the floor.**
Courtesy IISD/*Earth Negotiations Bulletin.*

within the same regime, the UNFCCC COP also serves as the protocol's MOP).[152] The first process, titled Dialogue on Long-Term Cooperative Action to Address Climate Change by Enhancing Implementation of the Convention, was established under the UNFCCC. In this process, parties were expected to exchange experiences and analyze strategic approaches for long-term cooperative action to address climate change.[153] The second process, the Ad Hoc Working Group on Further Commitments from Annex I Parties under the Kyoto Protocol, was established under the Kyoto Protocol to examine further commitments from Annex I parties.[154] As a working group established under the Kyoto Protocol, it would not consider commitments from developing countries (non–Annex I parties) and those Annex I countries that had not yet ratified the Kyoto Protocol, namely the United States. These issues could only be discussed under the UNFCCC process. This reveals why two processes were necessary: so that all types of potential future regime policies could be discussed by all the relevant countries.

Despite two years of preparatory negotiations and the release of the IPCC Fourth Assessment Report one month before (see Box 3.3), delegates had great difficulty reaching consensus in Bali. The resulting Bali Action Plan outlined a process and guidance for a series of meetings under both the convention and the protocol, with the aim of reaching agreement on a comprehensive framework for the post-2012 period in Copenhagen, Denmark, in December 2009. At the heart of the Bali Action Plan were the negotiating tracks to be pursued under the new Ad Hoc Working Group on Long-Term Cooperative Action (convention track) and the existing Ad Hoc Working Group on Further Commitments for Annex I Parties under the Protocol (protocol track).

The agenda under the convention track encompassed discussions on enhanced national and international action on reducing emissions (by both developed and developing countries), enhanced action on adaptation, technology transfer, and provision of financial resources and investment. Since the negotiations took place under the framework of the convention, they included all parties with major GHG emissions—including the largest developing countries and the United States. On the protocol track, the working group continued to analyze options for potential further commitments by Annex I parties and related issues, including the flexibility mechanisms.

During the two years between Bali and Copenhagen, the two working groups met eight times as they tried to overcome a host of obstacles standing in the way of an effective post-2012 climate regime. Many of the most difficult issues revolved around broad policy questions concerning the post-2012 period: Should the new commitments be legally binding or voluntary? Which countries would have to reduce their GHG emissions? What targets and timetables should be established? Should these be short-term or long-term targets, or both? Should the controls address GHG emissions in general, like Kyoto, or should they include action on specific sources of emissions, like cement production or deforestation? What types and levels of new technology transfer and financial assistance, if any, should be provided to developing countries? Should developing countries be required to adopt particular commitments in exchange for such assistance? Should the new agreement take the form of a new protocol, an extension of the Kyoto Protocol, an amendment to the convention, or some other agreement? How should the regime balance actions to mitigate climate change and those to help countries adapt to it?

Crisis in Copenhagen

When delegates arrived in Copenhagen, they had over two hundred pages of draft text before them—the output of the two working groups. Despite the preparatory work, however, negotiators were unable to resolve many of the core issues. One critical disagreement concerned the legal form of a Copenhagen outcome. The proposal by the industrialized countries for a single new agreement that combined the outcomes from the Kyoto and convention track negotiations was strongly opposed by developing countries, which stated that they would not allow "Kyoto to be killed."

The developing countries' position reflected, in part, their concern that the core principle of common but differentiated responsibilities must not be undermined or abandoned.[155] The disagreement reflected a negotiating dynamic that emerged in 2002, when European countries began pressing for action from developing countries. For the first decade of the regime, from 1991 to 2001, the negotiations focused almost exclusively on developed countries' emissions. The basic axis during this period was the EU-US split. Although developing countries engaged in these debates, the

BOX 3.3   INTERGOVERNMENTAL PANEL ON CLIMATE CHANGE'S
FOURTH ASSESSMENT REPORT

The IPCC's Fourth Assessment Report (AR4) was released in four installments during 2007. AR4 made a major scientific contribution toward the understanding of climate change and had an impact on the negotiations of the Bali Action Plan in December 2007.

Working Group I's contribution on climate-change science was released in February 2007. The document summarized progress in understanding human and natural drivers of climate change, observed climate change, climate processes, and estimates of projected future climate change. This was the strongest statement to date on the extent and causes of climate change. It expressed greater than 90 percent certainty that most of the observed warming over the past half century is caused by human activities. The report noted that the rate of warming and sea-level rise accelerated during the twentieth century and cited other important changes, such as more intense precipitation, drought, and tropical cyclones.

Working Group II's report, released in April 2007, focused on impacts, adaptation, and vulnerability. The IPCC summarized progress that has been made in understanding impacts of climate change on natural, managed, and human systems; their capacity to adapt; and their vulnerability. Particularly obvious impacts are widespread changes in ice and snow cover, earlier spring biological events in natural and managed ecosystems, and changes in water temperature and flows in rivers, lakes, and oceans.

The report presented projections of impacts on policy-relevant sectors, including water, ecosystems, food, coastal systems, industry, settlement and society, and health, and on major regions, including Africa, Asia, Australia and New Zealand, Europe, Latin America, North America, polar regions, and small islands.

The third installment to the IPCC Fourth Assessment Report was released in May 2007. The Working Group III report analyzed mitigation options for the main economic sectors in the near term. It provided information on long-term mitigation strategies, paying special attention to implications of different short-term strategies for achieving long-term goals, and also addressing the relationship between mitigation and sustainable development.

The final installment, the AR4 Synthesis Report, was released in November 2007. Key findings included the following:

- There is strong certainty that most of the observed warming of the past half century is due to human influences, and a clear relationship exists between the growth in human-made GHG emissions and the observed impacts of climate change.
- The climate system is more vulnerable to abrupt or irreversible changes than previously thought.

- Avoiding the most serious impacts of climate change—including irreversible changes—will require significant reductions in greenhouse gas emissions.
- Mitigation efforts must also be combined with adaptation measures to minimize the risks of climate change.

Sources: IPCC, *Fourth Assessment Report: Climate Change 2007* (Geneva: IPCC, 2007), www.ipcc.ch/ipccreports/assessments-reports.htm; Pew Center for Global Climate Change, "Highlights from *Climate Change 2007: Synthesis Report of the IPCC Fourth Assessment Report: Summary for Policy Makers*," www.pewclimate.org/docUploads/PewSummary _AR4.pdf.

negotiations were really about what developed countries would do.[156] However, in their second decade, the negotiations became increasingly about developing countries' commitments, an issue that moved to center stage in Bali in 2007, making the climate-change talks even more deeply divided over the principle of common but differentiated responsibilities.

Another factor that affected the negotiations in Copenhagen was a shift in power dynamics among key parties. The EU, long the leader in climate-change mitigation, was weakened by internal divisions and economic realities, making it more difficult for it to play a strong lead-state role. China had become far stronger economically and also passed the United States as the largest GHG emitter, strengthening the US position that China must take on binding obligations to reduce emissions. The G-77 had become increasingly fragmented on climate policy, split into different groups on different issues according to vulnerability to climate change, rates of economic development, levels of GHG emissions, and oil exports. G-77 and China subgroups now included:

- BASIC: Brazil, South Africa, India, and China, with fast-growing economies and increasing geopolitical status
- Least Developed Countries
- AOSIS: forty-two island and low-lying states, which are most vulnerable to sea-level rise and the strongest proponents of deep cuts in GHG emissions
- Organization of Petroleum Exporting Countries (OPEC): countries whose economies rely heavily on fossil-fuel extraction and export
- Bolivarian Alliance for the Peoples of Our America (ALBA): Venezuela, Cuba, Bolivia, Nicaragua, Ecuador, Dominica, Antigua and Barbuda, and St. Vincent and the Grenadines, which stress stronger developed-country commitments
- Central American Integration System
- Group of Mountain Landlocked Developing Countries

- Central Asia, Caucasus, Albania, and Moldova
- Coalition of Rainforest Nations, which strongly favors mechanisms that would pay developing countries to preserve large forests as carbon sinks
- African Group, which increasingly supports large GHG cuts and payments to developing countries to mitigate, and adapt to, climate change

The fragmentation of the G-77 meant that many nations focused more on their national interests rather than compromising to fit into the omnibus G-77 position. This created more complex negotiations, as more and more countries sought a seat around the key negotiating tables in the small contact groups that often hammer out the final deals, closed off from NGOs and the media.

The Copenhagen Climate Conference also faced significant logistical challenges produced by the presence of 115 heads of state and government, more than 40,000 delegates, and unprecedented public and media attention. A deeper and more problematic obstacle was the dispute between the world's two biggest GHG emitters and most powerful veto states: the United States and China. The United States insisted that a future agreement contain commitments by both developed and developing countries. China, supported by India, refused to accept any binding commitment to limit its emissions, even if they were differentiated. Meanwhile, most of the Annex I parties with Kyoto targets were unwilling to accept a second round of targets unless both the United States and the major emerging economies, in particular China, agreed to do their share under a legally binding global agreement.[157]

During the high-level segment in the final days of the talks, informal negotiations took place in a group consisting of major economies and representatives of regional groups. These negotiations were often characterized by mistrust, difficulties related to the immense agenda, and confusion produced by parallel informal negotiations taking place among diplomats and among senior officials and even heads of state. Through an extraordinary process, a very small group of extremely high-level representatives from the major economies, including China and the United States, and main UNFCCC negotiating groups reached consensus on a framework agreement, the Copenhagen Accord.[158] Indeed, these negotiations were so private that when President Obama announced the text to the media as the "Copenhagen outcome," most delegations had not yet seen it. When it was presented to the plenary for adoption, a long and acrimonious debate ensued, with parties unable to reach consensus. In the end, rather than formally adopt the Copenhagen Accord, parties agreed to merely "take note" of it. Some delegations, especially ALBA, that blocked adoption of the accord called the process "untransparent and undemocratic," since the text of the Copenhagen Accord had appeared "out of nowhere." For others, the most disturbing element was the consensus rule within the UNFCCC that allowed a few countries to prevent the accord from becoming part of the formal legal framework.[159]

In retrospect, the Copenhagen Accord represented a creative compromise that avoided a breakdown of the climate regime. The nonbinding agreement set forth a long-term, aspirational global goal of limiting temperature rise to no more than 2 degrees Celsius, established a process for recording voluntary mitigation targets and actions of both developed and developing countries, and agreed to increase funding for mitigation and adaptation by developing countries, including "fast start" money for the 2010–2012 period approaching $30 billion and a goal of mobilizing $100 billion per year by 2020.[160] To date, over 140 countries have endorsed the accord, and over 80 countries have submitted emissions targets and mitigation actions, as called for by the accord.

By establishing a process for listing both developed-country targets and developing-country actions, the Copenhagen Accord satisfied US demands for symmetry. By establishing only political commitments for developing countries, it satisfied China's rejection of legally binding obligations. And by focusing on a political rather than a legal outcome, it postponed the decision about whether to continue the Kyoto Protocol.[161] To fill in the details of how to operationalize key elements of the accord, the COP also extended the mandate of both working groups.

Rebuilding Trust

The two working groups met four more times before the parties reconvened in Cancun, Mexico, in December 2010. The main challenge was to restore the diplomatic trust that had been lost as a result of the "secretive" negotiations in Copenhagen. Even though a post-2012 climate deal was still beyond reach, the UNFCCC and Kyoto Protocol governing bodies did make steps toward a new climate agreement to replace the Kyoto Protocol. The Cancun Agreements included the following:

- formal affirmation of the IPCC-recommended global target to limit global warming to 2 degrees Celcius above preindustrial levels;
- agreement that scaled-up mitigation efforts are needed in order to work toward a global goal in 2011 to substantially reduce global emissions by 2050;
- establishment of an Adaptation Committee to enable enhanced action on adaptation and promote increased finance, technology, and capacity building;
- confirmation of the $30 billion fast-start pledges under the Copenhagen Accord and the newly established Green Climate Fund;
- establishment of a Technology Mechanism to improve technology transfer and development; and
- extending the mandate of the two working groups for another year.[162]

While the substantive outcome was viewed by many as far from perfect, and Bolivia went as far as to oppose the adoption of the Cancun Agreements because they would not reduce emissions sufficiently to prevent climate change,[163] most participants left Cancun with restored confidence in the UNFCCC process. [164] However, many also acknowledged that the meeting's achievements represented only small steps in combating climate change.[165]

After the frustrations in Copenhagen and the struggle to rescue the climate regime in Cancun, negotiators gathered in Durban, South Africa, one year later hoping to turn a corner and make more substantial progress.[166] The results were mixed. During the 2011 Durban Climate Change Conference, delegates agreed to the Durban Platform, which would launch a new negotiating process to develop a protocol or other agreement that would include all parties and address the post-2020 period but made no advances in finding solutions on the core issues.[167] They also agreed in principle to extend the Kyoto Protocol so there would be no gap in commitment periods between 2012 and 2020, but they could not agree on the details of how to do this.

One year later, and mere weeks before the end of Kyoto's first commitment period, governments met in Doha, Qatar. Governments set forth four key objectives for the 2012 Doha Conference: to ensure the seamless continuation of the Kyoto Protocol; to plan the work agreed to under the Durban Platform to reach a climate-change agreement covering all countries; to complete the Bali Action Plan; and to finalize the infrastructure for the Green Climate Fund and the Climate Technology Center and Network—mechanisms to help channel technology and financial resources to developing nations.[168]

When the conference concluded two weeks later, governments approved "The Doha Climate Gateway." The agreement launched a second eight-year commitment period under the Kyoto Protocol, which keeps Kyoto operational as a transitional measure; agreed on a timetable to adopt a universal global climate agreement by 2015 to cover the post-2020 period; endorsed the completion of new institutions and ways and means to deliver scaled-up climate finance and technology to developing countries; and established plans to address future "loss and damage" in developing countries that may result from rising sea levels, increased severe weather events, and other impacts of climate change.

Reactions to the outcome were predictably mixed. Many criticized the entire UNFCCC process as lacking the urgency needed to achieve meaningful progress and limit severe climate change. At the end of 2012—a year that included Hurricane Sandy, severe US droughts; flooding in Beijing, Manila, and the UK; and a record melting of ice in the Arctic Ocean—Greenpeace executive director Kumi Naidoo, representing the sentiments of many NGOs, commented,

PHOTO 3.6   Youth delegates at the climate-change negotiations in Doha call on delegates to reflect their demands.
Courtesy IISD/*Earth Negotiations Bulletin*.

Today we ask the politicians in Doha: Which planet are you on? Clearly not the planet where people are dying from storms, floods and droughts. Nor the planet where renewable energy is growing rapidly and increasing constraints are being placed on the use of dirty fuels such as coal. The talks in Doha were always going to be a modest affair, but they failed to live up to even the historically low expectations.[169]

Others were more nuanced: "The meeting brought no new agreement to limit the greenhouse-gas emissions that are set to warm the world still more, and no deal on new funds to help poor countries adapt. Yet the delegates left with some achievements that could, in time, come to matter."[170] Still others put a positive spin on the outcome, including EU Commissioner for Climate Action Connie Hedegaard, who said,

The EU wanted Doha to mark the transition away from the old climate regime, where only developed countries have the legal obligation to reduce emissions, to the new system where all countries developed and developing alike, will for the first time make legal commitments under the new global agreement. In Doha, we changed the very structure of our negotiations. Before, we had different working groups based on the sharp distinction between developed and developing countries. Now, we have one negotiation forum, the Durban Platform, for all countries.[171]

As attention shifts to actions at the domestic level and to future negotiations under the Durban Platform, real questions remain regarding the political will of governments to move to a low-emissions economy. Most believe that it is in their national interest to do so but short-term costs and international economic and political differences remain significant obstacles. The lead states and veto states, which have changed many times since the climate negotiations began in the early 1990s, will likely change again as economic, political, and climate-change realities sink in. The biggest challenge to achieving a universal agreement will likely be enabling the veto coalition of major GHG-emitting developing countries, particularly China and India, to move beyond their rigid view of the principle of common but differentiated responsibilities and accept some level of binding controls. Another is creation of national policy frameworks in the United States, the other major veto state, so that joining a global climate policy initiative becomes more desirable to key domestic political and economic actors. Either of these developments could open the door for other veto states to accept further emissions reductions. Only when these groups come together will a meaningful climate-change regime be possible.

CONCLUSION

These four regimes demonstrate how both state and nonstate actors can come together to address transboundary and atmospheric pollution problems. Each regime establishes binding controls, including in some cases specific targets and timetables, to limit emissions of specific substances. Each also demonstrates how regimes can strengthen over time but that such strengthening does not necessarily lead to fundamental success, as seen in the climate regime.

The negotiation of a strong global environmental regime almost always depends on inducing one or more key states in a veto coalition to go along with one or more of the core proposed provisions of the regime. By strong, we mean an agreement that includes obligations or norms that make it sufficiently clear that parties can be held accountable for implementing them and that calls for actions expected to have an impact on the problem. Whether a regime succeeds in addressing an environmental threat depends, of course, on the strength of the regime and the degree to which parties comply with its core provisions.

In these cases, numerous issues affected the negotiations. New scientific evidence helped move veto states on some issues (ozone and POPs) but far less on other issues (climate change). International political considerations played a role in the Basel Convention, where French and British desires to maintain close relations with former colonies factored into their views on the hazardous waste trade. Domestic political and ethical concerns played a key role in making Canada a lead state in the Stockholm Convention negotiations. Perceptions of economic interests changed significantly in the ozone regime, allowing for rapid strengthening while perceptions of other economic interests continue to slow significant strengthening of the climate regime.

Regime formation also requires leadership by one or more states committed to defining the issue and proposing a policy approach to address it. In these cases, states motivated by particular vulnerabilities played lead roles: African countries on hazardous waste; Canada and some European countries on POPs; AOSIS on climate change. However, only in the ozone case did arguably the most powerful state, the United States, play a lead role.

The ozone and climate regimes are often compared by scholars and policy makers as they share important similarities. Both address the Earth's atmosphere. Both attempt to prevent changes to a critical natural system. Each addresses a system that exists within a dynamic equilibrium but has certain tipping points. This means that human action can impact the ozone layer and global climate system to a certain degree without changing either significantly, but once these impacts reach a certain level, then it becomes essentially impossible to prevent significant negative changes to these systems or to reverse the changes (or "fix" the problem) for a very long time.

Both regimes started with framework conventions that established important goals, norms, institutions, and procedures. Governments then negotiated protocols that specified binding emissions reductions. Each has been significantly influenced by scientific bodies and economic interests. Both regimes impact important economic sectors and their control measures faced significant opposition from powerful national and international interests. Both include references to the importance of addressing their issues in a precautionary manner. Both follow the principle of common but differentiated responsibilities by mandating that industrialized countries address the issue first, since they are responsible for creating the problem and have the necessary resources to address it. Each includes provisions for developing countries to receive technical and financial assistance to help them meet their regime obligations.

The two regimes are also interrelated. Most of the chemicals that deplete the ozone layer and many of the substances developed to replace them are also powerful GHGs. Thus, by reducing CFC emissions, the ozone regime helped to address climate change, but by promoting certain CFC substitutes, such as HFCs, the ozone regime complicated matters and actually contributed to GHG emissions. At the same time, accelerating climate change is actually slowing recovery of the ozone layer. While climate change is warming the atmosphere nearest the Earth's surface, the troposphere, it is also cooling the stratosphere. A cooler stratosphere produces conditions that accelerate the chemical reactions that deplete ozone.

Yet, in other ways, the ozone and climate regimes are quite different. The ozone regime is widely considered to be among the most effective examples of international environmental policy. The climate regime has slowed the growth of GHG emissions but global emissions have still increased significantly since 1990, serious impacts of climate change are already being observed, and the odds have increased that very serious, even catastrophic, changes will occur in the future.

The regimes have also developed at very different speeds. Governments concluded negotiations on the framework treaty for the ozone regime in 1985, eleven years after the discovery that CFCs might threaten stratospheric ozone. Scientists discovered that increasing GHGs could warm the atmosphere one hundred years before the UNFCCC was adopted. The ozone regime quickly expanded its scope, has strong and effective control mechanisms, and covers all major emitters of ODS. The climate regime has developed at a slower pace. It does not yet include the rules necessary to mitigate climate change in the long term and does not yet place binding controls on all major GHG emitters. While both regimes have scientific bodies to advise them, they interact with them differently and as a result the scientific bodies have different impacts. The ozone regime has nearly eliminated many ozone-depleting chemicals, especially in the industrialized nations, and now focuses on implementing the remainder of its controls. While only five years younger, the climate regime must still go through many more difficult negotiations to create the controls necessary to prevent significant and damaging change to the Earth's climate.

While both regimes establish targets and timetables, in the ozone regime, all industrialized countries must meet essentially the same standards, while in the climate regime, different industrialized countries have very different targets for reducing emissions. Developing countries accepted binding controls to reduce the use of ODS under the Montreal Protocol, but there are no binding commitments on developing countries to reduce GHG emissions under the Kyoto Protocol. Finally, governments have expanded and strengthened the ozone regime, primarily because of scientific consensus and the availability of substitutes for ozone-depleting chemicals. In contrast, while the IPCC has provided the scientific consensus that climate change is occurring, many governments have refused to take significant action, in part because of concerns for the short-terms cost associated with reducing the use of coal, oil, and natural gas—fossil fuels that contribute most to CO_2 emissions.

These differences reflect a variety of factors, including characteristics of the issue area; the evolution of scientific consensus; the identity and interests of the major actors, especially the lead and veto states; the design of the respective regimes; the evolution of economic and political interests; and the presence or absence of well-known obstacles to effective cooperation (see Chapter 5). This contrasts somewhat with global regimes that address the conservation of natural resources. Chapter 4 examines six regimes for natural resource conservation and management and how they differ from pollution-control regimes. The conclusion to Chapter 4 will also review and compare all ten case studies presented in Chapters 3 and 4.

4

The Development of Environmental Regimes: Natural Resources, Species, and Habitats

Like the pollution-control regimes described in Chapter 3, regimes designed to conserve natural resources must also overcome conflicts between states' economic and political interests, concerns for protecting state sovereignty, and different opinions regarding the importance of the precautionary principle and the principle of common but differentiated responsibilities and how to implement these principles. Moreover, natural resource regimes face the additional challenge of trying to protect resources and species that are of international importance but exist within the boundaries of sovereign states or beyond the boundaries of any state.

The regimes described in this chapter focus on shared natural resources: physical or biological systems that extend into or across the jurisdictions of two or more states. Shared natural resources include nonrenewable resources (for example, underground pools of oil or waterways) subject to the jurisdiction of two or more states, renewable and biological resources (fish stocks, birds, mammals), and complex ecosystems (forests, regional seas, river basins, coral reefs, and deserts).[1] Many shared natural resources exist in or pass through the commons or the jurisdictional zones of two or more states. Many marine mammals, including whales, move through the waters of several coastal states as well as the waters that are part of the high seas, beyond a country's exclusive economic zone, the two-hundred-mile territorial waters under the jurisdiction of individual states.[2] Shared resources may also link states far removed from each other geographically, as in the case of migratory birds.

The international management of natural resources must also address transboundary externalities, which arise when activities that occur within the jurisdiction of an individual state produce results that affect the welfare of those residing in other states.[3] Such situations involve a very difficult question, one central not only to environmental but also to human rights and humanitarian issues: When does the international community have a legitimate interest, right, or obligation to seek significant changes in the domestic affairs of individual states because the activities occurring within their jurisdictions pose severe threats to the well-being of others or to international society as a whole? For example, should states still have unfettered rights to cut huge tracts of their forested land for timber or agriculture, since these forests benefit the entire world as biodiversity reserves and as carbon sinks that mitigate climate change? Do countries have a right to try to change how other states manage ecosystems with rich biological diversity because the loss of particular plants and animals could prevent the discovery of new drugs that might cure cancer or other diseases around the world? Do states have the right to tell other states to stop killing, buying, and selling endangered species because extinction is now a global concern? Should the ethical perspectives of a large group of countries regarding whales, elephants, or turtles affect the activities of a smaller set of countries that do not share these views?

In addition to national sovereignty issues, efforts to negotiate regimes to deal with biodiversity, endangered species, forests, fish stocks, and land management may also have consequences for particular economic-development strategies or efforts to promote free trade. Are states free to impose restrictions on imports from other countries if their production involves practices that are unacceptable on environmental grounds, such as catching shrimp in a way that endangers sea turtles? Should a country be prevented from developing a tropical timber industry, which could have major short-term economic benefits, because of the consequences of biodiversity loss?

Finally, pollution-control regimes, such as those for ozone and POPs, often include clear and measurable targets and timetables. Many natural resources regimes, especially those for biodiversity and desertification, do not lend themselves to those types of rules. Effective protection and management of natural resources often requires complex set of new policies that seek to address factors that threaten the resource. It is also often more difficult to develop effective indicators to measure implementation or to determine the impact of the regime.

The six cases examined in this chapter highlight different aspects of international natural resource management. The Convention on Biological Diversity (CBD) highlights North-South contrasts in the distribution of biodiversity resources and the many ways that natural resource management can conflict with important economic, social, and political interests. The International Convention for the Regulation of Whaling and the Convention on International Trade in Endangered Species of Wild Fauna and Flora (CITES) present two very different examples of regimes that manage endangered species, and they illustrate the politics and economics involved in the sustainable management of whales and elephants. The fisheries regime illustrates the importance and difficulty of managing resources that move between areas of national jurisdiction and the global commons. The desertification regime faces the challenge of improving land management that has an impact on environmental sustainability and economic and social development. Finally, the forests case demonstrates what happens when the international community cannot agree to establish a global regime and raises the question of whether legally binding treaties are always the solution for global environmental problems.

BIODIVERSITY LOSS

Biological diversity, or biodiversity, is most often associated with the earth's vast variety of plants, animals, and microorganisms, but the term encompasses diversity at all levels, from genes to species to ecosystems to landscapes. Approximately 1.75 million species have been identified, mostly small creatures, such as insects. Many scientists believe that there could be as many as 13 million species, although individual estimates range from 3 to 100 million. Ecosystems are another aspect of biodiversity. In each ecosystem, including those that occur within or between forests, wetlands, mountains, deserts, and rivers, living creatures interact with each other as well as with the air, water, and soil around them; in this way, they form an interconnected community. Biodiversity also includes genetic differences within species, such as different breeds and varieties, as well as chromosomes, genes, and genetic sequences (DNA).

The main anthropogenic threats to biodiversity include habitat destruction, overharvesting, pollution, invasive species, and human-induced climate change. According to the Millennium Ecosystem Assessment, humans have increased species extinction rates by as much as one thousand times over background, or natural, rates of extinction. Some 12 percent of birds, 23 percent of mammals, 25 percent of conifers, and 32 percent of amphibians are threatened with extinction.[4] Despite general acknowledgment of the importance of biodiversity and its value to the well-being of future generations, attempts to create an effective global regime for conserving biodiversity have suffered from differences concerning the definition of the problem, the application of the principle of national sovereignty versus that of the common heritage of humankind,[5] resistance to strong legal obligations by a veto coalition of developing states whose territory holds most of the world's biodiversity, and inconsistent support from the United States and several other key industrialized states.

In 1987, concern about the rate of species extinction led the governments that comprise UNEP's Governing Council to create a working group of experts to study an

PHOTO 4.1   Lack of effective implementation was also demonstrated in the international community's failure to meet the global target of significantly reducing the rate of biodiversity loss by 2010, during the International Year of Biodiversity. (Video message from UN Secretary-General Ban Ki-moon.)
Courtesy IISD/*Earth Negotiations Bulletin.*

"umbrella convention" to rationalize activities in biodiversity conservation. As the working group began the process of issue definition in 1990, the idea of a biodiversity convention became entangled in North-South struggles over plant genetic resources and intellectual property rights (IPR). The debate took shape around the "ownership" of genetic resources, with southern states arguing for explicit state sovereignty over the genetic resources within their borders and northern states arguing the view, previously accepted under international law, that these resources form part of the "common heritage of [hu]mankind." Some developing countries insisted that genetic resources belong to the states in which they are located and that access should be based on a "mutual agreement between countries." They also argued for the inclusion of provisions for noncommercial access to biotechnologies based on plant genetic resources found in the South as a central element in any biodiversity convention. Most industrialized countries initially opposed the inclusion of biotechnology in the convention and attempted to define the scope of the regime to include only the conservation of biodiversity in the wild and mechanisms to finance such efforts.[6]

Formal negotiations on what would become the Convention on Biological Diversity were completed in five sessions from July 1991 to May 1992. Four factors shaped the bargaining stage, polarized largely along North-South lines: the veto power of devel-

oping countries over biodiversity-conservation provisions, the veto power of industrialized countries over technology-transfer and financing provisions, the aggressive
role played by UNEP executive director Mostafa Tolba, and the implicit deadline imposed by the Earth Summit in Rio in June 1992.

During the final negotiating session in May 1992, Tolba, confronted with the
possibility that countries might fail to reach an agreement in time for the Earth
Summit, personally took over the negotiations. He replaced the designated chair
and drafted compromise texts. Tolba submitted the text to the delegations as a fait
accompli to be accepted or rejected shortly before the diplomatic conference that
would formally adopt the convention.[7] Although the industrialized countries had
concerns, most believed the proposed text offered the best agreement that could be
reached in time for the treaty to be opened for signature at the Earth Summit only
ten days later.

At the June 1992 Earth Summit, 153 countries signed the convention. The United
States refused to do so, citing the provisions on financing and IPR.[8] The United States
reversed its position after the Clinton administration came into office and signed the
convention in June 1993.[9] However, to date the United States has not ratified it and is
not a party.[10] The convention entered into force on December 29, 1993, and has been
ratified by 193 countries.[11]

The resulting regime has three objectives: the conservation of biological diversity,
the sustainable use of its components, and the fair and equitable sharing of benefits
arising out of the use of genetic resources. Parties are obligated to inventory and monitor biodiversity, incorporate the concepts of conservation and sustainable development into national strategies and economic development, and preserve indigenous
conservation practices. The unwillingness of key actors to consider quantitative targets
for the percentage of land that should be set aside for biodiversity conservation narrowed the scope of the CBD's conservation provisions. Germany informally raised the
idea early in the negotiations, but a veto coalition led by developing countries holding
a large proportion of the world's biodiversity (Brazil, Indonesia, and Mexico) vocifer-
ously opposed such stringent provisions. Interestingly, most European countries also
opposed such targets because they thought they would embarrass developed countries
that had already cut down most of their forests in past centuries.[12]

The convention takes a comprehensive, rather than sectoral, approach to the conservation of the biological diversity and the sustainable use of biological resources,
and this has proven to be an implementation challenge. The fact that the treaty encompasses socioeconomic issues, such as the sharing of benefits from the use of genetic
resources and access to technology, including biotechnology, has also led to implementation challenges. In order to implement and strengthen the CBD regime, the
Conference of the Parties (COP) has made decisions requiring implementation actions

by parties and negotiated protocols to establish concrete commitments on biosafety and the sharing of benefits from the use of genetic resources.

Regime Strengthening

Implementation decisions under the CBD have been less focused than in some of the other major global environmental regimes. This reflects the more diffuse nature of the regime's rules and norms, the absence of a strong lead-state coalition, the absence of an enforcement mechanism, and a general lack of political will. However, the COP has made progress in both identifying global conservation priority areas and developing work programs on conservation and/or sustainable use in particular sectors.

The COP developed seven work programs in critical areas that address sustaining biodiversity and providing critical ecosystem services: mountain regions, dry and sub-humid lands, marine and coastal areas, islands, inland waters, agricultural systems, and forests.[13] Drafting these work programs proved a long and arduous process. Discussions began at the first COP in 1994, but parties did not adopt the first program until 1998. Nevertheless, the programs' current conservation measures are largely ineffective because they lack precise, binding language. The formation of various veto coalitions based on common economic or political interests has further inhibited effective policy. For example, major forest-product–exporting countries, including Brazil, Canada, and Malaysia, ensured that the convention would not take the lead on forests by blocking the development of a strong work program in this issue area.

The programs of work are the main instruments that the parties use to implement their commitments under the convention. They include guidelines for national implementation, including recommendations for reform of national laws, policies, or administrative practices. They also identify tasks to be implemented at the international level by the COP and subsidiary bodies as well as opportunities for collaboration between the CBD and other treaties or processes.[14] However, the overall coherence of the programs of work has been obscured, according to some observers, by the "convoluted, repetitious and disorderly drafting of CBD COP decisions."[15] This is an obstacle for national officials who are responsible for implementing the convention. Furthermore, in a treaty that relies on national implementation, there is no mechanism to systematically and effectively monitor implementation at the national level. The COP does not even review national reports but, rather, offers conclusions on the basis of the secretariat's syntheses of reports submitted by parties.[16]

Lack of effective implementation was clearly demonstrated in the international community's failure to meet the global target of significantly reducing the rate of biodiversity loss by 2010. The COP adopted this target in 2002, and it was later endorsed by the World Summit on Sustainable Development and incorporated into the Millennium Development Goals.[17] The 2010 *Global Biodiversity Outlook* provided scientific evidence that the global target was not met. In particular, the authors noted:

- Species that have been assessed for extinction risk are on average moving closer to extinction. Amphibians face the greatest risk, and coral species are deteriorating most rapidly in status. Nearly a quarter of plant species are estimated to be threatened with extinction.
- The abundance of vertebrate species fell by nearly a third on average between 1970 and 2006, with especially severe declines in the tropics and among freshwater species.
- Natural habitats in most parts of the world continue to decline in extent and integrity.
- Extensive fragmentation and degradation of forests, rivers, and other ecosystems have also led to loss of biodiversity and ecosystem services.
- Crop and livestock genetic diversity continues to decline.
- The five principal pressures directly driving biodiversity loss (habitat change, overexploitation, pollution, invasive alien species [see Box 4.1], and climate change) are either constant or increasing in intensity.[18]

The causes of these failures include the insufficient scale of action to implement the convention, insufficient integration of biodiversity issues into broader policies, insufficient attention to the underlying drivers of biodiversity loss, and insufficient inclusion of the real benefits of biodiversity (and the costs of its loss) within economic systems and markets.[19]

Cartagena Protocol on Biosafety

Biosafety refers to a set of precautionary practices that seek to ensure the safe transfer, handling, use, and disposal of living modified organisms (LMOs) derived from modern biotechnology. By the early 1990s, most countries with biotechnology industries had domestic biosafety legislation in place, but there were no binding international agreements regarding genetically modified organisms that cross national borders. Biotechnology, particularly its agricultural applications, was a highly controversial issue. Policy responses varied widely in different legal orders, the most well-known example being the contrasting approaches of the United States and the European Union (EU), with the latter calling for a precautionary approach toward modern biotechnology. In 1999, several European governments joined European environmental nongovernmental organizations (NGOs) in calling for a moratorium on the import of genetically modified foods. Although the moratorium ended in 2004, it provoked a World Trade Organization (WTO) dispute between the United States and the EU, which was decided in favor of the United States in 2006.[20]

BOX 4.1   INVASIVE ALIEN SPECIES

Invasive alien species (IAS) are species whose introduction and/or spread outside their natural habitats threaten biological diversity. While only a small percentage of organisms transported to new environments become invasive, their negative impacts on food security; plant, animal, and human health; and economic development can be extensive and substantial.

Most nations already grapple with complex and costly invasive species problems. Examples include: zebra mussels affecting fisheries and electric power generation; the water hyacinth blocking waterways, decimating aquatic wildlife and the livelihoods of local people, and creating ideal conditions for disease and its vectors; rats exterminating native birds on Pacific islands; and deadly new disease organisms, such as avian influenza A (H5N1), attacking humans and animals, in both temperate and tropical countries. Addressing the problem of invasive alien species is urgent because the threat is growing daily, and the economic and environmental impacts are severe.

The problem of invasive alien species continues to grow, essentially due to global trade, transport, and travel, including tourism, at an enormous cost to human and animal health and the socioeconomic and ecological well-being of the world. Since the seventeenth century, invasive alien species have contributed to nearly 40 percent of all animal extinctions for which the cause is known. They pose the greatest threat to biodiversity on isolated ecosystems, such as islands, as these lack natural competitors and predators that usually control populations of invasives. The annual environmental losses caused by introduced pests in the United States, United Kingdom, Australia, South Africa, India, and Brazil have been calculated at over US$100 billion.

ECONOMIC IMPACT OF SOME INVASIVE ALIEN SPECIES

SPECIES	ECONOMIC VARIABLE	ECONOMIC IMPACT (ONE COIN=APPROX. US$20 MILLION)
Rats (*Rattus ruttus* and *R. norvegicus*)	US$19 million per year in losses and damages in the United States (Pimentel et al. 2005)	$
Feral pigs (*Sus scrofa*)	US$800 million per year in losses and damages in the United States (Pimentel et al. 2005)	$$$$$$$$$$$$$$$$$$$$ $$$$$$$$$$$$$$$$$$$$
Water hyacinth (*Eichhornia crassipes*) and other alien water weeds	US$100 million per year in costs related to water use to developing countries (GISP 2004b)	$$$$$
Vegetable leaf miner (*Liriomyza sativae*)	US$80 million per year for economic losses in China (Li and Xie 2002)	$$$$
Small Indian mongoose (*Herpestes javanicus*)	US$50 million in damages per year in Puerto Rico and the Hawaiian Islands alone (GISP 2004b)	$$
Coffee berry borer (*Hypothenemus hampei*)	US$300 million per year in India (GISP 2004b)	$$$$$$$$$$$$$$$

Source: Secretariat for the Convention on Biological Diversity, *Invasive Alien Species: A Threat to Biodiversity* (Montreal, Canada: Secretariat for the Convention on Biological Diversity, 2009), 6, http://www.cbd.int/doc/bioday/2009/idb-2009-booklet-en.pdf. Reprinted with permission of the Secretariat for the Convention on Biological Diversity.

Parties to the CBD began negotiations on the biosafety protocol in 1996 and planned to finish in 1999. However, in February 1999, when delegates convened in Cartagena, Colombia, for the planned final round of negotiations, a veto coalition called the Miami Group, which included the world's major grain exporters outside of the EU (Argentina, Australia, Canada, Chile, the United States, and Uruguay), blocked the agreement. The veto coalition argued that trade restrictions in the protocol would harm the multibillion-dollar agricultural export industry, imprecision in several key provisions would create uncertainty and difficulties implementing the treaty, countries would be able to block imports based on their own criteria rather than on sound scientific knowledge, and the increased documentation required under the protocol would create unnecessary and excessive procedures and financial costs.[21]

Informal consultations continued over the next year between the major coalitions, which included the Central and Eastern European Group, the Compromise Group (Japan, Mexico, Norway, Republic of Korea, and Switzerland, joined later by New Zealand and Singapore), the EU, the Like-Minded Group (an informal coalition that included the majority of developing countries but not the major grain exporters), and the Miami Group. Finally, after a week of formal negotiations in Montreal in January 2000, the major coalitions reached an agreement and adopted the Cartagena Protocol on Biosafety.[22] The protocol entered into force in September 2003. The protocol has since been supplemented by the 2010 Nagoya–Kuala Lumpur Supplementary Protocol on Liability and Redress to the Cartagena Protocol on Biosafety,[23] which provides international rules and procedures on liability and redress for damage to biodiversity resulting from LMOs. The supplementary protocol has not yet entered into force.

The successful implementation of the Cartagena Protocol depends on the interplay of economic interests. One example of this is the difficulty parties had in reaching agreement on documentation requirements for bulk shipments of living modified organisms intended for food, feed, and processing (LMO-FFPs). In order to adopt the protocol, negotiators put off an agreement on this issue; according to Article 18.2(a) of the protocol, parties are required to decide on the detailed requirements for such documentation within two years of entry into force. At the second Meeting of the Parties (MOP) in May 2005, exporting countries expressed concern that labeling shipments that *might* include LMOs could interfere with trade. Apart from fears that many commodity producers did not have the capability to account for small amounts of LMOs that a shipment might contain, there was widespread concern that stricter documentation requirements could prove costly, restrict market access, and have a negative impact on countries that rely heavily on agricultural exports. Meanwhile, importing countries wanted to set up documentation requirements that would state which LMOs actually were included in a shipment rather than a longer list of LMOs that might be included. Many developing-country importers, particularly African parties, stressed that documentation without guidance regarding which LMOs were most likely contained in the shipment posed significant capacity challenges to importing states to detect and monitor the content of incoming shipments.[24] New Zealand and Brazil played the role of veto states, later joined by Mexico, Paraguay, and Peru, and expressed serious objections to establishing any rule that would affect commodity trade in general.[25]

At MOP-3 in Curitiba, Brazil, in March 2006, Brazil shifted positions and, because of its role as host country, played the role of lead state by preparing drafts and promoting compromise to demonstrate its commitment to a successful outcome of the meeting. Under Brazil's leadership, parties agreed on a compromise package that balanced the interests of importing and exporting states as well as of developed- and developing-country parties. The Curitiba Rules request parties to take measures to ensure that documentation accompanying LMO-FFPs in commercial production clearly states that the shipment contains LMO-FFPs in cases where the identity of the LMO is known. In cases where the identity of the LMO is not known, the Curitiba Rules still allow documentation to state that the shipment may contain one or more LMO-FFPs, and they acknowledge that the expression "may contain" does not require a listing of LMOs of species other than those that constitute the shipment. The rules will be reviewed at MOP-7 in 2014.[26]

Considering that large agro-business and other economic interests, backed in most cases by their governments, did not want any agreement at all, the Cartagena Protocol is a historic achievement. For the first time under international law there is a requirement that countries take precautionary measures to prevent LMOs from causing harm to biodiversity and human health. Furthermore, at MOP-5 in 2010 a new phase in the international regulation of biotechnology began: one that focuses on cooperation in managing the risks associated with LMOs rather than on the struggle between those who see biotechnology as a solution for many of the world's pressing problems and those who oppose it because they consider the risks of LMOs greater than the benefits.[27] At the same time, however, to date only one member of the original veto coalition (Uruguay) has ratified the Cartagena Protocol, leaving many of the world's top grain exporters outside the regime, a situation that hinders the regime's effectiveness.

Access and Benefit Sharing

Genetic resources from plants, animals, and microorganisms are used for a variety of purposes ranging from basic research to consumer products to medicines. Those using genetic resources include research institutes, universities, and private companies operating in many different economic sectors, including pharmaceuticals, agriculture, horticulture, cosmetics, material science, and biotechnology. For example,

Calanolide A, a compound isolated from the latex of the tree *Calophyllum lanigerum var. auslrocoriaceum* found in the Malaysian rain forest, is used as a treatment for the human immunodeficiency virus type 1 (HIV-1).[28] An appetite suppressant has been derived from species of Hoodia, succulent plants indigenous to southern Africa and long used by the San people to stave off hunger and thirst.[29]

Since the convention's entry into force in 1993, developing countries have called for an increased focus on the convention's third official objective: fair and equitable sharing of benefits arising from the use of genetic resources.[30] This issue involves how foreign companies, collectors, researchers, and others gain access to valuable genetic resources in return for sharing the benefits of this access with the countries of origin and with local and indigenous communities. In 2004, the COP mandated the Working Group on Access and Benefit Sharing to elaborate an "international regime on access to genetic resources and benefit-sharing." In 2008, the COP agreed on a schedule of meetings to complete negotiations before its tenth meeting in 2010.[31]

Sharp divisions between the lead countries (the providers of genetic resources) and the veto coalition (user countries) plagued the access and benefit-sharing negotiations. Those arguing the position of provider countries, primarily the Like-Minded Group of Megadiverse Countries (see Box 4.2) and the African Group, claimed that the current distribution of benefits was unfair and sought to change it. Those regarded as user countries (i.e., those with industries that commercialize genetic resources)— mostly industrialized countries—were quite content with the status quo, in which access to genetic resources was arguably free.

After seven years of negotiations, parties adopted the Nagoya Protocol Access to Genetic Resources and the Fair and Equitable Sharing of Benefits Arising from Their Utilization in October 2010 in Nagoya, Japan. In a move that many criticized for its lack of transparency, the Japanese COP presidency convened a "secret" meeting of the African Group, Brazil, EU, and Norway in order to produce a draft to be considered by ministers. This enraged many delegations, in particular the Like-Minded Asia-Pacific and Latin American and Caribbean group members who felt excluded from this key meeting. Others, however, believed that the Japanese-brokered meetings— for better or worse—had produced an agreement that would have otherwise been impossible, as negotiations had ground to a halt.[32]

The final compromise text was characterized by many as a "masterpiece in creative ambiguity." Instead of resolving outstanding issues by crafting balanced compromise proposals—an endeavor that would have failed—the most contentious references were either deleted from the text or replaced by short and general provisions that allowed for flexible interpretation (but possibly also too wide a berth for implementation).[33]

Particularly contentious issues included the following:

- whether the scope of the protocol would extend beyond genetic resources to biological resources more generally;
- how the holders of traditional knowledge related to genetic resources would be involved in procedures of access to such knowledge;
- how far countries will cooperate with one another when there are allegations of illegal uses;[34] and
- whether the scope of the protocol would extend to genetic resources acquired prior to the protocol's entry into force.

BOX 4.2   MEGADIVERSE COUNTRIES

The Like-Minded Group of Megadiverse Countries (LMMC) formed in 2002 as a consultation and cooperation mechanism to promote common interests and priorities related to the conservation and sustainable use of biological diversity. The megadiverse countries are primarily tropical countries that possess rich varieties of animal and plant species, habitats, and ecosystems. Up to 70 percent of the world's biological diversity is located in the megadiverse countries, which include Bolivia, Brazil, China, Colombia, Costa Rica, Democratic Republic of Congo, Ecuador, India, Indonesia, Kenya, Madagascar, Malaysia, Mexico, Peru, Philippines, South Africa, and Venezuela.

On the first point, some developed countries had insisted that derivatives of genetic resources be excluded from the protocol and instead negotiated in bilateral contracts. Developing countries, on the other hand, tried to ensure that derivatives, such as naturally occurring biochemicals, were included.[35] The final text states that the protocol shall apply to "genetic resources" and to the "benefits arising from the utilization of such resources,"[36] which includes research and development on the genetic and/or biochemical composition of genetic material. Research on the properties of extracts and molecules from plants, for example, and their development and commercialization as ingredients in pharmaceuticals or cosmetics will now have to meet access and benefit-sharing requirements.

With respect to the treatment of traditional knowledge, some developed countries had argued that traditional knowledge relating to genetic resources should be addressed by the World Intellectual Property Organization. However, others argued that leaving out traditional knowledge made little sense, as it is often used alongside genetic resources, and doing so would significantly reduce the benefits for developing countries and local communities.[37] The protocol states that its rules apply to "traditional knowledge associated with genetic resources within the scope of the Convention and to the benefits arising from the utilization of such knowledge."[38]

On international cooperation, developed countries had argued that the protocol should focus on compliance with national legislation instead of creating international regulations. However, since only about twenty-five developing countries have legislation on access and benefit sharing in place, it was argued that such a requirement would further weaken the effectiveness of the protocol.[39] The final text encourages transboundary cooperation and provides that each party shall take "appropriate, effective and proportionate legislative, administrative or policy measures" to provide that genetic resources and traditional knowledge used within their jurisdiction have been accessed in accordance with "prior informed consent and that mutually agreed terms have been established."[40]

To resolve the question of sharing benefits from new and continuing uses of genetic resources acquired prior to the entry into force of the protocol—one of the key demands of the African Group—delegates also resorted to creative ambiguity. While there is no direct reference to this issue, a provision envisages creation of a global multilateral benefit-sharing mechanism to address benefit sharing in transboundary situations or situations in which it is not possible to grant or obtain prior informed consent. Such a mechanism, once established, could cover benefits arising from genetic resources acquired outside the framework of the CBD.[41]

In the end, the main strength of the Nagoya Protocol is also its weakness: the creative ambiguities could lead to differing interpretations at the national level, create legal uncertainties, and hinder implementation. Depending on how these issues are addressed, the protocol may or may not become a powerful tool for a more balanced implementation of the CBD's three objectives.[42]

Moving Forward

Although parties have made progress on important issues, the biodiversity regime remains surprisingly weak. The complexity of the biodiversity crisis, the multiple levels at which it can be addressed (e.g., ecosystem, species, genes), the North-South contrasts in the distribution of biodiversity resources, and the many ways that biodiversity protection can conflict with important economic, social, and political interests make reaching agreement on action-forcing language a contentious and intractable process. Numerous work programs, working groups, and subsidiary bodies have served to increase the number of meetings each year and decrease parties' focus on strengthening and implementing the convention.

A few steps were taken at COP-10 and COP-11 to address these and other issues. Parties adopted a new Strategic Plan for Biodiversity 2011–2020.[43] The plan serves as the framework for revising, updating, and implementing National Biodiversity Strategies and Action Plans, which are the key national-level implementation plans.[44] The plan also tasks the COP to consider developing additional mechanisms, or possibly strengthening the Subsidiary Body on Science, Technical, and Technological Advice, to facilitate compliance with the convention.

Effective strengthening of the biodiversity regime will depend, in part, on greater commitments by states with significant economic, political, or biodiversity resources. Some European states have been active in trying to strengthen the regime, but without greater clout—and the support of developing countries as well as the United States, which remains a nonparty to the regime—the convention could remain unfocused and ineffective.

WHALING

The history of global policy to safeguard whales illustrates the transformation of an international regime from one that allowed virtually unregulated exploitation into a framework for global conservation, despite resistance from a strong veto coalition. Despite this transformation, however, the international whaling regime has been at a crossroads for more than a quarter of a century. The balance of power in the regime's decision-making body, the International Whaling Commission (IWC), rests narrowly with the states favoring a whaling ban. The veto coalition, empowered by its ability to exit the regime at any time, remains strong. Although advances in population monitoring offer the prospect of developing a biologically sound management system, desires to uphold national sovereignty and strong emotions on both sides of the issue endanger the regime.

Emotions and concerns for national sovereignty influence the global debate on whaling far more than detailed scientific analysis or national economic interests (whaling no longer represents a significant economic enterprise on a global or even national basis). For some governments and many environmental NGOs, whaling is seen as both an act of unnecessary human cruelty to an intelligent species and a powerful symbol of environmental overexploitation. To whaling states, harvesting whales represents the right to preserve cultural traditions, maintain coastal livelihoods, and exercise national sovereignty. Humans have hunted whales for thousands of years. Increases in technology and the size of the whaling fleets, particularly in the nineteenth and twentieth century, reduced whale populations significantly. In 1946, whaling nations established the International Convention for the Regulation of Whaling. The convention prohibited killing certain endangered whale species, set quotas and minimum sizes for whales caught commercially, and regulated whaling seasons. The convention was not, however, an environmental regime but a club of whaling nations designed to manage the catch. The regime's designated decision-making body, the IWC, met in secret each year to haggle over quotas set so high that far more whales were being killed annually under the new regime than before the regulations had gone into effect. Indeed, the total number of whales killed more than doubled between 1951 and 1962. The IWC also had no power to enforce its regulations on the size of catch or even its ban on killing endangered species. Although the major whaling nations were members of the IWC, many developing countries, including Brazil, Chile, China, Ecuador, Peru, and South Korea, had refused to join or abide by its restrictions. Some allowed "pirate" whalers, often financed by sales to Japan, to operate freely.

The process of fact finding and consensus building played virtually no role in relations among IWC members. Scientific knowledge was usually subordinated to political and economic interests. The IWC's scientific committee routinely produced data and analyses supporting continued commercial exploitation, and no outside international organization existed that could facilitate a different framework for decisions based on the scientific facts on whaling. Given this situation, it is not surprising that by the 1960s the survival of the largest species, the blue whale, was in doubt; finback stocks were dwindling; and many other species were experiencing population declines, as whalers filled their quotas with younger and smaller whales.

Increasing public awareness of the diminishing stocks, including the potential extinction of blue whales, coincided with the emerging environmental movement to turn the tide against commercial whaling. The plight of the whales seized the imagination of many Americans, who were beginning to learn more about the intelligence of cetaceans, and the new awareness led to broad popular support for meaningful protection. Responding to the 1969 Endangered Species Act, the United States declared eight whale species endangered in 1970 and began to take the lead in defining the whaling issue internationally.[45]

Placing the issue of whaling in the context of the broader international environmental agenda, the United States first proposed an immediate moratorium on commercial whaling at the 1972 United Nations Conference on the Human Environment. Adopted by fifty-two of the countries attending the conference, the proposal signaled strong international support for a moratorium. However, because it had not been generated through the IWC, it carried no force within the whaling regime itself. In the IWC, the whaling states (Chile, Iceland, Japan, Norway, Peru, and the Soviet Union) not only constituted a powerful veto coalition (that could even choose to leave the regime if they wished) but also held a near majority. A proposal for a whaling moratorium was defeated in the IWC by a vote of six to four, with four abstentions.

Seeing the need to change the whaling regime itself, the United States, Sweden, and other lead states took advantage of the fact that the IWC does not limit membership to whaling nations and sought to overwhelm the veto coalition by recruiting nonwhaling states into the commission. Thus, rather than trying to transform the regime by building consensus within the IWC, lead states simply sought to assemble the three-fourths majority required to institute a whaling ban. To this end, between 1979 and 1982, the antiwhaling coalition recruited the Seychelles and a number of other developing states, most of which viewed the whaling issue from the perspective that the oceans and their natural resources are the common heritage of humankind.[46]

The United States also sought to weaken the veto coalition by threatening economic sanctions. It used domestic legislation to ban imports of fish products and to deny fishing permits within the United States' two-hundred-mile exclusive economic zone to countries that violated international whale-conservation programs. This action put pressure on Chile and Peru, both heavily dependent on US fishing permits and markets, to comply with the conservation programs.

By 1982, enough developing-country nonwhaling nations had joined the IWC to tilt the balance decisively. A five-year moratorium on all commercial whaling, to take effect in 1985, was passed twenty-five to seven, with five abstentions. Four of the veto-coalition states (Japan, Norway, Peru, and the Soviet Union), which accounted for 75 percent of whaling and almost all consumption of whale meat and other whale products, filed formal reservations to the moratorium but chose not to defy it openly when it went into effect.

Japan, Norway, and the Soviet Union ended their commercial whaling by the 1987–1988 whaling season. Soon after, however, Japan, Iceland, and Norway unilaterally began the practice of what they called "scientific" whaling, which is permitted under the IWC. Most IWC members found no scientific merit in this whaling, which is conducted by commercial ships, because it kills hundreds of minke whales annually. However, other economic and political interests weakened the ability of the United States and other countries to pressure whaling states to end this practice. For example, to avoid a probable Japanese retaliation targeting US fish exports, the United States decided not to ban imports of $1 billion in Japanese seafood annually as retaliation for Japan's whaling, instead choosing the lesser sanction of denying the Japanese permission to fish in US waters.

Although the adoption of "scientific" whaling programs allowed some whaling to continue, veto states had their sights set on the larger target of repealing the whaling moratorium. At the 1990 IWC meeting, after the United States had led a majority of IWC members in blocking a proposal to allow limited commercial whaling in the Atlantic, and instead extended the moratorium for another year, Iceland, Japan, and Norway threatened to leave the IWC if the moratorium was not overturned at the next meeting. When the IWC voted to retain the moratorium in 1992, Iceland followed through with the threat, leaving the IWC, only to return in 2002.

In 1993 Japan and Norway prepared another attempt to end the whaling ban. In advance of the IWC meeting, both governments spent large amounts of money and effort in nonwhaling countries to promote the position that minke whales were no longer endangered and that whaling villages, severely impoverished by the moratorium, were being denied the right to pursue a cultural tradition.[47] In addition, Japan induced six Caribbean IWC members to support its position by providing funds for new fishing vessels and paying their annual IWC membership fees.[48] Yet, despite these efforts, the IWC again voted to extend the whaling moratorium for another year.

Over the objections of the veto states, the IWC strengthened the regime in 1994 by adopting a no-catch area (even for scientific whaling) for all whales inhabiting waters below 40 degrees South latitude. The action created the Southern Ocean Whale Sanctuary, an Antarctic whale sanctuary that could protect up to 90 percent of the estimated 3.5 million remaining great whales. It is reviewed and open to change every ten years; changes require a 75 percent majority. The whaling nation most affected by the vote was Japan, which was taking three hundred minkes from the Antarctic annually, ostensibly for scientific purposes. However, Japan and Norway continued to defy both the whaling moratorium and the provisions for a no-catch area.[49]

Adopting the whaling moratorium and creating a no-catch area suggests a strong regime for the protection for whales. While certainly reducing the number of whales killed each year, the impact of the regime has been severely weakened by outright defiance of the whaling moratorium, incursions into the whale sanctuaries (in both the Southern and the Indian oceans), and the use of loopholes such as scientific whaling—all by nations that have strong environmental records on many other issues. Norway registered a formal reservation to the moratorium at the time of its passage, stating that this allowed it to ignore the ban. Despite significant international pressure, Norway has conducted commercial whaling outside the control of the IWC throughout the moratorium, capturing approximately two hundred to seven hundred whales each year between 1993 and 2011.[50] Iceland also registered a reservation and later dropped out of the IWC. As a conservation measure, Iceland set its own limits but significantly increased its self-targeted quotas in 2009, catching 193 whales since 2006.[51] Japan has conducted its whaling operations mostly under the banner of scientific whaling, with 13,920 whales captured since 1987, although the number of whales has decreased in recent years, largely a result of weather conditions and sabotage acts by NGO activists like Sea Shepherd Conservation Society[52] (see Figure 4.1). Japan defends its whaling by pointing to the large amount of scientific data it has generated. Some of these data, including stomach contents and reliable estimates of age, cannot be collected without taking whales. Nevertheless, many scientists contend that although the data are collected using a high degree of scientific rigor, the resulting information does not provide new and important information relevant to the management of stocks but instead largely supports previous knowledge.[53]

The fact that certain actors effectively ignore the regime has raised concern about the future of the IWC. The deep and "seemingly irreconcilable philosophical and political divisions" between the veto coalition and the lead states have led many to refer to the IWC as a dysfunctional regime.[54]

The lead states include Australia, New Zealand, the United States, twenty-six EU member countries,[55] and the so-called Buenos Aires group of thirteen countries from Central and South America. This coalition opposes the resumption of any commercial whaling and supports sanctuaries that also prohibit scientific whaling. Their position is that the convention needs "modernization" to, among other things, remove the article that allows members to unilaterally issue special permits to kill whales for research purposes.[56]

The key veto states are Iceland, Japan, and Norway, but their coalition has grown steadily since the 1990s. This expansion was engineered largely by Japan, which has engaged in what opponents label "vote buying"—that is, building support for its position on whaling through foreign aid and paying IWC membership fees for small-nation coalition members. The head of Japan's Fisheries Agency confirmed this practice, but government officials subsequently denied it.[57] The veto coalition asserts that whales should be managed just like other marine living resources and that opposition to whaling is contrary to the convention, since its purpose is to "provide for the proper conservation of whale stocks and thus make possible the orderly development of the whaling industry."[58] They believe that the moratorium and the establishment of the Southern Ocean Whale Sanctuary were adopted without a recommendation from the IWC's Scientific Committee that such measures were required for conservation

FIGURE 4.1   Scientific Whaling Catches, 1986–2012

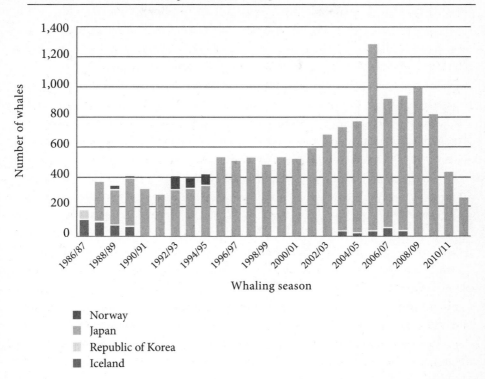

Note: In 1987–1988, Iceland had a scientific permit, and Japan and Norway caught whales in objection to the moratorium. Beginning in 1993–1994, Japan did all of the scientific whaling, and Norway continued to catch whales in objection to the moratorium (only its "scientific" whaling figures are included here). Iceland did not kill any whales from 1989 to 2003 but resumed whaling from 2003 to 2007, after rejoining the IWC in 2002.

Sources: International Whaling Commission, "Special Permit Catches Since 1985," accessed December 29, 2012, iwcoffice.org/table_permit, and "Japan Ends Whale Hunt with Less than a Third of Its Target Catch," *Telegraph* (London), March 9, 2012.

purposes. These positions were set out in a resolution, called the St. Kitts and Nevis Declaration, adopted by a vote of thirty-three in favor, thirty-two against, with one abstention, at its annual meeting in June 2006.[59]

In 2006 American William Hogarth, a fisheries biologist, took over as IWC chair for a three-year term. Determined to focus his efforts on the future of the IWC, Hogarth, like many others, recognized that for almost a quarter of a century the polarized views on whales and whaling had dominated discussions to the detriment of the effectiveness of the organization. At Hogarth's initiative the IWC convened an intersessional meeting in London in March 2008 to discuss the future of the IWC and to explore approaches to overcome this conflict. Three internationally recognized experts in the handling of challenging international issues, Special Adviser Calestous Juma, Ambassador Alvaro de Soto, and Ambassador Raul Estrada-Oyuela, were selected to offer guidance in the use of the consensus approach to conflict resolution.[60]

The results of the March 2008 meeting were presented to the IWC in Chile in June 2008 at its sixtieth meeting. Delegates agreed to set up a small working group on the future of the IWC to meet intersessionally. The task of the working group, which was chaired by Ambassador de Soto, was to "assist the Commission to arrive at a consensus solution to the main issues it faces, to enable it to best fulfill its role with respect to the conservation of whale stocks and the management of whaling."[61] The group met four times between December 2008 and March 2010. The result, a Proposed Consensus Decision to Improve the Conservation of Whales, was presented at the sixty-second meeting of the IWC, held in Agadir, Morocco, in June 2010.[62] After two days of private negotiations, delegates were unable to reach consensus on the question of the moratorium, the number of whales that might be taken, special-permit whaling, indigenous whaling, sanctuaries, and trade. Japan said the key stumbling block for them was the demand from the EU and the Buenos Aires group of Latin American countries that its Antarctic whaling program must end within a set time frame. For Japan, agreeing to reduce its quota from 935 in 2010 to 200 in ten years' time represented a significant step forward, which its representative thought ought to have been acceptable to its opponents.[63]

As discussions were suspended, the delegate from Japan noted that while many IWC members emphasized the importance of conservation and management based on science, public opinion against whaling was not based on science. In Japan's view, the two divergent positions on whaling should be mutually acceptable, and IWC members must be willing to accept that two strong views exist in order to avoid a continued impasse and restore the IWC.[64]

After a year's "period of pause and reflection" on the future of the IWC, the sixty-third meeting convened in June 2011. The United States and New Zealand submitted a proposed Resolution to Maintain Progress at the IWC.[65] Rather than getting into another prolonged debate, they hoped that governments would support the "notion that the Commission continue to try and encourage a dialogue and to build trust and consensus so that it could make progress and help the organization to evolve." So rather than having a lengthy debate on the resolution, its text was included in the report of the chair. In doing so, the commission "acknowledged that very different views exist among the members regarding whales and whaling and that this difference had come to dominate the time and resources of the Commission at the expense of effective whale conservation and management." To maintain progress, delegates agreed to fur-

PHOTO 4.2   The Sea Shepherd Conservation Society and other NGOs protested outside the IWC meeting in Jersey in 2011.
Courtesy Robert Read, Sea Shepherd UK.

ther dialogue, trust building, and cooperation, "notwithstanding their different views regarding the conservation of whales and the management of whaling."[66]

At its 2012 meeting, the IWC made little substantial progress on its future prospects. However, the mood was much improved over previous years, and votes were taken without grandstanding and walkouts. Many observers called it the most functional IWC meeting in years.[67] The commission adopted amendments permitting aboriginal subsistence whaling in the Bering-Chuckchi-Beaufort Seas, in the North Pacific, and off St. Vincent and the Grenadines. The commission rejected an amendment for Greenland hunts, after concern that too much of the whale meat from such hunts has been sold commercially in Europe. The commission also decided that it would no longer meet annually and instead hold meetings every two years, in an effort to make the commission more functional and efficient. Delegates concluded by selecting their first ever female chair, St. Lucia's Jeannine Compton-Antoine.[68]

Over the years, the IWC has evolved from a "whalers' club," which created quotas based on the power of the competing economic interests of whaling nations, into an international body divided into whaling and antiwhaling states in which "reliance on arguments grounded in moral beliefs have decreased the . . . whaling states' commitment to the process of collective decision making."[69] This shift in discourse has been driven by strong emotions. Both groups feel entirely justified in refusing to compromise for fear of an outcome undesirable to "their" side.[70] Pro-whaling countries fear losing their sovereign right to take ocean resources in international waters outside territorial limits. There is concern that the moratorium on whaling is the first step down a slippery slope whereby other depleted fish stocks will become off-limits. On the other hand, antiwhalers fear that any exception to the moratorium will degenerate into an open season on whales. For antiwhaling nations and NGOs, whaling is emblematic of the short-sighted degradation of the planet. They argue that whaling is inexcusably cruel and endangers an already scarce species, compounding the threats whales face from global warming, noise and chemical pollution, physical strikes by ships, and net entanglements.[71]

Coalition building on both sides has been characterized more by political maneuvering than by a process that values fact finding and consensus building. Science appears to have played a marginal role in decision making, with its credibility diminished by the practice of commercial whaling being carried out under the banner of scientific whaling. However, recent advances in the ability to monitor whale populations and a less contentious mood at the 2012 IWC meeting may help to break this deadlock.

INTERNATIONAL TRADE IN ENDANGERED SPECIES

The regime governing trade in endangered species centers on the Convention on International Trade in Endangered Species of Wild Fauna and Flora, commonly known as CITES. The treaty combats overexploitation of wild animals and plants by delineating threatened species, establishing rules regarding their trade, and imposing trade sanctions against violators.[72]

CITES is really an umbrella regime containing a multitude of smaller "regimes within regimes" that address specific species. Under this umbrella, proponent and veto coalitions vary across the specific agreements on individual species (or groups of species) and often cross traditional North-South divisions.[73] In contrast to the broader biodiversity regime, CITES focuses on a single cause of species loss (trade) and contains generally clearer, stronger, and more straightforward protection targets and corresponding regulations.

Adopted in 1973, CITES currently protects roughly 5,000 species of animals and 29,000 species of plants. There are currently 178 parties to the convention. A COP meets every two to three years to decide how to regulate trade in species in different degrees of danger. CITES divides threatened species into three categories, with various levels of controls for each category. Species listed in Appendix I are threatened with extinction and are not to be traded except for scientific or cultural endeavors. Species listed in Appendix II, while not yet endangered, are considered to be affected by international trade that, if left unregulated, would endanger them. Before a country can allow exports of an Appendix II species, a scientific authority must determine that the proposed export will not be detrimental to the survival of the species. The decision to list a particular species in Appendix I or II requires a vote by the parties. Species listed in Appendix III are listed voluntarily by range states (states within which the species live) seeking cooperation in the control of international trade, and they do not require a vote. As of 2012, Appendix I lists more than 900 species; Appendix II, over 33,000; and Appendix III, more than 250.[74]

In the negotiations that created CITES, countries expressed strong support for the overall goal of protecting endangered species. Nations where the traded species live also supported (and continue to support) CITES because it helps protect their valuable wildlife resources from poachers and illegal traders. Importing countries supported (and continue to support) the regime because it protected the interests of their legitimate dealers. Differences arose, however, concerning how to list specific species that would be restricted from trade. Many countries wanted a system that would require all parties to protect a species if a majority voted to list it. Others insisted on a system that would protect both economic interests and the principle of sovereign control.

In the end, a potential veto coalition forced the convention's strongest proponents to allow a party to enter a reservation to (i.e., opt out of) the listing of a species as controlled or banned if the party claimed an overriding economic interest in continuing to exploit it. Such a reservation makes that party, in effect, a nonparty with regard to that particular species. Listing decisions are made on a two-thirds supermajority voting system, so member states' option to enter a reservation to a specific Appendix I or II listing constrains negotiations. In certain circumstances, this can give some states de facto veto power over a listing. If one or a few states control the great majority of trade in a species, they can essentially veto the effectiveness of a listing by entering a reservation to it. However, it takes two countries (an exporter and an importer) to overcome a CITES listing, and in cases where reservations exist by range states, it is not unusual for importing countries to pass national laws that are stricter than CITES in an effort to prevent loopholes. The effects of the so-called veto power are, however, more evident when dealing with marine species: in that case species are introduced directly from the sea, and the two-party relationship does not take place.

All member parties are required to adopt national legislation that corresponds to the species listings of CITES. They have to designate two authorities on a domestic level: a management authority and a scientific authority. The scientific authority advises the management authority, which is in charge of issuing permits and certificates, in keeping with the CITES appendices. These authorities work in correlation with customs offices, police departments, and other appropriate agencies to record species trading and report to CITES. Thus, the operation and enforcement of CITES can be compromised when national and local officials do not, or cannot, enforce it.

CITES has three main operational bodies: the Standing Committee, the Animals Committee, and the Plants Committee. The Standing Committee oversees and helps to coordinate the workings of other bodies with policy guidance and budget management. The Animals and Plants Committees work between COPs and report to the COP about their respective mandates. The main implementation tool used by these bodies to monitor CITES's effectiveness is a review of significant trade (RST), a process whereby the bodies evaluate trade data pertaining to specific species, delving deeper if they notice anything out of place. However, CITES's capacity to actually reduce illegal trade using this process is minimal. The RST relies on data reported by countries through government agencies; these statistics include information only on legal trading. Since one of the major causes of species loss is illegal trading, these statistics do not reflect, or have much of an effect on, the illegal movement of species and their derivatives.

The more than 29,000 plant species protected under CITES's three appendices comprise 85 percent of all the species covered by the treaty. The collection of certain rare or commercially desirable plant species poses a major threat to their survival in the wild. Examples include trees that produce high-quality timber (e.g., big leaf mahogany, Brazilian rosewood), herbs for medicinal use (e.g., American ginseng, goldenseal), and unusual, exotic ornamental species, such as orchids, cacti, and cycads. For example, Brazilian rosewood produces a highly prized wood. Its red-brown timber is attractive, heavy, and strong, as well as highly resistant to insect attack and decay. Of more importance, however, is its high resonance—ideal for the production of musical instruments (see Box 4.3). The tree is also harvested for the construction of high-quality furniture and for its oils and resins. Brazilian rosewood was listed on CITES Appendix I in 1992, making trade in its timber illegal. Nevertheless, deforestation in its native habitat and illegal logging continued, and mature trees with thick trunks are now very rare.[75]

Another example is the African cherry (*Prunus Africana*), which is found in mountainous tropical forests in central and southern Africa and Madagascar. For centuries it has been harvested for its hard and durable timber as well as for its bark, which has medicinal properties and is used to treat malaria, fevers, kidney disease, urinary tract infections, and more recently prostate enlargement. As long as all the bark is not removed, the tree can bear repeated harvests and has been used sustainably for hundreds of years. Indigenous knowledge maintained that, postharvest, bark grows back more quickly on the side of the tree that faces the sunrise, and it was also believed that medicine made from this east-facing bark would heal a patient faster. Thus, traditionally,

BOX 4.3 GUITARS, CITES, AND THE LACEY ACT

Each party to CITES must pass domestic laws that implement the treaty. In the United States, Congress has passed a number of laws, including the Endangered Species Act, the Marine Mammal Protection Act, and the Wild Bird Conservation Act, which are administered by the US Fish and Wildlife Service, part of the Department of the Interior. Most relevant to CITES is the Lacey Act. Under the Lacey Act, it is unlawful to import or export fish, wildlife, or plants that are taken in violation of state or foreign law, including all species protected by CITES. In 2008, Congress amended the Lacey Act to include a wider variety of prohibited plants and plant products, including illegally logged woods.

Madagascar ebony is a slow-growing tree species that is considered threatened in its native environment as a result of overexploitation. Both legal and illegal logging of Madagascar ebony and other tree species have significantly reduced Madagascar's forest cover, home to many rare species of plants and animals. The harvest and export of ebony from Madagascar has been banned since 2006.

On November 17, 2009, US federal agents raided the Gibson Guitar Corporation's manufacturing facility in Nashville, Tennessee, as part of an investigation into the illegal trade of ebony from Madagascar. Gibson is one of the largest guitar manufacturers in the world. Among its iconic instruments are the Les Paul electric guitar, John Lennon's acoustic-electric dreadnought, banjos, mandolins, and even pianos under the Baldwin name. Gibson purchased "fingerboard blanks," consisting of sawn boards of Madagascar ebony from an exporter who did not have authority to export Madagascar ebony.

Two years later, on August 24, 2011, agents raided Gibson again, seizing pallets of ebony and rosewood fingerboards imported from India. Gibson's Nashville facility produces hundreds of guitars a day, and rosewood and ebony fingerboards, mostly imported from India, are essential components.

In August 2012, Gibson agreed to pay a $300,000 fine and donate $50,000 to the National Fish and Wildlife Foundation to promote the protection of endangered hardwood trees to settle the charges that it had illegally imported Madagascar ebony. In return, the government deferred prosecution for criminal violations of the Lacey Act. "Gibson has acknowledged that it failed to act on information that the Madagascar ebony it was purchasing may have violated laws intended to limit over-harvesting and conserve valuable wood species from Madagascar, a country which has been severely impacted by deforestation," said Ignacia S. Moreno, an assistant attorney general.

Sources: James McKinley Jr., "Famed Guitar Maker Raided by Federal Agents," *New York Times,* August 31, 2011; "Gibson Guitar to Pay $300,000 for Violating Lacey Act with Illegal Timber Imports from Madagascar," Mongabay.com, August 6, 2012; James McKinley Jr. "Gibson Guitar Settles Claim over Imported Ebony," *New York Times,* August 6, 2012.

only one side of the tree was stripped, yielding about 55 kilograms (121 pounds) of bark. But when completely stripped, a large tree may yield up to a metric ton of bark—worth considerably more on the international market. Harvest limits and protective folklore have therefore given way to market demand, and the African cherry appears to be in steep decline, despite its inclusion in CITES Appendix II.[76]

Despite CITES the illegal wildlife trade is also growing and estimated to be worth at least $5 billion and potentially in excess of $20 billion annually. Some of the most lucrative illicit wildlife commodities include tiger parts, elephant ivory, rhino horn, and exotic birds and reptiles. Demand for illegal wildlife is ubiquitous and growing[77] (see Table 4.1). Illicit wildlife trade uses complex distribution networks that connect source states and producers of wildlife products to customers in other states.[78] Illicit wildlife trade networks can involve a combination of any of the following: (1) village hunters, who trade small wildlife as a source of subsistence cash income or kill some wildlife to protect people and crops from attacks; (2) wildlife experts; (3) criminal entities, sometimes including terrorists, rebels, and drug traffickers, who are able to evade detection and transport and secure the products as well as launder the proceeds; (4) legitimate businesses serving as a front for the trade; (5) corrupt government officials to facilitate import and export; and (6) consumers willing to pay for the contraband.[79] Traffickers are connected globally to certain suppliers of exotic animals in developing countries, consumers at upscale art galleries, safari operators guiding hunters to illegal animal trophies, and international and interstate networks of wildlife exporters, taxidermists, and wildlife retailers.[80]

The Internet has contributed to the growth of the illegal wildlife trade, providing an unprecedented technological platform for a burgeoning, undocumented trade in endangered animals, alive and dead[81] (see Box 4.4). The ability to scan the globe for buyers or sellers without leaving one's office, to mask one's identity with increasingly sophisticated technology and software, and to buy and sell online, without ever having to meet even a middle man, are just three aspects of Internet-based endangered-species crime that challenge the abilities of national and international law enforcement officials. In addition, many national laws aimed at regulating wildlife trade to ecologically sustainable levels do not yet address aspects of illicit Internet sales, and some countries have few laws governing Internet commerce at all. Even where laws exist, enforcement is often inadequate because officials do not have the capacity to address Internet crime or because they are not focused on online trafficking in wildlife. One such case is the African elephant.

African Elephants

The case of African elephants illustrates CITES's efforts to curb species loss and exemplifies the difficulties inherent in negotiations between numerous parties.

TABLE 4.1   Selected Illicit Wildlife Trade and Estimated Retail Value

Elephants	$1,800 per kilogram of ivory[a]
Rhinos	$97,000 per kilogram of rhino horn[b]
Snakes	$235,175 per liter of snake venom[c]
Big Cats	$1,300–$35,000 per tiger or snow leopard skin[d]; up to $70,000 for tiger remains[e]
Bears	$200,000 per pound of bear bile[f]
Sharks	$400 per pound of shark fin[g]
Reptiles (often live)	$10,600 per iguana[h]; $4,400 per Komodo dragon[i]; $4000 per ploughshare tortoise[j]; $10,000 per tortoise from Madagascar[k]; $20,000 per golden coin turtle[l]
Fish	$200,000 per Asian arowana fish (dragon fish)[m]
Great Apes (often live)	$40,000 per baby gorilla[n]; $45,000 per orangutan[o]
Birds	$31,000 per black cockatoo[p]

Source: For this and other information, see Havocscope, "Endangered Animals and Wildlife Prices," accessed August 9, 2012, www.havocscope.com/black-market-prices/animals-wildlife/.

[a] "Asian Ivory Trade Poses Danger to African Elephant," ABC News, May 15, 2010.

[b] Esther Addley, "Epidemic of UK Rhino Horn Thefts Linked to One Criminal Gang," *Guardian* (London), August 8, 2011.

[c] P. Vijian, "Smugglers Deliver Deadly Bite into Snake Population," *Bernama* (Kuala Lumpur), August 27, 2011.

[d] Bryan Walsh, "How U.S. Soldiers Are Fueling the Endangered Species Trade," *Ecocentric Blog, Time*, February 27, 2012; Bhalin Singh, "Plight of the Bengal: India Awakens to the Reality of Its Tigers—and Their Fate," Mongabay.com, June 6, 2010.

[e] Rhett Butler, "Laos Emerges as Key Source in Asia's Illicit Wildlife Trade," *Yale Environment 360*, February 26, 2009.

[f] Victoria Kim, "Woman Staying in Los Angeles Accused in Bear Bile Importation," *Los Angeles Times*, March 28, 2009.

[g] John Berman and Sarah Rosenberg, "'Sharkwater': Turning the Page on 'Jaws,'" ABC News Nightline, October 26, 2007.

[h] "Man 'Steals Iguanas in Fake Leg," BBC News, September 22, 2007.

"Komodo Dragon Costs Rp 40 M on Black Market," *Jakarta Post*, March 23, 2011.

[j] David Adam, "Monkeys, Butterflies, Turtles . . . : How the Pet Trade's Greed Is Emptying South-East Asia's Forests," *Observer* (London), February 21, 2010.

[k] Hannah McNeish, "Madagascar's 'Tortoise Mafia' on the Attack," BBC News, June 27, 2011.

[l] Fergus O'Sullivan, "Threatened Species on the Menu Worldwide," *National* (Abu-Dhabi), July 17, 2011.

[m] "7 Charged in LA with Smuggling Endangered Fish," *Houston Chronicle*, May 11, 2010.

[n] Miguel Llanos, "Baby Gorilla on Black Market for $40,000 Is Rescued," MSNBC, October 11, 2011.

[o] Diana Wright, "Domestic Black Market for Endangered Wildlife Thrives in Indonesia," Mongabay.com, September 18, 2005.

[p] Carolyn Barry, "Australia's Wildlife Blackmarket Trade," *Australian Geographic*, August 16, 2011.

BOX 4.4   ENDANGERED SPECIES ONLINE

The International Fund for Animal Welfare (IFAW) conducted four investigations into potentially illegal trade in endangered species on the Internet from 2004 to 2008. The most recent investigation spanned three months in 2008 and involved investigations into 183 publicly accessible websites in eleven countries, looking at both wildlife products and live animal trade in primates, birds, reptiles, big cats, bears, elephants, rhinoceros, sharks, Tibetan antelopes, and sturgeon.

IFAW investigators tracked 7,122 online auctions, advertisements, and communiqués offering trade in wildlife listed in CITES Appendix I and offered for sale both domestically and internationally, as well as a notable number of species listed in Appendix II. The combined price for the advertised wildlife was approximately $3.8 million, and nearly $450,000 in sales took place. Actual figures are probably much higher, as many sites do not provide the means for tracking final sales.

Ivory represented more than 73 percent of the activity monitored, and 83 percent of the ivory items found worldwide in the investigation were for sale on eBay sites. Following the report, eBay instituted a global ban on ivory sales on all its websites. IFAW's ongoing work with other major online marketplaces has resulted in Alibaba.com, the world's largest online business-to-business trading platform for small businesses, and the German sites markt.de and hood.de implementing a ban on all ivory products. Kleinanzeigen.ebay.de, a subsidiary of eBay, has also agreed to implement a ban on living specimens listed on CITES Appendix I.

eBay Numbers (US)

Total Ivory Items Tracked	3,667
Total Ivory Final Sales Recorded	1,847 (50.37%)
Dollar Value of Recorded Ivory Transactions	$369,885.39
Estimated Annual Ivory Commerce	$3.2 million
Estimated Ivory Listing Fees	$3,278
Estimated Commission on Ivory Sales	$11,445.87
Estimated eBay Ivory Profit per Year	$127,606.87

Results of the IFAW Investigation
(includes websites in the United States, United Kingdom, China, France, Canada, Germany, Russia, and Australia)

Number of Websites Tracked	126
Number of Ads	7,122
Number of Ads for Elephant Products	5,223
Number of Ads for Exotic Birds	1,416
Percentage of Total US Ads	70%
Advertised Monetary Value of All Ads	$3,871,201.45
Value of Final Sales Recorded	$457,341.68

Sources: International Fund for Animal Welfare, *Killing with Keystrokes: An Investigation of the Illegal Wildlife Trade on the World Wide Web* (Yarmouth Port: MA: IFAW, 2008), www.ifaw.org/sites/default /files/Killing%20with%20Keystrokes.pdf; and International Fund for Animal Welfare, *Killing with Keystrokes 2.0: IFAW's Investigation into the European Online Ivory Trade* (Yarmouth Port, MA: IFAW, 2011), www.ifaw.org/sites/default/files/FINAL%20Killing%20with%20Keystrokes%202.0%20 report%202011.pdf.

The fact-finding stage led to the African elephant's listing under CITES Appendix II in 1977. Beginning in the early 1980s, African elephant populations began to decline precipitously, falling from 1.3 million in 1979 to 625,000 in 1989.[82] In 1985, CITES established a system of ivory export quotas in the countries with elephant herds. Declines continued, however, and a study sponsored by WWF and Conservation International concluded that African elephants were being harvested at a rate far exceeding that considered sustainable. This rate of loss, driven primarily by the international trade in ivory, led to increasing calls to place African elephants in Appendix I of CITES and establish a worldwide ban on trade in African elephant ivory.

The bargaining stage began at the seventh CITES COP in October 1989, when an odd international coalition consisting of Austria, Gambia, Hungary, Kenya, Somalia, Tanzania, and the United States initiated an effort to list the African elephant in Appendix I and ban trade in ivory products entirely. Another unlikely coalition, uniting foes in southern Africa's struggle over apartheid (Botswana, Malawi, Mozambique, South Africa, Zambia, and Zimbabwe), opposed the listing. Underlying their resistance was the fact that several southern African herds had grown in the 1980s as a result of conservation efforts financed through limited hunting of elephants and commercial trade of elephant parts. Despite this resistance, a two-thirds majority of all CITES parties voted to place all African elephant herds in Appendix I.[83] The southern African states lodged reservations against the ban and announced plans to sell their ivory through a cartel, with the proceeds to be used to finance conservation.[84]

It was Japan, however, not the African states, that determined the viability of the regime. In 1989, the worldwide ivory market was worth an estimated $50 to $60 million annually. Japan dominated this market, importing more than 80 percent of all African ivory products, making it the potential leader of an effective veto coalition.[85] As the major consumer nation, Japan had been expected to enter a reservation, allowing a significant portion of the ivory market to remain viable and effectively vetoing the ban. However, facing heavy pressure from the United States, the European Community (EC), and national and international NGOs, Japan eventually decided not to oppose the ban. World prices for raw ivory eventually plunged by 90 percent.[86]

In the 1990s, three southern African countries (Botswana, Namibia, and Zimbabwe) called for ending the ivory trade ban, proposing that the African elephant be "downlisted" from CITES Appendix I to Appendix II. Their efforts were unsuccessful at CITES meetings in 1992 and 1994.[87]

At the tenth COP in June 1997 in Harare, Zimbabwe, the three southern African range states, with support from Japan, again proposed a "split" downlisting of the elephant populations in their countries. The resulting debate was long and acrimonious. The three range states argued that their herds had grown to a combined total of about

150,000 and that their inability to exploit the herds commercially was costing them revenues that could be used to increase their conservation budgets. The United States and other parties feared that even partial easing of the trade ban would result in a new flood of illegal trade in ivory and cited deficiencies in enforcement and control measures in the three African countries and Japan that had been identified by the CITES panel of experts. They pointed out that, without adequate controls in place, it would be extremely difficult to track where elephant tusks originated.

In the end, a committee of nineteen CITES members worked out a compromise under which each of the three states could get permission to sell a strictly limited "experimental quota" of ivory under a stringent set of conditions.[88] A heavily regulated one-time sale of ivory from these countries was also approved after monitoring deficiencies were adequately addressed. All experimental sales went to Japan, with all funds obtained by the sale to be invested in elephant-conservation efforts.[89]

At the twelfth COP in 2002, Botswana, Namibia, and South Africa proposed another limited sale of ivory. This proposal was accepted after the establishment of strict monitoring and verification conditions. In 2004, at COP-13, Namibia proposed a two-thousand-kilogram annual quota of raw ivory, in addition to the trade of worked ivory, leather, and hair products. The proposal involving raw ivory was rejected, but Namibia was allowed to participate in trade in leather and hair products and noncommercial trade in worked ivory amulets known as *ekipas*.[90]

At COP-14 in 2007, the Trade Records Analysis of Flora and Fauna in Commerce (TRAFFIC) reported that illegal trade in ivory had increased since 2005 and implicated the countries of Cameroon, China, the Democratic Republic of Congo, Nigeria, and Thailand as the major players. Four proposals on African elephants were also presented. After negotiations, an all-African consensus was reached that kept the allowance of the one-off sale approved at COP-12, along with the trade in leather, hair products, and *ekipas* approved at COP-13. In addition, Botswana, Namibia, South Africa, and Zimbabwe received permission to have a one-off sale of raw ivory that had been registered in government stocks prior to January 31, 2007.[91] The decision also bars additional proposals for ivory trade for nine years following the one-off sale and allows the Standing Committee to stop the agreed-on trade if noncompliance arises. The Standing Committee was also tasked with proposing a decision-making mechanism for ivory trade in time for consideration at COP-16 in 2013 and requested the secretariat to establish a specific fund for African elephants.[92]

In July 2008, at the fifty-seventh meeting of the CITES Standing Committee, delegates gave the go-ahead for the one-off sale of ivory and agreed that China could join Japan as an approved bidder on the ivory. Combined, Botswana, Namibia, South Africa, and Zimbabwe were allowed to sell 108 tons.[93] The secretariat visited all four African countries to verify the quantity and legality of ivory stocks before allowing

PHOTO 4.3   **Examining poached elephant tusks.**
Photo by Rob Barnett/TRAFFIC.

the sale to proceed. The sale took place in October and November 2008 with a total profit of nearly $15.5 million to the four southern African states.[94]

In May 2012, CITES published a report showing that elephant poaching levels were the worst in a decade and recorded ivory seizures were at their highest levels since the ivory ban was approved in 1989.[95] While the global ban briefly halted the decline, poaching, especially in central Africa, now leads to the loss of as many as sixty thousand elephants each year. Some conservationists are concerned that without intervention, African elephants could be nearly extinct by 2020.[96] According to the *New York Times*, "elephants are getting squeezed in a deadly vise between a seemingly insatiable lust for ivory in Asia, where some people pay as much as $1000 a pound, and desperate hunters and traffickers in central Africa. . . . Poverty, as well as greed, is killing Africa's elephants."[97]

At the sixteenth meeting of the COP in March 2013, delegates addressed the unprecedented challenges through a comprehensive "package on elephants." While delegates did manage to revise and modernize the "rules of the game" for the trade in elephants and elephant products, including through addressing e-commerce, employing DNA analysis, monitoring ivory stockpiles, controlling live-elephant trade, and dealing with countries that are persistently involved in illegal trade in ivory, COP-16 did not resolve the debate on one-off ivory sales. Participants disagreed strongly on the impact and wisdom of such sales as a strategy to protect elephants. Proponents laud one-off sales as a way of funding conservation efforts and fulfilling demand through controlled means, while opponents see them as stimulating demand

and increasing incentives for poaching and black markets. While CITES programs to assess the impact of these sales, such as Monitoring the Illegal Killing of Elephants (MIKE) and Elephant Trade Information System (ETIS), found no clear connection between the sales and illegal markets, several delegates pointed to the limited number of one-off sales as providing insufficient evidence for such a conclusion. Parties remained split on whether to even discuss a potential CITES decision-making mechanism to standardize decisions on whether and when to allow one-off sales, with some countries opposing any move toward allowing such sales. As a result, the COP postponed the decision on one-off ivory sales until COP-17, which will be held in South Africa in 2016.[98]

Controlling International Trade in Endangered Species

The case of African elephant ivory illustrates several distinctive features of the CITES regime. First, and as noted above, CITES is actually an umbrella regime enveloping a multitude of "mini regimes" across which states' political and economic interests vary from species to species. These mini regimes, while sharing a common organizational structure, are all characterized by an individual set of developmental stages, proponents, and coalitions that often consist of unusual alliances. Veto coalitions can be led by producer nations, consumer nations, or a coalition of both producer and consumer nations, as is the case with elephant ivory. In addition, not all producer or consumer nations share the same interests. In the elephant case, range states split over listing, largely reflecting differences in the viability of central versus southern African elephant populations. Consumer nations also split, with the largest consumer of elephant ivory at the time, Japan, opposing the listing because of commercial concerns, but others, including the United States, in support.

Second, the role that science plays in the listing of species can also vary by species. While logically associated with the issue-definition and fact-finding stages, scientific knowledge can also play an important role in bargaining and regime strengthening (as seen in the ozone case in Chapter 3). The case of African elephants demonstrates an important scientific role in issue definition and fact finding, via the documentation of the initial population crashes, as well as in the bargaining and regime-strengthening stages, via the documentation of different population trajectories for southern and eastern African elephant populations.

Third, although scientific knowledge can inform debates, economic and political factors often determine specific outcomes. Strong commercial interests on the part of consumer nations or issues such as national sovereignty may lead nations to oppose listings or other conservation measures despite strong evidence of declining populations. In this regard, the elephant case is similar to the whaling case.

Finally, the impact that a CITES listing has on controlling population declines also varies by species. A CITES listing can be ineffective in stopping overexploitation, particularly if important trading countries file a reservation to the listing, trade is predominantly domestic rather than international (e.g., trade in Chinese tigers and tiger parts), factors other than trade are more important in driving population loss (e.g., habitat loss), or monitoring is difficult because of the type of product traded (e.g., sawn wood or plant extracts).

While the case of African elephants presents mixed results, many other listed species have seen significant and positive impacts from CITES listing. Consequently, CITES is widely considered to be among the more effective global environmental regimes, despite the powerful commercial interests involved and the ability of parties to opt out of regulation by entering reservations on particular species. This case, like those of whaling and ozone depletion, illustrates the effectiveness of bans or prohibitions as a mechanism for regulating activities that threaten the environment, natural resources, or wildlife. At the same time, the threats to endangered species continue to multiply, and a black market for trade in endangered species continues to proliferate, driven by both greed and poverty, presenting significant challenges to many endangered species even if they are already part of the CITES regime.

FISHERIES DEPLETION

For centuries, the ocean's bounties were viewed as limitless. But for the past three decades, the world's marine fisheries have been in crisis: overexploited to the point that the most valuable fish stocks have been depleted and some virtually eliminated. About 30 percent of the world's marine fish stocks are considered overexploited.[99] The biggest declines are in demersal fish, which live near the bottom of the sea, including key commercial species such as flounder, sole, turbot, halibut, cod, hake, redfish, haddock, and bass. Pelagic fish, including tuna and mackerel, which live near the surface, are also in decline (see Figure 4.2). Because fishing fleets can overexploit one fishery and then move on to another, and because fleets continued to catch high levels of lower-value fish even after depleting the most desirable stocks, the fisheries crisis was disguised for many years by the continuing increase in the total global catch figures, which grew from 16.8 million tons in 1950 to a peak of 86.4 million tons in 1996. Since then, the global catch has leveled off and fluctuated between 77 and 86 million tons.[100]

The primary reason for the worsening condition of fishery resources is the significant increase in the number of fishing vessels and increasingly effective fishing

FIGURE 4.2   **Fish Stocks in Different Status by Three Groups in 2009**

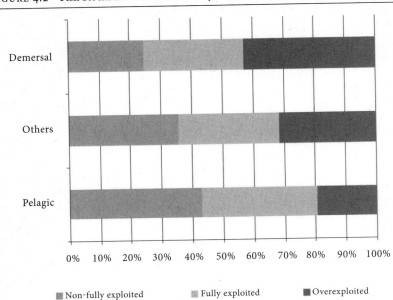

Source: Food and Agriculture Organization of the United Nations, *Review of the State of World Marine Fishery Resources*, FAO Fisheries and Aquaculture Technical Paper No. 569 (Rome: FAO, 2011). Reprinted with permission.

technologies, such as electronic fish-finding equipment, bigger nets, larger storage capacity, more powerful engines, and mechanized hauling gear, all of which give fleets far more catching power than fisheries can support. By the early 1990s, the global fishing fleet had as much as two and a half times more capacity than could be used sustainably.[101] Inadequate regulations on catch and enforcement and illegal, unreported, and unregulated (IUU) fishing also contribute to the fisheries crisis.

Fishery resources are found either under national jurisdiction or in international waters, and often in some combination of the two. This situation complicates the politics of forming a regime. So too does the fact that countries with "distant-water" fishing fleets (China, Japan, Poland, the Republic of Korea, Russia, Spain, and Taiwan) are responsible for the majority of the catch in international waters, providing them with the potential for effectively vetoing a global agreement to address overfishing.

Of the global fish catch, 95 percent is taken within the two-hundred-mile exclusive economic zones (EEZs) that are under the national jurisdiction of individual coastal states. But some important fish stocks, such as cod and pollack, straddle EEZs and adjacent areas of the high seas. Highly migratory fish stocks, especially tuna and swordfish, move long distances, passing through both the high seas and the EEZs of multiple coastal states each year. These straddling and highly migratory fish stocks are particularly important on the Challenger Plateau off the coast of New Zealand, off Argentina's Patagonian Shelf, off the coasts of Chile and Peru, in the Barents Sea, off the coast of Norway, in the Bering Sea, in the Sea of Okhotsk, in the South Pacific Ocean, and on the Grand Banks of Newfoundland outside Canada's two-hundred-mile nautical zone. As many straddling stocks and highly migratory fish stocks have dwindled, coastal and distant-water states each blame overfishing by the other group as the cause.

The first binding global agreement to address overfishing is often referred to as the United Nations Fish Stocks Agreement.[102] Not surprisingly, the agreement arose from conflicts over straddling and highly migratory fish stocks. Canada was the lead state in putting the issue of a global management regime for these stocks on the political agenda.

Canada was motivated to push for formal agreement limiting the freedom of distant-water fishing fleets to exploit these stocks because of a dispute with the EU, especially Spain, about the Spanish fleet's overfishing of the stocks on the Grand Banks outside Canada's EEZ. The regional fisheries management organization responsible for regulating fishing in the Grand Banks area, both within Canada's EEZ and on the high seas, is the Northwest Atlantic Fisheries Organization (NAFO), founded in 1979. From 1986 to 1990, the NAFO failed to enforce high-seas catch limits agreed to by the organization on most of the straddling stocks because the EC had exercised its right to opt out of the regional quotas; Canada, therefore, appealed to the broader international community to adopt a global policy governing the problem.

During preliminary negotiations for the United Nations Conference on Environment and Development (UNCED), a paper from coastal states proposed that new conservation rules should be established for high-seas fisheries but not for fisheries under national jurisdiction. Canada proposed language calling for recognition of the special interests of coastal states in highly migratory stocks and stocks that straddle national EEZs and international waters. The Europeans, as veto states, disagreed, producing a diplomatic deadlock on the issue. The issue remained unresolved until the Rio conference, when the United States brokered a compromise between Canada and the Europeans. The result was an agreement to hold an intergovernmental conference under UN auspices "with a view to promoting effective implementation of the provisions of the Law of the Sea on straddling and highly migratory fish stocks." The Europeans agreed to that formula because its diplomats believed the Convention on the Law of the Sea guaranteed the sovereign right of states to fish on the high seas. Canada hoped that the need for conservation would trump that traditional sovereign right.

The United Nations Conference on Straddling Fish Stocks and Highly Migratory Fish Stocks opened in July 1993 under the authority of the United Nations General Assembly (UNGA). The main conflict of interest was between the seventy coastal fishing states and the ten distant-water fishing states. The lead states were coastal states, led by the "like-minded" caucus (Argentina, Australia, Canada, Chile, Iceland, New Zealand, Norway, and Peru), which accused the distant-water fishing states of abusing their right to fish to the detriment of straddling stocks. The veto coalition was composed of distant-water fishing states, led by the European Commission (on behalf of its distant-water fishing states),[103] Japan, and the Republic of Korea, which argued that mismanagement of national fisheries by coastal fishing states was just as much to blame for the most serious problems of stock depletion.[104] Both sides were only half right, a conclusion based on the Canadian–EC case: the evidence is clear that there was gross mismanagement and overfishing within the Canadian EEZ and that from 1986 to 1989 the Spanish and Portuguese fleets were consistently catching several times the EC's NAFO allocation of groundfish (demersal fish) catch.[105]

As they had during the UNCED negotiations, the like-minded caucus proposed a legally binding agreement that would prescribe conservation rules for high-seas fishing that affected straddling stocks and highly migratory stocks. Coastal states also objected to proposed international rules that would limit their freedom to manage their EEZs. Distant-water states called for nonbinding conservation guidelines that would apply equally to coastal state fisheries and the high seas. They had long argued that the regulation of fishing practices on the high seas should be left to regional or subregional organizations.

Both groups of states were thus, in a sense, separate veto coalitions that were prepared, at least initially, to block agreement on needed measures to conserve stocks effectively. The United States, which is both a coastal fishing state and a distant-water fishing state, was in a pivotal position to play the role of lead state in negotiating the regime. Initially, however, the United States was ready to join with the distant-water states to oppose a binding convention because of its close historic ties with the EU and Japan on Law of the Sea issues. The United States had clashed with Canada and other coastal states during the negotiations on the Law of the Sea treaty. But in 1994, officials in the White House and the National Oceanic and Atmospheric Administration who had a strong commitment to conservation intervened after being lobbied by NGOs. As a result, the United States came out for a binding agreement and began playing the role of lead state.

One of the US contributions to the text was a proposal that the "precautionary approach" to fishing be applied by requiring the adoption of "reference points" (target levels of fishing effort aimed at conserving fish stocks) and measures for rebuilding the stocks, including reduced fishing efforts, if the reference points are exceeded. Canada resisted the application of precautionary reference points within fisheries under national jurisdiction, along with other conservation requirements, as a violation of national sovereignty. The United States pushed Canada and the like-minded caucus to accept certain basic conservation principles and guidelines for their application to straddling stocks on the high seas and within areas under national jurisdiction, but the issue remained unresolved after four negotiating sessions in April 1995.

The like-minded caucus also pressed the issue of coastal states' right to board and inspect fishing vessels in international waters. It argued that such a right was necessary to ensure compliance with international conservation measures. Traditionally, the enforcement of legal obligations on the high seas had been in the hands of the "flag state" (the state in which the vessel was registered), and distant-water fishing states wanted to maintain the status quo. The United States again sided with the like-minded caucus in supporting wider latitude for high-seas inspection by states other than the flag state under certain circumstances. The distant-water states resisted until the last session.

Before the negotiations could be completed, tensions between Canada and the EU escalated dramatically over Spanish fishing for turbot, allegedly in violation of NAFO quotas. In September 1994, the thirteen members of NAFO voted to reduce the annual total allowable catch of rapidly declining stocks of turbot by 38 percent and reallocated much of the EU share of the quota to Canada. The EU used its right to opt out of the quota and set its own, much higher, unilateral quota. In response, in February 1995, the Canadian fisheries minister warned that Canada would not let EU vessels "devastate turbot the way it devastated other ground fish stocks."[106] In March 1995, Canadian ships aggressively pursued and seized or cut the nets of Spanish trawlers outside the Canadian EEZ.

The Canadian actions angered the EU and temporarily polarized the conference. The March–April 1995 round of negotiations was still deadlocked on the issue of the right of coastal states to board ships on the high seas that they suspect of having violated a regional fisheries-conservation measure. The draft agreement allowed wider latitude for such high-seas boarding and inspection than the distant-water states were prepared to accept.

However, as tensions eased, a Canadian-EU agreement reached immediately after that round may have contributed to a successful conclusion of the negotiations. Canada agreed to give the EU the same quota as Canada, instead of one-fifth of the Canadian quota that had been authorized by NAFO. Canada also dropped charges against the Spanish trawler it had seized and repealed legislation authorizing such actions in international waters. In return, the EU agreed to a new regime of independent inspectors onboard every EU ship in the NAFO area to ensure that conservation rules were being followed.[107]

In the fifth and final negotiating session in August 1995, distant-water fishing states were still resisting high-seas boarding and the "precautionary approach" to fisheries management. The distant-water fishing states had agreed to boarding and inspecting in principle, but there were still differences about whether the regional fisheries organizations had to reach agreement on procedures governing such boarding and inspecting: Canada insisted that it would not require prior agreement on procedures by the organizations, whereas Japan and South Korea both insisted on regional agreement as a precondition for boarding and inspection. A compromise was ultimately adopted: states that were parties to regional fisheries management organizations could board and inspect vessels on the high seas of parties to the Fish Stocks Agreement suspected of violating regional conservation measures without prior regional agreement, but only if the regional organization had failed to adopt procedures for such boarding and inspection for two years prior to the boarding.

As discussed in Chapter 1, the precautionary principle states that scientific uncertainty should not be used as a reason for postponing or failing to take effective conservation measures if an action could produce significant environmental harm. Japan was concerned that coastal states would use the precautionary approach as an open license to adopt moratoria on fishing as the new management norm and was reluctant to see the principle enter into a binding international agreement. But Japan finally accepted the precautionary approach, perhaps because it did not want to be blamed for the collapse of the negotiations.[108]

After receiving ratifications from the required thirty signatories, a process that took nearly six years, the United Nations Fish Stocks Agreement entered into force in December 2001. By March 2013, eighty countries had ratified the treaty, but only four of the top ten fishing states (India, Japan, Russia, and the United States) and the EU are parties to the agreement. China and the Philippines signed but have not ratified and remain nonparties. Many of the other most important fishing states, including Peru, Chile, Malaysia, Mexico, Thailand, and Vietnam, also remain nonparties. Although these countries' support was not needed for the Fish Stocks Agreement to enter into force, their compliance is essential if the treaty is to be effective.

The agreement represents a major step forward in global cooperation for conservation of fish stocks, but it does not effectively address three key global management issues. First, regional fisheries management organizations that make decisions on management measures such as catch quotas normally allow member states simply to opt out of the decision if they don't like it—this was the weakness that prompted Canada's original push for a new regime. The second problem is overcapacity in the global fishing fleet. Although the agreement calls for states to take measures to "prevent or eliminate excess fishing capacity," it does not spell out this obligation or set up a mechanism for implementation. Finally, the agreement does not apply to all fish stocks under national jurisdiction but only to those referred to in the title, or approximately 20 percent of the global fish catch.

States have created several nonbinding agreements to supplement the regime. In October 1995, governments adopted an international Code of Conduct for Responsible Fisheries, which provides principles and standards applicable to the conservation, management, and development of all aspects of fisheries, such as the capture, processing, and trade of fishery products, as well as fishing operations, aquaculture, fisheries research, and the integration of fisheries into coastal-area management. To support implementation of the code of conduct, the FAO Technical Guidelines for Responsible Fisheries were elaborated.[109]

The FAO also developed international plans of action addressing specific issues in implementing the code of conduct. The 1999 International Plan of Action for the Management of Fishing Capacity aims to reduce excess fishing capacity in world fisheries. The 2001 International Plan of Action to Prevent, Deter and Eliminate Illegal, Unreported and Unregulated Fishing recommends good practice and calls upon states to adopt national plans of action to combat IUU fishing (see Box 4.5).[110] Although voluntary instruments such as these can be useful, a key problem is their nonbinding nature, which significantly impedes their effectiveness. Thus far, efforts to achieve the fine balance between encouraging widespread and international participation and the effective implementation of the guidelines and measures outlined in these voluntary instruments have not been that successful.

In May 2006, the United Nations held a review conference to assess implementation of the Fish Stocks Agreement. The conference recommended integrating ecosystem considerations into fisheries management, an urgent reduction in the world's fishing capacity to levels commensurate with the sustainability of fish stocks, urgent strengthening of the mandates of regional fisheries management organizations to implement modern approaches to fisheries, a commitment to develop a legally binding instrument on minimum standards for port-state measures and a comprehensive global register of fishing vessels, expanded assistance to developing countries, and a continuing dialogue to address concerns raised by nonparties, including issues related to boarding fishing vessels and inspections.[111]

The review conference convened again in 2010. This meeting focused on the role of flag states and agreed to develop criteria for assessing flag states' performance and to address the persistent failure of flag states to carry out their responsibilities. Progress was also made on deep-sea fisheries, with adoption of an EU proposal on establishing long-term conservation and management measures in accordance with the 2008 FAO International Guidelines on Deep-Sea Fisheries in the High Seas. This strengthened the agreement's principle of promoting the protection of habitats of special concern. However, the lack of state compliance with the agreement's provisions still constitutes an impediment to the recovery of such stocks, as well as associated and dependent species and habitats of special concern.

The review conferences also demonstrated that much has changed since the treaty's 1995 adoption. Parties and nonparties alike now accept certain principles of

BOX 4.5   ILLEGAL, UNREPORTED, AND UNREGULATED FISHING

Illegal, unreported, and unregulated (IUU) fishing is a global threat to sustainable fisheries and marine biodiversity. IUU fishing includes fishing that is against the laws and regulations of a country or an international agreement, misreporting catches to the relevant national or regional authority, and fishing in a way that undermines management efforts to conserve marine species and ecosystems. IUU fishing occurs globally and is thought to account for up to 30 percent of catches in some areas. However, since these catches are not recorded, the exact amounts are hard to quantify.

IUU fishing has enormous consequences. Not only are these poachers decimating valuable fish populations, but they are also killing tens of thousands of marine animals as bycatch and destroying habitats through their unregulated use of damaging and illegal fishing practices. Annual global economic losses from IUU fishing are estimated to be between $10 billion and $23 billion, representing eleven million to twenty-six million tons of fish.

IUU fishing is often an organized criminal activity. For example, a pirate vessel may be owned by a company in the Caribbean that is then owned by someone in Europe or Asia, it may have a Russian skipper and a crew from the Philippines or China, and it may be registered in Togo. IUU fishing boats use various strategies to evade detection and apprehension, and they often disguise the origin of their illegal catch so well that the fish is often sold legitimately into consumer markets in Japan, the European Union, and the United States.

To combat IUU fishing, countries and international organizations have emphasized the importance of enhanced port state control. In 2009, the FAO Conference approved the FAO Agreement on Port State Measures to Prevent, Deter and Eliminate Illegal, Unreported and Unregulated Fishing. The agreement aims to prevent illegally caught fish from entering international markets by requiring foreign vessels to provide advance notice and request permission for port entry. Port country officials will then conduct regular inspections in accordance with universal minimum standards, and offending vessels will be denied use of port or certain port services and information shared through new international networks.

Sources: Environmental Justice Foundation, "Pirate Fishing," accessed September 20, 2012, www .ejfoundation.org/oceans/issues-pirate-fishing; Food and Agriculture Organization of the United Nations, *Agreement on Port State Measures to Prevent, Deter and Eliminate Illegal, Unreported and Unregulated Fishing* (Rome: FAO, 2009), www.fao.org/fileadmin/user_upload/legal/docs/1_037t-e.pdf; and WWF, "Fishing Problems: Pirate Fishing," accessed September 20, 2012, wwf.panda.org/about _our_earth/blue_planet/problems/problems_fishing/fisheries_management/illegal_fishing.

the treaty, such as the ecosystem and precautionary approaches to management, that were agreed to only after long hours of negotiations in 1995. Overall, the discussion revealed a shift in dynamics from the original negotiations, which had been divided between the distant-water fishing states and the coastal states. In 2010, the divide was between the lead coalition of parties and a potential veto coalition of nonparties, whose continued refusal to ratify the agreement threatens the status of remaining fish stocks.[112]

The history of the fisheries regime includes several particularly interesting features. One of the key factors in the agenda setting, at least for one important actor, was less a concern for conservation of straddling and highly migratory fish stocks than it was Canada's desire to overcome the EU's ability to determine its own catch levels in the Grand Banks fishery. In the original negotiations two different veto coalitions—the like-minded caucus of coastal states and the major distant-water states—initially opposed key provisions of the regime. The US shift from veto state to lead state proved a major factor in overcoming the resistance of the two veto coalitions and gave greater impetus to the adoption of innovative conservation measures. And the willingness of Canada to use physical force on the high seas in its dispute with the EU, with the result that the EU agreed to onboard inspectors on the high seas, helped put the issue of boarding and inspecting in a different light for key veto states. Finally, the refusal to ratify the agreement by some of the main fishing states (such as Chile, China, and Peru, to name a few), continues to impede the regime's effectiveness.

DESERTIFICATION

Desertification affects the lives of two billion people living in drylands in more than 110 countries. It has been the subject of international attention for nearly three decades. Yet it has never been a priority issue on the global environmental agenda, despite efforts by many African countries. Indeed, it was put on the UNCED agenda only because African countries persisted. When the desertification convention became the first treaty to be negotiated after UNCED, some looked at it as a test of whether developed-country governments had the political will to follow up on some of the Agenda 21 commitments of greatest interest to developing countries.

Complexity, vagueness, and disagreement on whether desertification was indeed a global problem plagued the issue-definition stage. UNEP and most specialists defined desertification as sustained land degradation in arid, semiarid, and dry subhumid areas resulting mainly from adverse human impact[113] (see Box 4.6.). But the term *desertification* evokes images of deserts advancing and destroying productive land, whereas scientists have found no evidence to support claims that the Sahara is expanding at an alarming rate.[114] Foes of a convention exploited that fact: at one point in the UNCED negotiations, the United States proposed that negotiators discard the term *desertification* and suggested substituting *land degradation*. Some donor countries objected that the designation "global" might imply that treaty-implementation efforts would be eligible for Global Environment Facility (GEF) funding.[115]

PHOTO 4.4   *Despair.* **Severe land degradation and desertification has a huge impact on the livelihoods of some of the poorest people on the planet.**
2005 UNCCD photo contest, photo by Kushal Gangopadhyay, reprinted with permission.

African countries encountered other problems in defining desertification. First, desertification does not involve resources or life-support systems of global interest, as do other environmental issues on which major global treaties have been negotiated. It affects countries not suffering from desertification only because it threatens the economies and societies of many other countries. Second, a bewildering array of natural and social factors have an impact on land degradation in drylands, including overpopulation, climatic cycles, social and economic structures, poor pastoral or agricultural practices, bad government and donor policies, and North-South economic relations. It was difficult, therefore, to articulate in a simple and clear way either the nature of the problem or the international actions needed to address it.

In addition, for many African countries, there is a strong link between poverty alleviation and desertification control. Consequently, the African countries' definition of the problem emphasized the need for additional funding but for as-yet-unidentified activities. These countries hoped that a desertification convention would help them gain access to additional funding.[116] It was unclear to many developed countries exactly why such assistance should be provided.

Finally, the African countries' attempt to define the desertification issue was hampered because the earlier Plan of Action to Combat Desertification, launched in 1977, was generally acknowledged as a failure. A UNEP evaluation of the plan had blamed the failure on African governments and the donor community for not giving the issue

BOX 4.6   DRYLANDS FACTS

- The total population of the world's drylands is more than two billion. Drylands are home to almost one of every three people living in the world today.
- The majority of the world's dryland population is in developing countries.
- Drylands support 50 percent of the world's livestock.
- Drylands comprise 44 percent of all cultivated land.
- Plant species endemic to drylands make up 30 percent of the plants under cultivation today.
- The largest dryland areas are in Australia, China, Russia, the United States, and Kazakhstan.
- At least 99 percent of the surface area of six countries (Botswana, Burkina Faso, Iraq, Kazakhstan, Moldova, and Turkmenistan) is classified as drylands.
- Drylands store 46 percent of the planet's carbon inventory.

Source: United Nations Convention to Combat Desertification (UNCCD), *Desertification: A Visual Synthesis* (Bonn: UNCCD Secretariat, 2011), 10.

---

priority and for gross mismanagement. UNEP had found that only $1 billion of the $9 billion provided by donor agencies from 1978 to 1983 had been spent directly on projects in the field.[117]

When the issue of creating a desertification convention was first raised during the UNCED process, only France, with its historic ties to Africa, expressed support for the idea. Most industrialized countries and the World Bank argued that the primary problems were the macroeconomic policies of African governments (such as levying excessive taxes on agriculture and failing to grant enforceable property rights) and that policy reforms, better planning, and more popular participation would achieve better results than a new international program or formal agreement.[118]

Despite these problems in the definition of desertification, UNCED put it on the global agenda because of African persistence and because the United States unexpectedly supported the African position. After opposing a desertification convention throughout the negotiations leading up to the Earth Summit, the United States shifted its position in Rio, backing language calling for a convention in the hope of winning African support on forests and on other issues in the Rio Declaration.[119] Other industrialized countries then followed suit, and the call for a desertification convention became part of Agenda 21.[120]

Negotiations began in May 1993 and were completed in fifteen months. A formal fact-finding process was attempted through an "information-sharing segment" at the first session of the Intergovernmental Negotiating Committee, but the process focused primarily on socioeconomic strategies for slowing and reversing desertification and on reports from individual countries rather than on the scientific understanding of the problem. That process produced general agreement on the importance of such strategies as the integration of arid and semiarid areas into national economies, popular participation in antidesertification efforts, and land-tenure reform.[121] As a result, the convention would be the first to call for affected countries to provide for effective participation by grassroots organizations, NGOs, and local populations in the preparation of national action programs.[122]

The bargaining stage revolved not around commitments to environmental conservation actions but around financial, trade, institutional, and symbolic issues. The African countries were the lead states and presented detailed draft language for every section of the convention, some of which were accepted as the basis for negotiation.

Whether to include debt and trade matters within the scope of the convention became a central issue in the negotiations. African and other developing countries asserted that external debt burdens and commodity prices, among other international economic policy issues, affected their ability to combat desertification. The industrialized countries argued that those North-South economic issues could be negotiated only in other international forums. They did agree to general obligations to "give due attention" to the trade and debt problems of affected countries and so create an "enabling international economic environment" for those countries.

Differences over financial resources and the financial mechanism nearly caused the negotiations to collapse. As in other global negotiations, some members of the G-77 and China demanded commitments to "new and additional" financial resources and creation of a special fund for desertification as the centerpiece of the convention. Industrialized countries acted as a united veto coalition in rejecting provisions for new and additional financing, agreeing only to ensure "adequate" financial resources for antidesertification programs. The developed countries felt they bore no responsibility for desertification, unlike ozone depletion and climate change, and were therefore unwilling to accept binding obligations to increase their financial assistance to the affected countries.[123] They insisted that existing resources could be used more effectively.

The deadlock on a funding mechanism was broken only after the United States proposed the Global Mechanism (GM) under the authority of the conference of the parties, to be housed within an existing organization, which would improve monitoring and assessment of existing aid flows and increase coordination among donors. Developing countries remained dissatisfied because such a mechanism would not increase development assistance to African and other countries suffering from desertification. They ultimately accepted the GM, as it was the only compromise acceptable to donor countries.[124]

The United Nations Convention to Combat Desertification (UNCCD) was opened for signature in October 1994 and entered into force on December 26, 1996. Today, 194 countries and the European Union are parties. The convention recognizes the physical, biological, and socioeconomic aspects of desertification, the importance of redirecting technology transfer so that it is demand-driven, and the importance of local populations in efforts to combat desertification. The core of the convention is the development of national and subregional/regional action programs by national governments in cooperation with donors, local populations, and NGOs.

Implementing and Strengthening the Convention

The UNCCD faced significant challenges during its first six years. These included establishing and operationalizing the GM and reconciling the convention's emphasis on "bottom-up" approaches with involvement at all levels by all relevant actors with the logistical requirements for operating an effective international coordinating body. At the national level, challenges included assisting countries affected by desertification to develop effective action programs in conjunction with donor countries, international organizations, local communities, and NGOs.[125]

Between 1997 and 2003, the COP set up institutional mechanisms to enable effective implementation of the convention. This work and the lack of a dedicated financing mechanism in the convention meant that the first five COPs spent time on procedures and institutions rather than on substance. During this period, the COP established two subsidiary bodies: the Committee on Science and Technology and the Committee for the Review of the Implementation of the Convention. After a long-fought battle, the convention designated the GEF as the financial mechanism for the convention once the GEF agreed to establish a program to fund projects to combat desertification.

It took ten years for the convention to make the transition from awareness raising to implementation, but by 2005 it appeared as though crucial building blocks required for success were in place. Eighty-one affected countries had submitted national action programs, synergies had been developed with the climate change and biodiversity conventions, new initiatives were under way, and there seemed to be a growing understanding in the international community that the Millennium Development Goals could not be achieved without addressing the root causes of rural poverty, many of which were brought on or exacerbated by desertification and drought.[126]

When COP-7 convened in Nairobi in October 2005, however, delegates resumed the acrimonious debates on many of the same issues that had plagued the convention since its negotiation. To some extent, this reflected the fact that unlike the other treaties discussed in this chapter, desertification does not involve concerns for preserving natural resources. Many of the political problems in this regime, the only multilateral environmental agreement driven by developing countries, stem from the fact that land degradation is not a priority issue for donor governments. As one developing country official put it, the "scorching breath of the desert is not readily felt by the prosperous public of the rich North."[127]

The tone in Nairobi was also shaped by the critical report of the United Nations Joint Inspection Unit (an external oversight body). At COP-6 in Havana, parties had requested the Joint Inspection Unit to review the activities of the UNCCD Secretariat. The report confirmed, among other things, that the convention had a major identity crisis. "In the course of the review, it appeared to the Inspectors that from the outset there has been a lack of common understanding and recognition of the Convention in its true and proper perspective."[128] The report stated that it seemed unclear whether the convention is environmental, developmental, or both and whether it concerns problems of a purely local or a global nature. "The very name of the Convention may perhaps be misleading since the fundamental problem is one of land degradation, of which desertification is a key element. The failure and/or unwillingness to recognize the Convention in its proper perspective have inevitably led to undesirable consequences."[129] Some of these consequences include the lack of access to financial support, the lack of a stable financial commitment by the developed-country parties, the failure to mainstream UNCCD programs and activities into their respective development-support initiatives, and the lack of prioritization in affected country parties, which have had little success in integrating UNCCD objectives into overall national development plans. The inspectors also noted that in many developed countries, the ministry of cooperation or foreign affairs has responsibility for the UNCCD, but these ministries rarely see desertification as a priority issue. Furthermore, in developing countries, desertification is generally the responsibility of relatively weaker environment ministries. Officials designated as UNCCD focal points in both developed and developing countries are usually not sufficiently senior in their ministries to effectively promote the convention. As a result, the convention has difficulty getting the necessary recognition and support.[130]

The Nairobi meeting ended with agreement that in response to the Joint Inspection Unit's report, parties should adopt a long-term strategic plan for implementation of the convention at the next COP. While many admitted that this was not a panacea to the UNCCD's problems, they also hoped that it would help to strengthen the regime.

The strategic plan was developed at a series of intersessional meetings in 2006 and 2007 and brought forward for adoption at COP-8 in Madrid in September 2007. The strategic plan strives to link the work programs of the convention's institutions to a common vision, clarifies their mandates and methods of work, and institutionalizes a results-based management approach. It also sets out operational objectives on issues including awareness raising, policies, improving the flow of science and technology, and capacity building and further defines the coordination and respective mandates of the secretariat and the GM so as to enhance coordination and integration.[131]

The UNCCD still faces a number of significant challenges to its successful implementation. One is bringing more scientific and technological input into its operations. Since the convention's inception, the role of scientists has been marginalized. In its existing institutional architecture, scientific and technological input has been predominantly channeled to the COP through its subsidiary Committee on Science and Technology and a roster of independent experts nominated by the parties. However, the science and technology committee's large and diverse membership renders it rather unwieldy. Different people attend each meeting, and the discussions rarely include detailed, focused, and meaningful exchanges on specific scientific issues. Government representatives, many of whom lack the training or expertise to engage in substantive scientific debates, typically dominate the meetings. Committee sessions are also often marred by procedural quarrels resulting in low-profile, nonauthoritative outputs with little relevance for either the COP or the scientific community.[132]

In short, the UNCCD process lacks an efficient operational mechanism to process and channel practical and scientific expertise for political decision makers. The COP fails to tap the information potentially available from the scientific community, which in turn is unable to draw the attention of the parties to the scientific aspects of the issues on the COP's agenda.[133]

To address this problem, COP-8 called for "scientific-style" conferences. Two such conferences have been held so far. The first convened in Argentina in 2009 and focused on "bio-physical and socio-economic monitoring and assessment of desertification and land degradation, to support decision-making in land and water management." The second was held in Germany in 2013 and focused on "economic assessment of desertification, sustainable land management and resilience of arid, semi-arid and dry sub-humid areas." There have also been calls for the provision of independent scientific policy advisory services from outside the immediate UNCCD process, referring to the role of the Intergovernmental Panel on Climate Change vis-à-vis the United Nations Framework Convention on Climate Change as a promising model.

A second major challenge is uncertainty regarding the proper focus of the regime. While the UNCCD has carved a niche for itself at the interface of environment and development, it still suffers from an identity crisis. The UNCCD seeks to address poverty, both a cause and a consequence of dryland degradation, as well as problems pertaining to sustainable land management, combating desertification, and mitigating the effects of drought. Many parties, in fact, consider the UNCCD a development rather than an environmental treaty, stressing that its primary objective is to fight poverty. This dual emphasis reflects serious differences of opinion between developing and developed countries, hindering the effective implementation of the convention.

Developed countries have been reluctant to acknowledge desertification as a global commons problem and to commit substantive financial resources. The UNCCD's future success will arguably depend on the effective mediation of divergent perspectives on the environment-poverty nexus and improved understanding of the interlinkages between development and the environment.[134]

Unlike other regimes, the UNCCD's implementation has not been hindered by issues of national sovereignty or scientific uncertainty. In fact, the knowledge and technical skills exist to halt several causes of desertification, but political and economic factors determine whether the expertise is ever put into practice. Implementation has proven difficult because of the nature of the problem, lack of political commitment, and bureaucratic mistrust, often demonstrated by the developed countries, which serve as a veto coalition exploiting the power of the purse. The UNCCD will have to consider which issues in the desertification battle should be addressed in the bureaucratic, virtual world of international meetings and which are best addressed in the real world, at the national and local level. Unless the secretariat and the parties can effectively address these issues, and the UNCCD can refocus on implementation, within the context of reduced financial contributions and wavering political commitment from some donor parties, the future of the first "sustainable development" convention may be bleak indeed.

FORESTS

The issue of forests is unique among these case studies in that it continues to defy the creation of a comprehensive global regime. The main reasons for this are linked to the complexity of the issue and the successful efforts of a veto coalition. As in several other cases, the makeup of a veto coalition changed over time, but only in this issue has the veto coalition changed so much in both membership and rationale yet still blocked the adoption of a global treaty.

Forests cover four billion hectares, or about 31 percent of the total land area of the world. The five most forest-rich countries (the Russian Federation, Brazil, Canada, the United States, and China) account for more than half of the total forest area. Approximately thirteen million hectares of forests were lost globally between 2000 and 2010, although this was down from the sixteen million hectares lost in the 1990s.[135] The thirteen million hectares of the world's forests lost from deforestation every year account for up to 18 percent of the global greenhouse gas (GHG) emissions that contribute to global warming. The world's forests and forest soils store more than one trillion tons of carbon—twice the amount found in the atmosphere.[136]

FIGURE 4.3   **Annual Forest Cover Change, 1990–2010**

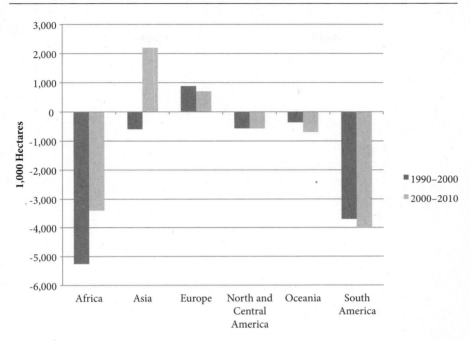

Sources: United Nations Food and Agriculture Organization (FAO), *State of the World's Forests, 2009* (Rome: FAO, 2009); FAO, *Global Forest Resources Assessment 2010* (Rome: FAO, 2010).

The World Bank estimates that more than half a billion people depend on forests for their livelihood. The forest-product industry is a major source of economic activity and employment. Each year $186 billion of forest products are traded internationally. Despite the global decline, in Asia forest area has actually expanded since 2000 (see Figure 4.3), largely because of an increase in forest plantations. Generally cultivated for industrial purposes, plantations now constitute 7 percent of the total forest area. Primary forests, or forests largely undisturbed by human activity, now comprise only about one-third of global forest area.[137]

Most forests are cut down to provide land for food and cash crops. Other causes of deforestation and forest degradation include overharvesting (of both industrial wood and fuelwood), overgrazing by livestock (which degrades the soil and has other impacts), insect pests and diseases (which are both expanding their range because of climate change), fires, storms, and air pollution. Fuelwood is the main cooking fuel for two to three billion people, including the world's poorest. Wood is essential for construction and a host of other uses. Timber exports are a source of foreign exchange for many countries.

Although cutting trees and clearing forests make perfect sense to those engaged in these practices, they have a negative impact on many people. As trees disappear, forest dwellers, often the poorest and most vulnerable members of society, are deprived of their homes and livelihoods. Fuelwood and other forest products become harder to obtain. Flooding results, land is eroded, and lakes and dams are filled with silt. With fewer trees to soak up carbon dioxide from the atmosphere, the risk of climate change increases. As plant and wildlife species become extinct, biological diversity is reduced.[138]

Countries have discussed forest-policy issues within the UN system since the end of World War II.[139] The FAO Conference was the principal global forum for the discussion of international forestry issues from the mid-1940s until 1971, when the FAO established the Committee on Forestry. Since its first session in 1972, this committee has met regularly at two-year intervals to review forestry problems of "an international character."[140] Forest industries and the restoration of timber supplies were prominent topics of early conferences and remain on the committee's agenda along with logging and the marketing and use of forest products.

Other milestones in the global dialogue on forest policy include the adoption of the International Tropical Timber Agreement in 1983 and the establishment of the International Tropical Timber Organization in 1986. These initiatives sought to promote international trade in tropical timber, the sustainable management of tropical forests, and the development of forest industries. The organization's membership represents 90 percent of world trade in tropical timber and 80 percent of the world's tropical forests.

The 1992 Earth Summit marked a turning point in the international forest-policy dialogue. Negotiations on forests during the UNCED Preparatory Committee quickly became polarized. Three competing public claims to the world's forests were made during the negotiations. The developed countries, which had called for a forest convention in 1990 in the European Parliament and at the Group of Seven Houston summit meeting, ventured that forests could be seen as a global commons because all humanity has a stake in forest conservation. On the other side, the G-77, led by Malaysia and India, claimed that forests are sovereign national resources to be used in line with national development objectives. NGOs and indigenous peoples' groups made a third claim: forests should be seen as local commons, and the best way to achieve forest conservation is to grant secure land-tenure rights to local communities whose livelihoods depend directly on the conservation of forest resources.[141] With rejection of a treaty by the G-77 dooming negotiations on a formal convention, delegates instead negotiated two non–legally binding agreements on forests: the Forest Principles[142] and Chapter 11 of Agenda 21, titled "Combating Deforestation."[143]

During the UNCED negotiations on the Forest Principles, the United States and Canada tried to link the principle of the sovereignty of countries over their own forest resources with the principles of national responsibility and global concern for forests. Canada, with huge forest resources under rapid development, proposed the principle that forests are of interest to the international community, that international standards should be implemented in forest management, and that targets and time frames should be included in national forestry plans. But Malaysia and India saw these formulations as an effort to establish the legal principle that forests are "global commons," or part of the "common heritage of [hu]mankind," a status that might eventually give industrialized countries the right to interfere in the management of the tropical-forest countries' resources.[144]

The final version of the Forest Principles only hints that forests are a global environmental issue and omits both the idea of international guidelines for forest management and all references to trade in "sustainably managed" forest products. It gives blanket approval to the conversion of natural forests to other uses. Developed countries widely regarded the agreement as worse than no declaration at all because it appeared to legitimize unsustainable forest-management policies.[145] The Forest Principles and Chapter 11 of Agenda 21 both reaffirmed the rights of sovereign nations to use their forests in accordance with their national priorities and policy objectives. The Rio agreements also stress the cross-sectoral nature of forests and point out that forests simultaneously provide a wide range of socioeconomic benefits as well as environmental values and services.

The Forest Principles agreement and the North-South confrontation over the issue seemed to shut the door on global negotiations on forests. By 1995, however, a series of lower-profile international meetings and initiatives, including several joint North-South collaborations, began a new process of maneuvering over sustainable forest management.[146] The result was agreement to begin the next phase of fact finding and bargaining.

Interim Solutions

With Canada and Malaysia acting as lead states, the UN Commission on Sustainable Development (CSD) established the Intergovernmental Panel on Forests (IPF) in 1995. The IPF was given a two-year mandate to build consensus on priority issues in five interrelated categories: implementation of UNCED decisions related to forests at the national and international level; international cooperation in financial assistance and technology transfer; scientific research, forest assessment, and development of criteria and indicators for sustainable forest management; trade-and-environment issues relating to forest products and services; and international organizations and instruments, including the possibility of a forests convention.[147]

By the time the IPF completed its work in February 1997, it had developed more than one hundred proposals for action on issues related to sustainable forest management.[148] These recommendations, however, did not effectively leverage changes in forest-management policies and practices. The IPF created no mechanism for reporting or follow-up on the recommendations, further limiting their impact on policy.

In addition, the debate about the need for a global forest convention remained as polarized as it was in 1992, although there was now a new alignment of country preferences. Malaysia and Canada, the lead states, supported elements of a convention in the hope that a global agreement on sustainable forestry could provide the basis for an officially sponsored, international ecolabel system for wood products that would be more amenable to their timber industries than other proposed or existing certification systems. Canada's forestry industry, the country's largest export sector, had been facing pressure from environmental protests and boycotts over clear-cutting of old-growth forests.[149]

The European Union still officially supported the negotiation of a binding treaty. Some of its key member states (France, Germany, and Italy) had long been the staunchest supporters of a global forest treaty. But by 1996 some environmental groups and aid agencies in EU member states had begun to oppose a binding agreement, in part because they saw that no new money would be forthcoming to support it. Germany had started to view it as a potentially dangerous agreement, pushed by some of the very states that had opposed meaningful norms of forest management at UNCED.[150]

Some developing countries, including Costa Rica, Indonesia, Papua New Guinea, and the Philippines, also changed their position to support a convention in the hope that it would generate new sources of development assistance for forests. There was also some movement from the African countries in favor of a convention. However, with the major South American countries remaining firmly opposed (led by Brazil), the G-77, which seeks to speak with one voice, maintained that it was too early to start negotiations for a convention, but that the desirability of a convention would be reassessed at a later stage.[151]

The United States, which had supported a convention in Rio, now opposed it and so became one of the leaders of the veto coalition. The influence of the corporate sector, which opposed a convention on the grounds that it would be interventionist and regulatory, was largely responsible for this shift.[152] Japan, which had endorsed a convention at UNCED without actively supporting it, now opposed the idea, as did Australia and New Zealand. As another leader of the veto coalition, Brazil's strong resistance to a binding treaty on forests reflected similar fears about environmental requirements. The forest convention issue thus shows how different states—and the timber industry in different countries—can share the same political and economic interests (in this instance freedom from third-party certification by a system that the industry didn't trust) but come out on opposite sides of the issue because of differing assessments of the situation.

A major shift also occurred within the NGO community. In Rio, many international NGOs tended to favor a convention if it contained strong conservation commitments and firm provisions respecting the rights and traditions of indigenous forest peoples. But at the IPF, NGOs issued a declaration against a convention. They had noticed the shift by major tropical timber producers such as Malaysia and Indonesia in favor of a convention. Coupled with the long-term support from the Canadian government and the Canadian forest industry, along with support from Finland and Russia, this led NGO campaigners to question which interests and values the convention would actually promote.[153] In the end, the IPF was unable to agree on recommendations for a global forest convention. Instead, in June 1997 the UNGA established an Intergovernmental Forum on Forests (IFF) under the auspices of the CSD.[154] In other words, governments supported the need for dialogue but could advance matters no further than the status quo.

The IFF, which concluded its work in February 2000, was charged with promoting and facilitating implementation of the IPF's proposals for action; reviewing, monitoring, and reporting on progress in the management, conservation, and sustainable development of all types of forests; and considering matters left pending by the panel, particularly trade, finance, technology transfer, and a possible forest convention. The same issues that stymied the IPF continued to prove difficult for the IFF. Canada did not give up its aim of securing agreement on a global forest convention, but the veto coalition of industrialized and developing states opposed to negotiating a forest treaty doomed the Canadian effort. Delegates finally agreed to recommend to the CSD that the UN establish an intergovernmental body called the United Nations Forum on Forests (UNFF) and, within five years, "consider with a view to recommending the parameters of a mandate for developing a legal framework on all types of forests." The language is sufficiently obscure that the lead and veto coalitions both felt they had achieved a successful outcome to the negotiations.

United Nations Forum on Forests

The United Nations Economic and Social Council established the UNFF in 2000 with the goal of promoting "the management, conservation and sustainable development of the world's forests, and to strengthen long-term political commitment to this end."[155] The Collaborative Partnership on Forests was also established to support the work of the UNFF and its member countries and to foster increased cooperation and coordination on forests.[156] When discussion on a forests convention or other "international arrangement on forests" convened at UNFF-5 in May 2005, the session was supposed to review the effectiveness of the current international arrangement on forests, including the UNFF itself, and also to consider whether negotiations on a global forest convention could be initiated. However, many of the most ardent proponents of a global forest convention were already conceding that a consensus was unlikely to emerge for any type of legally binding agreement.[157] The coalitions that had emerged in 1997 remained largely unchanged in 2005, and the debate appeared as polarized as ever. There was agreement that the global forest agenda had made some progress under the UNFF and that deforestation and forest degradation continued at an unsustainably high rate, but there was no consensus on how to proceed.

Developing countries, although divided on the need for a treaty, were united in their call for industrialized countries to implement commitments related to financial resources, capacity building, and technology transfer, which they saw as critical to advancing the management, conservation, and sustainable development of all types of forests.[158] Canada, the EU, Malaysia, and Switzerland continued to act as lead states, although they recognized that a treaty might not be possible and started to look for alternative proposals. The veto coalition, led by Brazil, continued to oppose a treaty, calling instead for the continuation and strengthening of the UNFF and the Collaborative Partnership on Forests. Several compromise proposals began to emerge. Some countries called for a non–legally binding voluntary code of conduct with clear overarching goals and a limited number of targets. Canada, Switzerland, and the United States, among others, supported this proposal, but Brazil and others rejected quantifiable goals and argued that the UNCED Statement of Forest Principles was a code of conduct. Negotiations on targets and timetables began, but although there was tentative agreement about goals and the possibility of negotiating a voluntary code, there was no consensus on the details. NGOs argued that members had engaged in policy talks for too long while deforestation continued unabated and unchallenged. They argued that governments must adopt clear, measurable targets; provide the necessary resources to implement actions to achieve them; and ensure broad participation of NGOs and indigenous peoples.

In the end, countries recognized that without the support of two key players in the veto coalition—the country with the largest timber industry (the United States) and the country with the world's largest tropical forest (Brazil)—no treaty would be possible. Other options were put on the table, but there was still no consensus on the adoption of targets, a voluntary code of conduct, or the consideration of a treaty in the future. With no agreement possible, delegates agreed to reconvene at UNFF-6 in 2006 to try, yet again, to reach consensus on an international arrangement on forests.

UNFF-6 finally secured the next step in strengthening the international arrangement on forests by deciding to develop a voluntary instrument. To this end, delegates agreed on four "global objectives" on forests: reversing the loss of forest cover and increasing efforts to prevent forest degradation, enhancing forest benefits and their contribution to international development goals, increasing the area of protected forests and areas of sustainably managed forests, and reversing the decline in official development assistance (foreign aid) for sustainable forest management. They also agreed to continue the work of the UNFF at least through 2015 and to conclude and adopt at its seventh session "a non–legally binding instrument on all types of forests."[159] So, fourteen years after Rio, the idea of a binding forest treaty seemed to have disappeared off the agenda, despite the efforts of a few staunch supporters, including the Canadians. Most countries seeking a legally binding treaty had no intention of abandoning the UNFF, with many stating that a voluntary instrument was a good first step toward securing a more binding agreement.

Nine months later, UNFF-7 completed negotiation of a non–legally binding instrument covering all types of forests, which the UNGA endorsed and adopted in December 2007.[160] The instrument sets out a framework for accomplishing the global objectives on forests and defines its overall purpose as:

- to strengthen political commitment and action at all levels to implement effectively sustainable management of all types of forests and to achieve the shared global objectives on forests;
- to enhance the contribution of forests to the achievement of the internationally agreed development goals, including the Millennium Development Goals, in particular with respect to poverty eradication and environmental sustainability; and
- to provide a framework for national action and international cooperation.

The forum also agreed to consider a financial mechanism to support implementation at its 2009 session. The effectiveness of the international arrangement on forests will be reviewed in 2015, at which time a full range of options will be considered, including a legally binding instrument on all types of forests. UNFF-7 also adopted a focused, multiyear program of work from 2007 to 2015, during which period the forum would meet biannually to review implementation of the non–legally binding instrument, sustainable forest management, the global objectives on forests, and the IPF/IFF proposals for action.[161]

When UNFF-8 convened two years later in April 2009, the main agenda item was to reach agreement on how to finance implementation of the non–legally binding instrument. At this point, the negotiations reflected the North-South division characteristic

PHOTO 4.5   During UNFF-9, Felix Finkbeiner, presenting "Felix & Friends," a Plant-for-the-Planet Children's Initiative, highlighted that forests are the future for children today. He noted two crises exist, poverty and environment, and lamented that too little action on either of these is being taken.
Courtesy Benjamin Singer, United Nations Forum on Forests.

of other environmental negotiations because the focus was now on financing and not on the definition of *sustainable forest management* or the need for a forest treaty. The first cochairs' draft failed to capture the true magnitude of the chasm between these positions, downplaying the G-77 and China's proposal for a global forest fund, resulting in a time-consuming false start. An entrenched debate over "fund or no fund" dominated the remainder of the session's negotiations, which never progressed past this to discuss more nuanced details, such as how such a fund would be governed. In the end, even a decision to establish an expert group to consider the need for a fund was quashed by lack of agreement over the group's mandate and a timeline for its work. Developing countries, as lead states, pushed for a decision on a fund's establishment sooner rather than later, and donor countries, as veto states, agreed to consider the establishment of a fund only at UNFF-10.[162]

One of the donors' main arguments was that the forum would run a great reputational risk if it created a fund that might never receive any voluntary contributions, an argument similar to the one they made during the negotiations on the UNCCD. Donors took the position that a facilitative process was preferable, calling for developing countries to make better use of existing funds. Developing countries turned this argument around, saying that the reputational risk lay in failing to create the fund needed to implement the forest instrument.[163]

This argument did not convince donors, and some delegates stated that the UNFF was not even the venue in which donors were most likely to produce big results for forest funding. Many reserved such expectations for the climate regime and the anticipated financing mechanism for reducing emissions from deforestation and forest degradation, which some see as the only major hope for generating anywhere near the amount of funding needed to address deforestation in a meaningful way. While the source of funds might seem irrelevant at first, many within the forest community worry that a purely climate-oriented source of forest funding risks marginalizing the many other values delivered by forests.[164] They believe that forest-related climate-change options must recognize a comprehensive approach to sustainable forest management, which goes beyond forests' carbon-storage potential. If only one good or service under sustainable forest management—such as climate-change adaptation and mitigation—attracts significant financing, there is a risk that this will distort sustainable forest management to the detriment of other goods and services. Many developing countries and NGOs emphasized this issue in 2011 at UNFF-9, where the focus was on forests for people, livelihoods and poverty eradication, and how sustainable forest management can contribute to human well-being, income, and livelihoods in addition to environmental sustainability.

It is important to remember that UNFF is just one of many platforms for addressing global forest issues. Forests are also addressed under the Convention on Biological Diversity (as habitat), the Convention to Combat Desertification (as weapons against land degradation), the UN Framework Convention on Climate Change (as carbon sinks), the International Tropical Timber Organization (as commercial products), and the FAO Committee on Forestry. At the regional level, the European forest ministers agreed in 2011 to negotiate their own legally binding agreement on forests in Europe, to be completed in 2013.[165]

The governance challenge for the future may be one of coordinating these multiple instruments rather than negotiating a new global treaty. Based on the experiences of the past twenty years, a comprehensive forest treaty looks increasingly unlikely. The forests case demonstrates that it is not always possible to negotiate a treaty to address a particularly complex environmental issue. This case also demonstrates that coalitions have the ability to shift significantly over time as a result of changing perceptions of the problem and changing and competing economic interests. Given the track record of the other natural resources treaties addressed in this chapter, a global, legally binding instrument on forests may not even be the best solution.

CONCLUSION

The environmental regimes discussed in Chapter 3 and this chapter show that the negotiation of a strong global environmental regime almost always depends on inducing one or more key states in a veto coalition to go along with one or more of the core proposed provisions of the regime. By a *strong* or *effective* regime, we mean an agreement that includes obligations or norms that make it sufficiently clear that parties can be held accountable for implementing them and that calls for actions that can reasonably be expected to have an impact on the problem if they are implemented. Whether a regime succeeds in addressing an environmental threat depends, of course, on how strong the regime is and on the degree to which parties comply with its core provisions. Five developments are usually associated with success in overcoming the impact of veto states in global environmental negotiations:

1. A veto state changed its own understanding of the problem because of new scientific evidence.
2. A veto state changed its position because its economic interests changed.
3. A veto state had a change of government, and the new government had a different policy toward the issue.
4. A veto state came under effective domestic political pressure to change its policy.
5. A veto state feared negative reactions from other governments or adverse international opinion, which it regarded as more important than its interest in vetoing a specific provision of the regime.

As Table 4.2 shows, in some of these cases one or more veto states either agreed to the central obligation proposed by the lead-state coalition or accepted the regime in general, despite earlier rejection.

New scientific evidence helped move veto states on some issues (ozone depletion, climate change, and persistent organic pollutants) but has been secondary or irrelevant in others (whaling, hazardous waste trade, desertification, and African elephants). International considerations were primary in several cases. Japan's concern with economic and diplomatic ties with other major trading nations and its international image helped tilt its stance on the ivory ban. French and British desire to maintain close relations with former colonies factored into their policy on the hazardous waste trade. The leading distant-water fishing states dropped their resistance to key provisions in the Fish Stocks Agreement at least in part because they did not want to appear to be blocking the first major global agreement on sustainable fishing. Changing economic interests or new political strategies concerning how to pursue those interests can also

TABLE 4.2   Veto States and Regime Creation or Strengthening

ISSUE	KEY VETO STATES	BASIS OF VETO POWER	VETO-STATE CONCESSION
Ozone depletion	European Community, later China and India	Percentage of CFC production, future CFC production	Agreeing to 50 percent cut; agreeing to phaseout
Hazardous waste trade	United States, EU, Japan	Percentage of exports	Agreeing to ban exports
Toxic chemicals	Developing countries that use DDT for malaria control	Percentage of use of DDT; global support for increased malaria control	Acceptance of elimination of DDT but with blanket exception for disease control; acceptance of regular reviews on continued need for DDT
Climate change	United States	Percentage of CO_2 emissions	Agreeing to stabilization goal[a]
Whaling	Japan and Norway	Percentage of catch	Acceptance of ban on whaling against depleted populations
African elephant ivory	Japan, southern African states	Percentage of imports (Japan); elephant herds (southern African states)	No reservation to CITES uplist
Biodiversity loss	United States	Percentage of financing of the GEF; biotechnology	Signing the agreement[a]
Fisheries depletion	European Commission, Japan, and the like-minded caucus	Percentage of global catch of straddling and highly migratory stocks	Agreement to precautionary reference points and new enforcement measures
Desertification	European Community, United States	Percentage of official development assistance	Agreeing to create the Global Mechanism as a funding mechanism
Forests	Brazil and other Latin American countries, United States	Percentage of the world's forests; largest timber industry	No agreement

Notes: This chart outlines one aspect of the veto coalition situation for each case as a point of comparison.
[a]In both of these cases veto-state power has not totally been overcome because although the United States in each case made certain concessions in the negotiations, the result was a much weaker treaty.

lead veto states to change position. The United Kingdom and France dropped their opposition to phasing out CFCs in part because their chemical industries invented substitutes. Several veto states in the forest negotiations changed positions when they believed they might secure a treaty that would preserve market access or secure new sources of multilateral funding.

In many of these cases, domestic political developments played a key role in facilitating agreement. Business and industrial concerns have affected the US response to climate change as well as the dispute over methyl bromide in the Montreal Protocol. Concern about persistent organic pollutants in the Inuit communities of northern Canada pushed Canada to the forefront of the negotiations to ban certain types of these substances.

Regime formation also requires leadership by one or more states committed to defining the issue and proposing a detailed policy approach as the basis for the regime. Sometimes, that lead role is played by states motivated by particular vulnerability (the African countries on the hazardous waste trade and desertification; the small island states on climate change) and sometimes by a state that has an advantageous legal or economic status (the original US call for a phaseout of chlorofluorocarbons). The absence of lead states seeking to strengthen the regime is a major factor, along with the presence of veto states, that the language in the conservation provisions of the biodiversity treaty remains largely advisory rather than binding.

Lead and veto states are not all equal of course. Lead states with greater diplomatic clout, economic resources, or negotiating skill outperform those with fewer resources. In the case of desertification, although the African countries have formed an active lead-state coalition, their weak political and economic influence has contributed to the ineffectiveness of the regime. Veto states require the ability to keep the regime from being effective in order to have an impact. This can vary from issue to issue and sometimes provides small states with significant clout if, for example, they have a large distant fishing fleet or are the main home to particular species. In general, however, the states and coalitions with the largest economies and populations (such as Brazil, China, G-77, India, the EU, and the United States) are the most potent potential veto states.

Overall, as these cases show, the United States has greater diplomatic influence on other state actors and intergovernmental organizations than any other state, although the EU as a unit is comparable and China is rivaling both, especially within the climate change regime. When the United States has taken the lead, as it did on ozone depletion, whaling, or the African elephant, the result has been a much stronger regime than otherwise would have been established. In the case of the Fish Stocks Agreement, the lead role played by the United States was crucial to agreement on conservation norms for the high seas and within EEZs. But when the United States has been a veto state, as in the Basel Convention, the Biodiversity Convention, and the Kyoto Protocol, the result is a significantly weaker regime.

In two of the potentially far-reaching regimes, climate and biodiversity, veto power wielded by key states greatly weakened the original agreement and has not yet been overcome in the subsequent negotiations on regime strengthening. The result is two relatively weak regimes, given what is known regarding the magnitude of the problems they seek to address. In negotiations on strengthening the climate regime, the key veto states have been Brazil, China, India, Russia, and the United States, which together account for much more than half of global GHG emissions. The United States, hobbled by strong domestic political opposition to a meaningful commitment to emissions reduction, has consistently opposed ambitious targets for reducing GHG emissions and played a large role in preventing a more effective regime. The insistence of major developing countries, whose emissions already account for a large proportion of global emissions, that the principle of common but differentiated responsibilities prevents placing any obligations for controlling emissions on them also threatens the effectiveness of the climate regime. While many had hoped that the election of President Barack Obama in 2008 would enable the United States to play a lead role in the negotiations, the reality is that domestic economic and political concerns in the United States still do not support any agreement that does not include developing countries.

In the case of biodiversity, efforts by a coalition of veto states have combined with several other factors—the complexity of the issue, lack of high levels of media interest, less domestic lobbying by environmental NGOs, and a poorly designed regime with a proliferation of working groups—to prevent the regime from becoming significantly stronger and more effective over time. These reasons have also contributed to the Biodiversity Convention receiving far less high-level political attention in major states than do the ozone or climate treaties.

As indicated in the cases examined in Chapter 3 and this chapter, the international community has been able to negotiate an impressively large number of agreements to reduce environmental threats. Many of these regimes have also grown significantly since the creation of their first agreement. Governments continue to meet and negotiate to add new pollution controls (as in the ozone and chemicals treaties), list new species (CITES), and even negotiate entirely new protocols within the regime (the Liability Protocol under the Basel Convention, the Kyoto Protocol, the Cartagena Protocol on Biosafety, and the Nagoya Protocol on Access and Benefit Sharing).

Global environmental regimes now include conventions that enjoy nearly universal participation. Almost every country in the world is a party to the climate change, biodiversity, ozone, and desertification conventions. Finally, some of these regimes (climate, biodiversity, hazardous waste trade, toxic chemicals, and desertification) have the potential to affect economic development strategies, production technologies, and even domestic political processes in ways supportive of long-term sustainable development.

However, as these cases also demonstrate, not all of these agreements have been successful. Serious obstacles exist to negotiating strong, global environmental treaties. Moreover, negotiating a strong treaty on paper does not mean it will be effective in practice. All of the regimes discussed in these chapters face serious implementation challenges, including compliance, financing, technology transfer, and effective translation of regime rules into national policy. The next chapter focuses on these challenges.

5

Effective Environmental Regimes: Obstacles and Opportunities

Environmental issues are an important part of international relations. More than 150 major international environmental agreements have been negotiated, and over 1,150 multilateral and 1,500 bilateral agreements contain at least some provisions addressing the environment.[1] However, simply negotiating an agreement, or even creating an entire regime, does not guarantee environmental protection.

The most important measure of the effectiveness of an environmental regime—the extent to which it produces measurable improvements in the environment—is a function of three factors. First is regime design, particularly the strength of the key control provisions aimed at addressing the environmental threat, but also the provisions on reporting, monitoring, regime strengthening, noncompliance, and financial and technical assistance. Second is the level of implementation, the extent to which countries (and to a lesser extent international organizations) adopt formal legislation and other regulations to enact the agreement. Third is compliance, the degree to which countries and other actors actually observe these regulations and the extent to which their actions conform to the explicit rules, norms, and procedures contained in the regime.[2]

This chapter examines some of the factors that inhibit or promote effective international environmental regimes. The first section outlines obstacles that can make it difficult to create and implement effective regimes with strong, binding control measures. These obstacles primarily relate to factors at the international level. The second section looks at variables that inhibit effective implementation and compliance. These primarily concern national-level issues. The third section outlines potential avenues to improve compliance. The final section discusses options for increasing the financing available to implement global environmental regimes.

OBSTACLES TO CREATING
STRONG ENVIRONMENTAL REGIMES

There are six major categories of obstacles that can inhibit creation of strong and effective global environmental regimes: (1) systemic or structural obstacles that stem from the structure of the international system, the structure of international law, and the structure of the global economic system; (2) a lack of necessary and sufficient conditions, in particular, public or official concern, a hospitable contractual environment, and capacity; (3) procedural obstacles inherent in international environmental negotiations; (4) obstacles that stem from common characteristics of global environmental issues; (5) obstacles that result from the interconnections of environmental issues, including potential conflicts between solutions; and (6) obstacles to designing effective regimes.[3] Of course, when we think about these categories, it is important to see them as broad, indicative, and heuristic rather than exhaustive and exclusive. The categories and the individual causal factors are interrelated, both with each other and with other issues, and their individual and relative impacts vary significantly across countries and issue areas. They also do not prevent effective policy; they simply make it more difficult to achieve.

Systemic Obstacles

Some impediments to creating strong global environmental regimes result from inherent elements of the global political, ecological, legal, and economic systems. One of the broadest is the anarchical structure of international politics. Anarchy, as used here, means the absence of hierarchy, specifically the absence of a world government with recognized authority to maintain order and make rules. For thousands of years, notable statesmen, philosophers, historians, and political scientists have argued that aspects of this structure have broad consequences for international relations.[4] In particular, states tend to believe they can rely only on self-help to ensure their safety, states usually attempt to balance the power of other states through alliances and armaments, states prefer independence over interdependence, and states often find it difficult to achieve effective international cooperation.[5]

The last consequence is perhaps the most relevant to environmental regimes. Just as in security or economic issues, system structure places pressures on state actors that can make it difficult to create effective environmental regimes (although to a lesser extent than in security issues). Strong states sometimes attempt to dictate terms to weaker states. States worry that other countries might face fewer costs from an agreement (even if both sides benefit environmentally) or that others might gain more economically or politically.[6] For example, the administration of George W. Bush expressed concern for relative impacts with regard to climate change, arguing that the United

States would suffer competitively if it reduced greenhouse gases (GHGs) but China did not.

States can fail to agree when some fear others might "double cross" them by not fulfilling regime obligations or paying their share of the costs.[7] States sometimes try to avoid paying a fair share of the costs, or to free ride, for example, by continuing to emit a certain pollutant when others have agreed to stop, the fear of which can scuttle an agreement or render it ineffective.[8] States sometimes have incentives to pursue policies that appear rational on their own but that result in harming or destroying a common-pool resource, resulting in a "tragedy of the commons."[9] A current example is the depletion of ocean fisheries, where many countries allow fishing fleets to catch as much fish as they can in international waters, which is good for them individually in the short run, even as the resource is depleted for everyone in the long run. States sometimes fail to locate mutually advantageous policies because of suspicions, a lack of information, market failure,[10] or misperception of the motives, intentions, or actions of other governments.[11] Governments can also compromise environmental negotiations by linking them to unrelated international or domestic political, security, and economic issues.

Another systemic or structural obstacle is the lack of congruence between the global political and ecological systems. The structure of the global political system, which comprises independent sovereign states, is inherently incongruent with ecological systems and not well suited to address complex, interdependent, international environmental problems whose causes, impacts, and solutions transcend unrelated political boundaries. Pollution released into the air or water spreads easily to other countries. Chlorofluorocarbons (CFCs) deplete the ozone layer without respect to which country released them. Persistent organic pollutants (POPs) released in the United States or Mexico affect people, animals, and ecosystems in northern Canada. Some of the mercury released from coal-fired power plants in China, India, Indonesia, and many other countries becomes absorbed and concentrated in ocean species eaten by people all over the world. High-seas fisheries and atmospheric chemistry are outside the political control of any one state.

This structural conflict has affected negotiations on global and regional commons issues—such as the atmosphere (ozone depletion and climate change) and the high seas (fisheries and whales)—as well as negotiations on problems when air and water pollution cross national borders. For example, upwind and downwind states can hold different views regarding appropriate rules to control air pollution, as was apparent in efforts to develop specific protocols to the Convention on Long-Range Transboundary Air Pollution protocols and in the US-Canada acid rain negotiations. Similar problems exist in the management of transboundary waterways. Of the more than 260 river basins around the world, one-third of them are shared by more than two countries, and

PHOTO 5.1   **The International POPs Elimination Network (IPEN) informs delegates about the dangers of mercury at the first session of the Intergovernmental Negotiating Committee to Prepare a Global Legally Binding Instrument on Mercury.** Courtesy IISD/*Earth Negotiations Bulletin.*

19 major river basins are shared by five or more states.[12] This significantly complicates efforts to manage pollution, overfishing, and sustainable use. For example, ten African states rely on the Nile River and its tributaries. Cooperative management efforts date back to a 1902 agreement between Ethiopia and Great Britain, but significant disputes continue to threaten the river's health. Egypt has at times even threatened military action against Sudan, Ethiopia, and Uganda for what it perceives as illegal diversions of water from the Nile, which decrease the river's volume when it reaches Egypt.[13]

A similar conflict exists between the foundations of international law and the requirements for effective international environmental policy. Perhaps the most fundamental principle of international law is sovereignty. States have nearly unassailable control over activities within their borders, including the use of natural resources. At the same time, however, legitimate actions within one country can create environmental problems for another. Consequently, effective international environmental policy often requires limiting what a state does within its own borders. This conflict is embodied in Principle 21 of the 1972 Stockholm Declaration, often cited as one of the most important foundations of modern international environmental law. It reads, "States have, in accordance with the Charter of the United Nations and the principles of international law, the sovereign right to exploit their own resources pursuant to their own environmental policies, and the responsibility to ensure that activities within their jurisdiction or control do not cause damage to the environment of other states or of areas beyond the limits of national jurisdiction."[14] This principle later became Principle 2 of the 1992 Rio Declaration, but with the words "and developmental" inserted before "policies," making it even more self-contradictory.

Overcoming the inherent tension captured in this principle is one of the most fundamental challenges of global environmental politics. Many states strongly resist regime provisions that, although beneficial to the environment, compromise their national sovereignty. For example, many of the most controversial proposals during negotiation of the Biodiversity Convention involved potential restrictions on state control over genetic resources within their borders.[15] The debate over a forest convention has been strongly affected by states wanting to ensure that they maintain clear sovereignty over their forest resources. Concerns about potential infringements on national sovereignty led to the inclusion of veto clauses that allow each party to block third-party adjudication under the Basel Convention.[16] China, India, and the United States have argued that efforts to curtail GHG emissions should not hamper their right to economic growth or use of domestic coal reserves. Whaling nations maintain they have the sovereign right to kill whales in their territorial waters and on the high seas.

Some argue that elements of the international economic system also present a structural impediment to creating and implementing strong and effective global environmental regimes. Different discussions along these lines point to the system's emphasis on resource extraction, globalization, free trade, lowest-cost production, high levels of consumption and consumerism, and, especially, the failure to include the economic and other costs produced by environmental degradation in the cost of activities and products that cause the degradation.

Some aspects of these arguments seem well founded. For example, few of the economic costs associated with the environmental and human-health impacts of using toxic chemicals or burning coal or gasoline are included in their price. These costs are passed on to society as a whole, rather than paid by the actors actually producing the pollution. Thus, there is little economic incentive for an individual company to reduce pollution when everyone pays its costs. There is an increasing consensus among a variety of theorists and politicians from across the political spectrum regarding the need to include the economic costs of environmental degradation into the larger economic system, although they often reach different conclusions about how to accomplish this.

Many also agree that the emphasis placed by certain international economic forces on developing countries to maximize resource extraction, pay off foreign debts, and industrialize as quickly as possible has produced serious environmental problems. The ultimate impact of free trade and economic integration on certain aspects of the environment also faces scrutiny, particularly when domestic environmental laws, such as the European Union (EU) ban on Canadian fur imports from animals caught in leg-hold traps, are overruled by free trade rules under the General Agreement on Tariffs and Trade and the World Trade Organization (WTO)[17] (see Chapter 6).

Yet it is probably too simplistic to assert that the global economic system only inhibits strong environmental regimes (see Box 5.1). Indeed, when properly harnessed, these same forces can support effective regimes. For example, in the expansion of the ozone regime, the global economic system supported the introduction of more environmentally friendly technology into developing countries much more quickly than many had expected. The financial power amassed by the global insurance industry supports stronger action on climate change. Free trade rules and economic integration have likely improved overall energy efficiency in Europe. Introducing carbon taxes, while lowering other taxes, would very likely increase demand for clean energy.[18] Thus, the key may be to examine, case by case, how economic interests and systems run counter to, or potentially could support, the goals or operation of a particular environmental regime rather than reflexively assuming that economic interests and systems necessarily inhibit strong environmental policy goals.

The Absence of Necessary Conditions: Concern, Contractual Environment, and Capacity

As discussed by Peter Haas, Robert Keohane, and Marc Levy, effective environmental regimes require three necessary, but not sufficient, conditions.[19] First, there must be adequate levels of concern within governments, and perhaps among the public at large, so that states decide to devote resources to examining and addressing the problem and implementing potential solutions. Environmental problems compete with many economic, security, and social issues for space on national and international agendas. Concern must exist for the issue-definition, fact-finding, bargaining, and regime-strengthening phases to occur and be completed successfully.

Second, there must be a sufficiently hospitable contractual environment so that states can gather together, negotiate with reasonable ease and costs, make credible commitments, reach agreement on new policies, and monitor each other's behavior in implementing those policies. In other words, if too many of the negative consequences of system structure, such as fears of cheating or free riding, are present, or if transaction costs (the time, money, and effort involved in negotiating a treaty) are too high, then creating strong agreements is difficult.

Third, states must possess the scientific, political, economic, and administrative capacity to understand the threat; participate in creating the global regime; and then implement and ensure compliance with the regime's principles, norms, and rules. Capacity is essentially a measure of the necessary scientific, administrative, economic,

BOX 5.1 PROMINENT OBSTACLES TO CREATING STRONG AND EFFECTIVE ENVIRONMENTAL REGIMES

SYSTEMIC OBSTACLES

- Anarchical structure of the international political system
- Aspects of the structure of international economic systems
- Incongruence of global political and ecological systems
- Incongruence of fundamental principles of international law and fundamental requirements for effective environmental policy

THE ABSENCE OF NECESSARY CONDITIONS

- Inadequate concern
- Inhospitable contractual environments
- Insufficient capacity

PROCEDURAL OBSTACLES

- Slow-boat problem: time lags in regime development and implementation
- Lowest-common-denominator problem

CHARACTERISTICS OF GLOBAL ENVIRONMENTAL ISSUES

- Links to important economic and social activity and interests
- Unequal adjustment costs
- Scientific complexity and uncertainty
- Time-horizon conflicts
- Different core beliefs
- Large number of actors

INTERCONNECTIONS BETWEEN ENVIRONMENTAL ISSUES

- Solutions can require addressing multiple issues
- Solutions to one issue may exacerbate problems in another issue

REGIME DESIGN DIFFICULTIES

- Other political and economic issues influence regime design
- Regimes are not created by environmental experts
- Effective regime design is difficult

and political resources a country possesses to address a particular issue, as well as the physical and political ability to deploy those resources effectively.

Concern, contractual environment, and capacity are not obstacles themselves. The presence of each is a necessary but insufficient condition. Thus, it is their absence that significantly inhibits, if not prevents, the creation and implementation of strong environmental regimes. The concepts are easy to oversimplify, but concern, contractual environment, and capacity encapsulate important, even critical causal factors and are interconnected with many of the other issues discussed in this chapter.

Procedural Obstacles

Once states begin the bargaining or negotiation phase, two important obstacles emerge: the time-lag and lowest-common-denominator problems.[20] Each is a product of how international negotiations work, the structural obstacles outlined above, and varying levels of national concern for particular environmental issues.

The process to create and implement effective global environmental policy is neither easy nor speedy. The international agenda must be set, negotiations convened, appropriate policies identified, strong agreements reached, implementation strategies agreed to, treaties ratified, national and international policies implemented and reported on, environmental problems monitored, and international policies revised in light of new data and lessons learned. The common practice of starting with a framework convention and adopting subsequent protocols adds even more time. Enough governments must ratify the convention and protocols so that they can enter into force and be effective.

Each step in this series can be time-consuming. As discussed in Chapter 3, the environmental problems posed by hazardous waste shipments were identified in the 1970s, but the Basel Convention did not come into effect until 1992, and the Ban Amendment still requires additional ratifications to take effect. The United Nations Convention on the Law of the Sea, a complex treaty that contains provisions on most aspects of maritime law, took nearly ten years to negotiate and another twelve to receive enough ratifications to enter into force. The International Convention for the Prevention of Pollution from Ships (MARPOL) experienced a ten-year time lag from its negotiation to its entry into force, despite the decades of collaborative efforts on oil pollution leading up to it.

Knowledge of the greenhouse effect goes back more than 150 years. Joseph Fourier, a French mathematician and physicist, discovered in 1824 that gases in the atmosphere likely increase the surface temperature of the earth. In 1859, John Tyndall, an Irish physicist, explained the ability of various gases, including carbon dioxide (CO_2) and water vapor, to absorb radiant heat, proving that the earth's atmosphere has a natural greenhouse effect. In 1896 Svante Arrhenius, a Swedish scientist, published an article suggesting that temperatures would rise 5 degrees Celsius if atmospheric CO_2 doubled. In 1960, Charles Keeling published data clearly showing that CO_2 levels were rising. Nevertheless, formal negotiations on the United Nations Framework Convention on Climate Change did not begin until 1991, and more than twenty years later only modest global controls exist for GHG emissions. Scientists discovered the threat to the ozone layer in 1974, but negotiations did not begin until 1982, the first binding controls did not come into force until 1988, developing countries did not have to phase out most uses of CFCs until 2010, and hydrochlorofluorocarbons (HCFCs) will not be phased out completely for another twenty years.

Yet environmental issues do not wait for the policy process. As negotiations continue, more species become extinct, forests are cut down, land is degraded, GHGs are emitted into the atmosphere, toxic chemicals are released, and hazardous wastes are not properly managed, making it even more difficult to create and implement effective regimes.

The second procedural obstacle, the lowest-common-denominator problem, is created by veto states. Because all states are sovereign entities, they can choose whether to join a global environmental agreement. However, because active participation by many countries is required to address a global environmental problem, the countries most concerned with addressing a particular issue often need support from countries with far less interest. Thus, an environmental treaty can be only as strong as its least cooperative state allows it to be. The regime's overall effectiveness is undermined by the compromises made in persuading these states, the veto states, to participate.

For example, as discussed in Chapter 3, during the Stockholm Convention negotiations, countries critical to its long-term success insisted on specific exemptions so that they could continue using small amounts of certain POPs, even though the convention called for eliminating all production and use of these substances. This process repeated itself when parties expanded the convention by adding chemicals in 2009 and 2011. During negotiation of the 1991 Protocol on Environmental Protection to the Antarctic Treaty, which protects Antarctica from possible mineral exploitation, opposition from the United States resulted in a fifty-year moratorium rather than the initially proposed permanent protection.[21] As discussed in Chapter 3, from 1977 to 1989, the European Community (EC) acted as a veto state and set the lowest common denominator for global ozone policy, forcing lead states to accept much weaker rules in the 1985 Vienna Convention and 1987 Montreal Protocol than they had sought.

The lowest-common-denominator problem has affected the climate regime for many years. As discussed in Chapter 3, all the major emitters of GHGs, but especially China, Europe, India, and the United States, must cooperate for the regime to succeed. Until relatively recently, China, India, and the United States have been reluctant to discuss binding actions to curb their domestic emissions, and each has refused to finalize such terms. This has limited the ability of Europe, the Alliance of Small Island States, and other lead states to move forward with aggressive global policies. They could create an agreement without Chinese, Indian, and US participation, like the Kyoto Protocol, or act on their own domestically, as the EU has done, but effective global policy requires the eventual participation of the veto states—putting them in a position to continue to force a lowest-common-denominator agreement.

Characteristics of Global Environmental Issues

Another set of obstacles to creating strong regimes stems from common characteristics inherent in global environmental problems. Although they are certainly not unique to environmental issues and have impacts that are both interconnected and vary across countries and issue areas, these characteristics are important elements of global environmental politics and have the capacity to exacerbate many of the other obstacles outlined above.[22]

One of the most critical characteristics is that environmental issues are inextricably linked to important economic and political interests. Environmental issues, and therefore environmental negotiations, are not independent of other economic and political activities and interests; environmental issues exist because of these activities and interests. Environmental problems are produced as externalities of individuals, corporations, and nations pursuing other interests. They result from important local, corporate, national, and international economic and political activities such as energy production, mining, manufacturing, farming, fishing, transportation, resource consumption, livestock husbandry, urbanization, weapons production, territorial expansion, and military conflict.

Few, if any, individuals or organizations harm the environment as an end in itself. People do not get up in the morning, leave their homes, and announce, "I intend to pollute today." What people do say is, "I intend to manufacture, to produce energy, to farm, to drive my car to work." Environmental degradation is a consequence of these otherwise legitimate pursuits. The fact that many of these activities could be pursued successfully while doing less harm to the environment does not erase the links between the issues.

Creating strong international environmental regimes, therefore, often requires addressing economic, social, and even security interests that are important to certain countries or interest groups. Regardless of whether these interests are justified, the links creates obstacles to effective action. The presence of important economic interests can lower relative concern, make veto states more determined, and cause powerful domestic economic actors to lobby for their views. They can also enhance fears of free riding, create more opportunities for positional bargaining, and otherwise harm the contractual environment.

Examples of the obstacles posed by the links between environmental problems and economic interests are common. Protecting the earth's remaining biodiversity requires addressing the economic and political pressures that cause habitat destruction, something that has proved almost impossible to date. In the Nagoya Protocol negotiations, developing countries called for fair and equitable sharing of benefits arising from the use of genetic resources with the countries of origin and with local and indigenous communities, whereas foreign companies, collectors, researchers, and other users who profit greatly from derivatives of these resources preferred the status quo, where they could gain access essentially for free. A strong regime to address climate change will require significant changes in fossil-fuel consumption, which currently remain out of reach. Complete protection of the ozone layer requires a near total phaseout of methyl bromide emissions, but major agricultural interests, particularly in the United States, are hesitant to agree to this. Combating deforestation in some developing countries would have a significant impact on their timber industry. Addressing the serious decline in fisheries will affect the economies of both distant-water fishing states and coastal states.

Sometimes the linkages are particularly difficult to argue against, even for strong proponents of the environmental regime. For example, the total elimination of DDT would prevent its use as an inexpensive tool in the battle against malaria in Africa and Asia. Even those countries most committed to addressing POPs under the Stockholm Convention agree that the use of DDT should continue (although with methods that reduce the environmental impact of DDT) while alternative products and processes are developed. Similarly, the toxic chemical perfluorooctane sulfonate (PFOS) is used in certain medical devices. While strongly agreeing the substance should be eliminated as part of the expansion of the Stockholm Convention in 2009, the United States and Switzerland also successfully argued that given the interest in advancing medical care, an exception should be granted so that small amounts of the substance can be used in certain medical devices until replacements are developed. Eliminating all demand for mercury requires addressing or controlling its use in a very effective and low-cost preservative for vaccines.[23]

A second characteristic, and one closely linked to the first, is unequal adjustment costs. Addressing an environmental problem means changing the economic, political, and/or cultural activities that ultimately cause the problem. Making these changes, or "adjustments," can produce many benefits, but they also carry different economic and political costs in different countries. For example, the transition to using solar, wind, and geothermal energy to replace fossil fuels will clean the air of harmful pollutants, reduce CO_2 emissions, and create new, sustainable jobs in the alternative-energy industry, but countries, regions, companies, and individuals with strong connections to the old, polluting industries will experience higher costs during the transition than those that do not. Parts of the United States with significant solar or wind resources might find the transition relatively easy. Saudi Arabia and Russia, whose economies rely on fossil-fuel exports, will incur significant costs. While the overall transition will likely produce far greater long-term benefits for nearly all countries and the planet as a whole, it will involve changes, or adjustment costs, that certain regions, countries, and businesses will find objectionable.

Countries face different adjustment costs depending on the environmental issue. These variations can reflect differences in their contribution to the problem, their level of economic development, and the political and economic influence of the relevant industry, as well as their enforcement capability, existing level of regulation, resource base, trade profile, method of energy production, transportation policy, and a host of other factors.

Large variations in adjustment costs in countries essential to a regime act as obstacles to creating a strong regime. Indeed, they are part of the reason that veto coalitions form. Large and unequal adjustment costs exacerbate the difficulties inherent in international cooperation. In addition to concerns about the costs they will bear, states often also consider potential positional advantages or disadvantages produced by the relative costs to be borne by other states. Thus, states may reject solutions that ask them to bear a larger burden than other states. Alternatively they may demand special compensation for joining the regime, which in turn can weaken the regime.

Unequal adjustment costs exist in all the regimes outlined in Chapters 3 and 4, and addressing their impact is a critical and difficult part of global environmental politics. During negotiation of the Kyoto Protocol, many governments argued that their different levels of industrialization, energy profile, transportation infrastructure, core industries, and even local temperatures made adhering to one set of mandatory reductions in CO_2 emissions inherently unfair. As a result, the Kyoto Protocol contained no mandatory reductions of CO_2 emissions for developing countries and different, modest targets for developed countries. The prospect of unequal adjustment costs continues to pose huge problems for the climate regime, including efforts to craft a successor agreement to the Kyoto Protocol. Strong controls on carbon emissions mean enormous adjustment for oil-exporting states, as demand for oil will fall, as well as for countries that depend on cheap coal for energy, such as Australia, China, India, and parts of the United States, as they will have to capture the CO_2 before it is released or turn to other energy sources. However, adjustment costs would be far less for countries such as France, which relies on nuclear power for most of its electricity, or Iceland, which uses geothermal energy. Developing countries as a whole also face the challenge of altering their energy future at a crucial point in their economic development, a prospect they believe carries far higher adjustment costs than those faced by the industrialized countries, which, in general, have greater technological and financial resources. Reconciling these positions remains a huge challenge for global climate policy, even with the progress made in the negotiations in recent years.

Similar problems exist in other regimes. Different governments consistently seek to exclude certain substances from the toxic chemicals regime or press for special exemptions, arguing that a particular industry using the substance would bear higher and unfair burdens if forced to comply with the same standards as companies in other countries that do not use the substance. China, India, Indonesia, and others objected to rules requiring them to install state-of-the-art devices to prevent mercury emissions from existing coal-fired power plants in part because they would face far higher costs than the United States and the EU, where such devices were already common.[24] Iceland, Japan, Norway, and other countries that permit whaling argue that the economic, cultural, or scientific adjustment costs of stopping all whaling would place unfair burdens on particular groups. Some developing countries express concern that future efforts to protect biodiversity or a future forest convention will include attempts to prevent their use of large forested areas for traditional types of economic development—costs most industrialized countries would not bear.

A third obstacle is that environmental issues often involve significant scientific complexity and uncertainty regarding their scope, severity, impact, or time frame. Scientific complexity can challenge the capacity of government bureaucracies to understand the problem and design and implement effective solutions. Scientific uncertainty about an environmental problem can undermine concern and allow other, more certain economic or political interests to be prioritized in the policy hierarchy. Uncertainty and complexity can lead different states to perceive payoffs differently, perhaps reducing incentives to risk cooperation and increasing incentives either to free ride or to ignore the problem altogether, thereby harming the contractual environment.

For example, opponents of a strong regime for climate change emphasize not only the costs of such an agreement (including the links to important economic interests and unequal adjustment costs) but also what they argue are important uncertainties regarding the severity of the problem (the vast majority of scientists and the Intergovernmental Panel on Climate Change do not share this view). Lack of certainty regarding the impacts of long-term, low-level exposure to toxic chemicals inhibits the chemicals regime from expanding more quickly, despite increasing evidence that causes many experts to express significant concern. Biodiversity loss, biosafety, and ozone depletion are some of the other issues for which scientific complexity and uncertainty slowed or prevented the creation of strong regimes.

A fourth characteristic that can act as an obstacle to creating and implementing strong regimes is time-horizon conflicts. Because the most serious consequences of many environmental problems will not occur for many years (or this appears to be the case, even if it is proven incorrect later), policy makers sometimes find it difficult to create strong regimes with significant short-term costs, even if such action would be less expensive and more successful in the long run. That some environmental issues do not develop in a linear, predictable pattern complicates matters.

In addition, the impacts of some environmental problems do not occur simultaneously in all regions and in all countries. This can mask their global impact or cause some actors to remain less concerned about addressing them. The time-horizon obstacle is enhanced if concern for the problem is low, the nature of the threat is not well defined, or the costs of acting are very high. Ozone depletion, biodiversity loss, and climate change are obvious examples of issues affected by time-horizon conflicts. Efforts to add additional substances to the POPs regime also face this problem. While thousands of chemical spills occur each year,[25] sometimes resulting in large short-term exposure to POPs and other toxic substances, the most widespread threats posed by many chemicals, including potential impacts on reproductive health, could occur in the future as a result of long-term exposure from their slow accumulation in humans and the environment.[26] Preventing these impacts requires preventing the buildup, and this means accepting certain current costs for likely, but future, benefits.

In addition, the time structures of environmental systems and those of political and corporate systems are not congruent. Addressing environmental problems effectively often requires an informed, long-term perspective. Most political and corporate systems operate on much shorter timescales. Major political figures in the United States, for example, face elections every two years (members of the House of Representatives), four years (president and governors), or six years (senators). Most corporations release reports on their revenues, costs, and profits every three months—reports that can significantly affect their stock price and executive compensation. Thus, even if every political figure and corporate leader wanted to address an environmental issue, the time horizon for their most immediate approval processes (elections and quarterly reports) are not in tune with the long-term time horizons needed to address environmental problems.

Fifth, states and groups within states sometimes possess different core religious, cultural, or political beliefs and values relevant to environmental issues. Such conflicting beliefs and values can limit the creation of sufficient transnational concern, block potential policies, cause some actors not to participate or comply, and necessitate compromises that weaken the resulting regime. For example, as discussed in Chapter 4, some groups in Iceland, Japan, and Norway have strong cultural links to whaling. They do not view it as a moral issue and thus reject international attempts to curtail their whaling as inappropriate foreign intrusion on their rights and beliefs. Some individuals in Asia believe products from endangered animal species, such as rhino horn, have important medicinal, physical, or sexual properties. This creates a market for these animals and undercuts international controls designed to protect them. Some religious leaders oppose policies designed to control human population growth. Some political ideologies treat economic development and freedom from government regulations as higher priorities than environmental protection and resist cooperative solutions that they believe would restrict economic or personal freedom. Some nongovernmental organizations (NGOs) believe just the opposite.

Sixth, large numbers of actors must cooperate to create and implement effective global environmental policy. Social science has long acknowledged that reaching cooperative solutions to common problems becomes more difficult as the number of actors increases. More actors mean more heterogeneity of interests. The larger the number of actors, the more likely that an agreement, if concluded at all, will be "partial" in at least one of three ways: (1) covering only some of the agenda topics, (2) leaving some disagreement latent in an ambiguous text, or (3) being signed and accepted only by some states. In addition, the risk of suboptimal outcomes, or lowest-common-denominator agreements, seems to increase as the number of actors increases.[27]

Large numbers can also increase incentives for noncompliance, because of reduced fears of detection, particularly if the benefits of cooperation are suspect or the adjustment costs are high or uneven. Large numbers can be particularly dangerous to the success of a regime that seeks to protect the commons, such as the oceans or atmosphere, which all can use but no one controls. If some states fear that others will cheat, they may believe they face a "use it or lose it" scenario that compels them to use the resource, leading to its more rapid degradation.[28] The situation is compounded in cases in which many states need to control many private actors in order for the environmental policy to succeed. The Convention on International Trade in Endangered Species of Wild Fauna and Flora (CITES) faces obstacles with compliance because the number of potential violators is so large, especially with the advent of Internet sales of endangered species and their products. An immense number of ships can violate ocean pollution and fishing agreements. Thousands of companies in countries around the world work with toxic chemicals or create hazardous waste. The huge number of GHG emissions sources complicates global policy making.

Interconnections Between Environmental Issues

Environmental issues do not exist in isolation. Causes, impacts, consequences, and solutions are often interconnected in surprising ways. Sometimes these connections can inhibit successful action. This is the case when one environmental problem exacerbates another one, making the problem more difficult to solve because long-term success in that issue also requires successfully addressing the other issue. For example, climate change threatens millions of species with extinction, making the preservation of biodiversity more difficult. Similarly, coral reefs face serious threats from warming seas, increased runoff from land degraded by deforestation, and pollution released by industrial facilities. Each of these harms the reefs, exacerbating the impact of the others. Solving one threat to a reef will not save it unless the others are solved as well. Deforestation and land degradation are major contributors to biodiversity loss, through habitat destruction, and to climate change, through the release of CO_2 into the atmosphere and because the forested lands can no longer act as carbon sinks by absorbing CO_2 from the air. Thus, effective long-term global policies on biodiversity or climate change will also require action to combat the destruction of tropical forests and land degradation.

Interconnections also create obstacles if addressing one environmental problem causes another problem to worsen. For example, replacing coal-fired power plants with nuclear power plants decreases GHG emissions, but it also creates the potential for immense environmental problems if radiation is released as a result of a natural disaster (as happened in the aftermath of the tsunami that hit Japan in 2011), an accident at the plant (as occurred at the Chernobyl nuclear power plant in Ukraine in 1986), a terrorist attack, or a leak from the storage of the nuclear waste. Dams can also help address climate change by producing electricity without burning fossil fuels, but they can also produce harmful environmental impacts such as riparian habitat loss, erosion, impacts on river animal and fish populations, and potential declines in water quality. Biofuels can be used to replace gasoline and reduce GHGs, but some biofuels, such as those made from corn, soybeans, or other crops requiring good soil, divert land from food production and usually require significant quantities of water and fertilizer. Some biofuels require immense amounts of energy to gather, transport, and refine into fuel, negating their climate impact and adding to other problems. (Research continues on developing biofuels from plants that can grow on marginal land without fertilizer or from algae that can be grown in greenhouses with recycled water, alleviating many of these negative impacts.)

Several chemicals developed to replace ozone-depleting substances, and thus safeguard the ozone layer, have had an impact on other environmental problems. As outlined in Chapter 3, companies developed HCFCs and HFCs as substitutes for ozone-depleting CFCs. These chemicals proved crucial to protecting the ozone layer while requiring relatively small changes to the huge refrigeration and air-conditioning industries. Unfortunately, HCFCs and HFCs are far stronger GHGs than the CFCs they replaced. Thus, their invention and increased use, which occurred only as part of global attempts to protect the ozone layer, exacerbated climate change. HCFCs have been controlled under the amended Montreal Protocol, but HFCs, which do not deplete the ozone layer, have not. Similarly, when China eliminated the use of halons in 2008 (as noted in Chapter 3, halons are excellent fire suppressants but powerful ozone-depleting gases), they did so in part by using firefighting foam mixes that included PFOS. As outlined in Chapter 3, in 2009 parties to the Stockholm Convention added

PFOS to the list of chemicals slated for elimination, but China and others argued successfully that an exemption should be granted for use in firefighting foam, as it would not be economical to phase out this fire-control substance so soon after eliminating halons.[29] Thus, one solution to the problem of halons as ozone-depleting chemicals exacerbated the problems of toxics in the environment and complicated policy discussions within the Stockholm Convention regime.

Regime Design

Another obstacle to strong effective global environmental regimes is sometimes the design of the regime itself. As Ron Mitchell puts it, "Regime design matters."[30] Regime rules inappropriate to an issue area are unlikely to work. Control measures and reporting requirements that are too complex or extremely vague might not be implemented correctly. Treaties without enough flexibility cannot be adjusted in response to new scientific findings. Treaties with too much flexibility might be changed so often that some governments and industries, frustrated with the inability to make long-term plans, may begin to leave or ignore the regime.

Regime design is difficult. All the issues outlined in the previous sections can inhibit the design of an effective regime. The process requires a nuanced understanding of the science of the environmental issue, including its causes and consequences, how it interacts with other issues, and how it will evolve over time; the economic and social activities that give rise to the problem and will be affected by it; how to address the issue so that a long-term solution is environmentally, economically, and politically possible; and how to design the solution in the form of an international regime that can be implemented effectively at the national level. This last point is often overlooked. No matter how well-meaning a treaty's intention or how strong its control provisions are, it will not yield measurable environmental benefits if states cannot implement it.

Equally important is the fact that regimes are negotiated as much as they are designed—and negotiated by people and governments with concerns that might run counter to the requirements for a perfectly crafted environmental regime. Environmental treaties are not designed by a small group of experts whose only goal is to eliminate a global environmental problem. In reality, treaties result from negotiations involving hundreds of government representatives from different types of ministries whose collective job is to address the environmental issue but whose individual instructions also reflect concerns for other national and international economic and political goals. Delegates operate within frameworks established by instructions and briefing books given to them by their government. People from different parts of the government, with different perspectives on the regime negotiations, often participate in creating these frameworks. In the United States, for example, while Environmental Protection Agency officials might see the negotiations as a means to address

PHOTO 5.2   Bangkok Climate Change Conference, 2011. Treaties result from negotiations involving hundreds of government representatives from different types of ministries. Courtesy IISD/*Earth Negotiations Bulletin.*

the environmental issue, trade officials might want to make sure a tough stand in the negotiations does not affect relations with a crucial trading partner or upset relationships important to an upcoming trade negotiation. State Department officials might object to a particular regime component, even if it would be very effective, for fear that it will set a precedent that could be demanded in negotiations on other issues. Congressional staff and White House domestic political advisers might not want policies that would upset key political allies or donors to political campaigns. Budget officials might insist on limiting provisions of financial and technical assistance (FTA). None of this is improper—each person is simply attending to his or her government responsibility—but it does point out how the complexities underlying national positions can produce pressures that can influence national negotiation positions away from consensus on the optimal regime design for a given issue.

Consequently, government goals in global environmental negotiation are often broader than addressing the environmental issue under discussion. Some developing countries might try to use the negotiations to obtain general development assistance masked as environmental investments. Donor countries might try to limit financial obligations in general or to funnel assistance through the Global Environment Facility (GEF) because they think doing so will save money or that they can control the GEF more easily, regardless of what might be best for a particular regime. Some governments might push against a particular principle—for example, the precautionary principle—

because they do not want it to be accepted as a general principle of international law. Some might try to build global scientific networks as a means to increase scientific training in their countries. Some might push for a strong noncompliance regime because they support strong international adjudication procedures in general. Some countries might have disagreements with particular international organizations, NGOs, or other governments that affect their negotiating positions.

Thus, environmental regime design should not be seen as the equivalent of blueprints drawn by a small group of brilliant architects who specialize in building hospitals and have been given the time and money to create an outstanding facility that will address one particular disease. They are more like blueprints drawn by a group of several hundred architects who specialize in different types of design and who have been assigned the group task of designing a hospital to address one particular disease. Plus, many of the architects have other jobs and must make sure that parts of the planned hospital can also be used as a bank, training facility, research center, advertising agency, school, police station, courthouse, travel agency, or construction company. Moreover, they do not agree on which of these other uses is the most important, they do not have enough land or money to construct a building that could do all these things well, not all of them are particularly good architects, and they do not have a great deal of time before the disease spreads and many more people start to die. Creating and implementing effective global environmental policy is challenging.

OBSTACLES TO EFFECTIVE NATIONAL IMPLEMENTATION AND COMPLIANCE WITH GLOBAL ENVIRONMENTAL REGIMES

Treaties contain many different types of obligations. The most important are sometimes referred to as substantive obligations, particularly obligations to cease or limit a specific activity such as GHG emissions, CFC production, or the release of certain toxic chemicals. Also important are a variety of procedural obligations, such as monitoring and reporting requirements. Compliance refers to whether countries adhere to the mandatory provisions of an environmental convention and the extent to which they follow through on the steps they have taken to implement these provisions.[31]

Global environmental regimes employ a variety of mechanisms to promote implementation and compliance. These include using binding rules instead of voluntary measures, providing eligible countries with technical and financial assistance to build capacity and help them to fulfill particular regime obligations, requiring regular reporting by the parties, allowing for independent evaluation and public availability of such reports, reviewing regime implementation and effectiveness, calling noncomplying parties to account publicly, providing incentives, creating formal noncompliance procedures that have the potential to establish penalties, augmenting public education and awareness raising, and monitoring of compliance by NGOs and international organizations. Of course, not all regimes employ each measure, and their success varies significantly across regimes and among parties.

Most countries that sign and ratify an international convention do so with the intention of complying with its provisions, and most comply to the best of their ability.[32] Nevertheless, compliance sometimes turns out to be politically, technically, administratively, or financially impossible, even when a government remains committed to the regime. Sometimes compliance becomes sufficiently difficult that a state decides to focus time, effort, and resources in other areas; that is, compliance is still possible, but a state chooses not to comply because of other priorities. Only rarely does a state deliberately set out to sign and ratify a treaty with no intention of complying.

As attention turns from creating new global environmental regimes to implementing and strengthening existing ones, compliance has become an even more important issue. In addition to the general obstacles outlined above, the literature on implementation and compliance with international environmental agreements suggests that noncompliance can be traced to several different types of factors, including inadequate translation of regime rules into domestic law; insufficient capacity to implement, administer, or enforce relevant domestic policy; inability to monitor and report on implementation; the costs of compliance; misperception of the relevant costs and benefits; inadequate FTA; poorly designed regimes; and the large number of environmental conventions and the confusing and uncoordinated web of requirements they have produced.[33] As with the discussion of the obstacles to creating strong and effective regimes, these categories of implementation obstacles overlap significantly and are extremely interrelated. They are not listed in order of importance, as their impacts vary from country to country and issue to issue. Indeed, scholars and national officials have many different opinions about which obstacles are most important overall or most relevant to particular issue areas (see Box 5.2).

Inadequate Translation of Regime Rules into Domestic Policy

Some states are unable to or choose not to adopt the domestic legislation necessary to implement and fully comply with an international agreement. This can include failing to adopt any or all of the needed regulations or adopting poorly crafted regulations. For instance, Peter Sand noted that "the main constraint on the implementation of CITES in each Party has been the need to create national legislation. Although this is an obligation under [CITES], several countries have not complied. . . . Others have only incomplete legislation."[34]

The failure to enact domestic law can stem from a variety of factors. Sometimes domestic economic or political opposition that failed to block a country from negotiating or signing a particular treaty can nevertheless prevent the country from ratifying it. If national ratification depends on approval by a legislative branch, as in the United States, then treaty ratification, and consequently, the translation of international regime rules into domestic law, can be prevented by interest groups or lawmakers opposed to its goals or means, by politicians seeking leverage to achieve other political ends, by an overburdened legislative agenda, or by conflicts over resource allocations. For example, since the 1990s, opposition from powerful interest groups and key senators has prevented the US Senate even from holding formal ratification votes on several key treaties, including the Kyoto Protocol and the Biodiversity, Basel, Rotterdam, and Stockholm conventions.

Even when a treaty is ratified, interest groups or the political opposition might still manage to prevent or significantly weaken the necessary implementing legislation. Weak legislative and bureaucratic infrastructures or a lack of expertise on the issue can also prevent the most effective regulations from becoming law. Some of the chemicals treaties, for example, require relatively high levels of knowledge about toxic chemicals and their management to enact all their provisions effectively into domestic law. Inefficient legislative procedures or political or economic instability also can keep states from fully or accurately enacting necessary domestic legislation. Finally, in democracies with nonintegrated federal structures, the federal government may not always have the jurisdiction to implement international environmental agreements completely at the state or provincial level. For example, in Belgium, each of the autonomous regions must separately adopt environmental legislation. In Canada, the provinces, not the federal government, control many aspects of environmental policy.[35]

BOX 5.2   OBSTACLES TO EFFECTIVE NATIONAL IMPLEMENTATION

- **Inadequate translation of regime rules into domestic policy**
- **Insufficient capacity to implement, administer, or enforce domestic policy**
- **Inability to monitor and report on implementation**
- **Costs of compliance**
- **Misperception of relevant costs and benefits**
- **Inadequate or poorly targeted financial and technical assistance**
- **Poorly designed regimes**
- **Many regimes, little coordination**

Insufficient Capacity to Implement, Administer, or Enforce Domestic Policy

It is not enough simply to enact laws and regulations. They must also be effectively implemented, administered, and enforced. Doing so requires sufficient issue-specific skills, knowledge, technical know-how, legal authority, financial resources, and enforcement capacity at the individual and institutional levels. Therefore, a second reason for inadequate compliance is insufficient state capacity to implement, administer, or enforce the relevant domestic policies and regulations. Insufficient capacity is a particular problem for some developing countries, but it exists in all parts of the world and varies from issue to issue and country to country.

Examples of capacity problems inhibiting compliance are unfortunately common. CITES has provisions for trade measures to enforce its controls on wildlife trade, but many countries, including industrialized countries, lack the budgets or trained personnel needed to comply fully and effectively.[36] Compliance with the Convention on Biological Diversity (CBD) has been hindered by a lack of national capacity to manage protected areas and to analyze and control the impact of development projects on biodiversity. Russia did not comply with its obligations under the ozone regime for several years because its government temporarily lacked the capacity to stop the black-market production and export of CFCs. Full compliance with the Stockholm Convention includes locating, identifying, and destroying stockpiles of obsolete pesticides in an environmentally sound manner, something beyond the technical and financial ability of many countries. The central governments of Brazil, Indonesia, and some other countries have not demonstrated the consistent ability to prevent illegal logging and deforestation.[37] The Basel Convention contains no provision for international monitoring of the accuracy of hazardous waste labels or spot-checking shipments in the ports of receiving countries. Developing countries, whose inability to monitor and regulate trade led them to call for a ban on international waste shipments in the first place, often do not have the capacity to monitor this shipping themselves.[38] African countries continue to express concern that they are sometimes unable to prevent unwanted shipments of obsolete pesticides and products, toxic chemicals, and potentially hazardous wastes into their countries.[39] Several countries in Asia, Africa, and Central and South America express concern for their ability to prevent the use of mercury in illegal, small-scale gold mining operations.[40]

A related obstacle is a lack of respect for the rule of law by particular groups within some countries. This problem tends to arise more often in countries where severe economic pressures, political instability, and patterns of corruption lead particular groups, government officials, or the general public to ignore elements of the legal system.

For example, sections of the Central African Republic, Democratic Republic of Congo, and several other African countries are relatively lawless, making it difficult to preserve their significant biodiversity, forest, and ecosystem resources. Illegal deforestation in Bolivia, Brazil, Colombia, Indonesia, and other countries reflects not only lack of government capacity but also indifference to the law by those clearing the land.[41] In Kenya during the rule of Daniel arap Moi, from 1978 to 2002, systematic corruption, extreme poverty, and the absence of a meaningful democratic process caused many people to feel alienated from the lawmaking apparatus, undermining their respect for the law, including regulations on wildlife conservation.[42] Similarly, the epidemic of illegal logging in national parks in Indonesia following the 1998 financial crisis resulted, at least in part, in a breakdown of law and order combined with economic pressures in the affected areas.[43]

Inability to Monitor and Report on Implementation

Similarly, some states that want to comply can end up not doing so because they do not know what is happening domestically. Two principal sets of factors affect states' ability to monitor domestic compliance with environmental laws: (1) whether states have adequate feedback mechanisms, such as on-site monitoring by inspectors, reporting requirements, complaint mechanisms, or close working relationships with NGOs; and (2) the number and size of the potential violators whose conduct the government must monitor.[44] For example, the relatively high level of compliance with the Montreal Protocol results not only from the widely accepted science regarding the cause and potential impact of the problem but also from the manageable limits the regime places on the number of sources or sites that require monitoring. Monitoring long-term compliance with any post-Kyoto climate regime may prove far more difficult, however, because of the multitude of GHG emissions sources. Similarly, monitoring compliance with CITES remains difficult in part because the number of potential violators is so large.

Costs of Compliance

Domestic compliance with international environmental agreements is also affected by the costs of such compliance relative to the country's level of economic development, current economic situation, resource base, and budgetary preferences.[45] Affluent countries experiencing relatively strong economic growth are historically far more willing and able to comply with environmental regulations than poorer states or states with economies that are growing slowly or not at all. States with low per capita incomes are generally reluctant to commit significant funds to comply with commitments to reduce global threats, even if doing so is in the country's long-term interest, because such compliance would likely come at the expense of spending for economic and social development. Even in wealthy countries, competing economic and budgetary preferences or concerns about national economic rivals can inhibit implementation and compliance. The United States, for example, did not ratify the Kyoto Protocol in part because a majority of senators and President George W. Bush believed that implementing the agreement would prove too expensive and because the protocol did not place similar costs on China and other large developing countries. Countries experiencing economic and financial difficulties might refuse or become unable to comply with global environmental agreements. The Russian Federation, for example, did not immediately comply with the 1996 phaseout of CFCs because of its critical economic situation at the time. At different times, other countries have also failed to comply with particular aspects of the ozone regime because of what they perceived to be the relatively high costs of implementation relative to other immediate needs.[46] Structural adjustment programs instituted by the International Monetary Fund (IMF, see Chapter 2) can also have a negative impact because they usually involve budget cuts in the debtor countries and favor programs designed to promote exports rather than limit pollution, conserve resources, or protect biologically important areas. More broadly, the impact of the global financial crisis on national budgets has contributed to the failure by donor countries to meet collective, nonbinding pledges of financial support for broad sustainable development goals and increased the difficulty of reaching agreements in negotiations on the provision of financial support for implementing specific multilateral environmental agreements, including the POPs and mercury negotiations.

Misperception of Relevant Costs and Benefits

A related obstacle is a lack of understanding regarding the full set of economic costs and benefits of pursuing environmental goals. Many analyses indicate that even if policy makers wish to ignore nonmonetary concepts relating to environmental and human-health protections, purely economic arguments exist that support environmental protection. However, such arguments often do not win in domestic policy discussions. Business, industry, and other groups that would have to stop or change particular operations or incur economic costs make their case clearly in policy debates. Less clear, however, are the potential economic benefits of protecting natural resources; reducing human health impacts from pollution; using energy, water, and material resources more efficiently; and creating green jobs. These are often obscured by the importance placed on short-term adjustment costs (which, in some issues, could be substantial for certain actors), insufficient analysis of economic changes that will occur if more environmentally benign technology or practices are required, and a failure to include the negative economic impacts of environmental degradation.

For example, arguments in the late 1970s that eliminating CFCs from aerosol spray cans would be extremely costly proved inaccurate when new processes and products actually saved consumers money. Global efforts to remove lead from fuel have yielded annual economic benefits of approximately $2.4 trillion via the associated improvements in IQ, reductions in cardiovascular diseases, introduction of pollution-control devices (some are not usable on cars and trucks using leaded fuel), and other health and social benefits.[47] Forestry and logging in Kenya actually cost that country roughly $60 million in 2010 because the negative economic costs produced by deforestation, especially the impact on the quality and availability of fresh water, far surpassed the economic benefits from forestry and logging.[48] The National Academy of Sciences estimated that burning fossil fuels costs the United States about $120 billion a year in health costs, mostly from the health impacts and premature deaths caused by air pollution.[49]

More broadly, a groundbreaking 1997 study estimated the economic value of "ecosystem services" provided by natural ecosystems in the form of fresh water, cleaner air, pollination, food production, recreation, waste treatment, and other outputs at $16 trillion to $54 trillion per year (compared with the total global gross national product in 2007 of around $18 trillion per year).[50] In 2009, several studies by the United Nations concluded that investments in green infrastructure projects, while requiring short-term costs, would both stimulate national economies and pay for themselves in energy savings, new jobs, and reduced costs associated with the impacts of pollution.[51] The Economics of Ecosystems and Biodiversity project is a major international initiative to study and publicize the global economic benefits of preserving biodiversity and healthy ecosystems.[52] A 2012 report by organizations and researchers participating in this initiative highlighted how short-term economic gains from draining wetlands for farming, building, or excessive water use, or their degradation from excessive releases of fertilizers and pollutants in their watersheds, threaten the far larger, and many billions of dollars' worth of, economic and environmental benefits these wetlands provide in preserving water quality, providing habitats and nurseries for fisheries, conserving biodiversity, and mitigating climate change (via carbon storage in peatlands, mangroves, and tidal marshes).[53] A 2012 report by the United Nations Environment Programme's Finance Initiative in collaboration with a number of asset owners, investment managers, and information providers showed that consideration of the economic impact of environmental degradation and the depletion of natural resources has the potential to lower a country's sovereign debt rating, denoting the purchase of that country's bonds as a greater risk and increasing the interest rate a country might have to offer to attract buyers.[54]

Several large-scale studies estimate that while some efforts to reduce GHG emissions and thus mitigate more extensive climate change carry significant short-term costs, these actions would help prevent far more significant economic costs associated with sea-level rise, changes in rainfall patterns, droughts, more extreme weather, and an increase in the range of tropical diseases.[55] Similarly, in the United States, while many understand the economic costs of reducing GHG emissions, less widely acknowledged are the potential economic benefits of significantly reduced oil and gas imports, fewer health problems from air pollution, increased energy efficiency, and the creation of new jobs in the solar, wind, and geothermal industries.

For example, at least 5 percent of global electricity consumption, and the associated GHG emissions, could be saved every year by transitioning to efficient lighting, action that would entail short-term costs but also result in annual worldwide energy savings of over $110 billion.[56] Methane vented or leaked from oil and gas systems represent more than 20 percent of anthropogenic methane and $27 to $60 billion a year in lost potential revenue. One-third of these losses could be reduced at zero cost with existing technologies and practices, and moderate long-term investments could address much of the rest and likely pay for themselves with sales of the captured natural gas and reductions in associated pollution and GHG emissions.[57]

Furthermore, a recent study by a consortium of researchers from, among others, the European Commission, GEF, McKinsey & Company, Rockefeller Foundation, and Standard Chartered Bank estimates that without mitigation and adaptation efforts, the impacts of climate change will soon begin to carry significant economic costs and, under certain scenarios, could cost some nations up to 19 percent of their gross domestic product (GDP) as early as 2030.[58] A 2008 UN-commissioned study estimated that concerted efforts to address climate change and sustainable development would create 20 million additional jobs in the renewable-energy sector by 2030, and that a worldwide transition to make all buildings energy efficient would create 2 to 3.5 million more green jobs in Europe and the United States alone, with the potential much higher in developing countries.[59] A 2012 study by the UN's International Labor Organization estimated that systemic efforts to transform to a greener economy could generate 15 to 60 million additional jobs globally over the next two decades and lift tens of millions of workers out of poverty.

Inadequate or Poorly Targeted Financial and Technical Assistance

Many global environmental regimes—including those for ozone, climate, biodiversity, desertification, toxic chemicals, and mercury—contain specific measures for providing FTA to developing countries and so help them fulfill their obligations. Developing countries consistently argue that implementation and compliance with specific elements within some environmental regimes, including, for example, the Montreal Protocol and Stockholm Convention, depend on the provision of adequate FTA. For some developing countries, such measures are indeed critical to their financial ability to comply with the regime; for others, they provide an important boost; for some the political importance of assistance is as important as its economic impact. Outside the ozone regime, however, one can argue that the provision of FTA has not reached levels that ensure effective compliance. At the same time, rapid economic development in some developing countries, the increasing gap between the least developed countries and the newly industrialized developing countries, and the impact of the global financial crisis on donor countries have complicated regime negotiations on expanding financial assistance in several global environmental issues.

Poorly Designed Regimes

A party's failure to comply with a regime sometimes reflects problems with the regime itself. As discussed above, regime design matters. Control measures and reporting requirements that are too complex or too vague allow states to make honest or intentional errors when translating them to domestic law. Regimes without flexibility leave states with little recourse but to violate regime rules when domestic circumstances change significantly. Regimes that do not pay attention to states' ability to implement them, the relative costs of compliance, the importance of reporting and monitoring, the interconnections between environmental issues, or the need to provide appropriate FTA are vulnerable to failure. Implementation and compliance, to some extent, are also a function of regime design.

Several regimes with particularly vague requirements have encountered implementation problems. Vagueness can be due to simple mistakes, the consequence of a lowest-common-denominator compromise, or an intentional negotiating strategy designed to produce imprecise requirements that allow states significant choice regarding which, if any, concrete actions they will take. Regardless of the reason, if a treaty does not contain clear, implementable requirements, parties often have trouble translating the vague language into domestic rules or regulations, or parties can choose to interpret the vague requirements in ways that produce few adjustment costs. The language in the biodiversity and desertification conventions and their related compliance challenges illustrate this point. In both cases, while countries are called on to develop their own national plans, there is little guidance in how to enable these plans to actually be effective in conserving biodiversity or combating desertification.

Many Regimes, Little Coordination

Another obstacle to compliance is the sheer number of environmental treaties and the confusing and uncoordinated web of requirements they now include. Since all parties, particularly developing countries, have finite financial, technical, and political resources available to implement environmental treaties, the more complex and confusing the total set of obligations, the more likely compliance will suffer.

Each environmental regime, as well as many other international environmental policy initiatives, has its own set of control measures, reporting requirements, monitoring systems, assessment mechanisms, implementation procedures, meeting schedules, financing requirements, and review procedures. In addition, nearly all of these regimes and initiatives exist independently of each other. As such, they sometimes place uncoordinated and confusing obligations on states that are difficult to fulfill. One example is reporting requirements that sometimes conflict, or at least remain uncoordinated, in their schedules, procedures, units of analysis, and required methods and formats. This was an issue within the ozone regime for many years and remains an issue within the chemicals arena, although efforts are under way to remedy the problem.

In addition, some regimes establish contrary rules or incentives. For example, HFCs are considered a replacement for CFCs under the ozone regime, but they are also a GHG subject to mandatory controls under the climate regime. Some closely related regimes have uncoordinated membership and regulatory gaps that potentially impede effectiveness. As discussed in Chapter 3, several treaties and other international initiatives exist to address hazardous waste and toxic chemicals, including the global Basel, Rotterdam, and Stockholm conventions, amendments to these conventions, and regional agreements. Although efforts are under way to increase coordination of the Basel, Rotterdam, and Stockholm conventions, different ratification patterns exist, meaning that certain countries have pledged to fulfill obligations under some chemicals agreements and amendments but not others. This pattern could become more pronounced if parties continue adding new chemicals to the Stockholm Convention and some countries opt out of the new controls.[60] This could threaten the effective implementation of the agreements, individually and as a package, because each treaty focuses on different aspects of the chemical life cycle (production, use, emissions, trade, destruction, and disposal) and a slightly different set of chemicals and wastes. Parties that implement one convention but not another allow certain chemicals or certain parts of their life cycles to escape global control.

OPPORTUNITIES TO IMPROVE EFFECTIVE IMPLEMENTATION AND COMPLIANCE

Several options exist to strengthen compliance with global environmental agreements. No single option, however, can address all the obstacles discussed in the previous two sections. Furthermore, whether these options or incentives can actually lead a government to comply depends on the willingness of states and other actors to take action.

However, existing experience with global environmental regimes, academic research, and deductive logic indicates that regime implementation, compliance, and effectiveness can be improved (see Box 5.3).

Raise Awareness and Concern

One of the most important factors in improving implementation and compliance is elevating awareness, concern, and knowledge among government elites and the general public regarding environmental issues. For each issue discussed in Chapters 3 and 4, sufficient expert knowledge exists on key aspects of the problem to demonstrate the scientific seriousness of the issue; the availability of technological, economic, and policy tools to address it; and the long-term environmental, human-health, and, in many cases, economic benefits of doing so. Significant obstacles remain to implementing solutions, however, in part because concern for environmental issues remains relatively low compared to other economic or political interests. The effectiveness of, and compliance with, international environmental regimes likely cannot increase significantly until public officials raise the priority of these issues or until elevated public concern and concerted individual action forces them to do so.

Create Market Incentives

As discussed in Chapter 1, most economic forces at work today still reward rather than punish unsustainable activity because the local and global costs of pollution and unsustainable resource use carry little or no economic costs to those responsible. There is broad agreement that changing this situation so that market forces reward environmentally friendly activities would greatly assist implementation of major environmental regimes and the pursuit of sustainable development goals and practices.

Important technologies that are essential to global sustainable development become profitable if the environmental and health costs are included in the price of the unsustainable option currently in use. Clean energy is the most obvious example. Wind, solar, and geothermal energy sources are all likely economically superior to fossil fuels if one includes the full costs of the health impacts of the air pollution from fossil fuels, the climate impacts of their CO_2 emissions, and the broader environmental and national security impacts of finding, extracting, and transporting them. Placing a price on CO_2 emissions, therefore, is widely seen as a critical step toward addressing climate change.[61] The same can be said for addressing most aspects of air and water pollution, rapacious resource use, and some types of deforestation.

Establishing market prices (through taxes, permits, incentives, tradable emission credits, or other measures) for pollution and unsustainable activity can reward efficiency and emission avoidance, encourage innovation, create a level playing field for non-

BOX 5.3   OPPORTUNITIES TO IMPROVE EFFECTIVE
IMPLEMENTATION AND COMPLIANCE

- **Raise awareness and concern**
- **Create market incentives**
- **Build domestic capacity**
- **Improve effectiveness of financial and technical assistance**
- **Support secretariat stability and capacity**
- **Augment coordination between regimes and conventions**
- **Improve monitoring and reporting**
- **Consider sanctions**
- **Generate publicity**

polluting and sustainable technology options, induce the use of low-emission and zero-emission technologies, and reduce the overall, system-wide cost of sustainable economic growth. Any negative, systemic economic impact of the additional costs could be offset by tax reductions in other areas, such as income taxes or sales taxes on particularly sustainable products or services.

Countries can exploit market forces on their own, through agreements with neighbors or trading partners, or through international agreements. Individual regimes, the United Nations Environment Programme (UNEP), United Nations Development Programme (UNDP), World Bank, IMF, and other institutions could expand efforts to raise awareness of the broad benefits of employing market mechanisms and perhaps provide incentives. However, efforts by a regime, a group of countries, or a single state to use market forces for environmental goods can run afoul of the WTO if they affect free trade (see Chapter 6). Broad agreement exists that the global trade regime need not stand in the way of more ambitious national and international environmental policy, including market mechanisms, to address climate change or other issues, but the precise frameworks need clarification.[62] Similarly, it is not always clear under which circumstances a country can exclude or tax certain imports for environmental reasons or when a country with a particular type of pollution tax relevant to the manufacture of certain products can introduce a tariff on the import of similar products that carry a price advantage because the country of its manufacture has no such tax. This could be particularly relevant to climate change, as some political figures in the EU and the United States have called for consideration of tariffs on goods imported from countries without GHG-reduction policies.[63]

Build Domestic Capacity

Improved compliance sometimes requires programs that strengthen the capacity of developing countries to implement environmental conventions. It also requires commitment by developing countries so that the assistance provided helps to develop permanent infrastructure.

Governments and international organizations recognize this need. GEF projects on biodiversity and climate change focus on capacity building or integrate capacity-building components into investment projects. Capacity-building activities also exist within particular regimes. For example, the CITES capacity-building strategy "trains the trainers" in a country by holding seminars and providing training materials.[64] The ozone regime supports significant capacity building through its Multilateral Fund. The Basel Convention and Stockholm regional centers act as nodes for capacity-building programs on issues relating to hazardous wastes and toxic chemicals. The creation of the United Nations Framework Convention on Climate Change's Durban Forum on Capacity Building reflects the need for a dialogue among all stakeholders involved in capacity building. In addition to filling in the information gaps, this dialogue provides an overview of the type of capacity-building support parties provide and their corresponding implementation efforts.

Despite these efforts, many of which are productive, results to date indicate that additional, well-targeted capacity building can augment regime compliance and effectiveness. Areas of particular need include environmental assessment and analysis, monitoring, regulatory infrastructure, enforcement, science education, public education and communication, and the use and maintenance of a wide variety of environmentally friendly technologies. Capacity building can also increase government concern for an issue by expanding awareness of the issue within the bureaucracy and increasing the number, skills, and visibility of people working on the issue. At the same time, experience shows the importance of ensuring that the funds actually go to focused capacity building directly related to addressing the environmental issue.

Improve Effectiveness of Financial and Technical Assistance

The line between capacity building and other types of FTA is largely an artificial one. In general, however, capacity building refers to permanent improvements in the ability and self-sufficiency of a country, whereas financial and technical assistance refers to help regarding specific instances of compliance. As noted above, providing effectively targeted FTA remains one of the most important avenues toward improving compliance and regime effectiveness. Key areas include obtaining access to new products and processes; technology transfer; developing new or expanded implementation plans, legislation, and regulations; purchasing scientific, monitoring, administrative, and communications equipment; financing individual implementation projects; properly disposing of hazardous wastes and toxic chemicals; and introducing substitute technologies.

The mere availability of increased or better targeted FTA is not a panacea. Increased and more effective compliance also requires more effective assistance: that is, assistance targeted toward the most important needs, monitored to avoid waste, provided conditionally in stages to promote real action, continually assessed and reviewed so that procedures can be improved, and coordinated within and across regimes to achieve potential synergies and to avoid duplication and unintended negative consequences.

Support Secretariat Stability and Capacity

Environmental regimes rely on treaty secretariats to fulfill a variety of key functions. Secretariats coordinate and facilitate day-to-day regime operations, organize meetings of the parties and subsidiary bodies, draft background documents on relevant policy issues, facilitate communication among parties, manage regime reporting, gather and disseminate information on treaty implementation, maintain clearinghouse mechanisms and websites, and support public education. Yet secretariat staffs tend to be small and their budgets minuscule in comparison with formal international organizations and most national bureaucracies (the Climate Secretariat is an exception). Combined with problems caused by late payment of or defaults on financial pledges by some parties, the small staffs and limited budgets decrease the ability of many secretariats to perform these functions. For example, the use of short-term contracts (one to six months) for staff positions in some secretariats, a practice caused by budget uncertainties and funding constraints, negatively affects secretariat productivity, reduces institutional memory, and limits the development of long-term working relationships with national officials so important to effective implementation.[65] Efforts by donor countries and foundations to stabilize funding for secretariats of global environmental conventions, to switch some donor funding from large organizations to more focused secretariats, and to end the practices of late payment and nonpayment of country pledges would allow secretariats to provide greater support to the regime.

Augment Coordination Between Regimes and Conventions

The broadest issue areas in global environment politics involve multiple, overlapping global and regional regimes, international organizations, and soft-law guidelines and procedures. Indicative examples include the atmosphere (ozone, climate, and regional air pollution agreements); chemicals and wastes (the Basel, Rotterdam, and Stockholm conventions; various regional treaties; and the Strategic Approach to International Chemicals Management [SAICM]); biodiversity, wildlife, and habitat protection (CBD,

CITES, Ramsar Convention, the Convention on Migratory Species, and a host of wild-life-specific treaties); oceans (the Law of the Sea, the London Convention, and MAR-POL); and fisheries (the Fish Stocks Agreement, the FAO Code of Conduct for Responsible Fisheries, and numerous regional fisheries agreements). In addition, some conventions span several issue areas. The Desertification Convention, for example, contains provisions that address biodiversity, climate change, forests, and freshwater resources.

Improved coordination among treaties and organizations would improve regime implementation and compliance by (1) helping to remove the obstacles produced by the lack of such coordination (outlined above), (2) allowing for more effective use of limited resources, (3) avoiding unnecessary duplication of tasks, and (4) potentially creating unforeseen opportunities where efforts for joint initiatives could improve reporting, monitoring, environmental assessments, financing, and implementation.

The potential for such activity is broadly recognized. UNEP has repeatedly addressed the issue, and environmental ministers have discussed it in a variety of fora.[66] The United Nations Conference on Environment and Development and the World Summit on Sustainable Development both endorsed the concept. A variety of secretariats consult regularly. As noted in Chapter 3, a formal initiative to increase coordination in the chemicals sector is well under way. But much more can be done. Donor countries in particular are pushing for enhanced coordination as a way to reduce duplicated bureaucratic costs so that available resources can be targeted at implementation programs that achieve measurable environmental results. Opportunities for enhanced coordination that have received particular attention and exhibit promise include examining and eliminating regulatory gaps or conflicts, coordinating reporting schedules and formats, co-locating secretariats and relevant international organizations that work in related issues, integrating certain operations within co-located secretariats, coordinating the scheduling of the conferences of the parties (COPs) of related regimes, supporting ratification to remove membership gaps, integrating appropriately related implementation activities, and establishing common regional centers and other programs for capacity building and the provision of FTA.

Improve Monitoring and Reporting

Monitoring and reporting on environmental issues and regime implementation are essential components of regime effectiveness. Without regular and accurate monitoring and reporting by parties, it is difficult to assess the baseline, trends, and current status of an environmental problem; to assess current levels of regime implementation; to identify specific instances or patterns of noncompliance or ineffectiveness; and to develop potential solutions. Studies on institutional effectiveness indicate that regimes employing systems of regular monitoring and reporting have better levels of domestic implementation and compliance than those that do not.[67]

Most environmental regimes require parties to submit data and reports on issues related to the environmental problem as well as on their implementation of the regime. Secretariats often compile this information and make it available to other parties and the public. Unfortunately, not all countries submit the required data and reports, and significant variations exist in the quality and timeliness of those that do. In addition, because most countries rely on existing national systems to gather information for regime reporting, the reports sometimes define, estimate, and aggregate the required data in different ways, making comparisons and analyses difficult.

As a result of these problems, some regimes have large information gaps. For example, reporting from parties under the Basel Convention, while improving, has often been incomplete, late, and sometimes based on different standards of measuring (or estimating) the generation, management, and disposal of hazardous wastes.[68] Large data gaps exist regarding the production, use, trade, management, and potential environmental and human-health consequences of many chemicals.[69]

Efforts to emphasize and improve national reporting and associated monitoring, combined with the ability of secretariats and COPs to review, publicize, and act on the information in a timely fashion, will likely increase regime compliance and effectiveness. In addition to stronger provisions within regimes, another method to pursue these goals is to increase the coordination and perhaps integration of the monitoring and reporting requirements between related regimes. For example, observers believe that regular and harmonized reporting from parties to the Basel, Rotterdam, and Stockholm conventions (if this occurs as part of the effort to augment coordination) could allow for far more accurate assessments of global levels and trends in the production, use, generation, transport, management, and disposal of hazardous chemicals. It would also make it easier to monitor progress in implementing these conventions and improve the ability to direct international policies toward areas where they would have the most impact.[70] Furthermore, harmonized reporting could help reduce the overall volume of reporting requirements, which could free up human and financial resources to improve compliance.

Another method is to expand formal and informal relationships with NGOs, intergovernmental organizations, academics, and industry to help monitor environmental issues and regime implementation and compliance. For example, in addition to government reporting, several major private-sector actors and NGOs have monitored aspects of compliance with the Montreal Protocol.[71] International NGOs also work closely with the CITES Secretariat to monitor wildlife trade. The Trade Records Analysis of Flora and Fauna in Commerce (TRAFFIC)—the wildlife-trade–monitoring program of WWF and the International Union for the Conservation of Nature and

PHOTO 5.3   Rifles and
ivory tusks taken from
poachers in Kenya, with
the assistance of the NGO
TRAFFIC.
Photo by Rob
Barnett/TRAFFIC.

Natural Resources—helps ensure that wildlife trade remains at sustainable levels and in accordance with domestic and international laws and agreements. Established in 1976, TRAFFIC employs more than one hundred people in thirty countries and assists in criminal investigations and enforcement actions; provides expertise for creating, reviewing, and improving wildlife-trade legislation; and works with wildlife consumers, producers, and managers to help dissuade unsustainable and illegal trade.[72]

Consider Sanctions

Improving compliance may require additional sticks (sanctions) as well as more carrots (capacity building, FTA, and other incentives). This could include applying sanctions—such as trade restrictions, tariffs, fines, or prohibitions on receiving FTA—against parties found to be in willful noncompliance with regime rules. Sanctions could also be used against countries that choose to remain outside of a particular regime in an effort to discourage or punish "free riders." The ozone regime includes such provisions, prohibiting parties from exporting or importing ozone-depleting chemicals or products that use them to or from nonparties.

To be effective, sanctions must be credible and potent. States in conscious violation of a treaty or measures adopted by a multilateral environmental agreement (MEA) must be convinced not only that they will face penalties for the violation but also that the costs of the violation will exceed the gains expected from it.[73]

Currently, little support exists among governments for expanding the use of sanctions as a remedy for treaty violations. Some argue they would make sense in situations such as illegal, unreported, and unregulated fishing, in which sanctions (in this example, curbs on fishing rights or imports) could be directly related to the failure to comply with a treaty. Many developing countries, however, oppose the potential use of sanctions, arguing that under the United Nations Charter and the Rio Declaration, such sanctions violate national sovereignty and, equally importantly, could be used as a disguised form of trade protectionism.[74]

Although some treaties, such as the Montreal Protocol and CITES, include the possibility of sanctions as a potential punishment for noncompliance, the potential for broader use is the subject of debate within MEAs and the WTO. The key question is under what conditions should the WTO and other agreements allow national governments to pursue ecological goals by restricting international trade in certain goods?[75] Resolving this issue requires balancing the principles, norms, and rules of the trade and environmental regimes (see Chapter 6).

Generate Publicity

Fear of negative publicity has sometimes proven a meaningful deterrent to treaty violations. Environmental conventions could create mechanisms through which negative publicity would become a more prominent consequence of refusal to participate in a global regime or failure to implement specific provisions.[76] The Internet, social networking, global television networks, and improved telecommunications make it easier, cheaper, and faster than ever to collect and distribute information, and evidence exists that such campaigns could have an impact in some cases. Countries go to significant lengths to deny or explain implementation lapses during many COPs and to avoid potential embarrassments in meeting reports, which shows they might be sensitive to systematic exposures. Norway lost money and public support when the European Union boycotted Norwegian fish products because of Norway's position on whaling. Iceland stopped whaling for two years because of a public campaign of negative publicity and boycotts. Negative publicity can also be used to expose and deter corporate noncompliance with national laws. In Europe and the United States, for example, environmental groups sometimes act as important watchdogs, reporting violations of environmental regime rules to the public, national authorities, and regime secretariats.

Positive publicity can also improve compliance, and some diplomats argue that efforts should be made to publicize compliance more effectively.[77] Regimes could create mechanisms through which positive publicity or other benefits would flow as the result of meeting particular standards. The intention would be to create competition to achieve certain levels of implementation and environmental status. Other mechanisms could reward special achievements. For example, in 2007 representatives from wildlife enforcement agencies in Cameroon and Hong Kong received Interpol's Ecomessage Award in recognition of the extraordinary level of cooperation that they provided in the investigation surrounding the 3,900-kilogram cache of ivory smuggled out of Cameroon and seized in Hong Kong. Interpol's Ecomessage Award comes with a prize sponsored by the International Fund for Animal Welfare valued at $30,000.[78]

Several broader efforts, such as the Environmental Performance Index, rank countries according to various environmental and sustainability criteria.[79] Supporters of such initiatives hope that these types of measures can replace, or at least augment, traditional gross national product rankings and that countries will take steps to attempt to rise in the rankings, or at least avoid being placed near the bottom.

INCREASING FINANCIAL RESOURCES FOR IMPLEMENTING GLOBAL ENVIRONMENTAL REGIMES

The issue of financial resources has been at the center of global environmental politics for many years and will continue to be for the foreseeable future. Implementing many of the opportunities outlined in the previous section for improving regime compliance requires additional financial and technical resources. More broadly, the successful expansion and implementation of MEAs, including those for climate, biodiversity, desertification, fisheries, and chemicals, require transitions to environmentally sound technologies and new strategies for natural resource management. As noted above, although these technologies and strategies could (and in many cases likely will) yield long-term economic benefits, such transitions require significant investments in the short run to implement, to ease the transition for those hardest hit, and to overcome resistance from powerful economic and political interests.

Most developing countries consider FTA to be an economic or political necessity for agreeing to new global environmental commitments and implementing existing obligations. For many, the major obstacle to effective implementation is the lack of adequate financial and technical resources to fulfill treaty obligations.[80] These countries simply do not have the resources to comply effectively. For others, such as India or South Africa, it provides valuable economic assistance so that resources can flow to other social needs. FTA also provides some developing countries, including those with large growing economies, with important political assistance, easing domestic objections regarding adjustment costs. More broadly, regime mechanisms that provide FTA are a crucial international political issue for many developing countries. Such measures fulfill the principle of common but differentiated responsibilities and represent a prerequisite to their participation in MEAs, especially those that address problems caused primarily by industrialized countries. This remains the position of large and increasingly prosperous developing countries such as Brazil and China.

On the other hand, many donor countries face financial and political challenges that limit their ability to fund large new initiatives or make significant new commitments to assist developing countries in implementing existing programs. Many donor countries also want both to target assistance more narrowly to focus on specific actions that will have permanent impacts and to take into account the large economic differences among developing countries when creating and implementing FTA programs.[81]

Most environmental treaties have no separate funding mechanism; the ozone regime is the exception. The Montreal Protocol was the first regime in which the financing mechanism was a central issue in the negotiations. It demonstrated that donor and recipient countries participating in a global environmental regime can devise a financial mechanism that equitably distributes power and effectively links financial assistance with compliance.

The GEF, which the biodiversity, climate, desertification, and chemicals regimes use as their financial mechanism, has developed a somewhat similar governance structure but faces more difficult issues in trying to link assistance with global environmental benefits. As discussed in Chapter 2, governments created the GEF in 1991 essentially as an arm of the World Bank, with UNEP and UNDP providing technical and scientific advice (see Box 2.5). The grants and concessional funds disbursed complement traditional development assistance by covering the additional costs (also known as agreed incremental costs) incurred when a national, regional, or global development project also targets global environmental objectives. At the GEF's replenishment in 2010, donor countries pledged \$4.25 billion to fund its operations through 2014.

However, given the immense challenges ahead, the GEF is unlikely to receive sufficient funds from donor countries to enable it to help developing countries achieve full compliance with the biodiversity, climate change, desertification, and chemicals conventions if their controls expand. In addition, although official development assistance (ODA) levels rose in the last decade after falling in the 1990s, most of this money was directed toward traditional development activities, not toward implementing global environmental priorities. Indeed, the total investment needed to fulfill current envi-

---

BOX 5.4   OPPORTUNITIES TO INCREASE FINANCIAL RESOURCES FOR IMPLEMENTING GLOBAL ENVIRONMENTAL REGIMES

- **Focus multilateral and bilateral assistance toward sustainable development**
- **Develop revenue from regime mechanisms**
- **Create new revenue streams from coordinated pollution taxes**
- **Exchange debt obligations for sustainable development policy reforms and investments**
- **Eliminate counterproductive subsidies**

---

ronmental regime obligations and achieve the broad sustainable development goals related to Agenda 21 and the Millennium Development Goals (MDGs) is already many times higher than total current ODA levels. In addition, the global recession that started in 2008 put tremendous pressure on national budgets. Major donors' aid to developing countries fell by nearly 3 percent in 2011, breaking a long trend of annual increases dating back to 1997.[82] Even if such funding is possible economically, and one could argue that a workable coalition of industrialized countries, international organizations, and fast-growing developing countries possess the resources,[83] countries do not seem to have the interest to make such investments on a systematic basis.

So what potential sources exist that could provide significant increases in financial resources for implementing global environmental regimes? This section outlines several possibilities proposed by government officials, NGOs, or other experts in different international fora. (See Box 5.4.) Each is theoretically possible, but each would also face significant obstacles before it could become policy.

Focus Multilateral and Bilateral Assistance Toward Sustainable Development Goals

Existing ODA and loan guarantee programs, which dwarf environmental funding in size, could systematically apply resources to programs that also enhance environmental goals. Overall ODA flows would not need to be reduced or enlarged under this proposal. Instead, governments and international organizations such as the World Bank would funnel aid to proven programs with shared environmental and development goals. Thus, ODA programs focused on industrialization or energy production would support only projects that produce or use green energy (such as solar, wind, geothermal, or tidal power) rather than oil or coal, employ significant energy-conservation measures, and emit low levels of air or water pollution. Many developing countries have tremendous renewable energy resources, including outstanding conditions for cost-efficient solar power plants in large sections of northern and southern Africa, the Arab states, and parts of Pakistan and India. Excellent resources for constructing geothermal facilities exist in East Africa and the Pacific Rim, including Indonesia, the Philippines, and the west coasts of Mexico, Central America, and South America. Significant wind-power resources exist in many places, including the coasts of Brazil, China, India, South America, and southern Africa.

Similarly, cleaning and redeveloping "brownfields"—former industrial properties containing hazardous substances, pollutants, or contaminants—would enjoy priority over clearing land for construction or agriculture. Projects that would clear tropical forests or place roads into or near protected areas would not be funded, nor would products that use or produce toxic chemicals. Reuse and recycling projects would be emphasized over mining projects or production processes that require large amounts of raw materials. Funding would increase to countries that followed these types of guidelines in their own policies and decrease to countries that continued "business as usual." Sustainable agriculture that produces food for local consumption on a regular basis would receive priority over boom-and-bust industrial export agriculture that consumes significant quantities of water and fertilizer and can leave countries as net importers of food. Energy-efficiency projects that train people in this increasingly profitable industry, that save the target country money in energy savings, and that reduce GHG emissions would be supported over other types of job-training programs with more limited reach.

Donors or recipients wishing to focus all or part of their ODA programs on health and social issues could effectively pursue these goals while also promoting the social bases of sustainable development, including basic health and nutrition, vaccinations, family planning, land preservation, and education (especially for women and girls). Indeed, better health and education are widely shown to contribute to smaller, healthier families, more productive agriculture, higher incomes, and less stress on the environment and natural resources. Many governments, international organizations, and foundations have efforts in these areas, but many observers agree that a broad-based commitment to make sustainable development a co-priority in all ODA initiatives would significantly affect sustainable development.

Develop Revenue from Regime Mechanisms

Environmental regimes have the potential to develop mechanisms to capture certain cost savings that result from environmental protections or to collect fees from services or permits. For example, one potential source of financing for greater energy efficiency, zero-GHG-emission energy sources, technological innovation, and technological diffusion is GHG emissions trading (see Chapter 3).

By making emissions reduction a potential profit source, the competitive nature of market capitalism is employed to combat climate change. Title IV of the US Clean Air Act of 1990 established one of the first national systems for emissions trading for meeting sulfur dioxide emissions targets in the electric-power sector as a means to reduce acid rain in the United States. In Europe, the European Union Greenhouse Gas Emission Trading Scheme (EU ETS) commenced operation in January 2005 as the world's largest multicountry, multisector GHG-emissions-trading scheme worldwide.[84] State and regional GHG-trading schemes have been developed in the United States, such as the Regional Greenhouse Gas Initiative (RGGI) in the northeast (see Chapter 2),[85] and California and Quebec linked their CO_2 trading systems in 2013.

The central challenge to deploying an effective emissions trading system is designing and then continually improving the system so that it works at both the business and the environmental levels. The success of emissions-trading programs in the United States for sulfur emissions argues that this is possible, although maintaining an effective and efficient trading system for CO_2 presents a more difficult challenge. The EU ETS experienced difficulties for the first few years because an excess of permits drove prices too low. However, some of these problems have been fixed (the system is designed to be adjusted if needed), and the system expanded to cover emissions from more types of sources.

In successor agreements to the Kyoto Protocol, parties could seek to develop a more active trading system than they have to date. In such a system, countries or private corporations would be able to sell their excess rights to emit carbon dioxide if they significantly reduced their emissions through conservation, greater efficiency, or using wind, solar, or geothermal power. A very small percentage of each transaction could go into a fund for the poorest developing countries to pursue clean-energy options. If a robust global system does not develop under the climate regime, major national and regional schemes could link together, and the participating countries could agree to a similar levy within their trading systems.

The climate regime already includes a mechanism for raising revenues, and possibilities exist in other regimes. The Clean Development Mechanism allows industrialized countries to implement GHG-emissions-reduction projects in developing countries and receive saleable, certified emissions-reduction credits, which can be counted toward meeting their Kyoto targets. The climate regime's Adaptation Fund will receive proceeds from the equivalent of a 2 percent tax on these credits. While this will not raise anything close to the amount of money required for climate adaptation, it may provide a dedicated revenue stream from a regime mechanism. Similar efforts might be possible in other pollution-control regimes should they adopt trading schemes, provisions similar to the Clean Development Mechanism, or analogous methods.

Create New Revenue Streams from Coordinated Pollution Taxes

Many ideas exist for global or coordinated national taxes to raise new revenue for sustainable development and protection of the environment.[86] In nearly all the proposals, countries would impose similar taxes on pollution or other activities and then pool or use the money individually to finance sustainable development and environmental regimes. Taxes would be levied on activities harmful in their own right and therefore reasonable to discourage through taxes. In some proposals, the taxes would be set quite low, so as to not affect individual consumers, but still raise large sums through their aggregate impact, or their impact on consumers would be partially offset by related cuts in income or sales taxes.

In the early 1990s, the European Union called for a tax on air fuel used for international flights to raise funds for environmental projects.[87] In 2009, during the climate change negotiations, the group of least-developed countries proposed that developed countries should accept a compulsory levy on international flight tickets and shipping fuel to raise billions of dollars to help the world's poorest countries mitigate and adapt to climate change. The aviation levy, which proponents claim would increase the price of long-haul fares by less than 1 percent, could raise $10 billion a year.[88]

A coordinated global tax of $1 per barrel of oil could raise more than $30 billion annually, while acting as a further incentive for conservation. Similar amounts could be raised by equivalent tax rates on coal. An Ecuador-led initiative proposed a 3–5 percent tax on oil exported to industrialized countries. The annual proceeds of this tax, which could reach $40 billion to $60 billion annually, would finance climate-mitigation and adaptation activities in developing countries.[89] Another well-known proposal is to tax large-scale speculative currency trading. A levy of just 0.005 percent could generate $15 billion a year for environmental projects if enacted in countries through which most of such trading takes place. Larger levies, which have been proposed, would raise even more and also act as a small brake on such speculation, which some argue presents an unnecessary threat to the stability of national currencies.[90] Although the revenue will not flow to environmental projects, eleven European countries have agreed to levy a very small uniform tax on stock, bond, and derivative trading designed to discourage high-frequency speculative trading and raise funds for public projects.[91] Taxes on international arms sales could raise similar sums with appropriate ancillary benefits. Other possibilities include taxes on certain types of energy production, fossil fuel–powered transportation, transboundary shipments of hazardous waste, the production of particular substances, or the release of toxic chemicals, heavy metals, or other types of air or water pollution into the environment. In addition to raising funds for implementing globally agreed-on environmental goals, the taxes would create additional economic deterrents to unnecessary pollution. An analogous and successful domestic example is the excise tax on CFCs enacted by the United States to help implement its obligations under the ozone regime. The tax has raised several billion dollars for the US Treasury and acted as a significant incentive for companies to speed their transition to alternatives.[92]

Many practical and political issues exist concerning the adoption and administration of such taxes, and the system would be subject to significant concerns about free riders. In addition, some national governments might fear that they would lose revenue, that the money raised in their countries would be wasted on inefficient international projects, that the taxes would be used to create slush funds for use by international organizations outside their control, or that the mechanism could contribute to other losses of sovereign control. The US Congress, for example, passed legislation in 1999 making it illegal for the United States to participate in global taxes.[93] Although a national tax, albeit one enacted in concert with other governments and administered domestically by the United States with proceeds distributed only by the United States, might pass muster against this legislation and meet at least some of the concern expressed by other countries, it would still face formidable political obstacles.

Exchange Debt Obligations for Sustainable Development Policy Reforms and Investments

Debt obligations can place huge burdens on developing countries. Sometimes they are forced to exploit their natural resources at unsustainable rates and use budgetary resources for debt payments at the expense of environmentally sustainable development programs. Implementing aggressive debt-relief programs in concert with agreements by the debtor country to use a specific amount of the savings for environmental programs offers potential to tap an additional source of funds for problems largely neglected by most assistance programs, such as programs needed to combat desertification in Africa.

Several initiatives in this direction have been developed in the past two decades. Under pressure from poor countries and NGOs in September 1996, the World Bank and the IMF launched the Initiative for Heavily Indebted Poor Countries (HIPC), which seeks to ensure that no poor country faces a debt burden it cannot manage.[94] The HIPC initiative helps the poorest and most heavily indebted countries escape from unsustainable debt. It enables poor countries to focus their energies on building the policy and institutional foundation for sustainable development and poverty reduction. Unlike earlier debt-relief mechanisms, it deals with debt in a comprehensive way and involves all creditors, including multilateral financial institutions.

In 2005, to help accelerate progress toward the UN MDGs, the HIPC initiative was supplemented by the Multilateral Debt Relief Initiative, which allows for 100 percent relief on eligible debts from three multilateral institutions—the IMF, the World Bank,

PHOTO 5.4 NGOs from 350.org and AVAAZ.org delivered to the British prime minister a petition to end fossil-fuel subsidies. Courtesy Stephen Brown Images.

and the African Development Fund—for countries completing the HIPC initiative process. In 2007, the Inter-American Development Bank also decided to provide additional debt relief to HIPCs in the Western Hemisphere.

The 2005 Group of Eight (G-8) summit culminated an equally substantive process, when leaders of the world's eight leading industrialized countries agreed to cancel the debt of eighteen of the world's poorest nations and to increase overall aid to Africa.[95] This debt-cancellation pledge addressed the needs of some of the countries that were eligible for the HIPC or Multilateral Debt Relief initiatives but could not participate because of the domestic exigencies and the structural adjustments required by the program. Several broad alliances of religious, charitable, environmental, and labor groups (the best known being the Jubilee Network) continue to advocate for debt cancellation.[96] Although the HIPC, G-8, and other initiatives represent significant steps, public and private debt levels remain an impediment to successful environmental protection and sustainable development in many developing countries.

Eliminate Counterproductive Subsidies

One direct method for increasing the sustainability of agriculture, forestry, and fisheries is to eliminate subsidies that contribute to the unsustainable use and long-term degradation of the affected land, forests, and fish. The period from the 1960s through the 1980s saw a rapid, worldwide expansion of subsidies for natural resource production. Although some reductions in subsidies given to agriculture and fisheries occurred in the 1990s and early 2000s, the scale of environmentally harmful subsidies in the energy, road transport, water use, and agricultural sectors remains staggering. For example, a 2013 IMF report concluded that national energy subsidies totalled $1.9 trillion.[97]

Despite the overall financial and environmental advantages of ending such subsidies, governments tend to keep such policies in place in response to political pressure from key interest groups. The WTO Agreement on Subsidies and Countervailing Measures attempts to discipline the use of subsidies, but it concentrates only on subsidized imports that hurt domestic producers. It will take a concerted effort to fashion the necessary national and international consensus needed to end, or even severely limit, subsidies impeding conservation. Doing so, however, would release billions of dollars that currently subsidize environmental degradation, perhaps allowing some to be used for environmental protection.

CONCLUSION

The effectiveness of an environmental regime, that is, the extent to which it produces measurable improvements in the environment, is a function of regime design, particularly the strength of the key control provisions aimed at addressing the environmental threat, as well as the level of implementation (the extent to which countries adopt domestic regulations to enact the agreement) and compliance (the degree to which countries conform to these regulations and other regime rules and procedures). Many factors can inhibit or promote the effectiveness of an environmental regime. Among the most fundamental are six broad sets of obstacles that can make it difficult to create regimes with strong and binding control measures:

1. structural or systemic obstacles that arise from the structure of the international system, the structure of international law, and the structure of the global economic system;
2. the lack of sufficient concern, a hospitable contractual environment, or necessary capacity;
3. the time-lag and the lowest-common-denominator procedural obstacles;
4. obstacles that stem from the characteristics of global environmental issues themselves, including the inherent links between environmental issues and important economic and political issues, unequal adjustment costs, scientific complexity and uncertainty, time-horizon conflicts, the presence of different core values and beliefs, and the involvement of large numbers of actors;
5. obstacles that stem from the interconnections between environmental issues; and
6. regime-design difficulties.

Once regimes are created, certain factors can negatively influence national compliance with their requirements. These include inadequate translation of regime rules into domestic law; insufficient capacity to implement, administer, or enforce domestic policy; inability to monitor and report on implementation and compliance; the costs of compliance; misperception of relevant cost and benefits; inadequate or poorly targeted FTA; poorly designed regimes; and the lack of coordination among the increasingly large number of environmental conventions.

Despite these obstacles, options exist to strengthen compliance with environmental agreements. Among the most important are elevating concern, creating market incentives, augmenting domestic capacity, increasing and more effectively targeting technical and financial assistance, enhancing secretariat capacity, emphasizing and supporting improved reporting and monitoring, enhancing coordination between regimes and conventions, applying sanctions, and employing positive and negative publicity.

Issues of financial resources, including the politics and provision of FTA, are central issues in global environmental politics. Given the political and economic obstacles preventing significant increases in financing for environmental regimes, as well as the potentially large amounts needed to assure their effectiveness, it appears necessary for regimes to seek alternative sources for such resources. This chapter outlined several ways to increase funding for global environmental regimes, including focusing existing bilateral and multilateral assistance on projects directly supportive of environmental regimes and sustainable development; developing revenue from regime mechanisms such as emissions trading; creating new revenue streams from coordinated pollution taxes; canceling debts owed by poor countries; and eliminating counterproductive subsidies and shifting some of the savings to conservation.

In spite of daunting obstacles that prevent the creation and effective implementation of international environmental agreements, successful examples do exist. Examining the obstacles to creating strong agreements and options for increasing compliance provides insights into additional tools for creating effective global environmental policy. Although this chapter has outlined what leading experts see as policy prescriptions that could help solve these problems, it is not possible to understand the evolution of global environmental politics without a closer look at the economic and social development context within which these regimes operate.

6

Environmental Politics and Sustainable Development

As the case studies in this book demonstrate, global environmental politics cannot be studied in a vacuum. Environmental issues are inextricably linked with economic and social development issues. Increased awareness of environmental issues, improved scientific understanding of them, the increased number of countries involved in the negotiation of environmental treaties, and the relationships between environmental protection, economic development, and social development—the three dimensions or pillars of sustainable development—all contribute to the current global environmental landscape.

North-South economic issues are a crucial element of the political context of global environmental politics. In spite of the growth of many emerging economies, including China, Brazil, India, and South Africa, to name a few, many developing countries still perceive global economic relations as fundamentally inequitable. This often shapes their policy responses to global environmental issues and their negotiating strategies on subjects as different as elephants and climate.

Developing countries continue to insist that the industrialized countries, because of their historical dominance in the production and consumption of chlorofluorocarbons (CFCs), combustion of fossil fuels, and production of toxic chemicals and hazardous wastes, are responsible for environmental problems and should bear the responsibility for any solution. More generally, they identify the high levels of consumption in industrialized countries as a key cause of global environmental degradation. For example, according to the United Nations Development Programme, today there are more than nine hundred cars per thousand people of driving age in the United States and more than six hundred in Western Europe but fewer than ten in India. American households average more than two televisions. In Liberia and Uganda, less than one household in ten has a television. Domestic per capita water consumption in the richest countries averages 425 liters a day, more than six times the 67 liters per day average in the poorest countries.[1] The average person in an industrialized country, like the United States, accounts for nearly four times the carbon dioxide emissions of someone in China or India and nearly thirty times that of someone in Kenya. The average British citizen accounts for as much greenhouse gas (GHG) emissions in two months as a person in a least-developed country generates in a year.[2] Chinese per capita emissions are rising rapidly, but many of these emissions relate to the production and transport of products for consumption in the United States and Europe. Therefore, many developing countries argue that industrialized countries in the North must adopt more sustainable consumption and production patterns and significantly reduce the use of natural resources and fossil fuels before the South follows suit.

This chapter looks at global environmental politics within the context of sustainable development with a focus on three elements in this complex relationship: North-South relations, social development, and economic development and trade.

NORTH-SOUTH RELATIONS AND SUSTAINABLE DEVELOPMENT

Historically, developing countries perceived global environmental issues as a distinctively North-South issue and, sometimes, as an effort to sabotage their development aspirations. This perspective emerged back in 1971 at a seminar held in Founex, Switzerland, which laid the groundwork for the 1972 Stockholm Conference on the Human Environment. Equally important, the Founex Report that resulted from the conference was the first paper to identify key environment-development objectives and relationships, and contributed to locating and bridging the policy and conceptual differences that separated developed and developing countries.[3] The tone and substance of the report foreshadowed, nearly exactly, what soon became the South's rhetoric for forty years at global environmental conferences and regime negotiations. The Founex Report provides critical testimony that these interests (1) have remained unchanged over time, and (2) lie at the heart of today's global politics of sustainable development.[4] As the Founex Report puts it,

> The developing countries would clearly wish to avoid, as far as feasible, the [environmental] mistakes and distortions that have characterized the patterns of development of the industrialized societies. However, the major environmental problems of the developing countries are essentially of a different kind. They

are predominantly problems that reflect the poverty and very lack of development in their societies. . . . These are problems, no less than those of industrial pollution, that clamor for attention in the context of the concern with human environment. They are problems which affect the greater mass of mankind. . . . In [industrialized] countries, it is appropriate to view development as a cause of environmental problems. . . . In [the southern] context, development becomes essentially a cure for their major environmental problems.[5]

Although many developing-country officials, particularly in environment ministries, recognize the seriousness of local and global environmental degradation and how it can negatively affect their economic future, the viewpoints expressed in the Founex Report help to explain why many developing countries often regarded global environmental regimes as largely unrelated to their core concerns and even suspiciously—as a means by which industrialized countries will maintain control or even gain new control over resources and technology located in the South. The 1972 Stockholm Conference on the Human Environment treated the environment as part of the broader development process in order to allay these concerns. This helped to focus discussion on specific problems facing developing countries and implied that additional financial resources would be sought, primarily through existing development assistance channels.[6] Along these lines, the resulting Stockholm Declaration and Action Plan specifically noted (in Recommendations 102–109) that environmental concerns should not be a pretext for discriminatory trade policies or reduced access to markets and that the burdens of environmental policies of industrialized countries should not be transferred to developing countries. Recommendation 109, in particular, called on states to ensure that concerns of developed countries with their own environmental problems should not affect the flow of assistance to developing countries and that this flow should be adequate to meet the additional environmental requirements of such countries.[7]

Emergence of Sustainable Development

In the wake of the Stockholm Conference, the United Nations worked to raise international environmental awareness through governments, nongovernmental organizations, and the world's business and scientific communities. However, environmental and development issues were often addressed separately and in a fragmented fashion. Stockholm successfully brought international attention to the environmental crisis but did not resolve any of the inherent tensions in linking environmental protection with social and economic development.[8]

As noted in Chapter 1, in 1983 the UN General Assembly (UNGA) established an independent commission to formulate a long-term agenda for action on the broad issues of environment and development that had been discussed at the 1972 Stockholm Conference. Chaired by Norway's environment minister, Gro Harlem Brundtland, the commission conducted fifteen public hearings during the subsequent three years at locations around the world. Both governments and civil society participated in the hearings. The commission's 1987 report, *Our Common Future*, stressed the need for development strategies in all countries that recognized the limits of natural ecosystems to regenerate themselves and to absorb waste products. Recognizing "an accelerating ecological interdependence among nations,"[9] the commission emphasized the link between economic development and environmental issues, and it identified poverty eradication as a necessary and fundamental requirement for environmentally sustainable development. In addition, the report noted that the goals of economic and social development must be defined in terms of sustainability in all countries: developed or developing, market-oriented or centrally planned.[10] It also determined that a series of rapid transitions and policy changes would be required, including keeping population levels in harmony with the ecosystem, reducing mass poverty, increasing equity within and between nations, increasing efficiency in the use of energy and other resources, reorienting technology, and merging environment and economics in decision making.[11]

The Brundtland Report also called on the UN General Assembly to convene an international conference to review progress made and promote follow-up arrangements. This conference became the 1992 Earth Summit (formally known as the United Nations Conference on Environment and Development or UNCED), which achieved a pact, underpinned by a set of core principles that had their origins in the Brundtland Report, between countries of the North and South linking environmental and developmental concerns.

The Rio Principles

On the twentieth anniversary of the Stockholm Conference, governments gathered in Rio de Janeiro, Brazil, to move the sustainable development agenda forward. The 1992 Earth Summit attracted greater official and unofficial interest than had the Stockholm Conference. The summit and the preparatory work that preceded it showed that there were still significant differences between developed and developing countries on many environmental issues. Each group provided different inputs to the agenda-setting process. Developed countries wanted to focus on ozone depletion, global warming, acid rain, and deforestation. Developing countries preferred exploring the relationship between the sluggish economic growth, consumption levels, and production patterns in developing countries and the economic policies of the developed countries. They emphasized that an "environmentally healthy planet was impossible in a world that contained significant inequities."[12]

The major output of the Earth Summit was the global plan of action for sustainable development called "Agenda 21." As noted in Chapter 1, Agenda 21 demonstrated an emerging consensus on the issues affecting the long-term sustainability of human society, including domestic social and economic policies, international economic relations, and cooperation on issues concerning the global commons. The summit also produced the Rio Declaration on Environment and Development, which led to the institutionalization of several principles that have roots in Stockholm but have become a feature of all post-Rio global environmental treaties: additionality, common but differentiated responsibilities, and the "polluter pays" principles.

The first of these principles is additionality, which arose out of the southern concern that environmental issues would attract international aid away from traditional developmental issues. Developing countries were concerned that instead of raising new funds for addressing global environmental issues, the North and international financial institutions would simply divert resources previously targeted for development toward the environment. Thus, the principle of additionality sought to ensure that new monies would be made available to deal with global environmental issues.[13]

Despite assurances given to the South, however, this principle suffered a setback soon after the Earth Summit, during the negotiation of the desertification convention. Early in these negotiations, it became clear that the industrialized countries were not going to make new funds available. This dismayed developing countries, particularly those in Africa, and became a major source of contention during the negotiations. Ultimately, the Global Mechanism was established under the 1994 United Nations Convention to Combat Desertification (UNCCD), its role essentially being to use existing resources more efficiently to meet the action needs of the convention (see Chapter 4).[14] Even though in 2002 the Global Environment Facility (GEF) decided to include land degradation as a new work area, the fact that the UNCCD regime began without new and additional financial resources to combat desertification severely damaged the principle of additionality.[15]

The principle of additionality and the southern demands for "new and additional" funding for developing countries' implementation of environmental agreements was also harmed by a sharp reduction in official development assistance (ODA) levels in the 1990s. In response, developing countries started to use the threat of retreating from previous consensus agreements on global environmental issues as leverage against the donor countries. For example, at the Earth Summit +5 (the 1997 Special Session of the United Nations General Assembly to review the implementation of Agenda 21 and the other Rio agreements), the Group of 77 and China refused to oppose proposals by oil-exporting states to delete all references to reducing consumption

FIGURE 6.1   **Net Official Development Assistance from OECD Countries, 1992–2011**

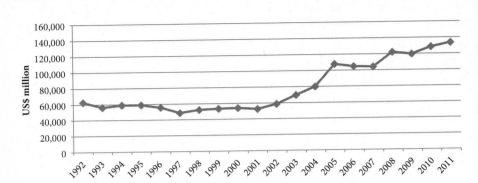

Source: OECD Development Assistance Committee (DAC) Statistical Tables, stats.oecd.org/qwids.

of fossil fuels. This tactic failed, however, to shake the veto exercised by donor countries on targets for ODA.[16]

Commitments made at the March 2002 United Nations Conference on Financing for Development reversed the ODA decline in 2003 and 2004. In 2005, donors committed to increase ODA at the Group of Eight summit in Gleneagles, Scotland,[17] and at the United Nations Millennium +5 Summit.[18] The pledges made at these summits, combined with other commitments, implied an increase in aid from nearly $80 billion in 2004 to nearly $122 billion in 2010. Until 2011, aid had been steadily increasing for more than a decade. Net ODA rose by 63 percent between 2000 and 2010, the year it reached its peak (see Figure 6.1). Yet, while ODA increased in 2011, it still represented only 0.31 percent of combined gross national income (GNI). This was also a 2.7 percent drop in real terms compared to 2010, the result of fiscal constraints in a number of countries as a result of the recession.[19]

In 2011, the largest donors were the United States, Germany, the United Kingdom, France, and Japan. However, Denmark, Luxembourg, the Netherlands, Norway, and Sweden remained the only countries to exceed the United Nations' ODA target of 0.7 percent of GNI (see Box 6.1). Moreover, environmental aid from both bilateral and multilateral aid agencies remains a small percentage of this figure. According to the Organization for Economic Cooperation and Development (OECD), out of $115 billion of total bilateral ODA in 2010 only 4.73 percent ($5.45 billion) was targeted for environmental aid.[20] So while there have been new and additional financial resources, the current and projected levels of ODA still fall far short of the estimates of what is necessary to achieve internationally agreed environmental goals.[21]

BOX 6.1   THE 0.7 PERCENT ODA TARGET

The best-known international target in the aid field is that of raising ODA to 0.7 percent of donors' national income. The target grew out of a proposal by the World Council of Churches in 1958 to transfer 1 percent of donor countries' income to developing countries. But it had a major problem: governments had no means of programming or even predicting the private element of capital flows, which in many years are more than half the total.

This drawback stimulated efforts to define a separate subtarget for official flows. The Dutch economist Jan Tinbergen led this work after he was appointed chair of the United Nations Committee on Development Planning in 1964. Tinbergen estimated the capital inflows developing economies needed to achieve desirable growth rates, and he proposed a target for official flows—both concessional (grants and subsidized loans) and nonconcessional—of 0.75 percent of GNP, to be achieved by 1972. Some, but not all, developed countries accepted this target, but without the date, at the second meeting of the United Nations Conference on Trade and Development (UNCTAD) in 1968.

This idea was then taken up by the Pearson Commission, appointed by World Bank president Robert McNamara. The commission's 1969 report proposed that ODA "be raised to 0.70% of donor GNP by 1975 and in no case later than 1980."

The late 1960s saw intense negotiations in the UN over a development strategy for the 1970s. Aid volume was a key sticking point between developed and developing countries. Developing countries pressed for the UNCTAD target of 0.75 percent of GNP in total official flows, but when negotiations stalled, they substituted the Pearson Commission target of 0.7 percent of GNP for ODA. This broke the impasse and, although most donor countries expressed reservations, in October 1970 they adopted UN General Assembly Resolution 2626 (XXV), which stated that "each economically advanced country will progressively increase its official development assistance to the developing countries and will exert its best efforts to reach a minimum net amount of 0.7% of its gross national product" by the mid-1970s.

The new target gained acceptance, with exceptions. The United States made clear that, while it supported the aims of the resolution, it did not accept specific targets or timetables. Switzerland was not a UN member at the time and did not adopt the target. All other developed countries have at one time or another accepted it, at least as a long-term objective, and it has been repeatedly reendorsed at international conferences to this day. However, to date, only Sweden, the Netherlands, Norway, Denmark, and Luxembourg have achieved the target. Finland achieved it once, in 1991. No other developed country has met the 0.7 percent target.

Sources: The information in this box is excerpted from OECD, *History of the 0.7% ODA Target*, 2010, www.oecd.org/dac/aidstatistics/45539274.pdf.

See also Lester B. Pearson, *Partners in Development: Report of the Commission on International Development* (London: Pall Mall, 1969), 18.

Developing countries also believe that the North should bear the financial burden of measures to reverse ecological damage. This is a key component of the principle of common but differentiated responsibilities. This principle states that global environmental problems are the common concern of all nations, and all nations should work toward their solution (common responsibilities), but responsibility for action should be differentiated in proportion to the responsibility for creating the problem and the financial and technical resources available for taking effective action (differentiated responsibilities). Since some nations have a greater and more direct responsibility for creating environmental problems, they have a greater responsibility to address them.

The principle of common but differentiated responsibilities enjoys broad support and has been explicitly acknowledged in nearly all international environmental agreements since the mid-1980s. It is reflected in specific regime rules, such as the different requirements for industrialized and developing countries under the Montreal Protocol (as discussed in Chapter 3, developing countries are given additional years before they have to phase out particular chemicals), the absence of developing-country commitments to reduce GHG emissions in the Kyoto Protocol, and provisions to provide developing countries with financial and technical assistance (FTA) to help them implement the ozone, climate, biodiversity, hazardous waste, and chemicals regimes.

At the same time, important differences exist regarding how countries believe the principle of common but differentiated responsibilities should influence global environmental policy both in general and on specific issues. Developing countries emphasize historical responsibilities for causing global environmental problems, the large disparities in current per capita contributions (e.g., in per capita GHG emissions or resource consumption), and their need to devote resources to lifting billions of people out of stifling poverty and underdevelopment. It would be unfair, counterproductive, and perhaps immoral, they maintain, for developing countries to devote scarce resources to combating global environmental problems at the expense of addressing development. Thus, many southern states argue that the principle of common but differentiated responsibilities not only demands that industrialized countries should take far more significant action far earlier than developing countries and provide greatly increased FTA but also that developing countries should participate in a global regime only to the extent that they receive sufficient FTA to allow them to implement the regime without having a negative impact on their economic development. This means, for example, that the FTA must meet the extra, or incremental, costs for using alternatives to the inexpensive ozone-depleting chemicals or coal-fired power plants that industrialized countries used during their economic development.

In contrast, while most industrialized countries allow that historical responsibility and current per capita emissions are relevant to policy discussions, they also emphasize the common responsibility of all countries to contribute to solving global environmental problems, which implies a need for developing countries to avoid duplicating the unsustainable historical development patterns of the industrialized world. They also point out that some developing countries are currently among the most important contributors to particular environmental problems and that it will be simply physically impossible to address these issues, in particular climate change, mercury pollution, and deforestation, if these developing countries do not act, and act soon. Thus, many industrialized countries maintain that while it is appropriate for them to act first and to provide FTA, developing countries must also take action; particular levels of FTA are not a precondition for developing countries to take responsible action; and developing countries experiencing rapid levels of economic growth or that have large impacts on particular environmental problems have more responsibility to act than other developing countries with regard to those problems.

These differences are on full display in the climate negotiations. The United States and some other countries believe that certain developing nations should agree to take significant action to reduce their GHG emissions from burning fossil fuels (e.g., China and India) and deforestation (e.g., Brazil and Indonesia). Many developing countries reject these arguments, citing their low per capita emissions, their need for energy and economic development, inadequate FTA provisions, and especially the responsibility of industrialized countries for creating the problem and the implications this should have on commitments to emissions reductions. During the Kyoto Protocol negotiations, for example, Brazil presented an analysis that compared the relative responsibility of Annex I (industrialized) countries and non–Annex I (developing) countries for climate change not just in carbon dioxide (CO_2) emissions in a given year but in CO_2 concentrations from historical emissions. It showed that the non–Annex I countries' responsibility for accumulated emissions would not equal that of Annex I countries until the middle of the twenty-second century.[22]

The third Rio principle is the "polluter pays" principle, which seeks to ensure that the economic and other costs of environmental action should be borne by those who created the need for that action. As with other Rio principles, the South has argued that the "polluter pays" principle has been steadily diluted. They point to an increasing pattern of pushing treaty implementation steadily southward, including in the climate, desertification, and biodiversity regimes, by seeking relatively fewer changes in behavior patterns in the North and relatively more in the South, even though northern behavior gave rise to most of the problems in the first place.[23]

Another consistent theme in developing-country views of global environmental issues is the inequality in governing structures of international organizations such as the World Bank, which allows a minority of donor countries to outvote the rest of the

PHOTO 6.1   NGOs reminding the developed countries about the principles of additionality and common but differentiated responsibilities.
Courtesy IISD/*Earth Negotiations Bulletin.*

world. Developing countries have demanded that institutions making decisions on how to spend funds on the global environment should have a "democratic" structure, that is, one in which each country is equally represented. Thus, developing countries did some of their toughest bargaining in negotiations relating to the environment when they resisted the donor countries' proposed governance structure for the GEF.

The South also has demanded that the transfer of environmental technologies on concessional or preferential terms be part of all environmental treaties. In the Montreal Protocol negotiations, for instance, developing states requested a guarantee from the industrialized countries that corporations would provide them with patents and technical knowledge on substitutes for CFCs. This has also been a major issue in the climate change and chemicals negotiations.

Needless to say, developing countries remain frustrated with global environmental politics, an attitude clearly related to convictions that the global economic system remains unfairly skewed in favor of the advanced industrialized countries. On the one hand, some argue that the concept of sustainable development has allowed developing countries to incorporate long-standing concerns about economic and social development into the environmental agendas; by doing so, they have influenced the nature of global environmental discourse.[24] On the other hand, the South claims that it has seen few benefits from its continuing involvement in global environmental politics. Much of North-South environmental relations in the more than twenty years since Rio has focused on what the South sees as the North's failure to deliver what was promised or implied at Rio: new and additional financial resources, technology transfer, and capacity building.

THE SOCIAL PILLAR OF SUSTAINABLE DEVELOPMENT

The social development pillar or dimension of sustainable development addresses issues of access to resources and opportunities, social justice and equity, participation and empowerment. A strong social pillar means that all development sectors are stronger, whether it is agriculture, infrastructure development, management of natural resources, or rural and urban development. A weak social pillar means weakness in other sectors as well.[25]

Developing-country concerns with social development, globalization, and other issues such as the HIV/AIDS epidemic led to a greater focus on the social development dimension of sustainable development as the millennium approached. There was growing recognition that the world was failing to achieve most of the goals for a more sustainable society set out in Agenda 21 and elsewhere. HIV/AIDS rolled back life expectancies in some countries to pre-1980 levels, and the number of people living with the disease approached the 40 million mark. The world's population climbed above 6.1 billion in 2000, up from 5.5 billion in 1992—a significant increase in just eight years. The total number of people living in poverty dropped slightly—from 1.3 to 1.2 billion—but most of the gains were in Southeast Asia, and virtually no progress was made in sub-Saharan Africa, where almost half the population lived in poverty. At least 1.1 billion people still lacked access to safe drinking water, and 2.4 billion lacked adequate sanitation.[26]

The world was also experiencing increasing globalization. Some viewed globalization as a threat, others as an opportunity. Many policy makers and industrialists in the developed world were (and remain) positive about the phenomenon. However, many living in developing countries and a variety of NGOs worried that environmental and labor standards were in a "race to the bottom" and that social and economic disparities were being exacerbated. Many NGOs were concerned that developing countries would eliminate or ignore environmental and labor standards in their efforts to attract foreign direct investment. There was a fear that if a host country demonstrated that it did not have strict pollution standards and did not condemn child labor or support an eight-hour work day, it would attract more corporate investment.[27]

In a speech delivered to the UNGA in April 2000 to launch the Millennium Report, then UN secretary-general Kofi Annan tackled the globalization issue. Observing that the opportunities provided by this phenomenon were being distributed unequally, he called for a candid debate on the positive and negative consequences of globalization and for discussions about how to make globalization work for all people in all countries. "How can we say that the half of the human race which has yet to make or receive a telephone call, let alone use a computer, is taking part in globalization?" he asked.[28]

The Millennium Assembly

The UNGA designated its fifty-fifth session, starting on September 6, 2000, as the Millennium Assembly and decided to hold a Millennium Summit of world leaders to address the pressing challenges facing the world's people in the twenty-first century. At the Millennium Assembly, world leaders agreed to a far-reaching plan to support global development objectives for the new century. The world's leaders reaffirmed their commitment to work toward peace and security for all and a world in which sustainable development and poverty eradication would have the highest priority. The agreement, set out in the Millennium Declaration, addressed a wide range of core international issues relating to fundamental values and principles; peace, security, and disarmament; development and poverty eradication; the protection of the environment; human rights, democracy, and good governance; the needs of the most vulnerable; the special needs of Africa; and the strengthening of the United Nations. Set against a backdrop of widespread concern about the social and ecological implications of globalization, the Millennium Assembly placed the relationship between poverty, environmental decline, and economic development firmly in the international spotlight.[29]

The following year, Secretary-General Annan presented his report, titled *Road Map Towards the Implementation of the United Nations Millennium Declaration* (UN document 56/326). The report contains, in an annex, eight development goals containing eighteen targets and forty-eight indicators, which are commonly known as the Millennium Development Goals (MDGs). The first seven goals are directed toward eradicating poverty in all its forms: halving extreme poverty and hunger, achieving universal primary education and gender equity, reducing the mortality of children under five by two-thirds and maternal mortality by three-quarters, reversing the spread of HIV/AIDS, halving the proportion of people without access to safe drinking water, and ensuring environmental sustainability. The final goal outlines measures for building a global partnership for development. The goals, targets, and indicators were developed following consultations held among members of the United Nations Secretariat and representatives of the International Monetary Fund, the OECD, and the World Bank in order to harmonize reporting on the development goals in the Millennium Declaration and the international development goals (see Figure 6.2).

In a relatively short period, the MDGs gained tremendous currency, primarily in development circles, but increasingly in related trade and finance spheres. Many actors counted on the MDGs to galvanize disparate and sometimes competing development agendas. Increasingly, stakeholders viewed the MDGs as a powerful political tool to hold governments and international institutions accountable. A key reason for this is that the Millennium Declaration and its MDGs clarified the shared and individual

FIGURE 6.2   The Millennium Development Goals

BY 2015, ALL UN MEMBER STATES HAVE PLEDGED TO

Eradicate extreme poverty and hunger

- Reduce by half the proportion of people living on less than $1 per day
- Reduce by half the proportion of people who suffer from hunger

Achieve universal primary education

- Ensure that all boys and girls complete a full course of primary schooling

Promote gender equality and empower women

- Eliminate gender disparity in primary and secondary education, preferably by 2005, and at all levels of education no later than 2015

Reduce child mortality

- Reduce by two-thirds the mortality rate among children under five

Improve maternal health

- Reduce by three-quarters the maternal mortality ratio

Combat HIV/AIDS, malaria, and other diseases

- Halt and begin to reverse the spread of HIV/AIDS
- Halt and begin to reverse the incidence of malaria and other major diseases

Ensure environmental sustainability

- Integrate the principles of sustainable development into country policies and programs and reverse the loss of environmental resources
- Reduce by half the proportion of people without sustainable access to safe drinking water
- Achieve a significant improvement in the lives of at least 100 million slum dwellers by 2020

Develop a global partnership for development

- Develop further an open trading and financial system that is rule based, predictable, and nondiscriminatory (This target includes a commitment to good governance, development, and poverty reduction, both nationally and internationally.)
- Address the special needs of the least developed countries (This includes tariff- and quota-free access for their exports, enhanced debt relief for heavily indebted poor countries, cancellation of official bilateral debt, and more generous ODA for countries committed to poverty reduction.)
- Address the special needs of landlocked countries and small island developing states
- Deal comprehensively with the debt problems of developing countries through national and international measures in order to make debt sustainable in the long term
- In cooperation with developing countries, develop decent and productive work for youth
- In cooperation with pharmaceutical companies, provide access to affordable essential drugs in developing countries
- In cooperation with the private sector, make available the benefits of new technologies, especially information and communications technologies

Source: "Millennium Development Goals," United Nations, www.un.org/millenniumgoals.

roles and responsibilities of key stakeholders. The declaration set out the responsibilities of governments to implement various specific goals and targets. It instructed the network of international organizations to marshal their resources and expertise in the most strategic and efficient way possible to support and sustain the efforts of partners at global and country levels. And it urged citizens, civil-society organizations, and the private sector to bring to the table their unique strengths for motivation, mobilization, and action.[30]

The World Summit on Sustainable Development

These issues came to a head at the World Summit on Sustainable Development (WSSD) in Johannesburg, South Africa, in 2002, held ten years after the Earth Summit in Rio to map out a detailed course of action for the further implementation of Agenda 21. Once again, the issue of sustainable development was on the negotiating table, and the MDGs definitely had an impact.

The WSSD took place in a difficult international climate compared to that of the Earth Summit. The optimism that had existed in 1992 about a large "peace dividend" that could be reallocated to sustainable development had deflated along with the rest of the world economy, especially in the year before the summit. One year after the September 11, 2001, terrorist attacks, the US government, preoccupied with the war on terrorism and laying the groundwork for the war in Iraq, was generally indifferent and sometimes even hostile to environmental causes and multilateralism. Developing countries were wary of, and frustrated with, industrialized countries. The failure to implement the Rio agreements effectively—especially the perceived lack of new and additional financial resources—had cast a long shadow and raised questions about the credibility and accountability of large, multi-issue global conferences.[31]

The summit produced three key outcomes. The first was the Johannesburg Declaration, a pledge by world leaders to commit their countries to the goal of sustainable development. The second was the Johannesburg Plan of Implementation, which sets out a comprehensive program of action for sustainable development and includes quantifiable goals and targets with fixed deadlines. Third, the summit produced nearly three hundred voluntary partnerships and other initiatives to support sustainable development. Many of the commitments and partnerships agreed to in Johannesburg echoed the MDGs. For example, countries agreed to commit themselves to halving the proportion of people who lack clean water and proper sanitation by 2015. In energy, countries committed themselves to expanding access to the two billion people who do not have access to modern energy services. In addition, although countries did not agree on a target for phasing in renewable energy (e.g., a target of 15 percent of the global energy supply from renewable energy by 2010), which many observers said was a major shortcoming of the summit, they did commit to green energy and the phaseout of subsidies for types of energy inconsistent with sustainable development.

On health issues, in addition to actions to fight HIV/AIDS and reduce water-borne diseases and the health risks caused by pollution, countries agreed to phase out, by 2020, the use and production of chemicals that harm human health and the environment. Many commitments were also made to protect biodiversity and improve ecosystem management. These included commitments to reduce biodiversity loss by 2010, to restore fisheries to their maximum sustainable yields by 2015, to establish a representative network of marine protected areas by 2012, and to improve developing countries' access to environmentally sound alternatives to ozone-depleting chemicals by 2010.[32]

Yet, among all the targets, timetables, and partnerships agreed on at Johannesburg, there were no silver-bullet solutions to aid the fight against poverty and a continually deteriorating natural environment. In fact, as an implementation-focused summit, Johannesburg did not produce a particularly dramatic outcome—no agreements emerged that led to new treaties, and many of the agreed targets had already been agreed on at the Millennium Assembly and other meetings—and did not carry the legal status of a binding treaty. As then UN secretary-general Kofi Annan told the press on the last day of the summit, "I think we have to be careful not to expect conferences like this to produce miracles. But we do expect conferences like this to generate political commitment, momentum and energy for the attainment of the goals."[33]

Among the summit's legacies was a shift in the balance of the three dimensions of sustainable development. During the previous decade, sustainable development more often than not equaled protection of the environment. Johannesburg was the first true summit on sustainable development in the sense that advocates of all three dimensions were under one roof arguing their cases, raising real issues, and confronting those with different interests and perspectives. It was not a social summit dealing only with poverty, exclusion, and human rights. It was not an economic and globalization summit addressing only trade, investment, finance, and the development and transfer of technology. And it was not an environmental summit focusing only on natural resource degradation, biodiversity loss, climate change, and pollution. Johannesburg was instead a summit about the intersections of all these issues.[34]

The Road to 2015:
Challenges in Implementing the MDGs

In 2005, world leaders gathered once again in New York to reaffirm the MDGs and discuss related issues. Among the outcomes, the heads of state and government expressed their commitment to achieve the MDGs by 2015, pledged an additional $50 billion a year by 2010 to fight poverty, and addressed such issues as innovative financing for development, debt relief and restructuring, and trade liberalization.[35]

Developing countries and many international organizations have adopted the MDGs as their framework for international development cooperation. There have also been significant contributions from the private sector and, critically, civil society in both developed and developing countries. These partnerships have resulted in sound progress in some areas, and some of the targets have been reached in advance of their target dates. *The Millennium Development Goals Report 2012* stated:

- Extreme poverty is falling in every region: the proportion of people living on less than $1.25 a day fell from 47 percent in 1990 to 24 percent in 2008—a reduction from over 2 billion to less than 1.4 billion.
- Preliminary estimates indicate that the global poverty rate ($1.25 a day) fell in 2010 to less than half the 1990 rate. If these results are confirmed, the first target of the MDGs—cutting the extreme poverty rate to half its 1990 level—will have been achieved at the global level well ahead of 2015.
- The target of halving the proportion of people without sustainable access to safe drinking water was also met by 2010, rising from 76 percent in 1990 to 89 percent in 2010. Between 1990 and 2010, over two billion people gained access to improved drinking water sources.
- The share of urban residents in the developing world living in slums declined from 39 percent in 2000 to 33 percent in 2012. More than two hundred million people gained access to either improved water sources, improved sanitation facilities, or more durable or less crowded housing. This achievement exceeds the target of significantly improving the lives of at least one hundred million slum dwellers, well ahead of the 2020 deadline.
- The world has achieved rough parity in primary education between girls and boys (although educational opportunities are less available for girls in a few countries).
- Enrollment rates of children of primary school age increased markedly in sub-Saharan Africa, from 58 to 76 percent between 1999 and 2010. Many countries in that region succeeded in reducing their relatively high out-of-school rates even as their primary school age populations were growing.
- Despite population growth, the number of children dying under the age of five fell from more than 12 million worldwide in 1990 to 7.6 million in 2010.
- Access to treatment for people living with HIV increased in all regions. At the end of 2010, 6.5 million people were receiving antiretroviral therapy for HIV or AIDS in developing regions. This constitutes an increase of over 1.4 million people from December 2009, and the largest one-year increase ever. The 2010 target of universal access, however, was not reached.
- Globally, tuberculosis incidence rates have been falling since 2002, and current projections suggest that the 1990 death rate from the disease will be halved by 2015.
- The estimated incidence of malaria has decreased globally, by 17 percent since 2000.[36]

PHOTO 6.2 NGOs marching in Johannesburg for access to better sanitation and clean water. Courtesy IISD/*Earth Negotiations Bulletin*.

In spite of this good news, progress has slowed for some MDGs, in part because the multiple financial crises since 2008 cut development assistance. Decreases in maternal mortality are far from the 2015 target. There have been important improvements in maternal health and reduction in maternal deaths, but progress is still slow. Reductions in adolescent childbearing and expansion of contraceptive use have continued, but at a slower pace since 2000 than over the decade before.[37]

Use of improved sources of water remains lower in rural areas. While 19 percent of the rural population used unimproved sources of water in 2010, the rate in urban areas was only 4 percent. And since dimensions of safety, reliability, and sustainability are not reflected in the proxy indicator used to track progress toward the MDG target, it is likely that these figures overestimate the actual number of people using safe water supplies. Worse, nearly half of the population in developing regions—2.5 billion—still lacks access to improved sanitation facilities.[38]

Hunger remains a global challenge. The most recent Food and Agriculture Organization (FAO) estimates of undernourishment set the mark at 850 million living in hunger in the world in the 2006–2008 period—15.5 percent of the world population. This continuing high level reflects the lack of progress on hunger in several regions, even as income poverty has decreased. The FAO assessment reveals that small countries, heavily dependent on food imports, were deeply affected by skyrocketing food prices—especially those in sub-Saharan Africa. Progress has also been slow in reducing child undernutrition. Close to one-third of children in Southern Asia were underweight in 2010.[39]

The number of people living in slums continues to grow. Despite a reduction in the share of urban populations living in slums, the absolute number has continued to grow from a 1990 baseline of 650 million. An estimated 863 million people now live in slum conditions.[40]

Perspectives on the MDGs and their implementation differ. Some argue that the MDGs form just another set of international development goals in a long history of nations' setting and failing to achieve such goals. To name just two examples, in the 1960s the United Nations set its sights on universal primary education by 1980. In 1980 it committed to achieving 6.5 percent economic growth throughout the developing world by 1990. During the 1980s and 1990s, there was economic growth, poverty reduction, improved schooling, and much else to celebrate in the developing world, but these impossible goals were not met. Some believe that these types of broad global goals focus attention away from what was accomplished (through sound domestic policies, aid, and other forms of cooperation), creating an unnecessary impression of failure.[41]

The Center for Global Development, a Washington, DC–based think tank, argues that the vast majority of developing countries, especially in Africa, will probably miss most of the MDG targets in 2015. But this should not be taken as a sign that poor countries have failed or that aid has been a waste. Nor will it result from a lack of ODA. In fact, during the first decade of the millennium, many of the world's poorest countries have made great progress in improving the quality of life of their people. For example, in 2007 Burkina Faso in Africa had net primary school enrollment of 40 to 45 percent. Should it be considered a failure if a country achieves only 60 percent enrollment by 2015 instead of the MDG of 100 percent enrollment? Such a feat would be extraordinary by historical standards—but still a failure to achieve the goal. By way of comparison, it took the United States over a century to transition from 40 percent enrollment to universal primary schooling.[42] As the Center for Global Development has argued, "development is a marathon, not a sprint."[43] From this perspective, failure to achieve the MDGs, provided that significant progress has been made, need not be seen as a failure in economic and social development.

Others argue that there needs to be a greater link between the MDGs and the environment. As noted earlier, there has been concern that the environmental pillar of sustainable development has been diminished in the context of the MDGs. In an influential article, Jeffrey Sachs and Walter Reid argue that development goals cannot be achieved and sustained without sound environmental management. Similarly, environmental goals cannot be achieved without development. Yet the world underinvests in both, and developing and developed countries tend to overlook the policy link between poverty reduction and the environment.[44] For example, investing in environmental assets and management is vital to cost-effective and equitable strategies to achieve goals relating to poverty alleviation, hunger, and disease. Investments in improved agricultural practices to reduce water pollution by runoff, as well as the use of chemical fertilizers and pesticides, can also boost the coastal fishing industry. Wetlands protection can meet the needs of rural communities while avoiding the costs of expensive flood-control projects. Yet these investments are often overlooked.[45]

So what do the MDGs mean for global environmental politics? Some believe that the tide has turned away from the environment and toward the economic and social-development pillars of sustainable development. The MDGs are a large part of the overall UN agenda, and most bilateral and multilateral aid programs focus on these two areas. Seeing this, many environmental regimes have tried to show how their priorities are in fact aligned with the MDGs so that they will continue to receive attention within the larger development agenda. In some respects, areas of "global environmental politics" have quite possibly become part of "global development politics."

ECONOMIC DEVELOPMENT AND TRADE

The third pillar of sustainable development is economic development. The relationship between the global economy and the natural environment goes a long way to explaining the evolution of global environmental politics. The global economy has changed dramatically over the past sixty years. The post–World War II economy of the 1950s and 1960s was essentially divided between developed or industrialized countries in the North and developing or nonindustrialized countries in the South. At that time, developed countries accounted for 90 percent of world manufacturing output and 90 percent of exports.[46] In addition to this imbalance in production and exports, there was an imbalance in living standards and political power.

By 1974, encouraged by a surge in commodity prices and the Organization of Petroleum Exporting Countries' successful manipulation of oil supplies in the early 1970s, developing countries attempted to restructure the global economic system. The South called for a bold but largely unrealistic plan, the New International Economic Order (NIEO), a list of demands for the redistribution of wealth, which would include a new system of international commodity agreements, a unilateral reduction of barriers to imports from developing states into industrialized countries, the enhancement of developing countries' capabilities in science and technology, increased northern financing of technology transfer, and changes in patent laws to lower the cost of such transfers.[47]

After the late 1970s, however, the NIEO faded from the global political agenda as economic trends turned against the South. Some officials in the North consequently felt even more strongly that it could disregard southern demands for change. Yet, although some northern observers might have considered the NIEO agenda "discredited,"[48] it remained unfinished business for much of the South and was still considered a goal "very much worth pursuing."[49]

In the 1980s, commodity prices, debt, and trade issues shaped the economic picture in developing countries. Falling commodity prices devastated the economies of countries heavily dependent on commodity exports. Between 1980 and 1991, the price of a weighted index of thirty-three primary commodities exported by developing countries, not including energy, declined by 46 percent.[50] Meanwhile, heavy debt burdens, taken on at a time when commodity prices were high and northern banks were freely lending dollars from Arab oil revenues, siphoned off much of the foreign exchange of many developing countries. By 1995, the total external debt of the least-developed countries was $136 billion, a sum that represented 112.7 percent of their gross national product that year.[51]

But the global economy was also changing. In 1992 the OECD countries' (industrialized) share of global gross national income (GNI) was 80 percent. By 2005, it was down to 75 percent. By 2010 it was 65 percent.[52] During this same period, OECD countries' share of exports declined from 70 to 59 percent of the global total,[53] as traditional production, trade, and finance patterns were replaced by new and more balanced configurations. Spurred by the revolution in information technology, trade liberalization, economic reforms, the entry of an estimated two billion people into the labor force as a result of the demise of the Soviet Union and the opening of China, and the increased movement of capital and technology from developed to developing countries, the global economy doubled in size from 1998 to 2008, increasing from $31 trillion to $62 trillion.[54] While this economic growth reached practically every region of the world, a handful of large developing countries—led by China, India, and Brazil—accounted for a major share of global growth. Other emerging economies, such as Indonesia, Mexico, Russia, Turkey, and Vietnam, also grew at a rapid pace. This enabled developing countries to expand their share of the global GNI, fueling speculation that the world's economic balance of power has shifted away from the United States and Europe toward Asia and Latin America.[55]

However, despite the growth of some economies, the income gap between the industrialized world and the developing world has not narrowed. The richest 25 percent of countries of the world (the so-called North) control about 62 percent of the world's income (see Figure 6.3). Furthermore, the richest 10 percent of the world controls 84 percent of global assets, with the top 1 percent alone accounting for 44 percent of global assets.[56] A few countries are seeing median household incomes rise, but most

FIGURE 6.3A   Global Adult Population Distribution, 2011

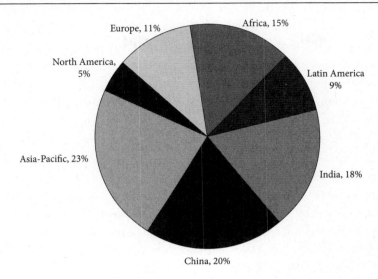

FIGURE 6.3B   Global Wealth Distribution, 2011

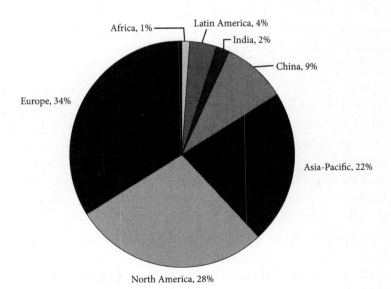

Source: United Nations Population Division, *World Population Prospects: The 2010 Revision* (New York: United Nations, 2011) and Credit Suisse Research Institute, *Credit Suisse Global Wealth Databook, 2011* (Zurich, Switzerland: Credit Suisse Research Institute, October, 2011).

are not, and the "cavernous divide" between the world's rich and poor is not closing.[57] In fact, most of the world's population earns an average annual income either below $1,500 or above $11,500.[58] The apparent lack of widespread economic mobility in the global division of labor has reinforced the popular perception in the poorest countries that the world is divided into haves and have-nots and that they exist solely on the world's periphery.[59]

Much of the economic growth in the emerging economies was the result of priority given to expanding the scope for trade and investment in adherence with neoliberal economics (a political-economic movement, increasingly prominent since 1980, that deemphasizes or rejects government intervention in the economy, focusing instead on achieving progress and even social justice through freer markets, especially an emphasis on economic growth). For example, neoliberals argue that the best way to protect the environment is by overcoming poverty through increased privatization, foreign direct investment, and free trade. As a result, the institutions governing the global economy have grown stronger, while those promoting social equity, poverty alleviation, and environmental cooperation remain weak.[60] The barriers to trade and investment began to fall, and the belief that poor countries could grow themselves out of poverty by boarding the liberalization express train took on an almost religious force—at least in many economic and policy circles within rich countries.[61] In other words, it was believed that if poorer countries supported trade liberalization, many of their economic development problems would be solved.

Yet many industrialized countries did not adhere to this philosophy in practice. During the early 1990s, trade barriers erected by industrialized countries against imports of manufactured and processed goods from developing countries increased even as most developing countries (under pressure from international financial institutions) were lowering their barriers to imports.[62] Tariffs on certain sectors of particular interest to developing countries, including agriculture, textiles, clothing, fish, and fish products, tended to be the highest in industrialized countries, limiting market access.[63] Furthermore, new kinds of nontariff barriers to trade (such as antidumping and countervailing duty actions), export-restraint agreements (such as the Multi-Fiber Arrangement), and direct subsidies were used to protect industries in the industrialized countries against imports from developing countries.

At the same time, trade liberalization raised the concerns of environmentalists about the potential impact on the Earth's ecosystems and on governments' development choices. They see liberalization as driving the demand for greater consumption of natural resources and as creating pressures to dismantle environmental regulations.[64] This perspective arose fairly recently. The global trade system evolved for decades without much thought about its impact on the environment. When the General Agreement on Tariffs and Trade (GATT), the central pillar of the international trading system, was negotiated just after World War II, there was no mention of the word "environment." For the next forty years, trade officials and their environmental counterparts pursued their respective agendas on nearly parallel tracks that rarely, if ever, intersected. Little attention was paid to potential connections between trade liberalization and environmental protection. The wake-up call for environmentalists occurred after the United States banned tuna from Mexico and Venezuela because their fleets did not meet US standards for minimizing dolphin kills in tuna fishing. In 1991, the GATT declared the US ban illegal under the rules of international trade. US environmentalists were alarmed that a national environmental law could be overturned by the GATT and began serious efforts to address the environmental implications of international trade policy.[65]

The GATT and the World Trade Organization (WTO) constitute a regime that seeks to promote a common set of international trade rules, a reduction in tariffs and other trade barriers, and the elimination of discriminatory treatment in international trade relations.[66] The WTO, which governments created in 1995, has the mandate to rule on a broad spectrum of issues from trade in goods and services to intellectual property rights, including issues affecting human health, the use of natural resources, and the protection of the environment.

The preamble to the treaty that established the WTO recognized that the organization should ensure "the optimal use of the world's resources in accordance with the objective of sustainable development."[67] This was a last-minute victory for environmentalists, although the statement is nonbinding. With this in mind, and with a desire to coordinate the policies in the field of trade and the environment, when trade ministers approved the treaty and the other results of the Uruguay Round of trade negotiations in Marrakech, Morocco, in April 1994, they also decided to begin a WTO work program on trade and environment. Their decision established the WTO's Committee on Trade and Environment (CTE) and ensured that the subject would have a place on the WTO agenda.

In November 2001, the WTO held its fourth ministerial conference in Doha, Qatar, and ministers agreed to set the current round of trade-liberalization negotiations in motion. They had attempted to start a new round of trade negotiations two years earlier at the third ministerial conference in Seattle, Washington, but were unable to agree on the agenda amid protests against the WTO and its policies by thousands of environmental, labor, and human rights activists. The Doha Ministerial Declaration launched a broad-based round of multilateral trade negotiations on nine topics, eight of which were supposed to be completed as a single undertaking by 2005: implementation, agriculture, services, industrial tariffs, subsidies, antidumping, regional trade agreements, and the environment. The declaration contained more language on both economic development and environmental issues, including fishing subsidies, than any of its predecessors.

However, WTO member states failed to complete their negotiations in 2005, and the trade talks were formally declared at an impasse at the end of 2011. With the ninth ministerial conference scheduled for December 2013 in Bali, Indonesia, WTO members are beginning to show signs of reengagement in the negotiations. This section examines some of the key issues along the trade-and-environment nexus, specifically, the relationship between environmental treaties and the WTO, how environmental issues have been dealt with in the dispute-settlement process, ecolabeling, standards and certification, subsidies and the environment, and liberalizing trade in environmental goods and services.

The Relationship Between Multilateral Environmental Agreements and the WTO

More than twenty multilateral environmental agreements (MEAs) incorporate trade measures to help them achieve their goals.[68] This means that the agreements use restraints on trade in particular substances or products, either between parties to the treaty or between parties and nonparties, or both. Although this represents a relatively small number of MEAs, they include some of the most important, including the Convention on International Trade in Endangered Species of Wild Fauna and Flora (CITES); the Montreal Protocol; the Basel, Rotterdam, and Stockholm conventions; and the Cartagena Protocol on Biosafety. Under all these treaties, trade in the specified products (e.g., endangered species, controlled ODS, hazardous wastes, toxic chemicals, or genetically modified organisms [GMOs]) is banned or restricted between parties or between parties and nonparties (see Box 6.2).

Trade-restricting measures in an environmental agreement may serve one of two broad purposes. First, they may control a type of trade perceived to be a source of the environmental damage that the convention seeks to address. CITES, which requires import and export licenses for trade in endangered species, is a good example. The Basel Convention seeks to restrict or ban the movement and trade of hazardous waste, seeing such movement as a source of environmental harm. The Rotterdam Convention calls on parties to notify other parties before they export certain substances and allows parties to ban certain imports, because the trade of toxic substances to countries unaware of their potential for harm can lead to environmental damage.

Second, environmental agreements may control trade as a means to ensure regime participation, compliance, and effectiveness. Some regimes use trade measures as an additional incentive to join and adhere to the MEA by barring nonparties from trading in restricted goods with parties. Nonparties to the Basel Convention, for example, cannot ship waste to any of the parties, nor can they import it from them. Some, like the Montreal Protocol, have provisions that would allow parties to impose trade sanctions on countries found to have significantly violated regimes rules (to date, this has not

BOX 6.2   SELECTED MEA TRADE MEASURES

CONVENTION ON INTERNATIONAL TRADE IN ENDANGERED SPECIES OF WILD FAUNA AND FLORA

- invokes trade restrictions against parties and nonparties to protect listed species of animals and plants threatened with extinction and endangerment
- uses a permit-and-listing system to prohibit the import or export of listed wildlife and wildlife products unless a scientific finding is made that the trade in question will not threaten the existence of the species

MONTREAL PROTOCOL ON SUBSTANCES THAT DEPLETE THE OZONE LAYER

- prohibits trade in ODS with nonparties unless the nonparty has demonstrated its full compliance with the control measures under the protocol
- uses trade provisions to encourage the phaseout of ODS and to discourage the establishment of "pollution havens" in which parties shift their manufacturing capabilities to nonparties

BASEL CONVENTION ON THE CONTROL OF TRANSBOUNDARY MOVEMENTS OF HAZARDOUS WASTES AND THEIR DISPOSAL

- uses trade measures to limit the market for the transboundary movement and disposal of hazardous waste between OECD and non-OECD countries
- provides that a party shall not permit hazardous waste or other wastes to be traded with a nonparty unless that party enters into a bilateral, multilateral, or regional agreement

ROTTERDAM CONVENTION ON THE PRIOR INFORMED CONSENT PROCEDURE FOR CERTAIN HAZARDOUS CHEMICALS AND PESTICIDES IN INTERNATIONAL TRADE

- allows parties to decide, from the convention's agreed list of chemicals and pesticides, which ones they will not import
- calls for labeling and information requirements to be followed when trade in the controlled substances does take place
- states that if a party decides not to consent to imports of a specific chemical, it must also stop domestic production of the chemical for domestic use, as well as imports from nonparties

CARTAGENA PROTOCOL ON BIOSAFETY

- states that parties may restrict the import of some living GMOs as part of a carefully specified risk-management procedure
- requires that living GMOs that will be intentionally released into the environment are subject to an advance informed agreement procedure, and those destined for use as food, feed, or processing must be accompanied by identifying documents

been used in the ozone regime). Some use trade restrictions as a means to enhance regime effectiveness, again by restricting trade in certain controlled substances (as a means to reinforce controls on production and use) or with nonparties. This prevents "leakage," that is, situations where nonparties or parties with exemptions simply increase production of a restricted good and ship it to the parties that have restricted their own production.[69]

The potential problem with using trade measures in MEAs is that they might conflict with WTO rules. An agreement that says parties can use trade restrictions against some countries (nonparties) but not against others (parties) could violate Articles I, III, and XI of the GATT (provisions addressing most-favored nations and national-treatment principles, as well as provisions on eliminating quantitative restrictions). Free-trade advocates worry that countries might use trade-restricting measures in an MEA as a means to seek economic gain or to reward friends and punish enemies rather than to protect the global environment. Environmentalists worry that countries affected by MEA trade restrictions might challenge their legitimacy before the WTO, which could weaken the MEA.

Most analysts argue that the latter is not particularly a problem when both countries involved are parties to the MEA. In such cases, both countries have voluntarily agreed to be bound by the MEA's rules, including the use of trade measures as spelled out in the agreement. However, problems can arise when the agreement spells out objectives only and leaves it to the parties to make domestic laws to achieve them. Parties to the Kyoto Protocol, for example, may fulfill their obligations (spelled out in the protocol) to lower GHG emissions by any number of trade-restrictive measures (not spelled out). The Nagoya Protocol to the Convention on Biological Diversity leaves it up to national governments to determine if changes are necessary to national patent laws for applicants to disclose the use of any traditional knowledge or genetic resources used in their invention. Although WTO members have expressed hope that disputes between parties might be settled within the MEAs themselves, a party complaining about the use of such nonspecific trade measures would almost certainly choose to take its case to the WTO.[70]

The situation is further complicated if a party to an MEA uses trade measures in the agreement against a nonparty, but both countries are WTO members. Here, the nonparty has not voluntarily agreed to be subjected to the MEA's trade measures. As with party-to-party measures, the trade-restricting party may be violating the nonparty's rights under WTO rules, but here the nonparty might take the matter to the WTO even if the measures are spelled out specifically in the MEA.

This raises the crucial question of which regime, the MEA or the WTO, should be accorded primacy when they conflict. The relationship between the WTO and MEA trade measures has been part of the CTE's agenda within the WTO since its creation in 1995. The current discussions are taking place under the mandate of paragraphs 31 and 32 of the Doha Ministerial Declaration, which address the relationship between existing WTO rules and the specific trade obligations set out in MEAs.[71] Thus far, parties have not made much progress, largely as a result of the overall state of the Doha round of trade negotiations. It remains to be seen if they can achieve an outcome that will equally benefit trade, the environment, and development.

Environmental Issues and the WTO Dispute Settlement System

Environmental policy increasingly affects, and is affected by, economic and trade policy. Consequently, it is not surprising that disputes between trade liberalization and environmental protection have increased in both number and diplomatic prominence. Indeed, the first case heard by the WTO Dispute Settlement Body involved an environmental dispute.[72]

An increasing number of domestic and international policies seek to regulate or restrict trade as a tool to address environmental problems. Such laws have been called environmental trade measures (ETMs) and include import prohibitions, product standards, standards governing production of natural resource exports, and mandatory ecolabeling schemes.[73] Exporters disadvantaged by such environmental measures sometimes charge that the policies are actually intended to protect domestic producers from foreign competition. Sometimes, the exporting countries bring such complaints to the WTO's dispute-resolution panels.

The United States has taken the lead in defending the right to use ETMs for domestic and international environmental objectives and has been the target of cases brought before WTO dispute panels. The United States used trade restrictions in conjunction with its lead-state efforts to end commercial whaling, to protect dolphins from killing by tuna fishermen, to improve protection of marine mammals from destructive drift nets, and to support CITES. For example, US threats to ban South Korean fish products from the US market and prohibit Korean fishing operations in US waters helped to persuade South Korea to give up whaling as well as drift-net operations in the Pacific Ocean.[74] The United States banned wildlife-related exports from Taiwan in 1994 after that country violated CITES by failing to control imports of rhino horn and tiger bone. Although environmentalists see these as justifiable protections, less powerful countries view the United States as throwing its weight around.

When a country believes that an ETM unfairly restricts market access, it can file a complaint, and a GATT/WTO dispute-resolution panel has the authority to determine whether a particular trade measure is or is not compatible with the GATT trade rules. The panels consist of trade specialists from three or five contracting parties with no stake in the issue and who have been agreed to by both parties to the dispute. Dispute panel rulings are normally submitted to the WTO Council (which includes all parties to the agreement) for approval. Decisions carry real weight. If a country fails to bring its law into conformity with the decision, other states are allowed to implement retaliatory trade measures. This is more threatening to small countries than large trading countries such as the United States. Few small countries will risk taking significant retaliatory measures on their own against the United States or the EU, as these could prove counterproductive.[75]

Domestic US laws that use trade measures to pursue environmental goals have been challenged before the GATT/WTO dispute-resolution panels on several occasions. The first panel decision, on the US-Mexican tuna-dolphin dispute, helped to shape the politics of trade-and-environment issues.

In 1991 Mexico filed a complaint with the GATT charging that a US embargo against Mexican yellowfin tuna was a protectionist measure put in place to benefit the US tuna industry. The embargo had been imposed under an amendment to the 1972 Marine Mammal Protection Act (MMPA), which allowed for the use of trade sanctions against countries that killed too many dolphins while catching tuna (the Mexican fleet killed dolphins at twice the rate of the US fleet). The Mexican complaint to the GATT argued that the amendment was simply a measure to protect the US tuna fleet and that US measures should not be allowed to apply to activities by other countries in international waters (where most tuna is caught). More broadly, Mexico, supported by Venezuela, asked why it should forgo export earnings and a low-cost source of protein for its own people to reduce the incidental impact on a marine mammal that was not an endangered species.[76]

The GATT panel ruled that the US ban was a violation of the GATT because it was concerned only with the process of tuna fishing rather than with the product. It also ruled that Article XX of the GATT, which allows trade restrictions for human health or the conservation of animal or plant life, could not justify an exception to that rule because the article does not apply beyond US jurisdiction, that is, in international waters. This was a historic decision. It also reflected the tendency of most trade specialists to view restrictions on trade for environmental purposes as setting dangerous precedents that could harm the world trade system. That eight governments or agencies spoke against the US tuna ban before the panel and not one party spoke for it may also have had an influence.[77]

The decision came at an embarrassing moment, when the United States and Mexico were negotiating the North American Free Trade Agreement. Because both governments really wanted the agreement, the United States was able to work out an agreement with Mexico that prevented the GATT panel decision from being presented to the GATT Council for formal approval and implementation.

In 1994, the EU brought a second complaint against the US tuna ban to a GATT dispute panel to secure resolution on the principle of extraterritorial unilateral actions. The EU charged that its exports of tuna were adversely affected by the MMPA's "secondary embargo" against imports of tuna from intermediary nations that fail to certify they do not buy tuna from nations embargoed under the law. The GATT panel again found the US ban incompatible with the GATT articles, but it accepted two key contentions of environmental critics of the GATT. It rejected the EU's arguments that dolphins are not an exhaustible natural resource and that Article XX applies only to the protection of resources located within the territory of the country applying the trade measure in question. But it held that such measures could be used only to conserve those resources directly and not to change the policy of another state—a distinction that is difficult, if not impossible, for policy makers to apply in practice—and thus found the US MMPA incompatible with the GATT.[78] Although Mexico won the case, the prospect that more refined versions of the MMPA's embargo would withstand WTO scrutiny made many developing countries even more determined to create international rules that would stand up against what they regarded as unfair trade restrictions masquerading as environmental policy.

Two other environmental complaints that have been brought under WTO dispute settlement rules are worth noting because of their precedent-setting nature. In the Venezuela reformulated-gasoline case, Venezuela and Brazil claimed they were discriminated against by a US Environmental Protection Agency rule under the Clean Air Act that required all refineries to make cleaner gasoline using the 1990 US industry standard as a baseline. Because fuel from foreign refineries was not as "clean" in 1990 as that from US refineries, the importing countries were beginning their cleanup efforts from a different starting point. The WTO panel ruled in 1997 for Venezuela and Brazil, and the Environmental Protection Agency revised its rules.[79]

In a second case, in January 1997, India, Malaysia, Pakistan, and Thailand charged that a US ban on the importation of shrimp caught by vessels that kill endangered migratory sea turtles violated WTO rules that no nation can use trade restrictions to influence the (fishing) rules of other countries. The United States argued that relatively simple and inexpensive turtle-excluder devices (TEDs) can be placed on shrimp trawlers to save the turtles. To implement the US Endangered Species Act, the US Court of International Trade, in response to a lawsuit brought by an NGO, the Earth Island Institute, ruled in December 1995 that in order to export mechanically caught marine shrimp to the United States, countries that trawl for shrimp in waters where marine turtles live must, from June 1996, be certified by the US government to have equipped their vessels with TEDs. TEDs have been mandatory on all US shrimp trawlers since December 1994. If properly installed and operated, TEDs, while minimizing loss of the shrimp catch, permit most sea turtles to escape from shrimp trawling nets before they drown. The United States argued the trade measure was necessary because sea turtles were threatened with extinction and the use of TEDs on shrimp nets was the only way to effectively protect them from drowning in shrimp nets.

In April 1998, the WTO dispute settlement panel held that the US import ban on shrimp was "clearly a threat to the multilateral trading system" and consequently was "not within the scope of measures permitted under the chapeau of Article XX." The United States appealed the decision. In October 1998, the appellate body found that the US ban legitimately related to the "protection of exhaustible natural resources" and thus qualified for provisional justification under Article XX(g). This decision represented a step forward for the use of unilateral trade measures for environmental purposes. But the decision also found that the US import ban was applied in an unjustifiably or arbitrarily discriminatory manner and cited seven distinct flaws in the legislation. It found, for example, that the requirement that exporters adopt "essentially the same policy" as that applied by the United States had an unjustifiably "coercive effect" on foreign countries. It also found that the United States had not seriously attempted to reach a multilateral solution with the four complaining countries and that the process for certification of turtle protection programs was not "transparent" or "predictable."[80]

The ruling left open the possibility that a unilaterally imposed trade ban in response to foreign environmental practices could be implemented in compliance with the GATT. But some trade law experts believed the procedural criteria in the ruling were unrealistic. The case once again underlined the question of whether a WTO panel, which lacks both environmental expertise and mandate, should pass judgment on trade measures for environmental purposes.

In response to the appellate body decision, the United States adjusted its policy. The new guidelines still prohibited the import of shrimp harvested with technology adversely affecting the relevant sea turtle species. But instead of requiring the use of TEDs by the exporting country, it allowed the exporting country to present evidence that its program to protect sea turtles in the course of shrimp trawling was comparable in effectiveness to the US program. The guidelines noted, however, that the Department of State was not aware of technology as effective as the TED.[81]

Ecolabeling, Standards, and Certification

The use of ecolabels—labeling products according to environmental criteria—by governments, industry, and NGOs is increasing. They help consumers exercise preferences for environmentally sound production methods for products, such as wood harvested from sustainably managed forests rather than clear-cutting or tuna caught with methods that do not kill large numbers of dolphins. However, within the WTO, concerns have been raised about the growing complexity and diversity of environmental labeling schemes. WTO members generally agree that labeling schemes can be economically efficient and useful for informing consumers, and tend to restrict trade less than other methods. However, these same schemes could be misused to protect domestic producers. For this reason, the schemes should not discriminate between countries and should not create unnecessary barriers or disguised restrictions on international trade.[82]

Although some ecolabels are conferred by product firms themselves or by trade associations, the ones with the most credibility are third-party ecolabels awarded by independent entities that use clear and consistent criteria to evaluate the process and production methods by which a product is made, grown, or caught. Some governments sponsor ecolabel programs, but some of the most important are private, voluntary schemes. Third-party ecolabels have already demonstrated their potential for attracting the attention of producers where international policy making has failed, as shown by the case of the Forest Stewardship Council (FSC) and timber products.

Certification and labeling became an international issue after the establishment in 1993 of the FSC, an independent NGO that created the world's first third-party ecolabeling scheme for wood products. By 1995, the FSC had begun to set standards for sustainable forest management and criteria for potential certifiers to meet and had released a label to show that a product has been certified by FSC standards. The FSC hoped to create a market for certified forest products among consumers and to use that market to leverage more sustainable forest management. Today, the FSC's governing body comprises more than eight hundred member organizations and individuals equally divided among environmental, social, and economic voting "chambers." FSC members include environmental organizations such as WWF, Greenpeace, and Friends of the Earth, as well as companies such as IKEA and Home Depot.

The FSC has the support of a large and growing number of companies that have united themselves in various countries into buyers' groups committed to selling only independently certified timber and timber products. The FSC-labeling scheme is the preferred scheme for buyers' groups in numerous countries, including Austria, Belgium, Brazil, Germany, Japan, the Netherlands, Switzerland, the United Kingdom, and the United States. This unprecedented alliance of major companies, NGOs, and other supporters has resulted in arguably greater levels of dialogue and progress than the formal international negotiations and has begun to change forest-management practices worldwide. As of February 2013, over 172 million hectares of forested land were FSC-certified in eighty countries around the world—the equivalent of more than 8 percent of the world's production forests. The value of FSC-labeled sales is estimated at over $20 billion, demonstrating that there is a demand for sustainably managed timber and timber products.[83]

FIGURE 6.4   **Examples of Ecolabels**

Forest Stewardship
Council

WaterSense

Green Restaurant
Association

Energy Star

Marine Stewardship
Council

Fairtrade

Similarly, the London-based Marine Stewardship Council (MSC) has developed an environmental standard for sustainable and well-managed fisheries. It uses a product label to reward environmentally responsible practices. Consumers concerned about overfishing can choose seafood products that have been independently assessed against the MSC standard and labeled to prove it. The MSC was developed in 1997 by Unilever, the world's largest buyer of seafood, and the environmental NGO WWF. It has operated independently since 1999. As of 2012, 170 fisheries had been certified, representing over 8 percent of global wild fisheries production for human consumption. Another 115 fisheries are currently undergoing assessment. More than one hundred major seafood buyers, including some large supermarket chains in France, Germany, the Netherlands, Switzerland, the United Kingdom, and the United States, have pledged to purchase MSC-certified seafood products. Worldwide, more than fifteen thousand seafood products bear the blue MSC ecolabel, ranging from fresh, frozen, smoked, and canned fish to fish-oil dietary supplements. This amounts to more than $2.5 billion in global annual sales, all of which can be traced back to certified sustainable fisheries.[84] However, it is worth noting that the annual world trade in fish and fishery products is about $109 billion,[85] and MSC proponents understand there is a very long way to go to ensure sustainable fish production.

In addition to the FSC and the MSC, there are over four hundred different types of ecolabels. The large number can certainly confuse consumers regarding which systems are the most valid (see Figure 6.4). Although the FSC, MSC, and some other initiatives have proven quite successful, ecolabeling systems do have the potential to be unfair and discriminatory. Consequently, labeling and related issues are under discussion within several WTO bodies.[86]

In May 2012, the WTO's highest court issued its first-ever ruling on ecolabeling. The court ruled that the US "dolphin-safe" label violates WTO law by discriminating against Mexican tuna. The judgment, which marked a tentative end to the decade-old conflict between Washington and Mexico City, was immediately lambasted by environmentalists and US consumer advocates who saw the judgment as an attack on US dolphin protection. However, the point of criticism was not necessarily the high standards used vis-à-vis Mexican products but rather the low standards used vis-à-vis all other products. The judges specifically criticized the US law for being unable to guarantee that non-Mexican products eligible for the label were, in fact, fished in a "dolphin-safe" manner. Thus, the label violated the WTO's Technical Barriers to Trade Agreement, which states that regulations must be implemented in a nondiscriminatory manner, treating foreign products no less favorably than domestic products. With this ruling, other labels, such as those pertaining to organic food, may have entered the realm of WTO law.[87]

Current discussions on environmental standards and certification requirements are also focusing on carbon footprint labeling, which show the quantity of carbon-dioxide emissions associated with making and transporting products. While the EU largely supports such carbon accounting efforts, developing countries fear that such schemes could be used as trade restrictions in disguise and impose burdensome and costly requirements, thus impeding their access to important export markets. There is also concern about the methodology for determining carbon footprints, in terms of both accuracy and consistency, and that carbon footprint certificates were mostly being awarded to agricultural products, fish, and raw materials, which have a greater impact on developing countries.[88]

Some countries are hostile to particular private ecolabeling schemes because they threaten to reduce markets for a domestic industry guilty of unsustainable practices. Both developed and developing countries have also expressed more justifiable concerns about some ecolabeling schemes that appear skewed in favor of domestic producers and against foreign competitors. This type of ecolabel scheme conveys an advantage to a domestic industry by virtually mandating a particular technology or production process, ignoring that another technology or process may be equally or more environmentally sound and more suitable in the country of origin. The transparency of official and private voluntary ecolabeling schemes and the ability of affected exporters to participate in their development is yet another North-South issue in the WTO.

Subsidies and the Environment

Another issue on the trade-and-environment agenda is what the CTE calls "the environmental benefits of removing trade restrictions and distortions"—a diplomatic euphemism for eliminating subsidies that harm the environment. A subsidy may be defined as any government-directed intervention that, whether through budgeted pro-grams or other means, transfers resources to a particular economic group. Subsidies distort markets by sending signals to producers and consumers that fail to reflect the true costs of production, thus misallocating financial and natural resources. Subsidies to goods traded internationally also give unfair advantages to exports that are subsi-dized over others.

Subsidies can have negative impacts on the environment, especially in the commod-ity sectors (agriculture, forests, fossil fuels, and fisheries). They draw a higher level of investment into these sectors and exacerbate the overexploitation of land, forests, and fish. They can also reduce the cost of particular practices, products, or technologies that harm the environment, such as flood irrigation, mining, fossil fuel extraction, or excessive use of pesticides.[89]

Fisheries subsidies are one of the factors that have led to massive overfishing (see Chapter 4). Fisheries subsidies total between $25 and $29 billion per year worldwide[90] (roughly 25 percent of the value of global fish catches). This not only negatively affects the world's fish stocks but also harms developing countries, as they confront the excess capacity exported from the mostly depleted fisheries of richer countries. The global fishing fleet ballooned in the past forty years, and government subsidies worldwide contributed to this growth.[91]

Since the establishment of the CTE, some members have focused on the elimination of fisheries subsidies as possibly the greatest contribution the multilateral trading sys-tem could make to sustainable development. In particular, the lead-state coalition known as the Friends of Fish (Australia, Chile, Ecuador, Iceland, New Zealand, Peru, the Philippines, and the United States) pointed to the "win-win-win" nature of such action: good for the environment, good for development, and good for trade. Their major argument is that subsidies are at least partly responsible for the alarming de-pletion of many fish stocks, because much of the money is spent on commissioning new vessels or enhancing the efficiency of older boats.[92] But a veto coalition consisting of heavily subsidizing members (EU, Japan, and South Korea) argued that the empir-ical evidence that eliminating subsidies would benefit the environment was still weak. Japan and South Korea insisted that poor fisheries management, rather than subsidies, was the root cause of stock depletion.

The Doha Ministerial Declaration explicitly called for negotiations aimed at clari-fying and improving WTO rules on fisheries subsidies. The mandate reflected con-cerns for the potentially harmful trade, the developmental and environmental effects of subsidies in the fisheries sector, and the benefits that stronger WTO rules would achieve. WTO negotiations on fisheries subsidies since Doha have taken place in the WTO's Rules Committee. After languishing for several years, there was a breakthrough agreement at the December 2005 WTO ministerial conference in Hong Kong.[93]

The ministerial declaration from the Hong Kong meeting called on the WTO Negotiating Group on Rules to "strengthen disciplines on subsidies in the fisheries sector, including through the prohibition of certain forms of fisheries subsidies that contribute to overcapacity and over-fishing."[94] In the two years following the Hong Kong ministerial, various WTO delegations submitted technical proposals on a range of fisheries subsidy topics. These submissions revealed convergence on some points and continued conflict on others. The first draft of a fisheries subsidies legal text was issued by the chair of the Negotiating Group on Rules in November 2007. The draft's proposals included:

- prohibiting a broad range of capacity- or effort-enhancing fisheries subsidies, as well as any subsidies affecting fishing on "unequivocally overfished stocks";
- exempting several specific classes of subsidies from the prohibition (e.g., for vessel safety or reducing fishing capacity);
- subjecting most permitted fisheries subsidies to the condition that basic fisheries management systems be in place;
- allowing developing countries to use most prohibited subsidies, subject to fisheries management and other conditionalities;
- creating a mechanism for involving the FAO in the review of measures taken to fulfill fisheries management criteria; and
- strengthening WTO notification rules regarding fisheries subsidies.[95]

While this text indicated significant progress, it soon became clear that many governments considered the proposal too strict. The chair of the rules group, Ambassador Guillermo Valles Galmés of Uruguay, subsequently released a more general "road map" for fisheries discussions in December 2008, hoping this would guide governments back toward an agreement. He indicated that the purpose of the road map was to allow delegates to take a step back from the most recent draft text—without abandoning it—and "reflect on the fundamental issues" of the mandate to "strengthen disciplines on subsidies in the fisheries sector" and establish "appropriate and effective" flexibilities for poorer countries.[96] Further WTO progress on these new rules on fisheries subsidies has been hindered because of the long-standing impasse in the Doha Round of trade negotiations.

Liberalizing Trade in Environmental Goods and Services

The final trade-environment issue to be discussed here is that of liberalizing trade in environmental goods and services. The 2001 Doha Ministerial Declaration instructs WTO members to negotiate the reduction or elimination of tariff and nontariff barriers on environmental goods and services. The WTO emphasizes that these negotiations will facilitate trade, since domestic purchasers will be able to acquire environmental technologies from foreign companies at lower costs. The environment will benefit because of the wider availability of less expensive products and technologies, which in turn will improve the quality of life by providing better access to clean water, sanitation, and clean energy. Finally, the liberalization of trade in environmental goods and services will help developing countries obtain the tools they need to address key environmental priorities as part of their ongoing development strategies.[97]

So what are environmental goods and services? And which ones should be the targets for easing trade restrictions? These are not straightforward issues. According to the OECD, "the environmental goods and services industry consists of activities which produce goods and services to measure, prevent, limit, minimize or correct environmental damage to water, air and soil, as well as problems related to waste, noise and ecosystems. This includes cleaner technologies, products and services that reduce environmental risk and minimize pollution and resource use."[98] While it is useful to understand what these categories are, they have not been universally accepted by all WTO members.

Indeed, the difficulty of defining environmental goods and services for the purposes of reducing trade barriers has plagued the negotiations since they began in 2002. Many states have provided lists of proposed environmental goods for tariff reductions. Proposals put forward thus far cover several broad categories, including air pollution control, renewable energy, waste management, water treatment, environmental technologies, and carbon capture and storage. While there is some overlap between the lists of products proposed by members, when compiled they comprise 514 individual environmental goods.[99] So far, the WTO discussions have focused on two broad categories: traditional environmental goods, which have a main purpose of addressing or remedying an environmental problem (for example, pollution control carbon capture and storage technologies), and environmentally preferable products, which include any product with environmental benefits over a similar product arising during the production, use, or disposal stages.[100]

These negotiations could have an impact on several MEAs. Their outcome could have far-reaching effects on the availability of technologies to replace ODS and persistent organic pollutants under the Montreal Protocol and Stockholm Convention, respectively. They could improve the availability of technologies for the environmentally sound management of hazardous wastes under the Basel Convention. The potential for liberalization in the area of low-carbon goods could significantly enhance implementation of the United Nations Framework Convention on Climate Change (UNFCCC), Kyoto Protocol, and any successor agreement. According to the World

Bank, removing tariffs on four basic clean-energy technologies (wind, solar, clean coal, and efficient lighting) in eighteen developing countries with high GHG emissions would result in trade gains of up to 7 percent.[101] Trade liberalization could also contribute toward fulfilling the technology-transfer mandates contained in the UNFCCC and similar provisions in other MEAs.

The Outlook for Trade and Environment

Depending on the progress (or lack thereof) in the Doha Round, many of the issues described in this chapter are likely to remain on the trade-and-environment agenda for many years. This is particularly true with regard to the relationship between trade rules and MEAs, labeling for environmental purposes, reducing fisheries, energy and agricultural subsidies, and liberalizing trade in environmental goods and services. The roles that developing countries and NGOs play within the context of the WTO will continue to evolve, as will the emphasis given to the relationship between trade and environment.

CONCLUSION

The evolution of global environmental politics cannot be understood completely outside the context of the three dimensions of sustainable development. The perception held by many developing countries that global economic relations are fundamentally inequitable often shapes their policy responses to global environmental issues and related negotiating strategies. As the linkages between environmental issues and economic and social development have multiplied, the boundaries of global environmental politics have broadened and now sometimes include the politics of economic and social development. The difficulty of sorting through environmental and development priorities carries through to the trade arena, where it has been difficult for countries to achieve a broadly acceptable balance between free trade and environmental protection within the context of the WTO, including on issues as diverse as endangered-species protection, fisheries subsidies, and environmental goods and services, to name but a few.

Despite the apparent tension between economic, social, and environmental goals in both developed and developing countries, many respected observers argue that in the long run economic health depends on social and ecological health. Some, including Walter Reid and Jeffrey Sachs,[102] make the case for pursuing sustainable development as envisioned in the Brundtland Report, arguing that environmental goals cannot be achieved without development, and development goals cannot be achieved without sound environmental management. The global economy cannot thrive in the face of the total devastation of our biospheric envelope, nor can it survive in the face of increasing poverty and disease. If the public and policy makers accept that fact, then there are two logical ways to resolve this tension: they can let it continue until the integrity of the environment and the economy deteriorate to the point they reach certain so-called tipping points and snap like old rubber bands, releasing all tension, or they can make the economic, social, and cultural changes that will support sustainable development at the community, national, and global levels. If this premise is correct, and the second option is deemed the better strategy, then the key questions might be: Do governments have the political will to make this shift? And do the people of the world have the will to accept, or even demand, the necessary change?[103]

7

The Future of Global Environmental Politics

Global environmental politics is at a crossroads. Forty years after the United Nations first addressed the "human environment" at the 1972 Stockholm Conference and twenty years after the 1992 Rio Earth Summit, there has been a transformation in how the international community approaches threats to the environment. By the time governments gathered again in Rio de Janeiro for the 2012 United Nations Conference on Sustainable Development (UNCSD or Rio+20), the optimism surrounding the promise of a paradigm shift to sustainable development had faded and, for some, had become downright pessimism. The excitement of negotiating new treaties to address global environmental problems had been replaced by implementation battles over such issues as common but differentiated responsibilities, finance, technology transfer, and accountability.

At the same time, the stakes continue to increase. Most global environmental problems are getting worse, not better.[1] The economic costs of both environmental degradation and the measures needed to reverse it continue to grow. Many global environmental regimes require greater changes in economic and social development strategies and production techniques to be effective. Accelerating globalization and trade liberalization create incentives that have a negative impact on the effectiveness of certain global environmental policies. The ambitious environmental agenda is in danger of being overwhelmed by economic forces that, in their current form, threaten the health of the planet.

Governments attempted to tackle these issues at Rio+20 and, in the eyes of many, failed. Critics argued that their inability to push for the necessary economic, social, and environmental policies called into question the effectiveness of UN multilateralism in the current geopolitical and economic context. This final chapter returns to the concepts of paradigm shift, examines the impacts of Rio+20 on global environmental politics, and looks toward the future.

SUSTAINABLE DEVELOPMENT AND
GLOBALIZATION: DUELING PARADIGMS

As described in Chapter 1, many of the world leaders attending the 1992 United Nations Conference on Environment and Development (UNCED or Earth Summit) believed it would be possible to move beyond the old world order and Cold War security paradigm and reap the benefits of what they believed would be a more balanced and peaceful international system. They sought to operationalize the new sustainable development paradigm that promised to enhance environmentally sound economic and social development. The Earth Summit presented the first post–Cold War test of whether the international community possessed the collective will and wisdom to develop sustainably and to improve the human condition. It was also a chance for the United Nations to prove that it could be an effective force in defining a new form of global peace. And it was the first significant opportunity for the North and the South to elaborate on how they might combine economic and social development concerns with those of environmental protection as governments struggled to put into action the concept of sustainable development.[2] Despite the optimism immediately following the Earth Summit that a new partnership had been struck between North and South, UNCED Secretary-General Maurice Strong acknowledged that time would tell whether it would produce historic changes in the way the human community ordered its affairs; the conference itself, he said, was only a beginning.[3]

The Earth Summit did launch a new era in the creation and expansion of international environmental treaty regimes. New conventions, protocols, and agreements emerged on climate change, biodiversity, desertification, fisheries, mercury, persistent organic pollutants, biosafety, access and benefit sharing of genetic resources, forests, and ozone depletion. Since 1992, environmental regimes have moved to the center of international affairs—an achievement that was best illustrated by the active engagement of 119 world leaders during the Copenhagen Climate Change Conference in December 2009.[4]

Yet these regimes have not led to significant environmental improvements in most issue areas. While it is likely conditions would be much worse if these agreements had not been negotiated, they have not proven a panacea, and as discussed in this book, many important obstacles still stand in the way of increasing the effectiveness of global environmental policies. Most governments realize that greater changes in economic and social development strategies and production techniques must occur if their collective environmental governance efforts are to be effective.[5] However, as described in Chapter 6, global economic forces and the policies that support them threaten the shift to a more environmentally sustainable future.

So how does globalization have an impact on the environment and on global environmental politics? There are two primary arguments in this debate. One contends that globalization can go hand in hand with sustainable development and is beneficial for the environment because it is an "engine of wealth creation." As societies become richer, the initial process of industrialization results in greater pollution. This happened in Europe and the United States and is happening now in many developing countries. As economic development continues, a point is eventually reached at which most material needs have been met and citizens enjoy general economic security, at least for a majority of the population. At this point, societies develop greater concern for pollution reduction and environmental protection, as Western Europe and the United States did in the 1970s. In addition, because of wealth creation, society has the economic and technical ability to implement the necessary measures to achieve these goals. Globalization, by delivering the development side of the sustainable development equation, can solve the social problems that contribute to environmental degradation. Along these lines, poverty is seen as a critical component of environmental degradation, and environmentalists who oppose globalization are sometimes condemned as "eco-imperialists" for trying to deny poor countries the right to develop.[6]

The opposing argument sees most aspects of globalization as contrary to sustainable development. By extending the exclusionist paradigm into all aspects of international economic relations, globalization promotes and accelerates the overconsumption of natural resources and overproduction of waste, and on a global scale. It advances the movement of capital, technology, goods, and labor to areas with high returns on investment without regard for the impact on the communities and people who live there or on the local environment. Globalization stretches the chains of production and consumption over great distances and across many locations, which increases the separation between sources of environmental problems and their impact. The division of labor associated with globalization increases the transport of raw materials, commodities, semiprocessed materials, parts, finished goods, and waste; requires greater energy consumption and more pollution, including higher carbon emissions; and increases the risk of localized pollution problems and even major environmental accidents.[7] Critics also argue that globalization reinforces the sharp inequalities between North and South discussed in Chapter 6, or at least the inequalities between rich and poor both nationally and internationally.

For example, the ready availability of every vegetable or fruit in your supermarket throughout the year is partly the result of a shift from subsistence farming in parts of many developing countries to intensive cash cropping, the wages and profits of which do not translate into sufficient food and social development in many local societies. In addition to the environmental externalities of flying these products to northern markets, cash crops bring questionable benefits to developing countries. Agribusinesses, not farmers, often reap the benefits and own the best-quality land. Chemical fertilizers and pesticides are relied on to produce uniform, export-quality produce; far fewer of these chemicals were needed to grow local and subsistence crops. Poor farmers of export crops also have perverse incentives, or are even forced by economic circumstances, to cultivate low-quality, marginal land, contributing to soil erosion, habitat destruction, and land degradation.[8] In addition, the reorganization of production under globalization has led to the creation of extended commodity chains that spread environmental impacts over many countries. For example, the production of cotton T-shirts can involve as many as six different countries, creating different types of pollution and environmental impacts in each one (see Box 7.1).

The exact relationship between the environment and globalization is of course more complex than either of these two archetypal arguments. Each contains elements of truth, and the specific impacts depend on national and international economic and policy choices. While the importance of the relationship between globalization and the environment is obvious, our understanding of how these twin dynamics interact remains weak. Much of the literature on globalization and the environment is vague (discussing generalities), myopic (focused disproportionately on trade-related connections), one-sided (examining the issue from only one of the two perspectives outlined above), or partial (highlighting the impacts of globalization on the environment but not vice versa). It is important to highlight that not only does globalization affect the environment, but the environment affects the pace, direction, and quality of globalization. At the very least, this happens because environmental resources provide the fuel for economic globalization, but it also happens because our social and policy responses to global environmental problems constrain and influence the context in which globalization happens.[9]

The dominant discourse on globalization has tended to highlight the promise of economic opportunity. On the other hand, there is a parallel global discourse on environmental responsibility. Is it possible to reconcile economic growth and the preservation of the environment without any significant adjustments in the market system?[10] Since 1992, the international community has tried to create the impression that only minor corrections to the market system are needed to launch an era of environmentally sound development, hiding the fact that aspects of the economic framework itself cannot accommodate environmental concerns without substantial reforms.[11] Themes such as consumption, equity, and the realities of externalities have often been ignored, while the logic of the market and trade has reigned supreme. As a result, a

BOX 7.1   COMMODITY CHAINS

The reorganization of production under globalization has led to the creation of extended commodity chains that spread environmental impacts over many countries. For example, the production of cotton T-shirts can involve as many as six different countries, creating different types of pollution and environmental impacts in each one.

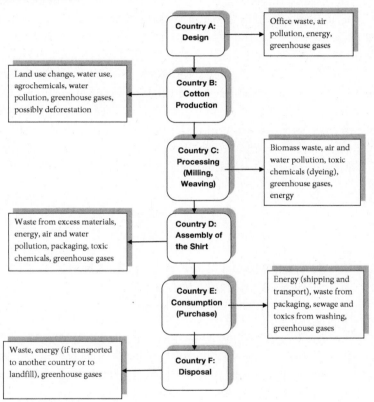

Source: Information on commodity chains and waste chains is from Ronnie D. Lipschutz, *Global Environmental Politics: Power, Perspectives, and Practice* (Washington, DC: Congressional Quarterly Press, 2004), 124.

large proportion of existing global environmental policy instruments is based on the creation, regulation, and management of traditional markets.[12] The most obvious examples are the direct trade-related instruments such as CITES and the Rotterdam and Basel conventions. The emissions-trading provisions of the Kyoto Protocol and the Convention on Biological Diversity's two protocols on biosafety and access and benefit sharing also operate largely within created or existing market logic.

So how do we develop a more nuanced understanding or paradigm, one that understands that some aspects of globalization are inevitable and seeks to actualize the positive opportunities offered by globalization while addressing global ecological responsibilities and advancing equity? As demonstrated throughout this book, effective global environmental policy is difficult to achieve. Ecosystem boundaries rarely overlap with national boundaries, pollution spreads beyond national jurisdictions, the requirements of effective international environmental policy often run up against issues of state sovereignty, and effective environmental policy, even if it assists the economy in the long run, necessitates short-term, and sometimes substantial, economic and social adjustment costs for powerful actors. Globalization and the need to address global environmental issues challenge elements of the architecture of the international system as it now exists. Global environmental governance, therefore, must evolve to respond to the challenges facing it.[13]

GLOBAL ENVIRONMENTAL GOVERNANCE IN A CHANGING INTERNATIONAL SYSTEM

Over the last forty years, the world has seen an unprecedented level of international activity and cooperation on environmental issues.[14] More governments and nonstate actors are active participants in environmental politics than in any other global issue area. The proliferation of multilateral environmental agreements (MEAs) represents an achievement in international diplomacy. However, activity does not necessarily produce success, cooperation does not necessarily produce effective action, and past accomplishments do not necessarily mean greater achievements in the future. What occurs in the future will depend in part on how global environmental politics intersects with not only increasing globalization but also several other complex realities of the twenty-first century.

The first involves the broad changes that are occurring in the international system. The East-West Cold War politics that dominated the 1972 Stockholm Conference were replaced by a North-South dynamic in 1992. At the Earth Summit there was a "simple" grand bargain: poor countries would become more environmentally sustainable if the rich countries would pay most of the costs.[15] This was codified in many MEAs, in-

TABLE 7.1   Top Twenty Countries Ranked by GDP, 1992 and 2011

Ranking	Country	1992 GDP ($ trillions)	Ranking	Country	2011 GDP ($ trillions)
1	United States	6,261.8	1	United States	14,991.3
2	Japan	3,852.7	2	China	7,318.5
3	Germany	2,064.3	3	Japan	5,867.1
4	France	1,372.9	4	Germany	3,600.8
5	Italy	1,271.9	5	France	2,773.0
6	United Kingdom	1,091.7	6	Brazil	2,476.6
7	Spain	612.5	7	United Kingdom	2,445.4
8	Canada	579.5	8	Italy	2,193.9
9	Russian Federation	460.2	9	Russian Federation	1,857.7
10	China	422.6	10	India	1,847.9
11	Brazil	390.5	11	Canada	1,736.0
12	Mexico	363.6	12	Spain	1,476.9
13	Netherlands	336.2	13	Australia	1,379.4
14	Korea, Rep.	329.9	14	Mexico	1,153.3
15	Australia	325.6	15	Korea, Rep.	1,116.2
16	India	293.2	16	Indonesia	846.8
17	Sweden	267.0	17	Netherlands	836.1
18	Switzerland	257.0	18	Turkey	774.9
19	Belgium	231.9	19	Switzerland	659.3
20	Argentina	228.8	20	Saudi Arabia	576.8

Note: GDP at purchaser's prices is the sum of gross value added by all resident producers in the economy plus any product taxes and minus any subsidies not included in the value of the products. It is calculated without making deductions for depreciation of fabricated assets or for depletion and degradation of natural resources. Data are in current US dollars. Dollar figures for GDP are converted from domestic currencies using single-year official exchange rates. For a few countries where the official exchange rate does not reflect the rate effectively applied to actual foreign exchange transactions, an alternative conversion factor is used.

Source: World Bank Databank, accessed December 26, 2012, data.worldbank.org/indicator/NY.GDP.MKTP.CD.

cluding the Montreal Protocol, the UN Framework Convention on Climate Change, the Convention on Biological Diversity, the Stockholm Convention on Persistent Organic Pollutants, and the Convention to Combat Desertification. Today the simple, two-sided world of rich countries and poor countries no longer exists. Consequently, Rio+20 could not achieve a similar grand bargain,[16] and individual MEAs are now struggling to determine which countries should take which actions and which countries should provide and receive financial and technical assistance.

The past twenty years has seen the rapid development of emerging economies led by China, Brazil, India, and Indonesia (see Table 7.1). China has surpassed Japan and many European countries to become the second largest national economy, has the second largest defense budget (after the United States), and emits the most greenhouse gases (GHGs). In this new world, the old model of OECD countries taking action first and paying the incremental costs for developing countries' action no longer makes sense. Brazil and China are very different from Bangladesh and Kenya. However, it is not yet clear how the world can operationalize new categories of common but differentiated responsibilities given current economic and political realities. Clearly the stalled climate regime reveals the downside of the world's failure to develop a new model.

A second reality is the proliferation of actors and stakeholders and the consequential difficulty of imposing top-down, system-wide policies. The 1992 model was based on the concept of a top-down global deal negotiated by governments through a consensus-seeking process.[17] That approach no longer works in today's multipolar world, especially one that lacks global environmental leadership from the most powerful countries, especially the United States. Instead, the 2012 model is essentially bottom-up, voluntary, and leader-driven across different stakeholder groups.[18] We see this occurring where NGOs are now playing key roles in global agenda setting and in regime implementation. As a result, the role of governments, while still primary, has diminished. We can see negative impacts of this in the United States, where powerful industrial concerns have prevented ratification of the three chemicals conventions (Basel, Stockholm, and Rotterdam) and the Convention on Biological Diversity; worked to build doubt among the public about the basic science of climate change; and negatively affected American implementation of the Montreal Protocol with regard to eliminating methyl bromide. On the positive side, some of the most dynamic forums at Rio+20 involved NGOs, the business community, community-based organizations, and other stakeholders discussing best practices for achieving sustainable development.[19] We can also see positive impacts of this phenomenon in cities and municipalities in the United States and elsewhere that are improving energy efficiency and reducing GHG emissions in accordance with the Kyoto Protocol even as their national governments refuse or are not able to do so.

A third reality is the fragmentation of global environmental issues. Far from a holistic, precautionary, and nonincremental approach, which was once deemed a requirement for global environmental governance, environmental policy has instead become fragmented into a series of separate and unequal regimes.[20] This has resulted in conflicting agendas and inconsistencies. In the ozone regime, as described in Chapter 3, connections with the response to climate change have come to the fore, notably in dealing with HFCs, but without resulting in effective action.[21] The biodiversity, desertification, and forest regimes are also major stakeholders in the evolving commitments under the climate-change regime on land-use change and forests. While debates over global environmental governance reflect the need for more urgent synergistic implementation, responsibility for negotiating and implementing solutions to global environmental problems is increasingly fragmented across both MEAs and government ministries.[22]

A fourth reality is that despite its flaws, the intergovernmental negotiating process itself is still a necessity. "Getting action in the United Nations," a diplomat once complained, "is like the mating of elephants. It takes place at a very high level, with an enormous amount of huffing and puffing, raises a tremendous amount of dust and nothing happens for at least 23 months."[23] Many who see the need for urgent action on environmental problems are skeptical of entrusting complete responsibility to the slow and often cumbersome, "huffing-and-puffing" multilateral negotiating process within the United Nations. While not every MEA has been negotiated within the UN system, since 1972 the United Nations or one of its specialized agencies—primarily the United Nations Environment Programme (UNEP)—has been recognized as the main venue for addressing global and regional environmental issues. Although there are frustrations inherent in this process and governments are not the only international actors, the international system is still centered on states. Yet, at the same time, governments are not ready to surrender environmental decision making and their own sovereignty to a supranational body with legislative and enforcement powers. As a result, the international community is forced to employ this slow method of intergovernmental cooperation.[24]

These realities had an impact on the ways that governments, NGOs, and other stakeholders addressed the two key themes of Rio+20: the green economy and the institutional framework for sustainable development. We examined the green economy as a possible new paradigm in Chapter 1. In the next section, we look at the impact of Rio+20 on global environmental governance within the institutional framework for sustainable development and the post-2015 United Nations "sustainable development" agenda.

THE CONTINUING EVOLUTION OF GLOBAL ENVIRONMENTAL GOVERNANCE

Since UNEP's establishment in 1972, the UN institutional framework for environmental issues has grown in its size and complexity, with an increasing number of institutions, agreements, meetings, reports, and actors. While governments have been discussing reform options for years with limited success, the debate entered a new phase in 2003, when French president Jacques Chirac announced to the UN General Assembly (UNGA) a proposal to create a United Nations Environment Organization (UNEO). This proposal was later emphasized in the 2007 Paris Call for

Action during the Citizens of the Earth Conference for Global Ecological Governance.[25] As President Chirac said, "This United Nations Environment Organization will act as the world's ecological conscience. It will carry out impartial and scientific assessment of environmental dangers. It will have policy-making terms of reference giving it the legitimacy to implement action jointly decided. It will lend greater weight and greater cohesion to our collective endeavors."[26] The UNGA responded by establishing a consultative process, chaired by the ambassadors of Switzerland and Mexico, to explore the possibility of a more coherent institutional framework for environmental activities in the UN system, including a UNEO, yet no consensus could be reached.[27]

The agenda for Rio+20 included consideration of the institutional framework for sustainable development as one of its two main agenda items, and some governments and NGOs hoped that this would provide the impetus for substantial UNEP reform. There were two main camps: institutional reformists who wanted to improve the system of treaty regimes and international institutions and those who believed far deeper changes, like a UNEO, were necessary. Among the former, some focused on strengthening key institutions in specific issue areas, negotiating stronger and more effective global regimes, and elevating the precautionary principle to an official guiding principle of global environmental policy. Increasing coherence and coordination among the goals and processes of the major global environmental, financial, trade, and development institutions and systems was also seen as a priority.[28]

Among the latter, France, Germany, and the European Union spearheaded support to create a UNEO with the status of a specialized agency. They argued this would increase the availability of financial resources and provide a more efficient and effective structure for governance and leadership. Some also argued that this model could bring the various environmental treaties together under a single roof. Other proposals were even more ambitious, such as creating a world environment agency that would counterbalance the WTO and operate as a type of global legislature, entrusted with setting international standards and given the authority to enforce them against laggard countries.[29]

After intense debate in Rio, the final agreement fell short of creating a UNEO or transforming UNEP into a specialized agency.[30] Rio+20 agreed to expand UNEP by allowing universal membership of the Governing Council (instead of only fifty-eight members) as well "as other measures to strengthen its governance as well as its responsiveness and accountability to member states," and to have "secure, stable, adequate and increased financial resources from the regular budget of the United Nations and voluntary contributions to fulfill its mandate."[31] Instead of UNEP becoming an umbrella organization for MEAs, the outcome merely "encourages" parties to MEAs to consider further measures to enhance coordination and cooperation.[32] The Euro-

PHOTO 7.1   **Artwork in RioCentro reminding governments of their responsibilities.**
Courtesy IISD/*Earth Negotiations Bulletin.*

pean Union and a number of African countries were not happy with the outcome and continued to hold onto their aspiration to see UNEP transformed into a UNEO with the status of a specialized agency in the belief that this would empower the standing of the environment pillar alongside the social and economic dimensions of sustainable development. Right up until the closing plenary in Rio, there were suggestions that one or two delegations might attempt to reopen the negotiated text in an attempt to reintroduce their demand for a UNEO, but in the end the text was adopted.[33]

The negotiations on the institutional framework for sustainable development also focused on the future of the Commission on Sustainable Development (CSD). The CSD, as described in Chapter 2, was established by the Earth Summit in 1992, but by 2012 the mandate and functioning of the CSD had been the subject of increasing contention.[34] Many called for the CSD's reform, and some even proposed that it should be replaced or abolished because of its lackluster performance. Others were also concerned that the low standing of the CSD and the ongoing stalemate in the climate-change negotiations "had sowed doubts regarding the ability of governments to collectively and effectively address crucial sustainable development issues."[35]

By June 2012, a clear consensus had emerged that the CSD had outlived its usefulness. To replace the CSD or, more accurately, to move beyond it, negotiations at Rio+20 focused on establishing a "high-level political forum" to "provide political leadership, guidance and recommendations for sustainable development."[36] The UNGA is finalizing the details of the new forum with a view to convening its first session in September 2013. The prospects for the successful implementation of the forum will rely on the UN's capacity to turn the language of the Rio+20 negotiated text into an "action-oriented agenda."

If the new forum has a sufficient mandate to act, a dynamic process for discussion and decision making, a strong secretariat, and high-level political backing, then the modest document coming out of Rio+20 could be transformed into meaningful change. Some are looking, in particular, to the UN secretary-general to champion a break from established UN patterns, such as those used by the CSD, that have too often resulted in consultative sessions and output documents that receive little attention and produce little change.[37]

Among the biggest obstacles to changing the system of global environmental governance is political will. Changes in policy and practice have been urged in numerous internationally agreed declarations and documents, but progress remains limited. Some of the political and economic leaders that oppose action appear to believe they live in isolation from fairly well accepted ecological, economic, and technological trends. They dismiss the idea that global warming, biodiversity loss, persistent organic pollutants, hazardous wastes, and ozone depletion undermine the future of their country or interests.[38] Other leaders worry that strengthening environmental governance could challenge fundamental issues of state sovereignty. Many express concern that environmental policies will hinder economic growth, at least in the short term. Some, however, agree that action is necessary and aspects of the system need to be changed, but they don't have either the political strength or the necessary resources to make it happen.

Given these constraints, it is perhaps not surprising that the outcomes from Rio+20 were not nearly as ambitious as many had hoped. Yet they also did not support the status quo. Whether the high-level political forum or the expanded UNEP Governing Council and "secure and stable" financial resources from the UN budget will strengthen global environmental governance remains to be seen. But as the international community continues to evolve, and as the understanding of the interrelationship between environmental and development issues continues to gain traction, the political will to further strengthen the structures of global sustainable development governance may follow.

FROM THE MILLENNIUM DEVELOPMENT GOALS TO SUSTAINABLE DEVELOPMENT GOALS?

Rio+20 also took another step that could have an impact on global environmental politics: the call for defining a set of Sustainable Development Goals (SDGs), similar to, and supportive of, the Millennium Development Goals (MDGs). During the Rio+20 preparatory process, the governments of Colombia and Guatemala proposed the SDGs to help provide a "concrete approach that delivers means for measuring—in accordance with the contexts and priorities of each country—both advances as well as bottlenecks in efforts to balance sustained socioeconomic growth with the sustainable use of natural resources and the conservation of ecosystem services." They noted, in particular, that the MDG experience demonstrated that when there are objectives to guide the international community's efforts toward a collective goal, it becomes easier for governments and institutions to work together to reach them.[39]

Supporters believed that the SDGs approach would generate a series of additional benefits. Internationally agreed objectives could eventually be underpinned by targets, as is the case with the MDGs, which reflect the realities and priorities at national levels and play a useful role in guiding public policies. The SDGs could also be important in identifying gaps and needs in countries: for example, in terms of means of implementation, institutional strengthening, and capacity building.[40]

Governments agreed at Rio+20 that the development of goals could

> be useful for pursuing focused and coherent action on sustainable development . . . [and] should address and incorporate in a balanced way all three dimensions of sustainable development and their interlinkages. They should be coherent with and integrated into the United Nations development agenda beyond 2015, thus contributing to the achievement of sustainable development and serving as a driver for implementation and mainstreaming of sustainable development in the United Nations system as a whole. . . .
>
> [The] sustainable development goals should be action oriented, concise and easy to communicate, limited in number, aspirational, global in nature and universally applicable to all countries while taking into account different national realities, capacities and levels of development and respecting national policies and priorities.[41]

The Rio+20 outcome called for the UNGA to create a working group to elaborate these goals and to coordinate with the UN's post-2015 development agenda. With the MDGs due to expire in 2015, the UN secretary-general established a High-Level Panel to advise on, and a UN System Task Team to develop, a post-2015 UN development agenda, in consultation with all stakeholders.[42]

In June 2012, the Task Team echoed many of the same concerns that surrounded the debate on the SDGs and are consistent with the battle between the sustainable development and globalization paradigms. Specifically, the Task Team said:

PHOTO 7.2   **Children's artwork was on display during Rio+20.**
Courtesy Pamela S. Chasek.

> Globalization offers great opportunities, but its benefits are at present very un-
> evenly shared. The continuous striving for improvements in material welfare is
> threatening to surpass the limits of the natural resource base unless there is a
> radical shift towards more sustainable patterns of consumption and production
> and resource use. Persistent inequalities and struggles over scarce resources are
> among key determinants of situations of conflict, hunger, insecurity and vio-
> lence, which in turn are key factors that hold back human development and ef-
> forts to achieve sustainable development.[43]

The Task Team recommended that the post-2015 development agenda focus on
end goals and targets—like the MDGs—but reorganized along four key dimensions:
(1) inclusive social development, (2) inclusive economic development, (3) environmental sustainability, and (4) peace and security. The report further states:

> The post-2015 UN development agenda should be conceived as a truly global
> agenda with shared responsibilities for all countries. Accordingly, the global
> partnership for development would also need to be redefined towards a more
> balanced approach among all development partners that will enable the trans-
> formative change needed for a rights-based, equitable and sustainable process

of global development. This would also involve reforms of mechanisms of global governance.

How the post-2015 development agenda and the SDGs will come together is far from certain. Perhaps the biggest question is if governments can agree on a common set of sustainable development goals that are "universally applicable to all countries"[44] in a world defined by the principle of common but differentiated responsibilities. Can developed and developing countries be held to the same set of goals? Can different sets of goals be established for different types of developing countries? Will the process get mired down by similar arguments as those that have recently plagued the climate-change and other environmental negotiations—that all developing countries should not be held to the same standard as industrialized countries? The MDGs did not have to deal with these challenges, since they focused on economic and social issues in developing countries and gave limited attention to the structural causes of poverty and sustainable development, including inequality, pollution, and resource scarcity.

The UN is holding extensive consultations on the vision for the post-2015 and SDG agendas. The challenge is to reach consensus on an agenda that adequately identifies the development needs of present and future generations and is capable of crystallizing these priorities in clear, easy-to-communicate sustainable development goals that will help guide coherent policy action at the global, regional, and national levels.[45]

CONCLUSION: THE PROSPECTS FOR GLOBAL ENVIRONMENTAL POLITICS

Over the last forty years, the international community's quest for improved planetary stewardship has produced a variety of intergovernmental, governmental, business, and civil-society initiatives. The results are mixed and, it is generally conceded, inadequate. Disturbing environmental trends and unsustainable development continues.

Can the international community develop effective cooperative efforts to address our major global environmental problems successfully? The case studies presented in this book show that, on some issues, states have taken collective actions that significantly reduced specific environmental threats, such as hunting endangered species of whales. In the case of the ozone layer, states have devised a regime that has been innovative in its rule making and largely effective in phasing out many of the chemicals responsible for the damage.

But the successful regimes have had favorable circumstances. The ozone case involved a relatively small number of interested economic actors and substitute technologies that turned out to be cost-effective. The initial whaling ban passed because only a few countries wanted to continue to hunt whales and there was no large world-wide market for whale products. The ivory ban initially succeeded because a few major countries were able to shut down most of the market for elephant ivory. At the same time, however, none of these regimes has completely solved the problems involved. The black market for ivory still exists, and elephant poaching has increased over the past year; Iceland, Japan, and Norway still hunt whales; and the ozone layer has not fully recovered.

In other cases we examined, the international community has not yet been able to reach an effective agreement, often because of the problem's links to major economic and social interests. The lack of progress toward a forest regime reflects the veto power wielded by a loose, ever-changing coalition of key developing and developed countries, which rely on the global trade in forest products. Slowing the hemorrhaging of the world's forests will require both wealthy countries and forest countries to consider what value the remaining forests have to present and future generations worldwide.

The climate regime faces another set of major economic and social interests, including requirements for major changes in energy production and use. Reluctance to increase commitments to reduce GHG emissions by one veto coalition, led by the United States, and a desire to uphold the principle of common but differentiated responsibilities by a second veto coalition, led by some of the larger developing countries, have seriously hampered discussion on achieving the necessary emissions reductions.

We have outlined the importance of continued efforts to improve the effectiveness of environmental regimes even after they are adopted. Parties can strengthen regimes by tightening the requirements for regulating activities that are causing the environmental disruption or resource depletion, by improving compliance with those requirements, or by broadening state participation in the regime. The regimes for biodiversity, desertification, and fisheries will need different kinds of strengthening in the next several years to become effective in reversing these environmental problems. For each threat, it will take unprecedented political commitments by major states to create a truly effective regime.

The biodiversity regime has focused work on seven thematic work programs addressing marine and coastal biodiversity, agricultural biodiversity, forest biodiversity, island biodiversity, the biodiversity of inland waters, dry and subhumid lands' biodiversity, and mountain biodiversity. Yet, despite this, the international community failed to meet the 2010 target for significantly reducing biodiversity loss.

The desertification regime faces considerable administrative and financial problems in fulfilling its mandate to reduce land degradation in the drylands. Although nearly universal ratification of the convention can be seen as recognition of the problem of drylands degradation, the issue is complicated by the fact that combating land degradation has to work hand in hand with efforts to address poverty eradication, water resources management, agriculture, deforestation, biodiversity conservation, climate change, and population growth. The success or failure of this regime is a key indicator for the overall success or failure of sustainable development.

The regime for global fisheries management needs a stronger compliance system and increased participation. The Fish Stocks Agreement lacks a conference of the parties, relying entirely on regional fisheries management organizations to track compliance, and most of the major distant-water fishing states have failed to ratify it.

But environmental regimes are not the only forces that influence the global environment. Multilateral institutions affect environmental politics and the development of regimes, be it by helping to set the global agenda (e.g., UNEP); bringing states together to negotiate (UNEP, Food and Agriculture Organization); monitoring global environmental trends (UNEP); conducting comprehensive scientific assessments (Intergovernmental Panel on Climate Change); or providing financial support for environmental activities (Global Environment Facility, World Bank, UN Development Programme). But these institutions do not always have the resources or the mandate to promote strong regimes. The Global Environment Facility has funding that can accomplish only a small fraction of what is needed to support effective international cooperation in biodiversity, climate, ozone protection, land degradation, and POPs. UNEP has been subject to the veto power and weak political will of key states.

The world's global trade and financial institutions—the World Trade Organization (WTO), the International Monetary Fund (IMF), and the World Bank—also play important roles. The stalemate in the Doha Round has left numerous issues unresolved: Will the WTO accommodate the use of trade measures by multilateral environmental agreements? How will trade in environmental goods and services be liberalized? And how may this affect the hazardous wastes, chemicals, ozone, and climate regimes, among others?

While the World Bank and the IMF have made some progress, critics point out that these institutions, which are controlled by developed countries, cannot be an effective tool for the environment without changing their power structures. Power in the World Bank is presently apportioned according to members' shares, just like in a corporation. Major decisions require 85 percent of the vote, and the United States, which holds about 16 percent of the shares (and controls the presidency), wields de facto veto power. The same is true of the IMF, whose presidency is controlled by Europe.[46] These institutions cannot be expected to change their policies further unless the finance ministries of the world's major industrialized countries instruct them to, something that will likely require domestic political pressure.

The leadership of the industrialized countries, especially the United States and European Union, is a key to effective regimes. The United States is the one state without whose leadership any environmental regime is certain to be much weaker. When the

United States has actively engaged in trying to achieve consensus on stronger institutions or actions, it has often been able to overcome reluctance on the part of other industrialized countries, as in the negotiations on ozone depletion, African elephants, whaling, and fish stocks. When the United States has been a veto state, as in the case of climate change and the hazardous waste trade, or has played a much lower-profile role, as in cases of desertification, POPs, and biodiversity, the resulting regime is negatively affected. The US executive branch wavered on these issues during the Bill Clinton, George W. Bush, and Barack Obama administrations, and Congress has remained a force for reducing US leadership.

The largest developing countries, too, must also show leadership and move beyond the traditional interpretation of the principle of common but differentiated responsibilities and participate fully in global environmental regimes. Developing countries need to take the initiative and accept new commitments in each of the major areas in return for financial or other forms of compensation, but the commitments and compensation need not be uniform for all developing countries. In the climate negotiations, for example, a successful regime requires a breakthrough in the discussions of developing-country commitments. As stated in Chapter 1, carbon dioxide emissions rose by 2.6 percent in 2012, fueled by major increases in China and India. This follows a record year in 2011, when countries pumped 3.1 percent more global warming pollution into the atmosphere—making it very likely that the world will surpass the 2 degrees Celsius warming threshold, which is the limit, scientists and international negotiators agree, to avoid particularly dangerous consequences.[47] The second commitment period for the Kyoto Protocol actually covers less than 15 percent of global emissions. If major developing countries do not take on GHG-reduction commitments, there is little that developed countries alone can do to prevent significant climate change.

There is increasing awareness among business groups regarding the implications of global environmental threats and global environmental regimes for their interests. As a result, more and more corporations and trade associations play active roles in global environmental politics. Because treaties could impose significant new costs or open up new opportunities, depending on their details, the business sector recognizes that early involvement in the negotiating process will often bring long-term benefits once a regime is in place. Sometimes this involvement is negative. Corporations and industry associations occasionally work to defeat strong international environmental measures. Exxon/Mobil reportedly once funded reports that minimized the seriousness and scientific proof of climate change.[48] The agro-industrial complex in the United States, along with the chemical companies producing methyl bromide, worked to prevent the phaseout of methyl bromide under the Montreal Protocol. At other times, corporate interests can assist creation of strong environmental regimes. During the Montreal Protocol negotiations, US chemical companies that manufactured chlorofluorocarbons realized significant regulations were on the way and started to develop alternatives. Their success enabled US negotiators to take a stronger position and emerge as a lead state in the negotiations.

Domestic political support for new political commitments on global environmental issues likely will not happen without environmental movements and the engagement of civil society that can influence national public opinion and push governments into action. At the international levels, NGO networks on climate change, chemicals, biodiversity, and desertification are mapping strategies for monitoring treaty implementation and encouraging public participation in national action programs and strategies. The Trade Records Analysis of Flora and Fauna in Commerce, or TRAFFIC, continues to monitor the international trade in endangered species. International NGOs such as Greenpeace and WWF are contributing substantial ideas on land-based sources of marine pollution, whales, and fisheries. Nevertheless, the most important challenge for NGOs will be to build political pressure on reluctant states to support participation in, or strengthening of, global environmental regimes. This has become increasingly challenging as fundraising for global environmental activities has become more difficult for NGOs, forcing many to focus on domestic priorities rather than global environmental problems.

Global environmental politics has grown significantly more complex since the first global environmental conference in Stockholm in 1972. Many more issues, treaties, institutions, and policy initiatives exist, and the environment is now integrated into a broad array of international economic, trade, and development issues. In some ways, this growth is a sign of the progress made in the last forty years by the international community in learning how to address global environmental issues.

Caution is necessary, however. Most of the spirit of Rio from 1992 has dissipated, as was demonstrated when the international community returned to Rio in 2012. The enthusiasm for environmental issues and the concept of sustainable development expressed by many governments in the early 1990s has waned. Although recent MEAs have applied the precautionary principle and made genuine efforts to grapple with equity issues, many observers believe these steps are not enough to meet the significant challenges of the twenty-first century.[49] The shift to a sustainable development paradigm—something that seemed imminent twenty years ago—has stalled.

This book has examined the principle paradigms, actors, issues, and challenges in global environmental politics. What the future will bring is still unclear. There are reasons for both optimism and grave concern. What we do know is that today's environmental challenges are global in nature, unprecedented in scope, and closely linked to economic and social development. The need for innovative and creative global solutions is greater than ever.

Notes

Chapter 1—The Emergence of Global Environmental Politics

1. WWF, *Living Planet Report 2012* (Gland, Switzerland: WWF, 2012), 36.

2. Ibid., 40.

3. Figures from United Nations Population Division, *World Population Prospects: The 2010 Revision* (New York: United Nations, 2011). For updated figures, reports, and searchable databases, see the website maintained by the UN Department of Economic and Social Affairs, Population Division: esa.un.org/wpp/wpp2012/wpp2012-1.htm

4. Figures in this paragraph from UN Population Division, "World Population to Exceed 9 Billion by 2050," March 11, 2009, www.un.org/esa/population/publications/wpp2008/press release.pdf.

5. Peter Dauvergne, *The Shadows of Consumption* (Cambridge, MA: MIT Press, 2008), 4.

6. United Nations Environment Programme (UNEP), *GEO 5: Global Environmental Outlook: Environment for the Future We Want* (Nairobi: UNEP, 2012).

7. WWF, *Living Planet Report 2012*, 56.

8. "UNEP-Hosted Global Partnership on Waste Management Answering Call as Municipal Waste to Grow to 2.2 Billion Tonnes per Year by 2025," UNEP Newsdesk release, November 6, 2012.

9. EIA, "U.S. Energy Facts Explained: U.S. Total Energy Statistics," 2011, www.eia.gov/energy explained/index.cfm?page=us_energy_home#tab3.

10. Alex Wilson and Jessica Boehland, "Small Is Beautiful: U.S. House Size, Resource Use, and the Environment," *Journal of Industrial Ecology* 9 (winter/spring 2005): 277–287.

11. United Nations, *Millennium Development Goals Report 2012* (New York: United Nations, 2012), 4.

12. United Nations Population Division, *World Population Prospects: 2010 Revision*, POP /DB/WPP/Rev.2010/02 (New York: United Nations, 2011), and US Energy Information Administration (EIA), *International Energy Statistics* (Washington, DC: EIA, 2012), www.eia.gov /countries; World Bank, *2009 World Development Indicators* (Washington, DC: World Bank, 2008), 128.

13. EIA, "U.S. Energy Facts Explained."

14. Ibid.

15. Ibid.

16. The figures in this paragraph refer to 2009. Simon Rogers and Lisa Evans, "World Carbon Dioxide Emissions Data by Country: China Speeds Ahead of the Rest," *Guardian* (London), January 31, 2011.

17. EIA, *International Energy Outlook 2009: Highlights* (Washington, DC: US EIA, June 2009).

18. UNEP, *GEO 5*.

19. Ibid.

20. EIA, *International Energy Outlook 2009*.

21. UNEP, *GEO 5*.

22. UNEP, *Vital Water Graphics: An Overview of the State of the World's Fresh and Marine Water*, 2nd ed. (Nairobi: UNEP, 2002).

23. National Intelligence Council, *Global Water Security* (Washington, DC: National Intelligence Council, 2012).

24. UNEP, *Global Environmental Outlook 4: Environment for Development* (Nairobi: UNEP, 2007), as cited in Peter Gleick, *The World's Water: 2008–2009* (Washington, DC: Island, 2008).

25. A hectare is 10,000 square meters.

26. Bertzy et al., *Protected Planet Report 2012: Tracking Progress Towards Global Targets for Protected Areas* (Gland, Switzerland, and Cambridge, UK: IUCN and UNEP-WCMC, 2012).

27. *Ecosystems and Human Well-Being: Biodiversity Synthesis* (Washington, DC: World Resources Institute, 2005).

28. Food and Agriculture Organization (FAO), *The State of World Fisheries and Aquaculture* (Rome: FAO, 2012), 11.

29. FAO, *Review of the State of World Marine Fishery Resources,* FAO Fisheries and Aquaculture Technical Paper No. 569 (Rome: FAO, 2011), 13–14, www.fao.org/docrep/015/i2389e/i2389e.pdf.

30. Ibid.

31. Secretariat of the Convention on Biological Diversity and the Scientific and Technical Advisory Panel–Global Environment Facility, *Impacts of Marine Debris on Biodiversity: Current Status and Potential Solutions*, Technical Series No. 67 (Montreal: Secretariat of the CBD, 2012). See also UNEP, *Marine Litter: A Global Challenge* (Nairobi: UNEP, 2009).

32. Information in this paragraph draws from two related reports: Daniela Russi et al., *The Economics of Ecosystem and Biodiversity for Water and Wetlands: A Briefing Note* (Geneva: UNEP The Economics of Ecosystems and Biodiversity, 2012); and Daniela Russi et al., *The Economics of Ecosystems and Biodiversity for Water and Wetlands: Final Consultation Draft*, UN Document UNEP/CBD/COP/11/INF/22, September 26, 2012.

33. Russi et al., *The Economics of Ecosystems*.

34. Asbjørn Eide, *The Right to Food and the Impact of Liquid Biofuels (Agrofuels)* (Rome: FAO, 2008), 14.

35. World Bank, *Global Monitoring Report 2012: Food Prices, Nutrition, and the Millennium Development Goals* (Washington, DC: World Bank, 2012), 30.

36. Eide, *The Right to Food*, 14.

37. Ibid., 44. Recent analyses of the links between climate change and weather, include Vladimir Petoukhov et al., "Quasiresonant Amplification of Planetary Waves and Recent Northern Hemisphere Weather Extremes," *Proceedings of the National Academy of Sciences* (March 1, 2013), doi: 10.1073/pnas.1222000110, www.pnas.org/content/early/2013/02/28/1222000110.full.pdf+html?sid=1fd59aed-5546-476e-8228-162da6389fda; C. B. Fields et al., eds., *Managing the Risks of Extreme Events and Disasters to Advance Climate Change Adaptation: Special Report of the Intergovernmental Panel on Climate Change* (Cambridge: Cambridge University Press for the IPCC, 2012); Department of Climate Change and Energy Efficiency, Government of Australia, *The Angry Summer* (Cannabera: Commonwealth of Australia, 2013); Hunter Cutting et al.,

"Current Extreme Weather and Climate Change," *Climate Communication Report*, September 7, 2011, climatecommunication.org/wp-content/uploads/2011/09/Extreme-Weather-and-Climate-Change.pdf.

38. International Resource Panel, United Nations Environment Programme, *Towards Sustainable Production and Use of Resources: Assessing Biofuels* (Nairobi: UNEP, 2009), www.unep .org/resourcepanel/Publications/tabid/54044/Default.aspx; Mireille Faist Emmenegger et al., *Harmonisation and Extension of the Bioenergy Inventories and Assessment* (Bern, Switzerland: EMPA [Swiss Federal Laboratories for Material Science and Technology], 2012), www.empa .ch/plugin/template/empa/*/125527; EMPA, "New Data on the Biofuel Ecobalance: Most Biofuels Are Not 'Green,'" EMPA Web, September 24, 2012, www.empa.ch/plugin/template /empa/3/125597/---/l=2; Damian Carrington, "Leaked Data: Palm Biodiesel as Dirty as Fuel from Tar Sands," *Guardian* (London), January 27, 2012.

39. Timothy A. Wise, "The Cost to Developing Countries of U.S. Corn Ethanol Expansion," Global Development and Environment Institute Working Paper No. 12-02, Tufts University, October 2012, 2, www.ase.tufts.edu/gdae/Pubs/wp/12-02WiseGlobalBiofuels.pdf.

40. Ibid.

41. Ibid.

42. UN Department of Economic and Social Affairs/Population Division, *World Urbanization Prospects: The 2011 Revision* (New York: United Nations, 2012), 2.

43. UNEP, *GEO 5*, 46–48.

44. "UNEP-Hosted Global Partnership on Waste Management."

45. Ibid., 6.

46. UN Habitat, "Urban Trends: 227 Million Escape Slums," Press Release, March 18, 2010, www.unhabitat.org/documents/SOWC10/R1.pdf.

47. Andrew Hurrell and Benedict Kingsbury, eds., *The International Politics of the Environment: Actors, Interests, and Institutions* (Oxford: Clarendon, 1992), 2; Pamela S. Chasek, *Earth Negotiations: Analyzing Thirty Years of Environmental Diplomacy* (Tokyo: United Nations University Press, 2001).

48. For an early effort to categorize environmental problems, see Clifford Russell and Hans Landsberg, "International Environmental Problems: A Taxonomy," *Science* 172 (June 25, 1972): 1307–1314.

49. Robert Dorfman and Nancy S. Dorfman, eds., *Economics of the Environment: Selected Readings*, 3rd ed. (New York: Norton, 1993), 75.

50. Garrett Hardin, "The Tragedy of the Commons," *Science* 162, no. 3859 (December 13, 1968).

51. Oran R. Young, *International Governance: Protecting the Environment in a Stateless Society* (Ithaca, NY: Cornell University Press, 1994), 19–26.

52. Susan Strange, "*Cave! Hic Dragones*: A Critique of Regime Analysis," *International Organization* 36 (spring 1982): 479–496.

53. Compare the definition and use of the term *regime* in John Gerard Ruggie, "International Responses to Technology: Concepts and Trends," *International Organization* 29 (1975): 557–583; Ernst Haas, "On Systems and International Regimes," *World Politics* 27 (1975): 147–174; Robert O. Keohane and Joseph Nye Jr., *Power and Interdependence: World Politics in Transition* (Boston: Little, Brown, 1977); Oran R. Young, "International Regimes: Problems of Concept Formation," *International Organization* 32 (1980): 331–356; Stephen D. Krasner, ed., *International Regimes*

(Ithaca, NY: Cornell University Press, 1983); Robert O. Keohane, *After Hegemony: Cooperation and Discord in the World Political Economy* (Princeton, NJ: Princeton University Press, 1984); Jack Donnelly, "International Human Rights: A Regime Analysis," *International Organization* 40 (1986): 599–642; Stephan Haggard and Beth A. Simmons, "Theories of International Regimes," *International Organization* 41 (1987): 491–517; Thomas Gehring, "International Environmental Regimes: Dynamic Sectoral Legal Systems," in *Yearbook of International Environmental Law*, vol. 1, ed. Günther Handl (London: Graham & Trotman, 1990); and David Leonard Downie, "Road Map or False Trail: Evaluating the Precedence of the Ozone Regime as Model and Strategy for Global Climate Change," *International Environmental Affairs* 7 (fall 1995): 321–345.

54. For influential discussions of the study of international cooperation, see and compare Friedrich Kratochwil and John Gerard Ruggie, "International Organization: A State of the Art on an Art of the State," *International Organization* 40 (1986): 753–776; James E. Dougherty and Robert L. Pfaltzgraff Jr., *Contending Theories of International Relations: A Comprehensive Survey*, 3rd ed. (New York: Harper and Row, 1990), ch. 10; and Joseph Grieco, "Anarchy and the Limits of Cooperation: A Realist Critique of the Newest Liberal Institutionalism," *International Organization* 42 (1988): 485–507.

55. Classic examples include Thucydides, Machiavelli, and Hobbes. Influential modern examples include Hans J. Morgenthau, *Politics Among Nations: The Struggle for Power and Peace*, 5th ed. (New York: Knopf, 1973); Robert Jervis, "Cooperation Under the Security Dilemma," *World Politics* 30 (1978): 167–186; Kenneth N. Waltz, *Theory of International Politics* (Reading, MA: Addison-Wesley, 1979); and Glenn Snyder, "The Security Dilemma in Alliance Politics," *World Politics* 36 (1984): 461–495.

56. Constitutionalists believed "international governance is whatever international organizations do; and formal attributes of international organizations, such as their charters, voting procedures, committee structures and the like, account for what they do" (Kratochwil and Ruggie, "International Organization," 755). The institutional process approach examines influence, how information is produced and digested, who speaks to whom, how decisions are made, and so on. It argues that the outputs of international organizations do not always reflect their charters or official procedures. A classic example is Robert W. Cox and Harold K. Jacobson, eds., *The Anatomy of Influence: Decision Making in International Organization* (New Haven, CT: Yale University Press, 1973).

57. For example, Richard A. Falk, *A Study of Future Worlds* (Princeton, NJ: Princeton University Press, 1975).

58. Important examples and discussions of functionalism include David Mitrany, *A Working Peace System: An Argument for the Functional Development of International Organization* (1943; rpt., Chicago: Quadrangle Books, 1966); David Mitrany, *The Functional Theory of Politics* (London: M. Robertson, 1975); and A. J. R. Groom and Paul Taylor, eds., *Functionalism: Theory and Practice in International Relations* (New York: Crane, Russak, 1975).

59. See and compare discussions in Kratochwil and Ruggie, "International Organization," 756–763; Dougherty and Pfaltzgraff, *Contending Theories of International Relations*, ch. 10; and Groom and Taylor, *Functionalism*, ch. 1.

60. Leading examples and discussion include Ernst B. Haas, *Beyond the Nation State: Functionalism and International Organization* (Stanford, CA: Stanford University Press, 1964); Ernst Haas, "The Uniting of Europe and the Uniting of Latin America," *Journal of Common Market*

Studies 5 (1967): 315–343; Philippe Schmitter, "Three Neo-Functional Hypotheses about International Integration," *International Organization* 23 (1969): 161–166; Ernst Haas, "The Study of Regional Integration: Reflections on the Joy and Anguish of Pretheorizing," *International Organization* 24 (1970): 607–646; Joseph S. Nye, *Peace in Parts: Integration and Conflict in Regional Organization* (Boston: Little, Brown, 1971); Kratochwil and Ruggie, "International Organization," 757–759; and Dougherty and Pfaltzgraff, *Contending Theories of International Relations*, 431–447. Influential comparisons of functionalism and neofunctionalism include Haas, *Beyond the Nation State*, and Groom and Taylor, *Functionalism*, chs. 11–12.

61. An example is Ernst B. Haas, "On Systems and International Regimes," *World Politics* 27 (1975): 147–174; and Ernst B. Haas, *When Knowledge Is Power: Three Models of Change in International Organizations* (Berkeley: University of California Press, 1990).

62. Robert O. Keohane and Joseph S. Nye Jr., eds., *Transnational Relations and World Politics* (Cambridge, MA: Harvard University Press, 1972); Robert O. Keohane and Joseph S. Nye Jr., "Transnational Relations and International Organizations," *World Politics* 27 (October 1974): 39–62.

63. Keohane and Nye, *Power and Interdependence*. Complex interdependence and turbulent fields share important concerns and insights.

64. John Gerard Ruggie, "International Responses to Technology: Concepts and Trends," *International Organization* 29 (1975): 570.

65. Haas, "On Systems and International Regimes," 147–174.

66. Keohane and Nye, *Power and Interdependence*, 5, 19.

67. Krasner, *International Regimes*, 2.

68. This paragraph is adapted from I. William Zartman, ed., *The 50% Solution: How to Bargain Successfully with Hijackers, Strikers, Bosses, Oil Magnates, Arabs, Russians, and Other Worthy Opponents* (1976; rpt., New Haven, CT: Yale University Press, 1983), 9–10.

69. Oran R. Young, *International Cooperation: Building Regimes for Natural Resources and the Environment* (Ithaca, NY: Cornell University Press, 1989), 13–14.

70. R. Michael M'Gonigle and Mark W. Zacher, *Pollution, Politics, and International Law: Tankers at Sea* (Berkeley: University of California Press, 1979), 58–59, 84–85, 93–96; Jan Schneider, *World Public Order of the Environment: Toward an International Ecological Law and Organization* (Toronto: University of Toronto Press, 1979), 33, 92–93.

71. Keohane, *After Hegemony*, provides an influential discussion of why it is easier to change international regimes to make them more effective than it is to create new ones.

72. For more information on the Convention on Migratory Species initiative on migratory sharks, see "CMS Convention on Migratory Species: Meetings on Migratory Sharks," Convention on Migratory Species, 2010, www.cms.int/bodies/meetings/regional/sharks/sharks_meetings.htm.

73. For an early analytical overview of these approaches, see Haggard and Simmons, "Theories of International Regimes."

74. Keohane and Nye, *Power and Interdependence*, 50–51.

75. For the former approach, see Robert Gilpin, *The Political Economy of International Relations* (Princeton, NJ: Princeton University Press, 1987); Grieco, "Anarchy and the Limits of Cooperation"; and Strange, "*Cave! Hic Dragones*," 337–343. Susan Strange, "The Persistent Myth of Lost Hegemony," *International Organization* 41 (summer 1987): 570, argues that inconsistency in US policy rather than loss of US global hegemony caused erosion of international regimes.

76. Oran R. Young, "The Politics of International Regime Formation: Managing Natural Resources and the Environment," *International Organization* 43 (summer 1989): 355.

77. Fen Osler Hampson, "Climate Change: Building International Coalitions of the Like-Minded," *International Journal* 45 (winter 1989–1990): 36–74.

78. See Peter Haas, "Do Regimes Matter? Epistemic Communities and Mediterranean Pollution Control," *International Organization* 43 (summer 1989): 378–403.

79. The issue of ocean dumping of radioactive wastes, in which scientific evidence was explicitly rejected as the primary basis for decision making by antidumping states, is analyzed in Judith Spiller and Cynthia Hayden, "Radwaste at Sea: A New Era of Polarization or a New Basis for Consensus?" *Ocean Development and International Law* 19 (1988): 345–366.

80. Robert Putnam, "Diplomacy and Domestic Politics: The Logic of Two-Level Games," *International Organization* 42, no. 3 (summer 1988): 427–460.

81. For example, David L. Downie, "Understanding International Environmental Regimes: Lessons of the Ozone" (PhD diss., University of North Carolina, Chapel Hill, 1996).

82. For an influential and accessible discussion of paradigm shifts, see Thomas S. Kuhn, *The Structure of Scientific Revolutions* (Chicago: University of Chicago Press, 1962). Our discussion of paradigm shifts in this section is not offered as a new theory to compete with existing theories of international regimes. Rather, this is meant to represent a supplementary set of lenses through which to discuss environmental issues.

83. Harold and Margaret Sprout, *The Ecological Perspective on Human Affairs, with Special Reference to International Politics* (Princeton, NJ: Princeton University Press, 1965); Kenneth E. Boulding, "The Economics of the Coming Spaceship Earth," in *Environmental Quality in a Growing Economy: Essays from the Sixth RFF Forum*, ed. Henry Jarrett (Baltimore: Johns Hopkins University Press, 1966).

84. For an analysis of neoclassical economic assumptions as they bear on environmental management, see Daniel Underwood and Paul King, "On the Ideological Foundations of Environmental Policy," *Ecological Economics* 1 (1989): 317–322.

85. See Michael E. Colby, *Environmental Management in Development: The Evolution of Paradigms* (Washington, DC: World Bank, 1990).

86. John McCormick, *Reclaiming Paradise: The Global Environmental Movement* (Bloomington: Indiana University Press, 1989), 67.

87. Lars-Göran Engfeldt, "The Road from Stockholm to Johannesburg," *UN Chronicle* 39, no. 3 (September–November 2002): 14–17.

88. See Clem Tisdell, "Sustainable Development: Differing Perspectives of Ecologists and Economists, and Relevance to LDCs," *World Development* 16 (1988): 377–378.

89. Donella H. Meadows et al., *The Limits to Growth: A Report for the Club of Rome's Project on the Predicament of Mankind* (New York: Universe Books, 1972); Council on Environmental Quality and Gerald Barney, *Global 2000: The Report to the President Entering the Twenty-First Century* (New York: Pergamon, 1980).

90. Julian Simon and Herman Kahn, eds., *The Resourceful Earth: A Response to Global 2000* (Oxford: Basil Blackwell, 1984).

91. For background on the sustainable development concept, see UN Center for Transnational Corporations, *Environmental Aspects of the Activities of Transnational Corporations: A Survey* (New York: United Nations, 1985).

92. World Commission on Environment and Development, *Our Common Future* (Oxford: Oxford University Press, 1987).

93. Jim MacNeill, "Sustainable Development, Economics and the Growth Imperative," paper presented at the conference The Economics of Sustainable Development, Smithsonian Institution, Washington, DC, January 23–26, 1990.

94. See Edith Brown Weiss, "In Fairness to Future Generations," *Environment* 32 (April 1990), and similar arguments made in the Latin American and Caribbean Commission on Development and Environment, *Our Own Agenda* (New York: Inter-American Development Bank, 1990).

95. See Alan Durning, "How Much Is Enough?" *Worldwatch* 3 (November–December 1990): 12–19.

96. See Yusuf Ahmad, Salah El Serafy, and Ernst Lutz, eds., *Environmental Accounting for Sustainable Development* (Washington, DC: World Bank, 1989). For an early example of natural resource accounting, see Robert Repetto et al., *Accounts Overdue: Natural Resources Depreciation in Costa Rica* (Washington, DC: World Resources Institute, 1991).

97. See Herman E. Daly, "Toward a Measure of Sustainable Social Net National Product," in Ahmad, Serafy, and Lutz, *Environmental Accounting for Sustainable Development*, 8–9; and Herman Daly and John Cobb Jr., *For the Common Good: Redirecting the Economy Toward Community, the Environment and a Sustainable Future* (Boston: Beacon, 1989), 368–373, 401–455. A similar effort to rate the distributive effects of national policies is embodied in the UNDP's human development indicators in its annual *Human Development Report*.

98. Centre for Bhutan Studies, *A Short Guide to Gross National Happiness Index* (Thimphu, Bhutan: Centre for Bhutan Studies, 2012), www.grossnationalhappiness.com/wp-content/uploads/2012/04/Short-GNH-Index-final1.pdf.

99. See World Bank, "Environmental Economics and Indicators: Green Accounting," May 28, 2010, go.worldbank.org/EPMTVTZOM0.

100. See OECD, "Measuring Well-Being and Progress," www.oecd.org/statistics/measuring well-beingandprogress.htm.

101. For information on the Environmental Sustainability Index, see www.yale.edu/esi.

102. Commission of the European Communities, *GDP and Beyond: Measuring Progress in a Changing World*, 20.8.2009 COM(2009) 433 final, Brussels, 2009, eur-lex.europa.eu/LexUri Serv/LexUriServ.do?uri=COM:2009:0433:FIN:EN:PDF. See also European Commission, "Indicators," epp.eurostat.ec.europa.eu/portal/page/portal/sdi/indicators.

103. See, e.g., Partha Dasgupta and Karl Goran Maler, "The Environment and Emerging Development Issues," paper presented at the World Bank Conference on Development Economics, April 26–27, 1990, 22; and Sander Tideman, "Gross National Happiness: Towards a New Paradigm in Economics," in *Gross National Happiness and Development: Proceedings of the First International Seminar on Operationalization of Gross National Happiness*, ed. Karma Ura and Karma Galay (Thimphu: Centre for Bhutan Studies, 2004), 222–246.

104. See Robert Repetto, *Promoting Environmentally Sound Economic Progress: What the North Can Do* (Washington, DC: World Resources Institute, 1990); and Daly, "Toward a Measure of Sustainable Social Net National Product."

105. UN Conference on Environment and Development, *Agenda 21, Rio Declaration, Forest Principles* (New York: United Nations, 1992).

106. Tideman, "Gross National Happiness," 229.

107. Martin Khor, "Globalisation and Sustainable Development: Challenges for Johannesburg," *Third World Resurgence* 139/140 (March–April 2002), www.twnside.org.sg/title/twr139a.htm.

108. Ibid.

109. James Gustave Speth, "Two Perspectives on Globalization and the Environment," in *Worlds Apart: Globalization and the Environment*, ed. James Gustave Speth (Washington, DC: Island, 2003), 12.

110. Ibid., 13.

111. UNEP, *Towards a Green Economy: Pathways to Sustainable Development and Poverty Eradication* (Nairobi: UNEP, 2011).

112. Ibid.

113. Ibid., 14.

114. United Nations, *Secretary-General's Report on Objectives and Themes of the United Nations Conference, UNDESA*, A/CONF.216/PC/7, December 22, 2010, 5, www.uncsd2012.org /index.php?page=view&type=400&nr=10&menu=45.

115. UNEP, *Towards a Green Economy*, 14.

116. Ibid., 16–17.

117. "Summary of the United Nations Conference on Sustainable Development: 13–22 June 2012," *Earth Negotiations Bulletin* 27, no. 51 (June 25, 2012): 21.

118. Martin Khor, "Global Debate on 'Green Economy,'" *Star* (Malaysia), January 24, 2011.

119. United Nations, "The Future We Want," A/66/L.56, July 24, 2012, 10, www.uncsd 2012.org/thefuturewewant.html.

120. Paul Raskin et al., *Great Transition: The Promise and Lure of the Times Ahead* (Boston: Stockholm Environment Institute, 2002). Compare to Kuhn's analysis of paradigm shifts in science in *The Structure of Scientific Revolutions*.

121. Ibid., x.

122. For updated information on EU sustainable development policy, see the relevant official websites, including European Commission, "Environment: Sustainable Development," ec.europa .eu/environment/eussd.

123. See, for example, Thomas Homer-Dixon, "On the Threshold: Environmental Changes as Causes of Acute Conflict," *International Security* 16, no. 2 (1991): 76–116; Thomas F. Homer-Dixon, "Environmental Scarcities and Violent Conflict: Evidence from Cases," *International Security* 19, no. 1 (1994): 5–40; Thomas F. Homer-Dixon and Jessica Blitt, eds., *Ecoviolence: Links Among Environment, Population and Security* (Lanham, MD: Rowman & Littlefield, 1998); and Thomas F. Homer-Dixon, *Environment, Scarcity, and Violence* (Princeton, NJ: Princeton University Press, 1999). Recent discussions that review the field include Larry Swatuk, "Security, Cooperation, and the Environment," in *Palgrave Advances in International Environmental Politics*, ed. Michele M. Betsill, Kathryn Hochstetler, and Dimitris Stevis (New York: Palgrave Macmillan, 2005); and Richard Matther, "Man, the State and Nature: Rethinking Environment Security," in *Handbook of Global Environmental Politics*, ed. Peter Dauvergne (Northampton: Edward Elgar, 2005). For current news and reports, see the Environmental Change and Security Program website: www.wilsoncenter.org/program/environmental-change-and-security-program.

124. UNEP, *Sudan: Post Conflict Environmental Assessment* (Nairobi: United Nations, 2007); Clionadh Raleigh, "Political Marginalization, Climate Change, and Conflict in African Sahel States," *International Studies Review* 12, no. 1 (2010): 69–86.

125. See Doug Hawley, "Drug Smugglers Curtail Scientists Work," *USA Today*, December 27, 2007.

126. Christian Nelleman, UNEP, and INTERPOL, *Green Carbon, Black Trade: Illegal Logging, Tax Fraud and Laundering in the World's Tropical Forests* (Nairobi: UNEP, 2012).

127. See, e.g., Carolyn Pumphrey, ed., *Global Climate Change: National Security Implications* (Carlisle, PA: Strategic Studies Institute, US Army War College, 2008); Geoffrey Dabelko and P. J. Simmons, "Environment and Security: Core Ideas and U.S. Government Initiatives," *SAIS Review* (winter/spring 1997): 127–146; Gen. Gordon Sullivan (Ret.) et al., *National Security and the Threat of Climate Change* (Alexandria, VA: CAN Corporation, 2007); German Advisory Council on Global Change, *Climate Change as a Security Risk* (Oxford: Earthscan, 2007); and Simon Dalby, *Security and Environmental Change* (Cambridge: Polity, 2009).

128. Oli Brown and Alec Crawford, *Climate Change and Security in Africa* (Winnipeg: International Institute for Sustainable Development, 2009), 2.

129. Oli Brown and Alec Crawford, *Rising Temperatures, Rising Tensions: Climate Change and the Risk of Violent Conflict in the Middle East* (Winnipeg: International Institute for Sustainable Development, 2009), 2.

130. For discussion, see J. Oglethorpe, J. Shambaugh, and R. Kormos, "Parks in the Crossfire: Strategies for Effective Conservation in Areas of Armed Conflict," *IUCN Protected Areas Programme: Parks* 14, no. 1 (2004): 2–8.

131. G. Debonnet and K. Hillman-Smith, "Supporting Protected Areas in a Time of Political Turmoil: The Case of World Heritage Sites in the Democratic Republic of Congo," *IUCN Protected Areas Programme: Parks* 14, no. 1 (2004): 11.

132. See, e.g., Talli Nauman, "Illegal Drugs Root of Evil for Conservation Community," *Herald Mexico*, August 1, 2006; Hawley, "Drug Smugglers Curtail Scientists Work."

133. "Rio Declaration on Environment and Development," in *Report of the United Nations Conference on the Human Environment*, Stockholm, June 5–16, 1972, ch. 1, www.un-documents.net/rio-dec.htm.

134. These concepts are adapted from David Kriebel et al., "The Precautionary Principle in Environmental Science," *Environmental Health Perspective* 109, no. 9 (September 2001): 871–876. See the article for a more complete discussion of these points.

135. Carolyn Raffensperger and Katherine Barrett, "In Defense of the Precautionary Principle," *Environmental Health Perspective* 109, no. 9 (September 2001): 811–812.

136. For a collection of examples, see Joel Tickner, Carolyn Raffensperger, and Nancy Myers, *The Precautionary Principle in Action: A Handbook*, Science and Environmental Health Network, www.sehn.org/rtfdocs/handbook-rtf.rtf.

137. Ministerial Declaration, Second International Conference on the Protection of the North Sea, London, November 24–25, 1987, seas-at-risk.org/1mages/1987%20London%20Declaration.pdf.

138. Preamble, Montreal Protocol, 26 ILM 1541, September 16, 1987, ozone.unep.org/new_site/en/montreal_protocol.php.

139. UN Framework Convention on Climate Change, United Nations, May 9, 1992, www.un-documents.net/unfccc.htm.

140. See Article 10 and Article 11 of the Biosafety Protocol, bch.cbd.int/protocol/text/.

141. Article 1 of the Stockholm Convention on Persistent Organic Pollutants, May 22, 2001, chm.pops.int/Convention/tabid/54/Default.aspx.

142. Communication from the Commission on the Precautionary Principle COM 1.1 final, Commission of the European Communities, February 2, 2000.

143. See Tickner, Raffensperger, and Myers, *The Precautionary Principle in Action*, 16–17.

144. Ibid.

145. Ibid.

146. Kenneth R. Foster, Paolo Vecchia, and Michael H. Repacholi, "Science and the Precautionary Principle," *Science* 288, no. 5468 (May 12, 2000): 2.

147. For example, the appellate body of the WTO in the beef hormones case refused "to take a position on whether the principle amounts to customary international law, commenting that the international status of the principle is 'less than clear'" (Philippe Sands and Jacqueline Peel, "Environmental Protection in the Twenty-First Century: The Evolution of Sustainable Development and International Law,'" in *The Global Environment: Institutions, Law, and Policy*, ed. Regina S. Axelrod, David Leonard Downie, and Norman J. Vig, 2nd ed. [Washington, DC: Congressional Quarterly Press, 2005], 56).

148. Personal observations by David Downie during negotiations related to the Montreal Protocol and the Rotterdam and Stockholm conventions.

149. Jon Van Dyke, "The Evolution and International Acceptance of the Precautionary Principle," in *Bringing New Law to Ocean Waters*, ed. David D. Caron and Harry N. Scheiber (Koninklijke, Netherlands: Martinus Nijhof, 2004), 357.

Chapter 2—Actors in the Environmental Arena

1. David Day, *The Whale War* (Vancouver: Douglas and MacIntyre, 1987), 103–107.

2. Reducing Emissions from Deforestation and Degradation (REDD) is a mechanism to create economic incentives for developing countries to protect and better manage their forest resources, thereby helping to combat climate change. REDD aims to make forests more valuable standing than they would be cut down, by creating a financial value for the carbon stored in trees. For information, see www.un-redd.org.

3. "7 Conglomerates Control 9M ha of Land in Indonesia," mongabay.com, May 5, 2011, news.mongabay.com/2011/0504-indonesia_conglomerates.html.

4. Richard Elliot Benedick, *Ozone Diplomacy: New Directions in Safeguarding the Planet*, 2nd ed. (Cambridge, MA: Harvard University Press, 1998), 59.

5. The German Green Party lost all of its parliamentary members in the first all-German elections since 1932 because it opposed reunification. It began to rebound by mid-1991, when polls showed it had the support of 6 percent of voters—above the 5 percent needed to achieve representation in the parliament. The Green Party won thirty-four seats in the German parliament in 1998 and made history by becoming part of a coalition government with the Social Democratic Party. In 2002, the Green Party won fifty-five seats and continued its role in the coalition government with the Social Democratic Party, which lasted until 2005.

6. *Earth Summit Update* 7 (March 1992): 3.

7. Detlev Sprinz and Tapani Vaahtoranta, "The Interest-Based Explanation of International Environmental Policy," *International Organization* 48, no. 1 (1994): 77–105.

8. Carolyn Thomas, *The Environment in International Relations* (London: Royal Institute of International Affairs, 1992), 228.

9. On EU ambitions for global leadership on the environment, see Brian Wynne, "Implementation of Greenhouse Gas Reductions in the European Community: Institutional and Cul-

tural Factors," *Global Environmental Change Report*, March 1993, 102; Yannis Paleokrassas is quoted in *Energy, Economics and Climate Change* 4, no. 7 (July 1994): 14.

10. Eugene Robinson and Michael Weisskopf, "Bonn Pushes Tough Stand on Warming; U.S. Puts Pressure on 3 Allies to Drop 2nd Stiff Initiative," *Washington Post*, June 9, 1992, A1.

11. Philippe Le Prestre and Evelyne Dufault, "Canada and the Kyoto Protocol on GHGs," *ISUMA* 2, no. 4 (winter 2001): 40.

12. Bill Curry and Shawn McCarthy, "Canada Formally Abandons Kyoto Protocol on Climate Change," *Globe and Mail* (Toronto), December 12, 2011.

13. For information, see the "U.S. Conference of Mayors Climate Protection Agreement," Mayors Climate Protection Center, 2008, www.usmayors.org/climateprotection/agreement .htm.

14. Seattle City Light, "Seattle Promotes Innovation in Achieving Energy Efficiency," press release, October 12, 2012, www.seattle.gov/light/news/newsreleases/detail.asp?ID=13172.

15. New York City, *PlaNYC: Update April 2011* (New York: Mayor's Office of Long-Term Planning and Sustainability, 2011), 146, www.nyc.gov/html/planyc2030/html/publications /publications.shtml.

16. Database of State Incentives for Renewables and Efficiency, "Incentives/Policies for Renewables and Efficiency," www.dsireusa.org/incentives/index.cfm?EE=1&RE=1&SPV=0&ST=0 &searchtype=RPS&sh=1.

17. See the Regional Greenhouse Gas Initiative website at www.rggi.org.

18. Ben Cubby, "Carbon Neutral NSW by 2020," *Sydney Morning Herald*, May 9, 2008.

19. See for example, Rheal Segun, "Quebec, California Setting Up Cap-and-Trade System to Reduce Emissions," *Globe and Mail* (Toronto), December 18, 2012.

20. See for example, the Clinton Climate Initiative, www.clintonfoundation.org/what-we -do/clinton-climate-initiative.

21. For a similar discussion that uses different terms, see David Leonard Downie, "UNEP and the Montreal Protocol: New Roles for International Organizations in Regime Creation and Change," in *International Organizations and Environmental Policy*, ed. Robert V. Bartlett, Priya Kurian, and Madhu Malik (Westport, CT: Greenwood, 1995).

22. Richard Elliot Benedick, "The Ozone Protocol: A New Global Diplomacy," *Conservation Foundation Letter* 4 (1989): 6–7; and Benedick, *Ozone Diplomacy*, 109–110.

23. For details on the challenges that UNEP faced in the latter half of the 1990s, see David L. Downie and Marc Levy, "The United Nations Environment Programme at a Turning Point: Options for Change," in *The Global Environment in the Twenty-First Century: Prospects for International Cooperation*, ed. Pamela Chasek (Tokyo: United Nations University Press, 2000).

24. UNEP, *State of the Environment and Contribution of the United Nations Environment Programme to Addressing Substantive Environmental Challenges: Report of the Executive Director*, UNEP/GC.23/3, October 21, 2004, www.unep.org/gc/gc23/working_docs.asp.

25. See UNEP, *United Nations Environment Programme Medium-Term Strategy 2010–2013*, UNEP/GCSS.X/8, 2007, www.unep.org/PDF/FinalMTSGCSS-X-8.pdf.

26. Stine Madland Kaasa, "The UN Commission on Sustainable Development: Which Mechanisms Explain Its Accomplishments?" *Global Environmental Politics* 7, no. 3 (August 2007): 114–115. For details on the consultative process, see "United Nations Open-Ended Informal Consultative Process on Oceans and the Law of the Sea," updated July 24, 2012, www.un.org /Depts/los/consultative_process/consultative_process.htm.

27. United Nations, "The Future We Want," A/RES/66/288, September 2012, sustainabledevelopment.un.org/futurewewant.html.

28. Gunnar Sjöstedt and Bertram Spector, conclusion to _International Environmental Negotiation_, ed. Gunnar Sjöstedt (Newbury Park, CA: Sage, 1993), 306.

29. Pamela Chasek, "Scientific Uncertainty in Environmental Negotiations," in _Global Environmental Policies_, ed. Ho-Won Jeong (London: Palgrave, 2001).

30. Ibid.

31. For information on the Millennium Ecosystem Assessment, see www.millenniumassess ment.org.

32. For information on IPBES, see www.ipbes.net.

33. Andrew Hurrell and Benedict Kingsbury, eds., _The International Politics of the Environment: Actors, Interests, and Institutions_ (Oxford: Clarendon, 1992), 2; Pamela Chasek, _Earth Negotiations: Analyzing Thirty Years of Environmental Diplomacy_ (Tokyo: United Nations University Press, 2001).

34. Food and Agriculture Organization of the United Nations, "Forestry," fact sheet, 2012, www.fao.org/docrep/014/am859e/am859e08.pdf.

35. UN Development Programme, "Environment and Energy," www.undp.org/content/undp /en/home/ourwork/environmentandenergy/overview.html.

36. This formulation is used in the context of a different conceptualization of the role of IGOs in global environmental policy making in Marc Levy, Robert O. Keohane, and Peter M. Haas, "Improving the Effectiveness of International Environmental Institutions," in _Institutions for the Earth: Sources of Effective International Environmental Protection_, ed. Peter M. Haas, Robert O. Keohane, and Marc Levy (Cambridge, MA: MIT Press, 1993), 400.

37. Steinar Andresen and Jon Skjaerseth, "Can International Secretariats Promote Effective Co-operation?" a background paper written for the United Nations University Conference on Synergies and Co-ordination Between Multilateral Environmental Agreements, Tokyo, Japan, July 14–16, 1999.

38. Rosemary Sandford, "International Environmental Treaty Secretariats: Stage-Hands or Actors," in _Green Globe Yearbook of International Cooperation on Environment and Development 1994_, ed. Helge Ole Bergesen and Georg Parmann (Oxford: Oxford University Press, 1994), 21.

39. Andresen and Skjaerseth, "Can International Secretariats Promote Effective Co-operation?" 15.

40. Discussion of these two topics has been based on the analysis presented in Steffen Bauer, Per-Olof Busch, and Bernd Siebenhüner, "Administering International Governance: What Role for Treaty Secretariats?" Global Governance Working Paper 29, October 2007, www.glo gov.org/images/doc/WP29.pdf.

41. This observation is supported by personal observations of the authors during attendance at various global environmental negotiations since 1990. For discussion, see Richard Elliot Benedick, "Perspectives of a Negotiation Practitioner," in _International Environmental Negotiation_, ed. Gunnar Sjöstedt (Newbury Park, CA: Sage, 1993), 224.

42. Bauer, Busch, and Siebenhüner, "Administering International Governance," 5.

43. Ibid., 18–19.

44. Ibid., 10.

45. UNFCCC website statistics, 2012, unfccc.int/essential_background/about_the_website /items/3358.php.

46. Oran R. Young, *International Governance: Protecting the Environment in a Stateless Society* (Ithaca, NY: Cornell University Press, 1994), 170.

47. Johan Kaufmann, *Conference Diplomacy: An Introductory Analysis*, 3rd ed. (London: Macmillan, 1996), 93–94.

48. Benedick, "Perspectives of a Negotiation Practitioner," 225. Downie also observed this while attending the 1990 ozone negotiations in London.

49. Farhana Yamin and Joanna Depledge, *The International Climate Change Regime: A Guide to Rules, Institutions and Procedures* (Cambridge: Cambridge University Press, 2005); Bauer, Busch, and Siebenhüner, "Administering International Governance."

50. Bauer, Busch, and Siebenhüner, "Administering International Governance," 13.

51. This observation is supported by personal observations of the authors and conversations with secretariat and government officials during attendance at global environmental negotiations since 1990.

52. See, for example, Steffen Bauer, "The United Nations and the Fight Against Desertification: What Role for the UNCCD Secretariat?" in *Governing Global Desertification: Linking Environmental Degradation, Poverty, and Participation*, ed. Pierre Marc Johnson, Karel Mayrand, and Marc Paquin (Aldershot, UK: Ashgate, 2006), 83.

53. For a critical analysis of the environmental impacts of various multilateral development bank loans, see Bruce Rich, *Mortgaging the Earth: The World Bank, Environmental Impoverishment, and the Crisis of Development* (Boston: Beacon, 1994).

54. Navroz Dubash and Frances Seymour, "World Bank's Environmental Reform Agenda," *Foreign Policy in Focus*, March 1, 1999, www.fpif.org/reports/world_banks_environmental_reform_agenda.

55. Ibid.

56. Ibid.

57. World Bank, *Making Sustainable Commitments: An Environment Strategy for the World Bank* (Washington, DC: World Bank, 2001).

58. Independent Evaluation Group–World Bank, *Environmental Sustainability: An Evaluation of World Bank Group Support* (Washington, DC: World Bank, 2008), xvi.

59. Frances Seymour, "Mainstreaming and Infrastructure," *Environment Matters 2004* (Washington, DC: World Bank, 2004), siteresources.worldbank.org/INTRANETENVIRONMENT /Resources/EM04Mainstreaming.pdf.

60. Independent Evaluation Group–World Bank, *Environmental Sustainability*, 71.

61. Ibid., 69.

62. World Bank, *Toward a Green, Clean, and Resilient World for All: A World Bank Group Environment Strategy 2012–2022* (Washington, DC: World Bank, 2012).

63. Ivy Mungcal, "New World Bank Environment Strategy Draws Mixed Reactions," Devex, June 8, 2012, www.devex.com/en/news/78385/print.

64. Ibid.

65. World Bank, "World Bank Group Unveils New Focus on 'Green, Clean, Resilient' Development," press release 2012/496/SDN, June 5, 2012.

66. "IMF Reviews Its Approach to Environmental Issues," *IMF Survey*, April 15, 1991, 124.

67. For information about the HIPC initiative, see "Debt Relief Under the Heavily Indebted Poor Countries (HIPC) Initiative," IMF Factsheet, January 10, 2013, www.imf.org/external/np /exr/facts/hipc.htm.

68. "Climate Change, Environment, and the IMF," IMF Factsheet, August 23, 2012, www.imf.org/external/np/exr/facts/enviro.htm.

69. Ved P. Gandhi, *The IMF and the Environment* (Washington, DC: IMF, 1998).

70. Belgium, West Germany, Luxembourg, France, Italy, and the Netherlands formed three organizations: the European Economic Community, the European Coal and Steel Community, and the European Atomic Energy Community.

71. The European Community (EC) has been a party to international conventions on environmental conservation since the 1970s. At present, it is a party to more than thirty conventions and agreements on the environment and takes an active part in negotiations. The EC also takes part in the activities and negotiations taking place within the context of international bodies or programs and in particular under the auspices of the United Nations.

72. European Union, *EUROPE 2020: A Strategy for Smart, Sustainable and Inclusive Growth*, 3.3.2010 COM(2010) 2020 final, 2010, eur-lex.europa.eu/LexUriServ/LexUriServ.do?uri=COM :2010:2020:FIN:EN:PDF.

73. Organization of American States, "Securing Our Citizens' Future by Promoting Human Prosperity, Energy Security and Environmental Sustainability," Declaration of Commitment of Port of Spain, Fifth Summit of the Americas, Port of Spain, Trinidad and Tobago, April 19, 2009, www.summit-americas.org/V_Summit/decl_comm_pos_en.pdf.

74. New Partnership for Africa's Development (NEPAD), *Action Plan of the Environment Initiative of the New Partnership for Africa's Development* (Midrand, South Africa: NEPAD, June 2003), www.unep.org/roa/Amcen/docs/publications/ActionNepad.pdf.

75. Asia-Pacific Economic Cooperation (APEC), "APEC Economic Leaders' Declaration," APEC Summit, Kuala Lumpur, Malaysia, November 18, 1998, www.apec.org/Meeting-Papers /Leaders-Declarations/1998/1998_aelm.aspx.

76. APEC, "Sydney APEC Leaders' Declaration" APEC Summit, Sydney, Australia, September 9, 2007, www.apec.org/Meeting-Papers/Leaders-Declarations/2007/2007_aelm.aspx.

77. APEC, "The Honolulu Declaration—Toward a Seamless Regional Economy," APEC Summit, Honolulu, Hawaii, United States, November 13, 2011, www.apec.org/Meeting-Papers/Leaders -Declarations/2011/2011_aelm.aspx.

78. Adil Najam, "The View from the South: Developing Countries in Global Environmental Politics," in *The Global Environment: Institutions, Law and Policy*, ed. Regina S. Axelrod, David Leonard Downie, and Norman J. Vig, 2nd ed. (Washington, DC: Congressional Quarterly Press, 2005).

79. This description is based on Group of 77, "About the Group of 77," www.g77.org/doc; and Najam, "The View from the South."

80. The organization was originally called the South Pacific Regional Environment Program. For information on SPREP, see its official website at www.sprep.org.

81. For additional information about the Central American Commission on Environment and Development, see its website at www.sica.int/ccad.

82. See Michele M. Betsill and Elisabeth Corell, eds., *NGO Diplomacy: The Influence of Nongovernmental Organizations in International Environmental Negotiations* (Cambridge, MA: MIT Press, 2008); Thomas G. Weiss and Leon Gordenker, eds., *NGOs, the UN, and Global Governance* (Boulder, CO: Lynne Rienner, 1996); Paul Wapner, "Politics Beyond the State: Environmental Actions and World Civic Politics," *World Politics* 47, no. 3 (April 1995): 311–340; Thomas Princen and Matthias Finger, eds., *Environmental NGOs in World Politics: Linking the Local and the*

Global (London: Routledge, 1994); and Barbara Bramble and Gareth Porter, "Non-Governmental Organizations and the Making of U.S. International Environmental Policy," in Hurrell and Kingsbury, *The International Politics of the Environment.*

83. Greenpeace, "About Greenpeace," 2013, www.greenpeace.org/international/en/about/.

84. Ramachandra Guha, "The Environmentalism of the Poor," in *Varieties of Environmentalism: Essays North and South*, ed. Ramachandra Guha and Juan Martinez-Alier (London: Earthscan, 1997), 15.

85. See Julie Fisher, *The Road from Rio: Sustainable Development and the Nongovernmental Movement in the Third World* (Westport, CT: Praeger, 1993), 123–128; and Monsiapile Kajimbwa, "NGOs and Their Role in the Global South," *International Journal of Not-for-Profit Law* 9, no. 1 (December 2006): 58–64.

86. Guha, "The Environmentalism of the Poor," 4.

87. Ibid.

88. See Third World Network, *The Battle for Sarawak's Forests* (Penang, Malaysia: World Rainforest Movement, 1989).

89. For representative press reports available online, see "Nine Villages Join Protest Against Illegal Logging," *Sarawak Mirror*, June 27, 2012, and "Villagers Protest Against Alleged Illegal Logging," *Borneo Post*, May 21, 2011.

90. For information about the Green Belt Movement, see its website: www.greenbeltmovement.org.

91. For information about Third World Network, see its website: www.twnside.org.sg.

92. For information on the Center for Science and Environment, see its website: www.cseindia.org.

93. For information on the International POPs Elimination Network, see its website: www.ipen.org.

94. Working with Merck and Genentech, the World Resources Institute, the World Wildlife Fund, and the Environmental and Energy Study Institute drafted an interpretive statement and persuaded President Clinton in 1993 to sign the treaty with such a statement attached.

95. For references to the boycott as well as broader discussion, see "Iceland," in *The Europa World Yearbook, 2004* (London: Taylor and Francis, 2004), 2049; Guillermo Herrera and Porter Hoagland, "Commercial Whaling, Tourism and Boycotts: An Economic Perspective," *Marine Policy* 30, no. 3 (May 2006): 261–269; Steinar Andresen, "Science and Politics in the International Management of Whales," *Marine Policy* 13, no. 2 (April 1989), 88–117; and "Burger Chain Targeted," *Los Angeles Times*, June 19, 1988.

96. Scott Couder and Rob Harrison, "The Effectiveness of Ethical Consumer Behavior," in *The Ethical Consumer*, ed. Rob Harrison, Terry Newholm, and Diedre Shaw (London: Sage, 2005), 89–104.

97. Robert Boardman, *International Organization and the Conservation of Nature* (Bloomington: Indiana University Press, 1981), 88–94.

98. Patricia Birnie, "The Role of International Law in Solving Certain Environmental Conflicts," in *International Environmental Diplomacy: The Management and Resolution of Transfrontier Environmental Problems*, ed. John Carroll (Cambridge: Cambridge University Press, 1988), 107–108.

99. Personal communication from a member of the US delegation to the biodiversity negotiations, February 1994.

100. Kal Raustiala, "States, NGOs and International Environmental Institutions," *International Studies Quarterly* 41 (1997): 728.

101. The *Earth Negotiations Bulletin* was initially published as the *Earth Summit Bulletin* and was created by Johannah Bernstein, Pamela S. Chasek, and Langston James Goree VI. For information, see www.iisd.ca.

102. Raustiala, "States, NGOs and International Environmental Institutions," 730. See also Pamela Chasek, "Environmental Organizations and Multilateral Diplomacy: A Case Study of the *Earth Negotiations Bulletin*," in *Multilateral Diplomacy and the United Nations Today*, ed. James P. Muldoon Jr. et al., 3rd ed. (Boulder, CO: Westview, 2005).

103. Laura H. Kosloff and Mark Trexler, "The Convention on International Trade in Endangered Species: No Carrot, but Where's the Stick?" *Environmental Law Reporter* 17 (July 1987): 10225–10226.

104. "BELC Company GHG Reduction Targets," Center for Climate and Energy Solutions, www.c2es.org/business/belc/climate-energy-strategies/targets.

105. See Gareth Porter, *The United States and the Biodiversity Convention: The Case for Participation* (Washington, DC: Environmental and Energy Study Institute, 1992). The Industrial Biotechnology Association merged with the Association of Biotechnology Companies in 1993 to form the Biotechnology Industry Organization.

106. *International Environment Reporter*, June 2, 1993, 416.

107. For example, in 2012, Swiss Re announced that insured losses came in at $60 billion in 2011, up from $5 billion forty years ago. The Climate Group, "Fostering Discussion on Climate Change Risks at Swiss Re Roundtable in New York," August 23, 2012, www.theclimategroup .org/what-we-do/news-and-blogs/fostering-discussion-on-climate-change-risks-at-swiss -re-roundtable-in-nyc/.

108. M'Gonigle and Zacher, *Pollution, Politics and International Law*, 58–62.

109. S. Res. 98, "A Resolution Expressing the Sense of the Senate Regarding the Conditions for the United States Becoming a Signatory to Any International Agreement on Greenhouse Gas Emissions Under the United Nations Framework Convention on Climate Change," 105th Congress, 1st Session, thomas.loc.gov/cgi-bin/bdquery/z?d105:SE00098. It is widely known as the Byrd-Hagel Resolution.

110. Day, *The Whale War*, 103–107.

111. Laura Eggerton, "Giant Food Companies Control Standards," *Toronto Star*, April 28, 1999.

112. Alon Tal, *Pollution in the Promised Land: An Environmental History of Israel* (Berkeley, CA: University of California Press, 2002), 305.

113. Interview with William Nitze, Alliance to Save Energy, June 20, 1994.

114. Jennifer Clapp, "Transnational Corporate Interests and Global Environmental Governance: Negotiating Rules for Agricultural Biotechnology and Chemicals," *Environmental Politics* 12, no. 4 (2003): 1–23. Prominent industry groups at the negotiations included the Biotechnology Industry Organization (a US-based biotechnology lobby group), BioteCanada, Japan Bioindustry Association, the International Chamber of Commerce, and the International Association of Plant Breeders for the Protection of Plant Varieties.

115. Alan S. Miller and Durwood Zaelke, "The NGO Perspective," *Climate Alert* 7, no. 3 (May–June 1994): 3.

116. *Daily Environment Reporter*, August 27, 1992, B2.

117. Examples include the Ceres Company Network (www.ceres.org/company-network), the Business for Innovative Climate and Energy Policy (www.ceres.org/bicep), and the Business Environmental Leadership Council (www.c2es.org/business/belc/climate-energy-strategies /targets).

118. Robert L. Paarlberg, "Managing Pesticide Use in Developing Countries," in Haas, Keohane, and Levy, *Institutions for the Earth*, 319.

119. See Stephen Schmidheiny, with the Business Council for Sustainable Development, *Changing Course: A Global Business Perspective on Development and the Environment* (Cambridge, MA: MIT Press, 1992).

120. See the World Business Council for Sustainable Development website at www.wbcsd.org.

Chapter 3—The Development of Environmental Regimes: Chemicals, Wastes and Climate Change

1. For discussion by an experienced negotiator on this dilemma, see Richard Benedick, "Perspectives of a Negotiation Practitioner," in *International Environmental Negotiation*, ed. Gunnar Sjöstedt (Newbury Park, CA: Sage, 1993), 240–243.

2. The number of ratifications necessary for a treaty to enter into force is specified in each treaty.

3. For early discussion of decision-making procedures in environmental regimes, see Glenn Wiser and Stephen Porter, *Effective Decision-Making: A Review of Options for Making Decisions to Conserve and Manage Pacific Fish Stocks* (Washington, DC: WWF–US, 1999), www.ciel .org/Publications/effectivedecisionmaking.pdf.

4. Ground-level ozone is a pollutant, a key component of urban smog produced by the interaction in sunlight of chemicals from factory emissions and automobiles, which contributes to respiratory problems and damages plants.

5. United Nations Environment Programme (UNEP), *Environmental Effects of Ozone Depletion and Its Interactions with Climate Change: 2010 Assessment* (Nairobi: UNEP, 2011), details the impacts of ozone depletion. This paragraph closely follows a similar summary in David L. Downie, "The Vienna Convention, Montreal Protocol, and Global Policy to Protect Stratospheric Ozone," in *Chemicals, Environment, Health: A Global Management Perspective*, ed. Philip Wexler et al. (Boca Raton, FL: CRC Press, 2012).

6. Mario Molina and F. Sherwood Rowland, "Stratospheric Sink for Chlorofluoromethanes: Chlorine Atomic Catalyzed Destruction of Ozone," *Nature* 249 (June 28, 1974): 810–812.

7. World Meteorological Organization (WMO) et al., *Scientific Assessment of Stratospheric Ozone: 2010* (Geneva: WMO, 2011), provides comprehensive discussion of the ozone layer and ozone-depleting substances.

8. The history and analysis of the ozone regime presented in this chapter explicitly follows, and builds on, previous writings by David Leonard Downie, including "Understanding International Environmental Regimes: The Origin, Creation and Expansion of the Ozone Regime" (PhD diss., University of North Carolina, Chapel Hill, 1996); "UNEP and the Montreal Protocol: New Roles for International Organizations in Regime Creation and Change," in *International Organizations and Environmental Policy*, ed. Robert V. Bartlett et al. (Westport, CT: Greenwood, 1995); "The Vienna Convention, Montreal Protocol and Global Policy"; and "Stratospheric Ozone Depletion," in *The Routledge Handbook of Global Environmental Politics*, ed. Paul Harris (New York: Routledge, 2013). Several sections in these publications are intentionally very similar.

Other detailed discussions of the development of the issue and the creation and expansion of the ozone regime include Lydia Dotto and Harold Schiff, *The Ozone War* (Garden City, NY: Doubleday, 1978); Sharon Roan, *Ozone Crisis: The 15 Year Evolution of a Sudden Global Emergency* (New York: John Wiley & Sons, 1989); Peter Haas, "Banning Chlorofluorocarbons: Epistemic Community Efforts to Protect Stratospheric Ozone," *International Organization* 46, no. 1 (winter 1992): 187–224; David L. Downie, "Comparative Public Policy of Ozone Layer Protection," *Political Science* 45, no. 2 (December 1993): 186–197; Karen T. Litfin, *Ozone Discourses: Science and Politics in Global Environmental Cooperation* (New York: Columbia University Press, 1994); Richard Benedick, *Ozone Diplomacy: New Directions in Safeguarding the Planet*, 2nd ed. (Cambridge, MA: Harvard University Press, 1998); Stephen Anderson and K. Madhavea Sarma, *Protecting the Ozone Layer: The United Nations History* (London: Earthscan, 2002); Penelope Canan and Nancy Reichman, *Ozone Connections: Expert Networks in Global Environmental Governance* (Sheffield, UK: Greenleaf, 2002); Edward Parson, *Protecting the Ozone Layer: Science and Strategy* (Oxford: Oxford University Press, 2003); and Ozone Secretariat, *Montreal Protocol on Substances That Deplete the Ozone Layer, 2012: A Success in the Making* (Nairobi: UNEP, 2012).

9. See in particular Iwona Rummel-Bulska, "The Protection of the Ozone Layer Under the Global Framework Convention," in *Transboundary Air Pollution*, ed. Cees Flinterman et al. (Dordrecht, Netherlands: Martinus Nijhoff, 1986), 281–296; and Benedick, *Ozone Diplomacy*.

10. For discussion of the early stages of the negotiations, see Downie, "Understanding International Environmental Regimes"; Benedick, *Ozone Diplomacy*; Roan, *Ozone Crisis*; Parson, *Protecting the Ozone Layer*; and Haas, "Banning Chlorofluorocarbons."

11. For analysis of this point, see David L. Downie, "The Power to Destroy: Understanding Stratospheric Ozone Politics as a Common Pool Resource Problem," in *Anarchy and the Environment: The International Relations of Common Pool Resources*, ed. J. Samuel Barkin and George Shambaugh (Albany: State University of New York Press, 1999).

12. Benedick, *Ozone Diplomacy*, stresses US leadership on this point. Benedick led the US delegation to these negotiations.

13. J. Farman et al., "Large Losses of Total Ozone in Antarctica Reveal Seasonal ClO_x/NO_x Interaction," *Nature* 315 (May 16, 1985): 207–210.

14. Disagreements exist in various historical accounts regarding the awareness and use of the satellite data. It is clear, however, that British scientists using ground-based measurements published the first peer-reviewed reports of the ozone hole.

15. For representative discussion, see Downie, "Understanding International Environmental Regimes," ch. 6; Litfin, *Ozone Discourses*, 96–102; Benedick, *Ozone Diplomacy*; and Roan, *Ozone Crisis*, 125–141, 158–188.

16. See, for example, Anderson and Sarma, *Protecting the Ozone Layer*, 93–94, as well as relevant discussions in Benedick, *Ozone Diplomacy*, and Roan, *Ozone Crisis*.

17. For example, *Executive Summary of the Ozone Trends Panel*, Office of Management, Scientific and Technical Information Division, NASA, March 1988.

18. WMO et al., *Scientific Assessment of Stratospheric Ozone: 1989* (Geneva: WMO, 1989).

19. For example, at the first Meeting of the Parties (MOP-1) in 1989, EC members joined eighty nations (including the United States but not Japan or the Soviet Union) to support a nonbinding declaration calling for a complete CFC phaseout by 2000.

20. For the text of the ozone treaties, amendments, and adjustments, as well as official reports from each Meeting of the Parties, visit the Ozone Secretariat's website: ozone.unep.org.

21. Countries with economies in transition (CEITs) include the countries in Eastern Europe formerly aligned with the Soviet Union, as well as Russia, Ukraine, and other countries created when the Soviet Union collapsed, which were transitioning from communist to capitalist economies. The Global Environment Facility (GEF) later took over most of the responsibility for assisting CEITs on ozone issues.

22. The fund has been replenished eight times: $240 million (1991–1993), $455 million (1994–1996), $466 million (1997–1999), $440 million (2000–2002), $474 million (2003–2005), $400.4 million (2006–2008), and $400 million (2009–2011 and 2012–2014). The extra $50 million in the 2012–2014 budget is leftover funds and interest. For these figures and details of the history and operation of the fund, see the Multilateral Fund homepage: www.multilateralfund.org.

23. David Downie's observations and conversations with national delegates during the ozone negotiations in 1995, 1997, and 1999.

24. The tiny amount allowed over the last ten years of the period is known as a "servicing tail" that allows for the continued use and servicing of equipment that uses HCFCs during this period.

25. HCFCs have shorter atmospheric lifetimes, and one HCFC molecule destroys far fewer ozone molecules than one CFC molecule. But ozone destruction by HCFCs takes place sooner.

26. The Implementation Committee Under the Non-compliance Procedure for the Montreal Protocol and the MOP have considered many cases of potential noncompliance, most involving countries with economies in transition, although more developing-country cases are occurring as their controls intensify. Although the regime allows for the application of specified trade sanctions in response to severe cases of intentional noncompliance, the committee and MOP decided that each instance fell below such a threshold and opted for consultation and targeted technical assistance to remove barriers to implementation and, on occasion, the equivalent of a public rebuke to try harder.

27. Brian Gareau, *From Precaution to Profit: Contemporary Challenges to Environmental Protection in the Montreal Protocol* (New Haven, CT: Yale University Press, 2012), provides detailed information on the methyl bromide debates. Information about the issue in this and the next paragraph is based on observations by David Downie and his conversations with Australian, EU, NGO, secretariat, US, and other officials during the ozone negotiations from 1992 to 1997. See also the official meetings of these MOPs (which Downie helped to write), available on the Ozone Secretariat website.

28. "Summary of the Nineteenth Meeting of the Parties to the Montreal Protocol: 17–21 September 2007," *Earth Negotiation Bulletin* 19, no. 60 (September 24, 2007). For other summaries of the HCFC debate and other developments at MOP-19, see *Report of the Nineteenth Meeting of the Parties to the Montreal Protocol on Substances that Deplete the Ozone Layer*, UN Document UNEP/OzL.Pro.19/7, September 21, 2007; Keith Bradsher, "Push to Fix Ozone Layer and Slow Global Warming," *New York Times*, March 15, 2007; and David Ljunggren, "Ozone Deal Hailed as Blow Against Climate Change," Reuters Newswire, September 22, 2007.

29. "Summary of the Nineteenth Meeting."

30. Many delegates still bring paper documents to the meeting, printed from the Internet, but the secretariat does not send paper copies to delegates prior to the meeting, nor does it, in general, print, copy, and circulate in-session paper documents during the meeting.

31. Downie, "Stratospheric Ozone Depletion."

32. For recent examples of this debate, see UNEP, *Report of the Twenty-Third Meeting of the Parties to the Montreal Protocol on Substances That Deplete the Ozone Layer*, UNEP Document

UNEP/OzL.Pro.23/11, December 8, 2011, paragraphs 15–17 and 103–119; UNEP, *Report of the Thirty-Second Meeting of the Open-Ended Working Group of the Parties to the Montreal Protocol on Substances That Deplete the Ozone Layer,* UN Document UNEP/OzL.Pro/WG.1/32/7, August 8, 2012, paragraphs 69–77; UNEP, *Report of the Twenty-Fourth Meeting of the Parties to the Montreal Protocol on Substances That Deplete the Ozone Layer,* UNEP Document UNEP/OzL.Pro .24/10, November 25, 2011; and ENB, "Summary of the Twenty-Fourth Meeting of the Parties to the Montreal Protocol on Substances that Deplete the Ozone Layer," *Earth Negotiations Bulletin* 19, no. 93.

33. UNEP, *Information Provided by Parties in Accordance with Article 7 of the Montreal Protocol on Substances that Deplete the Ozone Layer,* UNEP Document UNEP/OzL.Pro.23/7, September 16, 2011.

34. WMO et al., *Scientific Assessment of Stratospheric Ozone: 2010.*

35. Downie, "Stratospheric Ozone Depletion."

36. United Nations Environment Programme, "Backgrounder: Basic Facts and Data on the Science and Politics of Ozone Protection," press release, September 18, 2008, ozone.unep.org /Events/ozone_day_2008/press_backgrounder.pdf." See similar discussions based on computer simulations in WMO et al., *Scientific Assessment of Stratospheric Ozone: 2010*; and Paul Newman, Paul McKenzie, and Richard McKenzie, "UV Impacts Avoided by the Montreal Protocol," *Photochemical and Photobiological Science* 10, no. 7 (2011): 1152–1160.

37. UNEP, *Environmental Effects of Ozone Depletion and Its Interactions with Climate Change: 2010 Assessment,* 2010; US Environmental Protection Agency (EPA), *Protecting the Ozone Layer Protects Eyesight: A Report on Cataract Incidence in the United States Using the Atmospheric and Health Effects Framework Model* (Washington, DC: EPA, 2010); Arjan van Dijk et al., "Skin Cancer Risks Avoided by the Montreal Protocol: Worldwide Modeling Integrating Coupled Climate-Chemistry Models with a Risk Model for UV," *Photochemistry and Photobiology* 89, no. 1 (January–February 2013): 234–246.

38. For a representative discussion, see Guus Velders et al., "The Importance of the Montreal Protocol in Protecting Climate," *Proceedings of the National Academy of Science* 104, no. 12 (March 20, 2007): 4814–4819.

39. Ibid.

40. Ozone Secretariat, *Key Achievements of the Montreal Protocol to Date* (Nairobi: UNEP, 2012).

41. WMO, "Record Stratospheric Ozone Loss in the Arctic in Spring of 2011," WMO Press Release No. 912, April 5, 2011.

42. Downie, "The Vienna Convention, Montreal Protocol and Global Policy," 255.

43. WMO et al., Executive Summary, *Scientific Assessment of Stratospheric Ozone: 2010.*

44. Downie, "The Vienna Convention, Montreal Protocol and Global Policy," 255.

45. Downie, "Understanding International Environmental Regimes"; Downie, "Stratospheric Ozone Depletion."

46. Ibid.; Downie, "The Power to Destroy."

47. For detailed and sometimes differing analysis of the complex interrelationships between the development of scientific knowledge and policy developments, see, among others, Dotto and Schiff, *The Ozone War*; Downie, "Understanding International Environmental Regimes"; Downie, "Stratospheric Ozone Depletion"; Haas, "Banning Chlorofluorocarbons"; Litfin, *Ozone Discourses*; Benedick, *Ozone Diplomacy*; Anderson and Sarma, *Protecting the Ozone Layer*;

Canan and Reichman, *Ozone Connections*; Parson, *Protecting the Ozone Layer*; and Gareau, *From Precaution to Profit.*

48. Downie, "Stratospheric Ozone Depletion." For detailed and sometimes differing analysis of different aspects of the impact of changing economic interests on the development of ozone policy, see, among others, the works cited in the previous endnote and Kenneth Oye and James Maxwell, "Self-Interest and Environmental Management," *Journal of Theoretical Politics* 64 (1994): 599–630.

49. Ronald Mitchell, "Regime Design Matters: International Oil Pollution and Treaty Compliance," *International Organization* 48, no. 3 (summer 1994): 425–458.

50. For an extended discussion, see Downie, "Understanding International Environmental Regime, See also Downie, "The Vienna Convention, Montreal Protocols and Global Policy."

51. UNEP, *GEO 5: Global Environmental Outlook: Environment for the Future We Want* (Nairobi: UNEP, 2012), 223.

52. General analyses of the international hazardous waste issue and regime include: David Hackett, "An Assessment of the Basel Convention on the Control of Transboundary Movements of Hazardous Wastes and Their Disposal," *American University Journal of International Law and Policy* 5 (winter 1990): 313–322; Mark A. Montgomery, "Travelling Toxic Trash: An Analysis of the 1989 Basel Convention," *Fletcher Forum of World Affairs* 14 (summer 1990): 313–326; Jonathan Krueger, *International Trade and the Basel Convention* (Washington, DC: Brookings Institute, 1999); Katharine Kummer, *International Management of Hazardous Wastes: The Basel Convention and Related Legal Rules* (New York: Oxford University Press, 2000); Kate O'Neill, *Waste Trading Among Rich Nations: Building a New Theory of Environmental Regulation* (Cambridge: MIT Press, 2000); Henrik Selin, *Global Governance of Hazardous Chemicals: Challenges of Multilevel Management* (Cambridge: MIT Press, 2010). Information on hazardous waste and international policy is available from the Basel Convention website: www.basel.int. For information from a prominent NGO working on the waste issue, including links to news articles and reports, see the website of the Basel Action Network: www.ban.org.

53. Carol Annette Petsonk, "The Role of the United Nations Environment Programme (UNEP) in the Development of International Environmental Law," *American University Journal of International Law and Policy* 5 (winter 1990): 374–377; *International Environment Reporter*, April 1989, 159–161.

54. For the text of the convention, reports from the COP and other meetings, official documents, updated lists of signatories and ratifications, and other information on the regime, see the Basel Convention website (www.basel.int). For independent summaries and analyses of the COP meetings, see reports by the *Earth Negotiations Bulletin* at www.iisd.ca/vol20/.

55. See Hackett, "An Assessment of the Basel Convention"; and Montgomery, "Travelling Toxic Trash."

56. *International Environment Reporter*, 159–160.

57. *Greenpeace Waste Trade Update*, no. 3 (July 1989); and *Greenpeace Waste Trade Update*, no. 4 (December 1989).

58. To date, twenty-four African countries are party to the convention, which entered into force in 1998. For updated treaty information, see the African Union's official website: ww.au.int.

59. Only the republics of the former Soviet Union, desperate for foreign exchange and willing to disregard the health and environmental consequences, appeared openly willing to accept significant shipments of hazardous wastes. See Steven Coll, "Free Market Intensifies Waste

Problem," *Washington Post*, March 23, 1994; Tamara Robinson, "Dirty Deals: Hazardous Waste Imports into Russia and Ukraine," *CIS Environmental Watch* (Monterey Institute of International Studies) 7, no. 5 (fall 1993).

60. Greenpeace, *The International Trade in Wastes: A Greenpeace Inventory*, 5th ed. (Washington, DC: Greenpeace, 1990). See also "Chemicals: Shipment to South Africa Draws Enviro Protests," *Greenwire*, February 18, 1994; Michael Satchell, "Deadly Trade in Toxics," *U.S. News and World Report*, March 7, 1994, 64–67.

61. John Cushman Jr., "Clinton Seeks Ban on Export of Most Hazardous Waste," *New York Times*, March 1, 1994; "Basel Convention Partners Consider Ban on Exports of Hazardous Wastes," *International Environment Reporter*, March 22, 1994, A9.

62. Charles Wallace, "Asia Tires of Being the Toxic Waste Dumping Ground for Rest of World," *Los Angeles Times*, March 23, 1994, cited in *Greenwire*, March 23, 1994. For a detailed account of the Geneva meeting, see Jim Puckett and Cathy Fogel, "A Victory for Environment and Justice: The Basel Ban and How It Happened," Basel Action Network, September 1994, www.ban.org/about_basel_ban/a_victory.html.

63. Greenpeace, *The International Trade in Wastes: Database of Known Hazardous Waste Exports from OECD to Non-OECD Countries: 1989–March 1994* (Washington, DC: Greenpeace, 1994). See also Jim Puckett, "The Basel Ban: A Triumph over Business-as-Usual," Basel Action Network, October 1997.

64. A key dispute was interpretation of Article 17(5) of the Basel Convention and its impact on the number of ratifications required for the Ban Amendment to enter into force. Some countries supported the "current time" approach, in which the number of ratifications required for the Ban Amendment to enter into force would be based on the current number of parties to the Basel Convention. Other countries supported the "fixed time" approach, in which the number of ratifications required would be calculated on the basis of the number of parties to the convention when the Ban Amendment was adopted. For more analysis, see "Summary of the Ninth Meeting of the Parties to the Basel Convention: 23–27 June 2008," *Earth Negotiations Bulletin* 20, no. 31 (June 30, 2008). This debate was resolved at COP-10 in 2011.

65. Some of the strongest supporters of the Ban Amendment had hoped COP-9 would resolve the key legal and technical debates obstructing the amendment, issue a strong statement calling for ratification, or even declare the amendment in force. Such outcomes were unrealistic (ibid.).

66. "Summary of the Ninth Meeting."

67. For up-to-date information, see www.basel.int/ratif/protocol.htm.

68. See "Regional Centers," Basel Convention, www.basel.int/centers/centers.html.

69. In February 2007, the company that had leased the tanker, Trafigura, settled with the government for the equivalent of $198 million. As part of the agreement, the Côte d'Ivoire government released three jailed Trafigura executives, dropped criminal charges against the company and its executives, and sealed the investigation results. International Network for Environmental Compliance and Enforcement (INECE), "Côte d'Ivoire Toxic Waste Scandal Triggers Legal Action in 3 Countries," *INECE Newsletter* 14 (April 2007).

70. "Summary of the Ninth Meeting."

71. David L. Downie and Jessica Templeton, "Pesticides and Persistent Organic Pollutants," in *Routledge Handbook of Global Environmental Politics*, ed. Paul Harris (New York: Routledge, 2013).

72. Ibid.

73. "Summary of the Tenth Meeting of the Parties to the Basel Convention: 17–21 October 2011," *Earth Negotiations Bulletin*, 20, no. 37 (October 24, 2011).

74. Ibid.

75. Strategic Approach to International Chemicals Management (SAICM) was initiated at the 1976 International Conference on Chemicals Management. For information, see the SAICM website: www.saicm.org.

76. For official information, see the Synergies website: synergies.pops.int.

77. Downie and Templeton, "Pesticides and Persistent Organic Pollutants."

78. For information on COP-8, see the official report and documents from the meeting, available on the Basel Convention website (www.basel.int). See also "Summary of the Eighth Meeting of the Parties to the Basel Convention: 27 November–1 December 2006," *Earth Negotiations Bulletin* 20, no. 25 (December 4, 2006).

79. United Nations Environment Programme (UNEP), "Urgent Need to Prepare Developing Countries for Surge in E-Wastes," press release, February 22, 2010; UNEP, *Recycling: From E-Waste to Resources* (Nairobi: UNEP, 2009).

80. Ibid.

81. The Nairobi Declaration states that parties will work to promote awareness on e-waste, clean technology, and green design; encourage information exchange from developed to developing countries; improve relevant waste management controls; and prevent and combat illegal traffic of e-wastes.

82. For information on COP-9, see the official report and documents from the meeting, available on the Basel Convention website (www.basel.int). See also "Summary of the Ninth Meeting."

83. UNEP/Basel Convention Press Release, "Basel Convention Launches New Initiative on Computing Equipment," Bali, Indonesia, June 27, 2008. See also relevant documents from COP-9.

84. UNEP, "Urgent Need to Prepare Developing Countries"; UNEP, *Recycling*.

85. David Downie, personal observation and discussion during COP-7. Other officials echoed these remarks at several subsequent meetings of the Basel and Stockholm conventions attended by Downie.

86. Selin, *Global Governance of Hazardous Chemicals*, 40.

87. UNEP, *GEO 5*, 170.

88. Ibid., 174, citing *OECD Factbook: Economic, Environmental and Social Statistics* (Paris: Organization for Economic Cooperation and Development, 2010).

89. UNEP, *GEO 5*, 174.

90. Ibid., citing *OECD Factbook*.

91. Lowell Center for Sustainable Production, *Chemicals Policy in Europe Set New Worldwide Standards for Registration, Education and Authorization of Chemicals (REACH)*, 2003, cited in UNEP, *GEO 5*, 223.

92. EPA, *Guidelines for Carcinogen Risk Assessment*. Document EPA/630/P-03/001F (Washington, DC: EPA, 2005), cited in UNEP, *GEO 5*, 223.

93. Masanori Kuratsune et al., "Epidemiologic Study on Yusho, a Poisoning Caused by Ingestion of Rice Oil Contaminated with a Commercial Brand of Polychlorinated Biphenyls," *Environmental Health Perspectives* 1 (April 1972): 119–128.

94. Thomas R. Dunlap, *DDT: Scientists, Citizens, and Public Policy* (Princeton, NJ: Princeton University Press, 1981); Janna G. Koppe and Jane Keys, "PCBs and the Precautionary Principle,"

in *The Precautionary Principle in the 20th Century: Late Lessons from Early Warnings*, ed. Poul Harremoës et al. (London: Earthscan, 2002), 64–78.

95. The action plan produced at the conference called for improved international efforts to develop and harmonize procedures for assessing and managing hazardous substances and to make more resources available to developing countries for building domestic capacity.

96. Global agreements include the 1972 International Convention on the Prevention of Marine Pollution by Dumping of Wastes and Other Matter (London Convention) and the MARPOL Convention, which includes the 1973 International Convention for the Prevention of Pollution from Ships and its 1978 protocol. Early regional and river agreements include the 1972 Convention for the Prevention of Marine Pollution by Dumping from Ships and Aircraft (Oslo Convention); 1974 Convention for the Prevention of Marine Pollution from Land-Based Sources (Paris Convention); 1974 Convention on the Protection of the Marine Environment of the Baltic Sea Area (Helsinki Convention); 1976 Convention on the Protection of the Rhine Against Chemical Pollution; 1976 Protocol for the Prevention of Pollution of the Mediterranean Sea by Dumping from Ships and Aircraft; and the 1978 Great Lakes Water Quality Agreement.

97. Jonathan Krueger and Henrik Selin, "Governance for Sound Chemicals Management: The Need for a More Comprehensive Global Strategy," *Global Governance* 8 (2002): 323–342.

98. David Victor, "Learning by Doing in the Nonbinding International Regime to Manage Trade in Hazardous Chemicals and Pesticides," in *The Implementation and Effectiveness of International Environmental Commitments: Theory and Practice*, ed. David Victor et al. (Cambridge, MA: MIT Press, 1998), 228.

99. The IOMC includes UNEP, Food and Agriculture Organization, the International Labour Organization, World Health Organization, United Nations Industrial Development Organization, United Nations Institute for Training and Research, and OECD. Other global institutions active on chemicals include the GEF, UNDP, and the World Bank. Regional institutions include the Arctic Council, European Union, Great Lakes Program, Helsinki Commission, North American Agreement on Environmental Cooperation, and the Oslo-Paris Commission for the Protection of the Marine Environment of the North-East Atlantic.

100. For the text of the convention, official documents, reports from the COPs, and other information, see the Rotterdam Convention website: www.pic.int. Analyses of the development and content of the convention include Victor, "Learning by Doing"; Richard Emory Jr., "Probing the Protections in the Rotterdam Convention on Prior Informed Consent," *Colorado Journal of International Environmental Law and Policy* 23 (2001): 47–91; and Selin, *Global Governance of Hazardous Chemicals*.

101. For broader discussions of the science of POPs, see Arnold Schecter, *Dioxins and Health Including Other Persistent Organic Pollutants and Endocrine Disruptors* (Hoboken, NJ: Wiley and Sons, 2012); David Leonard Downie and Terry Fenge, eds., *Northern Lights Against POPs: Combatting Threats in the Arctic* (Montreal: McGill-Queen's University Press, 2003); Joe Thornton, *Pandora's Poison: Chlorine, Health, and a New Environmental Strategy* (Cambridge, MA: MIT Press, 2000); and Theo Colborn, Dianne Dumanoski, and John Peterson Myers, *Our Stolen Future: Are We Threatening Our Fertility, Intelligence, and Survival?—A Scientific Detective Story* (New York: Dutton, 1996).

102. For examples and discussion of these studies, see Downie and Fenge, *Northern Lights Against POPs*; and AMAP (Arctic Monitoring and Assessment Programme), *AMAP Assessment Report: Arctic Pollution Issues* (Oslo: AMAP, 1998).

103. For a discussion of the science and politics of this point, see Downie and Fenge, *Northern Lights Against POPs*.

104. These are personal observations and discussions by David Downie with UNEP chemicals and national government officials during this period and during the first negotiating session in 1998.

105. For official reports and other documents from the negotiations, see "Stockholm Convention Negotiations," Stockholm Convention, 2008, chm.pops.int/Convention/Negotiations/tabid/62/language/en-US/Default.aspx. For detailed secondary-source reports, see "Chemical Management," IISD Linkages, www.iisd.ca/linkages/chemical/index.html.

106. The World Health Organization (WHO) estimated that about 250 million new cases of malaria cases occur each year and nearly 1 million deaths. People living in the poorest countries are the most vulnerable. Malaria is a serious problem especially in Africa, where its effects lead to 20 percent of childhood deaths. An African child has on average between 1.6 and 5.4 episodes of malaria fever each year. And every thirty seconds a child dies from malaria ("10 Facts on Malaria," WHO, April 2012, www.who.int/features/factfiles/malaria/en/index.html). For detailed information and links, see "Health Topics: Malaria," WHO, 2012, www.who.int/topics/malaria/en.

107. The decision by the UNEP Governing Council to initiate the talks included specific mandates to address both issues.

108. Very small amounts of DDT can also be used as an intermediate in the production of the chemical dicoful if no DDT is released into the environment.

109. Aspects of this debate are addressed in Downie and Fenge, *Northern Lights Against POPs*.

110. For a detailed discussion of this process, including the original version of Figure 3.2, see Downie and Fenge, *Northern Lights Against POPs*, 140–142.

111. See in particular paragraphs 7(a) and 9 of Article 8 of the Stockholm Convention.

112. Information and analyses of the POP Review Committee (POPRC) include Jessica Templeton, "Framing Elite Policy Discourse: Scientists and the Stockholm Convention on Persistent Organic Pollutants" (PhD diss., London School of Economics and Political Science, 2011); Downie and Templeton, "Pesticides and Persistent Organic Pollutants"; official POPRC documents and meeting reports, available via the POPRC Secretariat's website (chm.pops.int/Convention/POPsReviewCommittee/Overview/tabid/2806/Default.aspx); and reports on POPRC meetings by the *Earth Negotiations Bulletin*. www.iisd.ca/vol15

113. Opt-in parties include Australia, Canada, China, India, Korea, and Russia. If it ratifies the convention, the United States would likely be an opt-in party. The "opt-in" and "opt-out" options could lead some parties being bound by controls on new substances while others are not. This could deter listing more live substances if some countries believe that doing so will put them at a competitive disadvantage versus opt-in states. Uneven patterns of ratification could also create legal uncertainties with regard to restricting trade in products made with or containing POPs. Downie and Templeton, "Pesticides and Persistent Organic Pollutants."

114. GEF, *Report of the GEF to the Fifth Meeting of the Conference of the Parties to the Stockholm Convention on Persistent Organic Pollutants* (Washington, DC: GEF, 2011). We extrapolated from the figures in that document. Updated figures can be found in GEF documents submitted to more recent biannual reports to the Stockholm Convention COP.

115. Updated information can be found on the Stockholm Convention's website: chm.pops.int.

116. Because the United States had already controlled the dirty dozen, its costs to implement the original treaty would be low. President Bush participated in a Rose Garden ceremony heralding the convention and stating his intention to push for ratification. In the absence of 9/11, it is logical that he would have done so, if for no other reason than to provide his administration with an environmental victory before the 2004 election. It is possible that Barack Obama or a subsequent president will submit the treaty for consideration.

117. David Downie, personal observation and conversations with delegates during Stockholm Convention COPs.

118. For information on the Stockholm Convention and documents and official reports from the COP and POPRC, see the Stockholm Convention's website (chm.pops.int). For third-party daily and summary reports, analyses, and photos, see the relevant issues of the *Earth Negotiations Bulletin* at www.iisd.ca/process/chemical_management.htm#pops.

119. For example, for a particular substance, nominations coming from a developing country might carry more influence with other developing countries or countries in a certain region. Or a government, having considered all factors, may favor nomination but not want to be a lead state in order to avoid, or at least delay, conflict with certain domestic lobbying groups.

120. The five are short-chained chlorinated paraffins, hexabromocyclododecane, chlorinated naphthalenes, hexachlorobutadiene, and pentachlorophenol.

121. "Summary of the Fourth Meeting of the Persistent Organic Pollutants Review Committee of the Stockholm Convention: 13–17 October 2008," *Earth Negotiations Bulletin* 15, no. 161 (October 20, 2008).

122. Ibid.; personal observations by David Downie during these meetings and subsequent COPs.

123. Downie and Templeton, "Pesticides and Persistent Organic Pollutants."

124. For details of the meeting, see background documents and the official meeting report on the Stockholm Convention's website (chm.pops.int) and the daily and summary reports provided by the *Earth Negotiations Bulletin* at www.iisd.ca/chemical/pops/cop4. This section draws heavily on personal observations and notes made by David Downie while attending the meeting, the official report of the meeting, and "Summary of the Fourth Conference of Parties to Stockholm Convention on Persistent Organic Pollutants: 4–8 May 2009," *Earth Negotiations Bulletin* 15, no. 174 (May 11, 2009).

125. David Downie, personal observations during the COP.

126. GEF, *Report of the GEF to the Fifth Meeting*, 4.

127. Ibid.

128. Downie and Templeton, "Pesticides and Persistent Organic Pollutants."

129. "Summary of the Third Meeting of the Stockholm Convention on Persistent Organic Pollutants: 30 April–4 May 2007," *Earth Negotiations Bulletin* 15, no. 154 (May 7, 2007).

130. Personal communication between David Downie and James Willis. Related to the synergies initiative in theme, but springing from a different legal and operational basis, is SAICM, which is discussed in the section on hazardous wastes.

131. WHO and UNEP, *State of the Science of Endocrine Disrupting Chemicals* (Geneva: WHO and UNEP, 2013); UNEP, *GEO 5*, 223.

132. US policy on toxic chemicals is generally strong, and the United States supports the convention financially. However, it is possible that over time the regime could move beyond US chemical policy, potentially creating a market haven for certain substances.

133. Downie and Templeton, "Pesticides and Persistent Organic Pollutants."

134. For an overview of the science of climate change, see IPCC, "Summary for Policy-makers," in *Climate Change 2007: The Physical Science Basis*, Contribution of Working Group I to the Fourth Assessment Report of the Intergovernmental Panel on Climate Change, ed. S. Solomon et al. (Cambridge: Cambridge University Press, 2007). For a broader overview of the issue, approved by government representatives, see IPCC, *Climate Change 2007: Synthesis Report*, Contribution of Working Groups I, II and III to the Fourth Assessment Report of the Intergovernmental Panel on Climate Change, ed. Core Writing Team, R. K. Pachauri, and A. Reisinger (Cambridge: Cambridge University Press, 2007).

135. For overview discussions of observed and potential climate-change impacts, see IPCC, *Climate Change 2007: Adaptation and Vulnerabilities*, Contribution of Working Group II to the Fourth Assessment Report of the Intergovernmental Panel on Climate Change, ed. M. L. Parry et al. (Cambridge: Cambridge University Press, 2007); C. B. Field et al., eds., *Managing the Risks of Extreme Events and Disasters to Advance Climate Change Adaptation: A Special Report of Working Groups I and II of the Intergovernmental Panel on Climate Change* (Cambridge: Cambridge University Press, 2012); Trevor Letcher, ed., *Climate Change: Observed Impacts on Planet Earth* (Amsterdam: Elsevier, 2009).

136. John Vidal, "Large Rise in CO_2 Emissions Sounds Climate Change Alarm," *Guardian* (London), March 8, 2013.

137. Svante Arrhenius, "On the Influence of Carbonic Acid in the Air upon the Temperature of the Ground," *Philosophical Magazine* 41 (1896): 237–276.

138. G. S. Callendar, "The Artificial Production of Carbon Dioxide and Its Influence on Climate," *Quarterly Journal of the Royal Meteorological Society* 64 (1938): 223–240.

139. Richard Houghton and George Woodwell, "Global Climatic Change," *Scientific American* 260 (April 1989): 42–43.

140. Lamont Hempel and Matthias Kaelberer, "The Changing Climate in Greenhouse Policy: Obstacles to International Cooperation in Agenda Setting and Policy Formulation" (unpublished paper, April 1990), 6; Daniel Bodansky, "The United Nations Framework Convention on Climate Change: A Commentary," *Yale Journal of International Law* 18, no. 2 (summer 1993): 461.

141. The IPCC is organized into three working groups: Working Group I on the climate system, Working Group II on impacts and response options, and Working Group III on economic and social dimensions. For more information, see the IPCC website: www.ipcc.ch.

142. See Matthew Paterson, *Global Warming and Global Politics* (London: Routledge, 1996), 77–82.

143. Japan subsequently backtracked by proposing a process of "pledge and review" in place of binding commitments. Individual countries would set for themselves appropriate targets that would be publicly reviewed. Most EC member states and NGOs opposed the idea. Bodansky, "The United Nations Framework Convention on Climate Change," 486.

144. For country GHG emissions, contributions to total emissions, and rankings at the time of the negotiations, see World Resources Institute, *World Resources, 1992–1993* (New York: Oxford University Press, 1992), 205–213, 345–355. For an early discussion of different methods of greenhouse gas accounting, see Peter M. Morrisette and Andrew Plantinga, "The Global Warming Issue: Viewpoints of Different Countries," *Resources* 103 (spring 1991): 2–6.

145. *Earth Summit Update* 9 (May 1992): 1; *Wall Street Journal*, May 22, 1992, 1.

146. "Status of Ratification of the Convention," UN Framework Convention on Climate Change, 2012, unfccc.int/essential_background/convention/status_of_ratification/items/2631.php.

147. See the Climate Secretariat website (unfccc.int) for text of the Kyoto Protocol. For a contemporary analysis, see Herman Ott, "The Kyoto Protocol: Unfinished Business," *Environment* 40, no. 6 (1998): 16ff.; Clare Breidenrich et al., "The Kyoto Protocol to the United Nations Framework Convention on Climate Change," *American Journal of International Law* 92, no. 2 (1998): 315.

148. See "The Mechanisms Under the Kyoto Protocol: Joint Implementation, the Clean Development Mechanism and Emissions Trading," UNFCCC, accessed October 19, 2012, unfccc.int/kyoto_protocol/mechanisms/items/1673.php.

149. For information on COP-7, see "Summary of the Seventh Conference of the Parties to the UN Framework Convention on Climate Change: 29 October–10 November 2001," *Earth Negotiations Bulletin* 12, no. 189 (November 12, 2001).

150. International Centre for Trade and Sustainable Development, "EU Attacks Bush's U-Turn on Climate Change," *Bridges Weekly Trade News Digest* 5, no. 11 (March 27, 2001), ictsd .org/i/news/bridgesweekly/81784.

151. See, for example, Alex Rodriguez, "Russian Move on Global Warming Treaty Sets Stage for Enactment," *Chicago Tribune*, October 1, 2004.

152. By tradition, conventions usually have "Conferences of the Parties," or COPs. Protocols usually have "Meetings of the Parties," or MOPs. The meetings serve the same function: to bring all parties together to conduct treaty business as specified by the treaty.

153. UNFCCC Secretariat, "Decisions Adopted by the Conference of the Parties," in *Report of the Conference of the Parties on Its Eleventh Session*, Montreal, November 28–December 10, 2005, Addendum, Part Two (FCCC/CP/2005/5/Add.1), Decision 1/CP.11.

154. UNFCCC Secretariat, "Decisions Adopted by the Conference of the Parties Serving as the Meeting of the Parties to the Kyoto Protocol," in *Report of the Conference of the Parties Serving as the Meeting of the Parties to the Kyoto Protocol on its First Session*, Montreal, November 28–December 10, 2005, Addendum, Part Two (FCCC/KP/CMP/2005/8/Add.1), Decision 1 /CMP.1.

155. The Climate Group, *The Copenhagen Climate Conference: A Climate Group Assessment*, January 2010, www.theclimategroup.org/_assets/files/TCG-Copenhagen-Assessment-Report -Jan10.pdf.

156. Daniel Bodansky, "The International Climate Change Regime: The Road from Copenhagen," Viewpoints, Harvard Project on International Climate Agreements, October 2010, belfercenter.ksg.harvard.edu/publication/20437/international_climate_change_regime.html ?breadcrumb=%2Fproject%2F56%2Fharvard_project_on_climate_agreements%3Fpage_id%3D 234.

157. Ibid.

158. "Summary of the Copenhagen Climate Change Conference: 7–19 December 2009," *Earth Negotiations Bulletin* 12, no. 459 (December 22, 2009): 1.

159. "Summary of the Cancun Climate Change Conference: 29 November-11 December 2010," *Earth Negotiations Bulletin* 12, no. 498 (December 13, 2010): 28.

160. UNFCCC, *Report of the Conference of the Parties on Its Fifteenth Session, Held in Copenhagen from 7 to 19 December 2009*, FCCC/CP/2009/11/Add.1, March 30, 2010.

161. Bodansky, "The International Climate Change Regime," 3.

162. Climate Focus, *CP16/CMP6: Cancun Agreements: Summary and Analysis*, January 10, 2011, www.climatefocus.com/documents/cp16cmp6_cancun_agreements; UNFCCC, "The Cancun Agreements," accessed October 20, 2012, cancun.unfccc.int.

163. Bolivian Ministry of Foreign Affairs, "Bolivia Decries Adoption of Copenhagen Accord II Without Consensus," press briefing, December 11, 2011, pwccc.files.wordpress.com/2010/12/press-release-history-will-be-the-judge.pdf.

164. "Summary of the Cancun Climate Change Conference: 29 November–11 December 2010," *Earth Negotiations Bulletin* 12, no. 498 (December 13, 2010): 1.

165. Ibid.

166. "Summary of the Durban Climate Change Conference: 28 November–11 December 2011," *Earth Negotiations Bulletin* 12, no. 534 (December 13, 2011): 1.

167. See UNFCCC, *Report of the Conference of the Parties on Its Seventeenth Session, Held in Durban from 28 November to 11 December 2011, Addendum, Part Two: Action Taken by the Conference of the Parties at Its Seventeenth Session*, FCCC/CP/2011/9/Add.1, March 15, 2012.

168. UNFCCC, "UN Climate Change Conference in Doha Kicks Off with Calls to Implement Agreed Decisions, Stick to Agreed Tasks and Timetable," press release, Doha, November 26, 2012, unfccc.int/files/press/press_releases_advisories/application/pdf/pr20102611_cop18_open.pdf.

169. Greenpeace, "Talks Fail to Meet Pace of Climate Change," press release, Doha, December 9, 2012, www.greenpeace.org/international/en/press/releases/Talks-fail-to-meet-pace-of-climate-change-Greenpeace.

170. "What Doha Did," *Economist* (International Edition), December 15, 2012.

171. Connie Hedegaard, "Why the Doha Climate Conference Was a Success," *Guardian* (London), December 14, 2012.

Chapter 4—The Development of Environmental Regimes: Natural Resources, Species, and Habitats

1. Oran R. Young, *International Environmental Governance: Protecting the Environment in a Stateless Society* (Ithaca, NY: Cornell University Press, 1994), 21.

2. Ibid., 21–22.

3. Ibid., 23.

4. Millennium Ecosystem Assessment, *Ecosystems and Human Well-Being: Synthesis Report* (Washington, DC: Island, 2005).

5. National sovereignty over natural resources implies that a government has control over its resources, such as oil, minerals, and timber. Common heritage implies that no one can be excluded from using natural resources, except by lack of economic and technological capacity; conversely, everyone has a right to benefit from the exploitation of the resources. This concept has been used for fisheries and mineral resources found in the high seas and more recently in the debate about genetic resources. See G. Kristin Rosendal, "The Convention on Biological Diversity: A Viable Instrument for Conservation and Sustainable Use," in *Green Globe Yearbook of International Cooperation on Environment and Development 1995*, ed. Helge Ole Bergesen et al. (Oxford: Oxford University Press, 1995), 69–81.

6. United Nations Environment Programme (UNEP), *Report of the Ad Hoc Working Group on the Work of Its Second Session in Preparation for a Legal Instrument on Biological Diversity of the Planet*, UNEP/Bio.Div2/3, February 23, 1990, 7.

7. Personal communication from a member of the US delegation to the biodiversity convention negotiations, October 21, 1994. See also Fiona McConnell, *The Biodiversity Convention: A Negotiating History* (London: Kluwer Law International, 1996).

8. For a detailed discussion, see Robert Blomquist, "Ratification Resisted: Understanding America's Response to the Convention on Biological Diversity, 1989–2002," *Golden Gate University Law Review* 32, no. 4 (2002): 493–586.

9. A coalition of nongovernmental organizations (NGOs) with major interests in biodiversity worked with several companies to pressure the Clinton administration to sign the treaty. See US Senate, *Convention on Biological Diversity: Message from the President of the United States, November 20, 1993*, Treaty Document 103-120 (Washington, DC: US Government Printing Office, 1993).

10. The Senate Foreign Relations Committee approved the ratification of the Convention on Biological Diversity by a vote of sixteen to three on June 29, 1994. However, in a dramatic move in September 1994, CBD ratification was removed from the Senate's agenda, and since then the ratification issue has never come up for a vote.

11. For updated information on the status of signatures and ratifications, see the official Convention on Biological Diversity website at www.cbd.int.

12. Personal communication from a member of the US delegation to the biodiversity convention negotiations, April 12, 1994.

13. "Thematic Programmes and Cross-Cutting Issues," Convention on Biological Diversity, accessed September 8, 2012, www.cbd.int/programmes.

14. Elisa Morgera and Elsa Tsioumani, "Yesterday, Today, and Tomorrow: Looking Afresh at the Convention on Biological Diversity," *Yearbook of International Environmental Law* 21, no. 1 (2010): 3–40.

15. Ibid., 8. As noted by Morgera and Tsioumani in footnote 42, "CBD parties have long complained of this (see, for instance, Decision X/12 on Ways and Means to Improve the Effectiveness of the Subsidiary Body on Scientific, Technical and Technological Advice, Doc. CBD UNEP/CBD/COP/10/27 (2010), para. 6, which reads: '[The COP] requests the Executive Secretary to streamline the texts of suggested draft recommendations for submission to the Subsidiary Body and encourages Parties to make these recommendations as short as possible so that the actions required are clear'). Note that the Subsidiary Body on Scientific, Technical, and Technological Advice's (SBSTTA) recommendations form the basis of the majority of the CBD COP decisions and that this problematic drafting practice is reflected across all of the other sub-processes that contribute to formulating the rest of the CBD COP decisions."

16. Ibid.

17. See Convention on Biological Diversity, COP Decision VI/26 on Strategic Plan for the Convention on Biological Diversity, Doc. CBD UNEP/CBD/COP/6/20 (2002) at para. 11; World Summit on Sustainable Development, Johannesburg Plan of Implementation, UN Doc. A/CONF.199/20, September 4, 2002, Resolution 2, Annex, para. 44; and United Nations General Assembly, 2005 World Summit Outcome, Resolution 60/1, October 24, 2005, para. 56.

18. CBD and UN Environment Programme–World Conservation Monitoring Centre, *Global Biodiversity Outlook* (Montreal, Canada: Secretariat of the Convention on Biological Diversity, 2010), gbo3.cbd.int.

19. Ibid., and Morgera and Tsioumani, "Yesterday, Today, and Tomorrow."

20. For analysis of the WTO ruling, see ITCSD, "A Preliminary Analysis of the WTO Biotech Ruling," *Bridges* 10, no. 7 (November 2006), ictsd.net/i/news/bridges/11680.

21. Nicholas Kalaitzandonakes, "Cartagena Protocol: A New Trade Barrier?" *Regulation* 29, no. 2 (Summer 2006): 18–25, www.cato.org/pubs/regulation/regv29n2/v29n1–4.pdf.

22. For a summary of the negotiations and a synopsis of the protocol, see "Report of the Resumed Session of the Extraordinary Meeting of the Conference of the Parties for the Adoption of the Protocol on Biodiversity to the Convention on Biological Diversity: 24–28 January 2000," *Earth Negotiations Bulletin* 9, no. 137 (January 31, 2000), www.iisd.ca/biodiv/excop.

23. *Nagoya–Kuala Lumpur Supplementary Protocol on Liability and Redress to the Cartagena Protocol on Biosafety* (Montreal: Secretariat of the Convention on Biological Diversity, 2011), bch.cbd.int/protocol/NKL_text.shtml.

24. "Summary of the Third Meeting of the Parties to the Cartagena Protocol on Biosafety: 13–17 March 2006," *Earth Negotiations Bulletin* 9, no. 351 (March 20, 2006), www.iisd.ca/download/pdf/enb09351e.pdf.

25. Ibid. Exporting parties' preexisting bilateral trade agreements with large nonparties, such as the United States, were widely acknowledged as one of the reasons why some Latin American parties emerged as the ones most likely to resist consensus.

26. Fifth meeting of the Conference of the Parties serving as the meeting of the Parties to the Cartagena Protocol on Biosafety (COP-MOP-5), "Handling, Transport, Packaging and Identification of Living Modified Organisms: Paragraph 2(a) of Article 18," Decision BS-V/8 (2010), bch.cbd.int/protocol/decisions/?decisionID=12321.

27. "Summary of the Fifth Meeting of the Parties to the Cartagena Protocol on Biosafety: 11–15 October 2010," *Earth Negotiations Bulletin* 9, no. 533 (October 18, 2010), www.iisd.ca/download/pdf/enb09533e.pdf.

28. For more information, see Rhett Butler, "Anti-HIV Drug from Rainforest Almost Lost Before Its Discovery," Mongabay.com, September 13, 2005.

29. See Kabir Bavikatte, Harry Jonas, and Johanna von Braun, "Shifting Sands of ABS Best Practice: Hoodia from the Community Perspective," United Nations University Institute of Advanced Studies, March 31, 2009, www.unutki.org/default.php?doc_id=137.

30. Article 1 of the CBD states, "The objectives of this Convention, to be pursued in accordance with its relevant provisions, are the conservation of biological diversity, the sustainable use of its components and the fair and equitable sharing of the benefits arising out of the utilization of genetic resources, including by appropriate access to genetic resources and by appropriate transfer of relevant technologies, taking into account all rights over those resources and to technologies, and by appropriate funding."

31. Convention on Biological Diversity, "Access and Benefit-Sharing: Background," www.cbd.int/abs/background.

32. "Summary of the Tenth Conference of the Parties to the Convention on Biological Diversity: 18–29 October 2010," *Earth Negotiations Bulletin* 9, no. 544 (November 1, 2010), www.iisd.ca/download/pdf/enb09544e.pdf.

33. Ibid., 27.

34. Sachiko Morita, "After 18 Years, a Protocol on Access to Genetic Resources Is Adopted at COP 10," World Bank, December 2010, go.worldbank.org/KWVLRFHC10.

35. Ibid.

36. Convention on Biological Diversity (CBD), *Nagoya Protocol Access to Genetic Resources and the Fair and Equitable Sharing of Benefits Arising from Their Utilization*, Article 3 (Montreal, Canada: CBD, 2010), www.cbd.int/abs/doc/protocol/nagoya-protocol-en.pdf.

37. Ibid.

38. CBD, *Nagoya Protocol Access to Genetic Resources*, Article 3.

39. Morita, "After 18 Years, a Protocol on Access."

40. CBD, *Nagoya Protocol Access to Genetic Resources*.

41. "Summary of the Tenth Conference," 27.

42. Ibid.

43. Convention on Biological Diversity, "Strategic Plan for Biodiversity 2011–2020, Including Aichi Biodiversity Targets," Decision X/2 (October 29, 2010), www.cbd.int/decision/cop /?id=12268.

44. Morgera and Tsioumani, "Yesterday, Today, and Tomorrow."

45. A revised version of the 1973 Endangered Species Conservation Act banned whaling in US waters or by US citizens, outlawed the import of whale products, and required that the United States initiate bilateral and multilateral negotiations on an agreement to protect and conserve whales.

46. The effort to build an IWC majority to ban whaling was stymied in the latter half of the 1970s because otherwise antiwhaling states such as Canada and Latin American states such as Mexico were primarily concerned about protecting rights to regulate economic activities within their own two-hundred-mile economic zones and opposed the jurisdiction of an international body over whaling.

47. Teresa Watanabe, "Japan Is Set for a Whale of a Fight," *Los Angeles Times*, April 20, 1993.

48. Paul Brown, "Playing Football with the Whales," *Guardian* (London), May 1, 1993. The Caribbean states cooperating with Japan were Grenada, St. Lucia, St. Kitts and Nevis, Antigua and Barbuda, Dominica, and St. Vincent.

49. "During Clinton's Watch Global Whaling Triples," Greenpeace, May 20, 1997, archive.greenpeace.org/majordomo/index-press-releases/1997/msg00126.html.

50. IWC, "Catches Under Objection Since 1985," accessed August 21, 2012, http://iwc office.org/table_objection.

51. Ibid.

52. "Japan Ends Whale Hunt with Less than a Third of Its Target Catch," *Telegraph* (London), March 9, 2012.

53. For example, see Dennis Normile, "Japan's Whaling Program Carries Heavy Baggage," *Science* 289, no. 5488 (September 29, 2000): 2264–2265.

54. Dan Goodman, "The 'Future of the IWC': Why the Initiative to Save the International Whaling Commission Failed," *Journal of International Wildlife Law & Policy* 14, no. 1 (2011): 64.

55. Since 2008, EU member countries of the IWC have been bound by a "common position," requiring that they all vote and speak in the same manner at meetings of the IWC (Denmark has an exception related to Greenland). IWC, *Revised Chair's Report of the 60th Annual Meeting* 6 (2008). This means that some of the EU countries that formerly expressed some support for sustainable whaling (Sweden, Finland, and Denmark) can no longer do so. As cited in Goodman, "The 'Future of the IWC,'" 66.

56. Goodman, "The 'Future of the IWC,'" 66.

57. Fisheries Agency head Masayuki Komatsu in an Australian Broadcasting Corporation radio interview. See "Japan 'Buys' Pro-Whaling Votes," CNN.com, July 18, 2001, edition.cnn .com/2001/TECH/science/07/18/japan.whale/index.html, and "Japan Denies Aid-for-Whaling Report," CNN.com, July 18, 2001, edition.cnn.com/2001/WORLD/asiapcf/east/07/19/japan .whaling. See also Andrew R. Miller and Nives Dolšak, "Issue Linkages in International Environmental Policy: The International Whaling Commission and Japanese Development Aid," *Global Environmental Politics* 7, no. 1 (February 2007): 69–96.

58. International Convention for the Regulation of Whaling, December 2, 1946, www.iwc office.org/cache/downloads/1r2jdhu5xtuswws0ocw04wgcw/convention.pdf.

59. Goodman, "The 'Future of the IWC'", 65. International Whaling Commission, "Resolution 2006-1: St. Kitts and Nevis Declaration," Fifty-Eighth Annual Meeting, St. Kitts and Nevis, June 16–20, 2006, www.iwcoffice.org/_documents/commission/IWC58docs/Resolution2006-1.pdf. The following countries sponsored the declaration: St. Kitts and Nevis, Antigua and Barbuda, Benin, Cambodia, Cameroon, Côte d'Ivoire, Dominica, Gabon, Gambia, Grenada, Republic of Guinea, Iceland, Japan, Kiribati, Mali, Republic of the Marshall Islands, Mauritania, Mongolia, Morocco, Nauru, Nicaragua, Norway, Republic of Palau, Russian Federation, St. Lucia, St. Vincent and the Grenadines, Solomon Islands, Suriname, Togo, and Tuvalu.

60. Calestous Juma, a Kenyan national, was professor of the practice of international development and director of the Science, Technology, and Globalization Project at Harvard University's Kennedy School. A former executive secretary of the UN Convention on Biological Diversity and founding director of the African Centre for Technology Studies in Nairobi, he served as chancellor of the University of Guyana. Ambassador Raúl Estrada-Oyuela had been a major player, in particular, with climate-change negotiations and the Kyoto Protocol and its implementation, chairing sessions to finalize the negotiations on the Kyoto Protocol. Ambassador Alvaro de Soto concluded twenty-five years' service at the United Nations, where he was deeply involved in a range of peace negotiations, his last role being the UN special coordinator for the Middle East Peace Process. *Chair's Report of the Intersessional Meeting on the Future of IWC, Renaissance London Heathrow Hotel, UK, 6–8 March 2008*, International Whaling Commission, iwcoffice.org/index.php?cID=intersession08.

61. Media release by William Hogarth, chair of the International Whaling Commission, Rome, March 11, 2009, iwcoffice.org/index.php?cID=33&cType=document.

62. IWC, *Annual Report of the International Whaling Commission 2010* (Cambridge, UK: IWC, 2011), 6, iwcoffice.org/cache/downloads/1anxqeu1b6ysk0wk4gs4ow0k4/AnnualReport 2010.pdf.

63. Richard Black, "Whaling 'Peace Deal' Falls Apart," BBC News, June 23, 2010.

64. IWC, *Annual Report 2010*, 7.

65. See IWC, "Resolution to Maintain Progress at the IWC," document IWC/63/7rev, January 30, 2012, www.iwcoffice.org/index.php?cID=644&cType=document.

66. IWC, *Annual Report of the International Whaling Commission 2011* (Cambridge, UK: IWC, 2012), 7, iwcoffice.org/cache/downloads/2poira6w2vaco8w008008ks4c/AnnualReport2011.pdf.

67. Richard Black, "Call for UN Debate Rejected as Whaling Talks End," BBC News, July 6, 2012.

68. Ibid.

69. Ronald B. Mitchell, "Discourse and Sovereignty: Interests, Science, and Morality in the Regulation of Whaling," *Global Governance* 4 (1998): 277.

70. Ibid.

71. Rebecca Goldman, "Notes from the IWC/60—Will Comity Save the Whales?" *Whales Alive* 17, no. 3 (July 2008): 3, csiwhalesalive.org/csi2008_07.pdf.

72. Detailed and updated information on the Convention on International Trade of Endangered Species (CITES), including its history, operation, species covered, current parties, and other issues, can be found on the regime's official website: www.cites.org.

73. Ed Stoddard, "CITES Does Not Follow Standard U.N. Divisions," Environmental News Network, October 14, 2004, www.enn.com/top_stories/article/169.

74. For updated lists and other information concerning the species listed in each appendix, see www.cites.org.

75. Suzanne Sharrock, *A Guide to the GSPC: All the Targets, Objectives and Facts* (Richmond, UK: Botanic Gardens Conservation International, 2012), 25, www.plants2020.net/files/Plants 2020/popular_guide/englishguide.pdf.

76. Ibid, 27.

77. Liana Sun Wyler and Pervaze A. Sheikh, *International Illegal Trade in Wildlife: Threats and U.S. Policy* (Washington, DC: Congressional Research Service, March 3, 2008), 1, fpc.state.gov/documents/organization/102621.pdf.

78. See, e.g., Greg Warchol, Linda Zupan, and Willie Clack, "Transnational Criminality: An Analysis of the Illegal Wildlife Market in Southern Africa," *International Criminal Justice Review* 13, no. 1 (2003): 7; Jolene Lin, "Tackling Southeast Asia's Illegal Wildlife Trade," *Singapore Year Book of International Law and Contributors* 9 (2005): 198; and Gavin Hayman and Duncan Brack, "International Environmental Crime: The Nature and Control of Environmental Black Markets," paper prepared for the Royal Institute of International Affairs, London, May 2002, 114, ec.europa.eu/environment/docum/pdf/02544_environmental_crime_workshop.pdf.

79. Wyler and Sheikh, *International Illegal Trade in Wildlife*, 7.

80. Ibid., 8.

81. International Fund for Animal Welfare, *Killing with Keystrokes: An Investigation of the Illegal Wildlife Trade on the World Wide Web* (Yarmouth Port, MA: IFAW, 2008), 4, www.ifaw.org/Publications/Program_Publications/Wildlife_Trade/Campaign_Scientific_Publications/asset_upload_file848_49629.pdf.

82. See Sarah Fitzgerald, *International Wildlife Trade: Whose Business Is It?* (Washington, DC: WWF, 1989), 3–8, 13–14.

83. David Harland, "Jumping on the 'Ban' Wagon: Efforts to Save the African Elephant," *Fletcher Forum on World Affairs* 14 (summer 1990): 284–300.

84. "CITES 1989: The African Elephant and More," *TRAFFIC Dispatches* 9 (December 1989): 1–3.

85. See World Resources Institute, *World Resources 1990–1991* (New York: Oxford University Press, 1990), 135.

86. "U.S. Ivory Market Collapses After Import Ban," *New York Times*, June 5, 1990, C2.; Raymond Bonner, *At the Hand of Man: Peril and Hope for Africa's Wildlife* (New York: Vintage Books, 1994), 157.

87. In each case the proposals were withdrawn prior to a formal vote. WWF, "The Challenge of African Elephant Conservation," *Conservation Issues*, April 1997.

88. "CITES and the African Elephants: The Decisions and the Next Steps Explained," *TRAFFIC Dispatches* (April 1998): 5–6.

89. CITES, "Verification of Compliance with the Precautionary Undertakings for the Sale and Shipment of Raw Ivory," Doc. SC.42.10.2.1, Forty-Second Meeting of the Standing Committee, Lisbon, Portugal, September 28–October 1, 1999.

90. "Summary of the Thirteenth Conference of the Parties to the Convention on International Trade in Endangered Species of Wild Fauna and Flora: 2–14 October 2004," *Earth Negotiations Bulletin*, 21, no. 45 (October 18, 2004): 16, www.iisd.ca/download/pdf/enb2145e.pdf.

91. Julie Gray, *TRAFFIC Report of the 14th Meeting of the Conference of the Parties to CITES*, TRAFFIC, 2007, www.traffic.org/cop-papers.

92. "Summary of the Fourteenth Conference of the Parties to the Convention on International Trade in Endangered Species of Wild Fauna and Flora: 3–15 June 2007," *Earth Negotiations Bulletin* 21, no. 61 (June 18, 2007): 21, www.iisd.ca/download/pdf/enb2161e.pdf.

93. CITES, "Ivory Sales Get the Go-Ahead," CITES, June 2, 2007, www.cites.org/eng/news /press/2007/070602_ivory.shtml.

94. CITES, *Report on the One-Off Ivory Sale in Southern African Countries*, SC58 Doc. 36.3, Fifty-Eighth Meeting of the Standing Committee, Geneva, Switzerland, July 6–10, 2009, www.cites.org/eng/com/SC/58/E58–36–3.pdf.

95. CITES, *Elephant Conservation, Illegal Killing and Ivory Trade*, SC62 Doc. 46.1 (Rev. 1), 2012, cites.org/eng/com/SC/62/E62–46–01.pdf.

96. Michael Casey, "Ivory Ban Wins Vote at U.N. Wildlife Convention," Associated Press (March 23, 2010).

97. Jeffrey Gettleman, "In Gabon, Lure of Ivory Is Hard for Many to Resist," *New York Times*, December 27, 2012, A8.

98. "Summary of the Sixteenth Meeting of the Conference of the Parties to the Convention on International Trade in Endangered Species of Wild Fauna and Flora: 3–14 March 2013," *Earth Negotiations Bulletin* 21, no. 83 (March 18, 2013): 26, www.iisd.ca/download/pdf /enb2183e.pdf; CITES Secretariat, "CITES Conference Takes Decisive Action to Halt Decline of Tropical Timber, Sharks, Manta Rays and a Wide Range of Other Plants and Animals," press release, Bangkok, Thailand, March 14, 2013, www.cites.org/eng/news/pr/2013/20130314 _cop16.php.

99. Food and Agriculture Organization of the United Nations (FAO), *Review of the State of World Marine Fishery Resources*, FAO Fisheries and Aquaculture Technical Paper No. 569 (Rome: FAO, 2011), 13, www.fao.org/docrep/015/i2389e/i2389e.pdf.

100. FAO, *The State of World Fisheries and Aquaculture* (Rome: FAO, 2012), 11.

101. See Gareth Porter, *Estimating Overcapacity in the Global Fishing Fleet* (Washington, DC: WWF, 1998).

102. Its official title is the United Nations Agreement for the Implementation of the Provisions of the United Nations Convention on the Law of the Sea of 10 December 1982 Relating to the Conservation and Management of Straddling Fish Stocks and Highly Migratory Fish Stocks.

103. According to European law, the European Commission, on behalf of the EU, negotiates fisheries agreements with third countries.

104. See, e.g., Commission of the European Communities, "Fishing on the High Seas: A Community Approach," Communication from the Commission to the Council and the European Parliament, SEC (92) 565, April 2, 1992, 5.

105. On Canadian mismanagement, see Raymond Rogers, *The Oceans Are Emptying: Fish Wars and Sustainability* (Montreal: Black Rose Books, 1995), 96–147; on EU allocations and Spanish and Portuguese catches, see Senate Standing Committee on Fisheries and Oceans, *Report on Straddling Fish Stocks in the Northwest Atlantic*, 37th Parliament of Canada, 2nd Session, June 2003, www.parl.gc.ca/Content/SEN/Committee/372/fish/rep/rep05jun03-e.pdf.

106. "Canada Hits EU's Atlantic Overfishing," *Washington Times*, February 19, 1995, A11.

107. Marvin Soroos, "The Turbot War: Resolution of an International Fishery Dispute," in *Conflict and the Environment*, ed. Nils Petter Gleditsch (Dordrecht, Netherlands: Kluwer Academic, 1997), 248.

108. "Summary of the Fifth Substantive Session of the UN Conference on Straddling Fish Stocks and Highly Migratory Fish Stocks: 24 July–4 August 1995," *Earth Negotiations Bulletin* 7, no. 54 (August 7, 1995), www.iisd.ca/vol07/0754000e.html.

109. To date there are twelve technical guidelines relevant to data in fisheries management: (1) fisheries operations, 1996; (2) precautionary approach to capture fisheries and species introductions, 1996; (3) integration of fisheries into coastal-area management, 1996; (4) fisheries management, 1997; (5) aquaculture development, 1997; (6) inland fisheries, 1997; (7) responsible fish utilization, 1998; (8) indicators for sustainable development of marine capture fisheries, 1999; (9) implementation of the International Plan of Action to deter, prevent, and eliminate illegal, unreported, and unregulated fishing, 2002; (10) increasing the contribution of small-scale fisheries to poverty alleviation and food security, 2005; (11) responsible fish trade, 2009; and (12) information and knowledge sharing, 2009. For more information and updates, see Fisheries and Aquaculture Department, "Technical Guidelines for Responsible Fisheries," FAO, accessed September 20, 2012, www.fao.org/fishery/publications/technical-guidelines/en.

110. The other international plans of action are the 1999 International Plan of Action for Reducing Incidental Catch of Seabirds in Longline Fisheries and the 1999 International Plan of Action for the Conservation and Management of Sharks. For more details, see FAO Fisheries and Aquaculture Department, Activities—Introduction, www.fao.org/fishery/activities/en.

111. "Summary of the UN Fish Stocks Agreement Review Conference: 22–26 May 2006," *Earth Negotiations Bulletin* no. 7, 61 (May 29, 2006), www.iisd.ca/download/pdf/enb0761e.pdf.

112. Ibid., and "Summary of the Resumed Review Conference of the UN Fish Stocks Agreement: 24–28 May 2010," *Earth Negotiations Bulletin* 7, no. 65 (May 31, 2010), www.iisd.ca/download/pdf/enb0765e.pdf.

113. UNEP, *Desertification: The Problem That Won't Go Away* (Nairobi: UNEP, 1992); Ridley Nelson, "Dryland Management: The 'Desertification' Problem," Working Paper 8, World Bank Policy Planning and Research Staff, Environment Department, September 1988, 2.

114. For a news report on these findings see William K. Stevens, "Threat of Encroaching Deserts May Be More Myth Than Fact," *New York Times*, January 18, 1994, C1, 10.

115. UN Governmental Liaison Service, "Second Session of Desertification Negotiations, Geneva, 13–24 September 1993," *E and D File* 2, no. 13 (October 1993).

116. "A Convention for Africans," *Impact* (Nairobi) 6 (September 1992): 3.

117. UNEP, *Desertification Control Bulletin* (Nairobi) 20 (1991); Mostafa K. Tolba, "Desertification and the Economics of Survival," statement to the International Conference on the Economics of Dryland Degradation and Rehabilitation, Canberra, Australia, March 10–11, 1986.

118. *World Bank News* (May 27, 1993): 4; *Crosscurrents* 5 (March 16, 1992): 13.

119. E. U. Curtis Bohlen, deputy chief of the US delegation, recalls that he made the decision personally without consulting with higher US officials. Private communication from Bohlen, August 15, 1994. On the earlier suggestion by African countries of a possible bargain linking African support for a forest convention with US support for a desertification convention, see *Crosscurrents* 5 (March 16, 1992): 13.

120. "A Summary of the Proceedings of the United Nations Conference on Environment and Development: 3–14 June 1992," *Earth Summit Bulletin* 2, no. 13 (June 16, 1992): 3, www.iisd.ca /download/pdf/enb0213e.pdf.

121. "Summary of the First Session of the INC for the Elaboration of an International Convention to Combat Desertification, 24 May–3 June 1993," *Earth Negotiations Bulletin* 4, no. 11 (June 11, 1993): 2–6, www.iisd.ca/linkages/vol04/0411000e.html.

122. "Summary of the Fifth Session of the INC for the Elaboration of an International Convention to Combat Desertification, 6–17 June 1994," *Earth Negotiations Bulletin* 4, no. 55 (June 20, 1994): 7–8, www.iisd.ca/linkages/vol04/0455000e.html.

123. "Summary of the Second Session of the INC for the Elaboration of an International Convention to Combat Desertification, 13–24 September 1993," *Earth Negotiations Bulletin* 4, no. 22 (September 30, 1993): 11, www.iisd.ca/vol04/0422000e.html.

124. "Summary of the Fifth Session of the INC," 9–10.

125. For more information on the challenges the convention faced, see "Summary of the Second Conference of the Parties to the Convention to Combat Desertification, 30 November–11 December 1998," *Earth Negotiations Bulletin* 4, no. 127 (December 14, 1998), www.iisd.ca /download/pdf/enb04127e.pdf.

126. "Summary of the Seventh Conference of the Parties to the Convention to Combat Desertification, 17–28 October 2005," *Earth Negotiations Bulletin* 4, no. 186 (October 31, 2005): 16, www.iisd.ca/download/pdf/enb04186e.pdf.

127. Ibid.

128. Even Fontaine Ortiz and Guangting Tang, *Review of the Management, Administration and Activities of the Secretariat of the United Nations Convention to Combat Desertification (UNCCD)* (Geneva: UN Joint Inspection Unit, 2005), 7, www.unjiu.org/data/reports/2005/en2005_5.pdf.

129. Ibid.

130. Ibid.

131. UNCCD, "Ten-Year Strategic Plan and Framework to Enhance the Implementation of the Convention (2008–2018)," document ICCD/COP(8)/16/Add.1, October 23, 2007, www .unccd.int/Lists/OfficialDocuments/cop8/16add1eng.pdf.

132. Steffen Bauer and Lindsay C. Stringer, "The Role of Science in the Global Governance of Desertification," *Journal of Environment & Development* 18, no. 3 (2009): 248–267.

133. Ibid.

134. Bauer and Stringer, "The Role of Science," 3.

135. FAO, *State of the World's Forests 2011* (Rome: FAO, 2011), 2.

136. World Bank, "Forests and Forestry," accessed September 28, 2012, go.worldbank .org/VIQE69YFZ0.

137. Ibid.; United Nations Environment Programme (UNEP), *GEO 5: Global Environmental Outlook: Environment for the Future We Want* (Nairobi: UNEP, 2012), 72; UNEP, *GEO 4: Global Environmental Outlook: Environment for Development* (Nairobi: UNEP, 2007), 88, www.unep .org/geo/geo4/media.

138. FAO, *The Challenge of Sustainable Forest Management* (Rome: FAO, 1993), 9.

139. Even prior to the formation of the United Nations, forests had been discussed as an international issue between Canada and the United States as early as the late nineteenth century. See R. Peter Gillis and Thomas R. Roach, *Lost Initiatives: Canada's Forest Industries, Forest Policy, and Forest Conservation* (Westport, CT: Greenwood, 1986). There is also a long history of international conferences on forestry convened by the British under the banner of "Empire Forestry." See Gregory Barton, *Empire Forestry and the Origins of Environmentalism* (Cambridge: Cambridge University Press, 2002).

140. FAO, "History of the Committee on Forestry," COFO/2005/INF/8, 2005, www.fao.org/docrep/meeting/009/J4566e.htm.

141. David Humphreys, "The Elusive Quest for a Global Forests Convention," *Review of European Community and International Environmental Law* 14, no. 1 (April 2005): 1–10.

142. This is a non–legally binding authoritative statement of principles for a global consensus on the management, conservation, and sustainable development of all types of forests (Rio de Janeiro, June 13, 1992).

143. Agenda 21, 1992 report of the United Nations Conference on Environment and Development (UNCED), I (1992), UN Doc. A/CONF.151/26/Rev. 1, ch. 11.

144. David Humphreys, "The UNCED Process and International Responses to Deforestation," paper presented to the Inaugural Pan-European Conference on International Studies, Heidelberg, Germany, September 16–20, 1992, 34–35.

145. *Earth Summit Update* 8 (April 1992): 7.

146. These initiatives included the Conference on Global Partnerships on Forests organized by Indonesia, the India–United Kingdom initiative to establish reporting guidelines for forests to the Commission on Sustainable Development, and the Intergovernmental Working Group on Global Forests, convened jointly by Malaysia and Canada, which met twice in 1994.

147. For a summary of the international initiatives in support of the IPF process, see Grayson and Maynard, *The World's Forests—Rio +5*, 29–46.

148. The IPF's report to the Commission on Sustainable Development (E/CN.17/1997/12) can be found at www.un.org/documents/ecosoc/cn17/ipf/1997/ecn17ipf1997-12.htm.

149. The former Canadian natural resources minister, Anne McLellan, said in a 1997 speech to the Canadian pulp and paper industry that Canada was leading a push for a forest convention to secure an internationally recognized ecolabel for wood-based products (see Chapter 5). She linked the project to the threat posed to pressures on the Canadian forest industry. See "Americans, Canadians at Odds over 'Sustainable Forestry' Plan," *Ottawa Citizen*, February 1, 1997.

150. NGO briefings on developments in Intergovernmental Panel on Forests (IPF) and the CBD at BIONET, January 26, 1996, and December 5, 1996.

151. Humphreys, "The Elusive Quest."

152. Ibid.

153. Interview with William Mankin, Global Forest Policy Project, fourth session of the UN Forum on Forests, Geneva, Switzerland, May 11, 2004, as cited in Humphreys, "The Elusive Quest."

154. "Summary of the Nineteenth United Nations General Assembly Special Session to Review Implementation of Agenda 21: 23–27 June 1997," *Earth Negotiations Bulletin* 5, no. 88 (June 30, 1997): 5–6, www.iisd.ca/download/pdf/enb0588e.pdf; David Humphreys, "The Report of the Intergovernmental Panel on Forests," *Environmental Politics* 7, no. 1 (spring 1998): 219–220.

155. United Nations Economic and Social Council Resolution E/2000/3, Economic and Social Council Official Records (2000), Supplement No. 1, para. 11.

156. The Collaborative Partnership on Forests currently comprises fourteen international organization members: Centre for International Forestry Research (CIFOR); FAO; International Tropical Timber Organization (ITTO); International Union of Forestry Research Organizations (IUFRO); Secretariat of the CBD; Secretariat of the Global Environment Facility (GEF); Secretariat of the UNCCD; Secretariat of the United Nations Forum on Forests (UNFF); Secretariat of the United Nations Framework Convention on Climate Change (UNFCCC); United Nations Development Programme (UNDP); UNEP; World Agroforestry Centre (ICRAF); World Bank; and World Conservation Union (IUCN).

157. Deborah S. Davenport and Peter Wood, "Finding the Way Forward for the International Arrangement on Forests: UNFF-5, -6 and -7," *Review of European Community and International Environmental Law* 15, no. 3 (2006): 317.

158. For more information on UNFF-5, see "Summary of the Fifth Session of the United Nations Forum on Forests: 16–17 May 2005," *Earth Negotiations Bulletin*, 13, no. 133 (May 30, 2005), www.iisd.ca/download/pdf/enb13133e.pdf.

159. ECOSOC Resolution E/2006/49, Economic and Social Council Official Records (2006), E/2006/INF/2/Add.1, www.un.org/esa/forests/pdf/2006_49_E.pdf.

160. See General Assembly Resolution 62/98, "Non–Legally Binding Instrument on All Types of Forests," January 31, 2008, www.un.org/esa/forests/about-resolutions.html.

161. Economic and Social Council, United Nations Forum on Forests, *Report of the Seventh Session, 24 February 2006 and 16 to 27 April 2007*, E/2007/42 (New York: United Nations, 2007), 13.

162. "Summary of the Eighth Session of the United Nations Forum on Forests: 20 April–1 May 2009," *Earth Negotiations Bulletin* 13, no. 174 (May 4, 2009): 9, www.iisd.ca/download/pdf/enb13174e.pdf.

163. Ibid.

164. Ibid.

165. For more information on these negotiations, see www.forestnegotiations.org.

Chapter 5—Effective Environmental Regimes: Obstacles and Opportunities

1. The commonly cited figure of 150 major multilateral agreements totally directed to environmental issues comes from United Nations Environment Programme (UNEP) data. See Harold K. Jacobson and Edith Brown Weiss, "A Framework for Analysis," in *Engaging Countries: Strengthening Compliance with International Environmental Accords*, ed. Edith Brown Weiss and Harold K. Jacobson (Cambridge, MA: MIT Press, 1998), 1, 18. The figures of 1,150 and 1,500 come from the International Environmental Agreements Database Project (iea.uoregon.edu), directed by Ronald Mitchell.

2. Broader and influential discussions of issues related to implementation and compliance include Weiss and Jacobson, *Engaging Countries*; James Caermon et al., eds., *Improving Compliance with International Environmental Law* (London: Earthscan, 1996); David Victor, Kal Raustiala, and Eugene Skolnikof, eds., *The Implementation and Effectiveness of International Environmental Commitments* (Cambridge, MA: MIT Press, 1998); Oran R. Young, ed., *The Effectiveness of International Environmental Regimes* (Cambridge, MA: MIT Press, 1999); Edward Miles et al., *Environmental Regime Effectiveness* (Cambridge, MA: MIT Press, 2001); Michael

Faure and Jürgen Lefevere, "Compliance with Global Environmental Policy," in *Global Environmental Policy: Institutions, Law and Policy*, ed. Regina S. Axelrod, Stacy D. VanDeever, and David Leonard Downie, 3rd ed. (Washington, DC: Congressional Quarterly Press, 2011); "The Oslo-Potsdam Solution to Measuring Regime Effectiveness: Critique, Response, and the Road Ahead," *Global Environmental Politics* 3, no. 3 (August 2003): 74–96; Ronald Mitchell, "Problem Structure, Institutional Design, and the Relative Effectiveness of International Environmental Agreements," *Global Environmental Politics* 6, no. 3 (August 2006); 72–89; and Oran R. Young, "Effectiveness of International Environmental Regimes: Existing Knowledge, Cutting-Edge Themes, and Research Strategies," *PNAS* 108, no. 50 (2011): 19853–19860.

3. The discussion of the first four sets of factors draws explicitly on research and publications by one of the coauthors. See particularly David L. Downie, "Understanding International Environmental Regimes: Lessons of the Ozone" (PhD diss., University of North Carolina, Chapel Hill, 1996); David Leonard Downie, "Road Map or False Trail: Evaluating the Precedence of the Ozone Regime as Model and Strategy for Global Climate Change," *International Environmental Affairs* 7 (fall 1995): 321–345; David Leonard Downie, "Global Environmental Policy: Governance Through Regimes," in *Global Environmental Policy: Institutions, Law, and Policy*, ed. Regina S. Axelrod, David Leonard Downie, and Norman J. Vig, 2nd ed. (Washington, DC: Congressional Quarterly Press, 2005).

4. Classic examples include Thucydides, Niccolò Machiavelli, and Thomas Hobbes. Influential modern examples include Reinhold Niebuhr; Henry Kissinger; Hans J. Morgenthau, *Politics Among Nations: The Struggle for Power and Peace*, 5th ed. (New York: Knopf, 1973); Robert Jervis, "Cooperation Under the Security Dilemma," *World Politics* 30 (1978): 167–186; and Kenneth N. Waltz, *Theory of International Politics* (Reading, MA: Addison-Wesley, 1979).

5. Waltz, *Theory of International Politics*.

6. For discussion of the impact of positional concerns on cooperation, see Joseph Grieco, "Anarchy and the Limits of Cooperation: A Realist Critique of the Newest Liberal Institutionalism," *International Organization* 42 (summer 1988): 485–507.

7. Jervis, "Cooperation Under the Security Dilemma"; Kenneth A. Oye, ed., *Cooperation Under Anarchy* (Princeton, NJ: Princeton University Press, 1986), 1–22.

8. Mancur Olson, *The Logic of Collective Action* (Cambridge, MA: Harvard University Press, 1965).

9. Garrett Hardin, "The Tragedy of the Commons," *Science* 162, no. 3859 (December 13, 1968): 1243–1248; J. Samuel Barkin and George Shambaugh, eds., *Anarchy and the Environment: The International Relations of Common Pool Resources* (Albany: State University of New York Press, 1999).

10. Robert O. Keohane, *After Hegemony: Cooperation and Discord in the World Political Economy* (Princeton, NJ: Princeton University Press, 1984).

11. Robert Jervis, *Perception and Misperception in International Politics* (Princeton, NJ: Princeton University Press, 1976).

12. M. A. Giordano and A. T. Wolf, "Sharing Waters: Post-Rio International Water Management," *Natural Resources Forum* 27 (2003): 163–164.

13. Elli Louka, *International Environmental Law: Fairness, Effectiveness, and World Order* (New York: Cambridge University Press, 2006).

14. 1972 Stockholm Declaration and Action Plan, UN Document A/CONF.48/14, 118.

15. Gary Bryner, *From Promises to Performance: Achieving Global Environmental Goals* (New York: Norton, 1997), 59.

16. Peter Sand, *Lessons Learned in Global Environmental Governance* (Washington, DC: World Resources Institute, 1990), 21.

17. Discussions of trade and environment include Chris Wold, Sanford Gaines, and Greg Block, *Trade and the Environment: Law and Policy* (Durham, NC: Carolina Academic, 2011); Erich Vranes, *Trade and the Environment: Fundamental Issues in International and WTO Law* (New York: Oxford University Press, 2009); Kevin Gallagher, *Handbook on Trade and the Environment* (Northampton: Edward Elgar, 2009); Jeffrey Frankel and Andrew Rose, "Is Trade Good or Bad for the Environment? Sorting Out the Causality," *Review of Economics and Statistics* 87, no. 1 (February 2005).

18. For general discussion, see the Carbon Tax Center's website (www.carbontax.org) and Eduardo Porter, "In Energy Taxes, Tools to Help Tackle Climate Change," *New York Times*, January 29, 2013.

19. Peter Haas, Robert O. Keohane, and Marc Levy, eds., *Institutions for the Earth: Sources of Effective International Environmental Protection* (Cambridge, MA: MIT Press, 1993). This discussion slightly expands their definition of the three conditions.

20. For discussion of these obstacles, see Lawrence Susskind, *Environmental Diplomacy: Negotiating More Effective Global Agreements* (New York: Oxford University Press, 1994), and Sand, *Lessons Learned in Global Environmental Governance.*

21. This point is also made by Susskind, *Environmental Diplomacy*, 156.

22. As with similar discussions in this book, the categories presented in this subsection should also be seen as indicative and heuristic rather than exhaustive and exclusive.

23. This paragraph is based on personal observations by David Downie during international negotiations on POPs and mercury emissions.

24. David Downie, personal observations during the mercury negotiations. See also the official reports of these negotiations (which Downie helped to draft), www.unep.org/hazardous substances/MercuryNot/MercuryNegotiations/tabid/3320/language/en-US/Default.aspx, as well as the *Earth Negotiations Bulletin*, www.iisd.ca/vol28.

25. Most spills occur in industrial facilities and laboratories and are relatively contained but can expose particular individuals to high doses. Large spills and area contaminations also occur as a result of industrial accidents; fires; accidents involving trains, ships, or trucks transporting chemicals; and inadequate pollution controls at production facilities. Some of the most famous chemical spills in history provide examples. In August 2008 a series of explosions at a large chemical plant in Guangxi Province, China, released toxic gas into the air and contaminated the Longjiang River, forcing evacuation of the nearby town. In 1991, seven train cars carrying the pesticide metam sodium derailed, spilling the chemicals into the Sacramento River and killing downriver plant and aquatic life for forty-three miles. In 1986, Ciba-Geigy accidentally discharged large amounts of toxic agricultural chemicals into the Rhine River in Europe. The next day a fire at a chemical warehouse in Basel, Switzerland, caused thirty tons of mercury-laden toxic waste to be sluiced into the Rhine. In December 1984, a cloud of poisonous gas escaped from a Union Carbide chemical plant that produced the pesticide Sevin in Bhopal, India, killing thousands of people and exposing hundreds of thousands. In 1983, the US government purchased the entire town of Times Beach, Missouri, and relocated more than 2,200 residents because the land was so badly contaminated from nearby industries.

26. WHO and UNEP, *State of the Science of Endocrine Disrupting Chemicals* (Geneva: WHO and UNEP, 2013).

27. See Knut Midgaard and Arild Underdal, "Multiparty Conferences," in *Negotiations: Social-Psychological Perspectives*, ed. Daniel Druckman (Beverly Hills, CA: Sage, 1977), 339; and Pamela S. Chasek, *Earth Negotiations: Analyzing Thirty Years of Environmental Diplomacy* (Tokyo: United Nations University Press, 2001), ch. 3.

28. Barkin and Shambaugh, *Anarchy and the Environment*.

29. Personal observation by David Downie during the fourth Conference of the Parties to the Stockholm Convention, Geneva, Switzerland, May 4–8, 2009.

30. Ronald Mitchell, "Regime Design Matters: Intentional Oil Pollution and Treaty Compliance," *International Organization* 48, no. 3 (summer 1994): 425–458. See also Ronald Mitchell, "Problem Structure, Institutional Design, and the Relative Effectiveness of International Environmental Agreements," *Global Environmental Politics* 6, no. 3 (August 2006): 72–89.

31. Jacobson and Weiss, "A Framework for Analysis," 4.

32. Abram Chayes and Antonia Chayes, "Compliance Without Enforcement: State Behavior Under Regulatory Treaties," *Negotiation Journal* 7 (1991): 311–330; J. Timmons Roberts, Bradley Parks, and Alexis Vásquez, "Who Ratifies Environmental Treaties and Why? Institutionalism, Structuralism and Participation by 192 Nations in 22 Treaties," *Global Environmental Politics* 4, no. 3 (August 2004): 22–64.

33. In addition to those cited above or below (in particular those by Faure, Lefevere, Jacobson, Sand, Weiss, and Young and Faure), prominent examples of this literature include Peter Sand, ed., *The Effectiveness of International Environmental Agreements* (Cambridge, MA: Grotius, 1992); Ronald Mitchell, *Intentional Oil Pollution at Sea* (Cambridge, MA: MIT Press, 1994); Victor, Raustiala, and Skolnikof, *International Environmental Commitments*; Michael Kelly, "Overcoming Obstacles to the Effective Implementation of International Environmental Agreements," *Georgetown International Environmental Law Review* 9, no. 2 (1997); Ronald Mitchell, "Compliance Theory: A Synthesis," *Review of European Community and International Environmental Law* 2, no. 4 (1993): 327–334; Patrick Bernhagen, "Business and International Environmental Agreements: Domestic Sources of Participation and Compliance by Advanced Industrialized Democracies," *Global Environmental Politics* 8, no. 1 (2008): 78–110; David McEvoy and John Stranlund, "Self-Enforcing International Environmental Agreements with Costly Monitoring for Compliance," *Environmental and Resource Economics* 42, no. 4 (2009): 491–508.

34. Sand, *International Environmental Agreements*, 82.

35. Kelly, "Overcoming Obstacles," 462–463.

36. For example, in an experiment conducted by WWF, volunteers declared or displayed a cactus to customs officials in several countries, including the United Kingdom, Switzerland, Germany, Sweden, Denmark, and the United States. Although virtually all cacti are protected under CITES, no questions were asked by officials in any of these countries about the species of the plant or its origins. See Bill Padgett, "The African Elephant, Africa and CITES: The Next Step," *Indiana Journal of Global Legal Studies* 2 (1995): 529, 538–540, as cited in Kelly, "Overcoming Obstacles," 469–470.

37. See, e.g., Duncan Brack, "Combating International Environmental Crime," *Global Environmental Change* 12, no. 2 (July 2002): 79–147; William Laurance et al., "Deforestation in Amazonia," *Science* 304, no. 5674 (May 21, 2004): 1109–1111; Christian Nelleman, UNEP, and INTERPOL, *Green Carbon, Black Trade: Illegal Logging, Tax Fraud and Laundering in the World's Tropical Forests* (Nairobi: UNEP, 2012).

38. David Mulenex, "Improving Compliance Provisions in International Environmental Agreements," in *International Environmental Treaty-Making*, ed. Lawrence Susskind, Eric Dolin, and J. William Breslin (Cambridge, MA: Program on Negotiation at Harvard Law School, 1992), 174.

39. Personal observations by David Downie during meetings of the Stockholm, Rotterdam, and Basel conventions and personal communications from senior environmental officials from several African countries during the Fourth Conference of the Parties to the Stockholm Convention on Persistent Organic Pollutants, Geneva, Switzerland, May 4–8, 2009.

40. Personal observations by David Downie during negotiations on creating a global mercury treaty.

41. Nelleman, UNEP, and INTERPOL, *Green Carbon, Black Trade*.

42. Andrew Heimert, "How the Elephant Lost His Tusks," *Yale Law Journal* 104 (1995): 1473, as cited in Kelly, "Overcoming Obstacles," 465.

43. Environmental Investigation Agency and Telepak, *The Final Cut: Illegal Logging in Indonesia's Orangutan Parks* (Washington, DC: Environmental Investigation Agency, 1999); David Brown, *Addicted to Rent: Corporate and Spatial Distribution of Forest Resources in Indonesia: Implications for Forest Sustainability and Government Policy* (Jakarta: Indonesia-UK Tropical Forest Management Programme, 1999).

44. David Vogel and Timothy Kessler, "How Compliance Happens and Doesn't Happen Domestically," in Weiss and Jacobson, *Engaging Countries*, 24.

45. Ibid., 35.

46. For specific and numerous examples, see reports of the ozone regime's Implementation Committee, available at the Ozone Secretariat's website: ozone.unep.org.

47. Peter Tsai and Thomas Hatfield, "Global Benefits from the Phaseout of Leaded Fuel," *Journal of Environmental Health* 75, no. 5 (December 2011): 8–14.

48. UNEP and Kenya Forest Service, *The Role and Contribution of Montane Forests and Related Ecosystem Services to the Kenyan Economy* (Nairobi: UNEP, 2012).

49. Matthew Wald, "Fossil Fuels' Hidden Cost Is in Billions, Study Says," *New York Times*, October 19, 2009; Committee on Health, Environmental, and Other External Costs and Benefits of Energy Production and Consumption, National Research Council, *Hidden Costs of Energy: Unpriced Consequences of Energy Production and Use* (Washington, DC: National Academies Press, 2010).

50. Robert Costanza et al., "The Value of the World's Ecosystem Services and Natural Capital," *Nature* 387 (May 15, 1997): 253–260.

51. *UNEP Year Book 2009* (Nairobi: UNEP, March 2009); UNEP, *Global Green New Deal: Policy Brief* (Nairobi: UNEP, March 2009).

52. For information, see the Economics of Ecosystems and Biodiversity (TEEB) website: www.teebweb.org.

53. See Patrick ten Brink et al., *The Economics of Ecosystems and Biodiversity for Water and Wetlands: A Briefing Note* (Geneva: UNEP TEEB, 2012); and Daniela Russi et al., *The Economics of Ecosystems and Biodiversity for Water and Wetlands: Final Consultation Draft*, UN Document UNEP/CBD/COP/11/INF/22, September 26, 2012.

54. UNEP FI and Global Footprint Network, *A New Angle on Sovereign Credit Risk: E-RISC—Environmental Risk Integration in Sovereign Credit Analysis* (Geneva: UNEP, 2012).

55. E.g., Nicholas Stern, *The Economics of Climate Change: The Stern Review* (Cambridge: Cambridge University Press, 2007); Frank Ackerman and Elizabeth Stanton, *The Cost of Climate*

Change: What We'll Pay If Global Warming Continues Unchecked (Washington, DC: Natural Resources Defense Council, 2008); Economics of Climate Adaptation (ECA) Working Group, *Shaping Climate Resilient Development: A Framework for Decision-Making* (Washington, DC: ECA, 2009).

56. UNEP-GEF, "New Countries to Start Phase-Out of Inefficient Lighting, with Major Economic and Climate Benefits," press release, June 21, 2012. Information on the initiative is available at www.enlighten-initiative.org. National data on the benefits of a transition to energy-efficient lighting can be viewed at www.unep.org/PDF/PressReleases/Table_Energy_Efficient _Lighting_Transition.pdf.

57. E.g., UNEP, "World-Wide Action on Black Carbon, Methane and Other Short-Lived Pollutants Grows as Seven More Countries Join New Coalition," press release, July 25, 2012. For more information on the coalition, see www.unep.org/ccac.

58. ECA Working Group, *Shaping Climate*.

59. Michael Renner et al., *Green Jobs: Towards Decent Work in a Sustainable, Low-Carbon World* (Nairobi: UNEP, 2008).

60. David Leonard Downie and Jessica Templeton, "Pesticides and Persistent Organic Pollutants," in *Routledge Handbook of Global Environmental Politics*, ed. Paul Harris (New York: Routledge, 2013).

61. For extensive discussion of this point, see Stern, *The Economics of Climate Change*, xvii and chs. 14–17.

62. For discussion, see UNEP and WTO, *Trade and Climate Change: A Report by the United Nations Environment Programme and the World Trade Organization* (Geneva: WTO Publications, 2009).

63. Such provisions were even included as part of proposed climate-change legislation that passed the US House of Representatives in 2009 (HR 2454: American Clean Energy and Security Act of 2009) but did not become law.

64. Edith Brown Weiss, "The Five International Treaties: A Living History," in Weiss and Jacobson, *Engaging Countries*, 115–116.

65. Ibid., 162. This conclusion is also supported by the personal observations of the authors and communications with secretariat and government officials.

66. Examples include the UNEP Governing Council, Open-Ended Intergovernmental Group of Ministers or Their Representatives on International Environmental Governance, Global Ministerial Environment Forum, and the synergies initiative under way in the chemicals sector.

67. See, e.g., Victor, Raustiala, and Skolnikoff, *International Environmental Commitments*.

68. For a full discussion, see Basel Convention Secretariat, *Global Trends in Generation and Transboundary Movement of Hazardous Wastes and Other Wastes: Analysis of the Data Provided by Parties to the Secretariat of the Basel Convention*, UN Publication Series, Basel Convention on the Control of Transboundary Movements on Hazardous Wastes and Their Disposal 14 (Geneva: Basel Convention Secretariat, 2004).

69. E.g., European Environment Agency and UNEP, "Chemicals in the European Environment: Low Doses, High Stakes?" in *The EEA and UNEP Annual Message 2 on the State of Europe's Environment* (Copenhagen: European Commission, 2001).

70. E.g., Jonathan Krueger, Henrik Selin, and David Leonard Downie, "Global Policy for Hazardous Chemicals," in Axelrod, Downie, and Vig, *Global Environmental Policy*; and personal communications from regime officials.

71. Examples include the Alliance for Responsible Atmospheric Policy, which tracked ODS production and use for many years and reports by the Environmental Investigation Agency's investigations of CFC smuggling (e.g., Environmental Investigation Agency, "Ozone Depleting Substances," www.eia-international.org.php5-20.dfw1-1.websitetestlink.com/our-work/global-climate/ozone-depleting-substances).

72. For additional information, see the TRAFFIC website: www.traffic.org. Also see the Environmental Investigations Agency website: www.eia-international.org.

73. For discussion, see Mitchell, *Intentional Oil Pollution at Sea*, 47–48.

74. For more information, see Martin Khor, *The Proposed New Issues in the WTO and the Interests of Developing Countries* (Penang, Malaysia: Third World Network, 2001).

75. For an overview of this issue, see Daniel Esty, "Economic Integration and Environmental Protection," in Axelrod, Downie, and Vig, *Global Environmental Policy*.

76. See, e.g., Susskind, *Environmental Diplomacy*.

77. Personal communications.

78. Ecomessage was created by Interpol in the 1990s as a reporting system to improve sharing of wildlife-crime information among international wildlife law enforcement agencies. The International Fund for Animal Welfare sponsors the Ecomessage Award. For information, see www.ifaw.org/international/our-work/fighting-wildlife-trade.

79. See the website of the Environmental Performance Index: www.epi.yale.edu.

80. For example, see Pamela S. Chasek, "Confronting Environmental Treaty Implementation Challenges in the Pacific Islands," *Pacific Islands Policy* 6 (2010).

81. Personal observation by the authors during recent global negotiations in the ozone, chemical, and mercury regimes. For specific examples, see recent meeting reports and *Earth Negotiations Bulletin* reports from the Montreal Protocol, Stockholm Convention, and mercury negotiations at www.iisd.ca/voltoc.html

82. OECD, "Development: Aid to Developing Countries Falls Because of Global Recession," press release, April 4, 2012, www.oecd.org/newsroom/developmentaidtodevelopingcountries fallsbecauseofglobalrecession.htm.

83. See particularly Jeffrey Sachs, *The End of Poverty: Economic Possibilities for Our Time* (New York: Penguin, 2005); and Jeffrey Sachs, *Common Wealth: Economics for a Crowded Planet* (New York: Penguin, 2008).

84. For official, detailed information on the EU Emissions Trading System, see ec.europa .eu/clima/policies/ets/index_en.htm.

85. See the Regional Greenhouse Gas Initiative (RGGI) webpage: www.rggi.org.

86. For an early example, see International Institute for Sustainable Development, "Financing Climate Change: Global Environmental Tax?" *Developing Ideas* 15 (September–October 1998).

87. UN Commission on Sustainable Development, *Financial Resources and Mechanisms for Sustainable Development: Overview of Current Issues and Developments, Report of the Secretary-General*, E/CN.17/ISWG.II/1994/2, February 22, 1994, 24.

88. "Levy on International Air Travel Could Fund Climate Change Fight," *Guardian* (London), June 8, 2009, 13.

89. See, for example, John Vidal, "Oil Nations Asked to Consider Carbon Tax on Exports," *Guardian* (London), November 21, 2012.

90. The original proposal, by Nobel Prize–winning economist James Tobin, was for a 0.5 percent tax on speculative currency transactions that would raise $1.5 trillion annually and was

aimed at deterring such transactions. The UNDP proposed reducing the tax to 10 percent of the original level. See UNDP, *Human Development Report 1994* (New York: Oxford University Press, 1994), 69–70; Martin Walker, "Global Taxation: Paying for Peace," *World Policy Journal* 10, no. 2 (summer 1993): 7–12.

91. Floyd Norris, "A Tax That May Change the Trading Game," *New York Times*, February 21, 2013.

92. Stephen R. Seidel and Daniel Blank, "Closing an Ozone Loophole," *Environmental Forum* 7 (1990): 18–20; "Effect of Ozone-Depleting Chemicals Tax Could Be Wide-Ranging, IRS Attorney Says," *Environment Reporter* 21 (November 2, 1990): 1257.

93. See section 921 of the United Nations Reform Act of 1999, commonly referred to as "Helms-Biden."

94. Updated information on HIPC can be found on the World Bank and IMF websites: www.worldbank.org/debt and www.imf.org/external/np/exr/facts/hipc.htm.

95. Jim VandeHei, "G-8 Leaders Agree on $50B in Africa Aid," *Washington Post*, July 9, 2005.

96. See the Jubilee USA Network's website: www.jubileeusa.org.

97. See Institute for European Environmental Policy, *Reforming Environmentally Harmful Subsidies*, final report to the European Commission's DG Environment, March 2007; Organization for Economic Cooperation and Development (OECD), *Environmentally Harmful Subsidies: Challenges for Reform* (Paris: OECD Publishing, 2005); Maura Allaire and Stephen Brown, *Eliminating Subsidies for Fossil Fuel Production: Implications for U.S. Oil and Natural Gas Markets*, Issue Brief 09–10 (Washington, DC: Resources for the Future, 2009), www.rff.org/RFF /Documents/RFF-IB-09-10.pdf; *IMF, Energy Subsidy Reform: Lessons and Implications* (Washington, DC: IMF, 2013).

Chapter 6—Environmental Politics and Sustainable Development

1. United Nations Development Programme (UNDP), *Human Development Report 2011, Sustainability and Equity: A Better Future for All* (New York: Palgrave Macmillan, 2011), 27.

2. Ibid., 24.

3. *Development and Environment* (Paris: Mouton, 1971), report and working papers of experts convened by the secretary-general of the UN Conference on the Human Environment, Founex, Switzerland, June 4–12, 1971.

4. Adil Najam, "The View from the South: Developing Countries in Global Environmental Politics," in *The Global Environment: Institutions, Law and Policy*, ed. Regina Axelrod, David Downie, and Norman Vig, 2nd ed. (Washington, DC: Congressional Quarterly Press, 2005), 224–243.

5. *Development and Environment*, 5–6, as cited in Adil Najam, "Why Environmental Politics Looks Different from the South," in *Handbook of Global Environmental Politics*, ed. Peter Dauvergne (Cheltenham, UK: Edward Elgar, 2005), 111–126.

6. Lars-Göran Engfeldt, *From Stockholm to Johannesburg and Beyond* (Stockholm: Government Offices of Sweden, 2009), 81.

7. Ibid., 67; United Nations, *Report of the United Nations Conference on the Human Environment*, A/CONF.48/14/Rev 1 (1973), www.un-documents.net/unche.htm.

8. Pamela S. Chasek, "Sustainable Development," in *Introducing Global Issues*, ed. Michael Snarr and D. Neil Snarr, 5th ed. (Boulder: Lynne Rienner, 2012), 256–257.

9. World Commission on Environment and Development, *Our Common Future* (New York: Oxford University Press, 1987), 5.

10. World Commission on Environment and Development, *Our Common Future*, 43.

11. Engfeldt, *From Stockholm to Johannesburg*, 111.

12. Marian Miller, *The Third World in Global Environmental Politics* (Boulder: Lynne Rienner, 1995), 9.

13. Najam, "The View from the South."

14. Pamela S. Chasek, "The Convention to Combat Desertification: Lessons Learned for Sustainable Development," *Journal of Environment and Development* 6, no. 2 (1997): 147–169.

15. Najam, "The View from the South."

16. See *Outreach* 1, no. 24 (April 22, 1997).

17. See the final communiqué from the Gleneagles Summit, 2005, www.g7.utoronto.ca /summit/2005gleneagles/communique.pdf.

18. See the outcome document from the 2005 UN summit, www.un.org/summit2005.

19. "Development: Aid to Developing Countries Falls Because of Global Recession," Organization for Economic Cooperation and Development (OECD), April 4, 2012, www.oecd.org /newsroom/developmentaidtodevelopingcountriesfallsbecauseofglobalrecession.htm.

20. Data from OECD StatExtracts, 2010, stats.oecd.org/index.aspx?DataSetCode=CRS1. The figures represent total ODA in 2010 for all sectors and total for environmental protection.

21. United Nations Environment Programme (UNEP), *GEO 5: Global Environmental Outlook: Environment for the Future We Want* (Nairobi: UNEP, 2012).

22. "Proposed Elements of a Protocol to the United Nations Framework Convention on Climate Change, Presented by Brazil in Response to the Berlin Mandate," Ad Hoc Group on the Berlin Mandate, seventh session, Bonn, July 31–August 7, 1997, 22.

23. Najam, "The View from the South." See also Anil Agarwal and Sunita Narain, *Global Warming in an Unequal World: A Case of Environmental Colonialism* (New Delhi: Center for Science and Environment, 1991); Anil Agarwal, Sunita Narain, and Anju Sharma, eds., *Green Politics: Global Negotiations*, vol. 1 (New Delhi: Center for Science and Environment, 1999).

24. Najam, "The View from the South."

25. Sha Zukang, "Remarks on the Opening Session of the 50th Session of the Commission for Social Development," United Nations, New York, February 1, 2012, www.un.org/en/development /desa/usg/statements/commission-for-social-development-2.html.

26. United Nations Department for Public Information, "Press Summary of the Secretary-General's Report on Implementing Agenda 21," press release, January 2002.

27. Chasek, "Sustainable Development," 252.

28. "Addressing Inequities of Globalization 'Overarching Challenge' of Times Says Secretary-General, Presenting Millennium Report to General Assembly," press release SG/SM/7343, United Nations, April 3, 2000, www.un.org/News/Press/docs/2000/20000403.sgsm7343.doc.html.

29. Pamela S. Chasek and Richard Sherman, *Ten Days in Johannesburg: A Negotiation of Hope* (Cape Town: Struik, 2004); and International Institute for Sustainable Development (IISD), *Millennium Review Meeting Bulletin* 104, no. 2 (March 16, 2005), www.iisd.ca/sd/ecosocprep1 /sdvol104num2e.html.

30. Ibid.

31. James Gustave Speth, "Perspectives on the Johannesburg Summit," *Environment* 45, no. 1 (2003).

32. Department of Economic and Social Affairs, United Nations, "The Johannesburg Summit Test: What Will Change," September 25, 2002, www.un.org/jsummit/html/whats_new/feature _story.html.

33. Ibid.

34. Speth, "Perspectives on the Johannesburg Summit," 24–29.

35. See the 2005 World Summit website: www.un.org/summit2005.

36. United Nations, *Millennium Development Goals Report 2012* (New York: United Nations, 2012), 4.

37. Ibid.

38. Ibid.

39. Ibid., 12.

40. Ibid., 56.

41. Michael Clemens and Todd Moss, "What's Wrong with the Millennium Development Goals?," CGD Policy Brief (Washington, DC: Center for Global Development, 2005), 3.

42. Ibid.

43. Ibid., 4.

44. Jeffrey Sachs and Walter Reid, "Investments Toward Sustainable Development," *Science* 312 (May 19, 2006): 1002.

45. Ibid.

46. Raymond Ahearn, "Rising Economic Powers and the Global Economy: Trends and Issues for Congress," Congressional Research Service Report 7–5700 (Washington, DC: Congressional Research Service, 2011).

47. See Karl Sauvant and Hajo Hasenpflug, eds., *The New International Economic Order: Confrontation or Cooperation Between North and South?* (Boulder: Westview, 1977).

48. James Sebenius, "Negotiating a Regime to Control Global Warming," in *Greenhouse Warming: Negotiating a Global Regime*, ed. Jessica Tuchman Mathews (Washington, DC: World Resources Institute, 1991), 87.

49. South Commission, *The Challenge to the South: The Report of the South Commission* (Oxford: Oxford University Press, 1990); Mohammed Ayoob, "The New-Old Disorder in the Third World," *Global Governance* 1, no. 1 (1995): 59–77; Adil Najam, "An Environmental Negotiation Strategy for the South," *International Environmental Affairs* 7, no. 3 (1995): 249–287; Najam, "The View from the South," 224–243.

50. This was part of a longer-term decline in the real prices of primary products in the world market, caused by slow growth in demand, the development of cheaper substitutes, and overproduction. See UNDP, *Human Development Report 1992* (New York: UNDP, 1992), 59.

51. UNDP, "Financial Inflows and Outflows," *Human Development Report 1998* (New York: Oxford University Press, 1998). The term *least-developed countries* (LDCs) was originally used at the United Nations in 1971 to describe the "poorest and most economically weak of the developing countries, with formidable economic, institutional and human resources problems, which are often compounded by geographical handicaps and natural and man-made disasters." There are currently fifty LDCs.

52. World Bank, "World Development Indicators and Global Development Finance," 2012, databank.worldbank.org/data/home.aspx.

53. Ibid.

54. Ahearn, "Rising Economic Powers and the Global Economy," 1.

55. M. Ayhan Kose and Eswar Prasad, *Emerging Markets: Resilience and Growth Amid Global Turmoil* (Washington, DC: Brookings Institution Press, 2010), 1.

56. Credit Suisse Research Institute, *Credit Suisse Global Wealth Databook, 2011* (Zurich: Credit Suisse Research Institute, 2011), 10, infocus.credit-suisse.com/data/_product_documents /_shop/323525/2011_global_wealth_report.pdf.

57. J. Timmons Roberts and Bradley Parks, *A Climate of Injustice: Global Inequality, North-South Politics, and Climate Policy* (Cambridge, MA: MIT Press, 2007), 12.

58. Ibid.

59. Roberts and Parks, *A Climate of Injustice*; Najam, "The View from the South."

60. Chasek, "Sustainable Development," 262.

61. Mark Halle, "Sustainable Development Cools Off: Globalization Demands Summit Take New Approach to Meeting Ecological, Social Goals," *Winnipeg Free Press*, July 29, 2002.

62. World Bank, *Global Economic Prospects and the Developing Countries* (Washington, DC: World Bank, 1992), 13.

63. "Barriers to entry" are any obstacle that impedes a potential new entrant (a company or country) from entering a market to produce or sell goods or services. Barriers to entry shelter incumbent companies against new entrants. They can include government regulations, subsidies, intellectual property rules, restrictive practices, preexisting supplier or distributer agreements, control of resources, economies of scale, advantages independent of scale, consumer preferences, and other factors.

64. Kevin P. Gallagher, "The Economics of Globalization and Sustainable Development," in "Trade, Environment and Investment: Cancún and Beyond," special issue, *Policy Matters* 11 (September 2003).

65. Steve Charnovitz, "Environmentalism Confronts GATT Rules," *Journal of World Trade* 28 (January 1993): 37; Daniel C. Esty, "Economic Integration and the Environment," in *The Global Environment: Institutions, Law, and Policy*, ed. Norman Vig and Regina Axelrod (Washington, DC: Congressional Quarterly Press, 1999), 192.

66. General Agreement on Tariffs and Trade (GATT) and World Trade Organization (WTO), preamble to "Agreement Establishing the World Trade Organization," WTO, 1994, www.wto.org/english/docs_e/legal_e/04-wto.pdf.

67. Ibid.

68. For a matrix of selected MEAs and their trade provisions, see WTO, "Matrix on Trade Measures Pursuant to Selected Multilateral Environmental Agreements," WT/CTE/W/160/Rev.5 TN/TE/S/5/Rev.3, June 15, 2011, docsonline.wto.org/DDFDocuments/t/tn/te/S5R3.doc.

69. UNEP and IISD, *Environment and Trade: A Handbook* (Winnipeg: IISD/UNEP, 2000).

70. Ibid.

71. "Doha Ministerial Declaration," WT/MIN(01)/DEC/1, WTO, November 20, 2001, www.wto.org/english/thewto_e/minist_e/min01_e/mindecl_e.htm.

72. Richard Tarasofsky, "Trade, Environment, and the WTO Dispute Settlement Mechanism," report commissioned by the European Commission, June 2005, 4, ecologic.eu/download/projekte/1800-1849/1800/4_1800_cate_wto_dispute_settlement.pdf.

73. The term *environmental trade measures* is used in Steve Charnowitz, "The Environment vs. Trade Rules: Defogging the Debate," *Environmental Law* 23 (1993): 490. Charnowitz lists all these forms of ETMs except mandatory ecolabeling.

74. Sang Don Lee, "The Effect of Environmental Regulations on Trade: Cases of Korea's New Environmental Laws," *Georgetown International Environmental Law Review* 5, no. 3 (summer 1993): 659.

75. One exception was when Ecuador sought WTO approval for retaliatory sanctions against the EU for the EU's failure to comply with the WTO ruling on its banana-import regime, which discriminated against a number of South and Central American banana-exporting countries. However, realizing that, as a small country, imposing punitive tariffs on EU imports would have

had little impact on the EU but a devastating effect on Ecuador's consumers, Ecuador said it would seek to target intellectual property rights and services for retaliation. See International Centre for Trade and Sustainable Development (ICTSD), "Ecuador, U.S. Reject EU Banana Proposal; Ecuador to Cross-Retaliate," *Bridges Weekly Trade News Digest* 3, no. 45 (November 15, 1999).

76. Daniel C. Esty, *Greening the GATT: Trade, Environment and the Future* (Washington, DC: Institute for International Economics, 1994), 188. In an ironic twist, research undertaken by the Inter-American Tropical Tuna Commission found that "dolphin-safe" tuna fishing results in catching tuna at least thirty-five times more immature (because young tuna do not school beneath groups of dolphins as mature tuna do) and thus threatens to deplete tuna fisheries. See Richard Parker, "The Use and Abuse of Trade Leverage to Protect the Global Commons: What We Can Learn from the Tuna-Dolphin Conflict," *Georgetown International Environmental Law Review* 12, no. 1 (1999): 37–38.

77. For environmental critiques of the decision, see Steve Charnovitz, "GATT and the Environment: Examining the Issues," *International Environmental Affairs* 4, no. 3 (summer 1992): 203–233; Robert Repetto, "Trade and Environment Policies: Achieving Complementarities and Avoiding Conflict," *WRI Issues and Ideas* (July 1993): 6–10. For an alternative view of the decision, see John H. Jackson, "World Trade Rules and Environmental Policies: Congruence or Conflict?" *Washington and Lee Law Review* 49 (fall 1992): 1242–1243.

78. For an excellent summary, see Donald M. Goldberg, "GATT Tuna-Dolphin II: Environmental Protection Continues to Clash with Free Trade," *CIEL* 2 (June 1994).

79. Janet Welsh Brown, "Trade and the Environment," in *Encyclopedia of Violence, Peace and Conflict*, vol. 3, ed. Lester Kurtz (San Diego: Academic Press, 1999), T12–14.

80. The appellate body also noted that the United States had failed to sign the Convention on Migratory Species and the United Nations Convention on the Law of the Sea; nor had it ratified the Convention on Biological Diversity or raised the issue of sea turtles during recent CITES conferences. These inconsistencies in the US record on protection of endangered species do not prove, of course, that the US intention in the shrimp/turtle case was not to protect endangered sea turtles.

81. See "Revised Guidelines for the Implementation of Section 609 of Public Law 101-162 Relating to the Protection of Sea Turtles in Shrimp Trawl Fishing Operations," Public Notice 3086, *Federal Register*, July 1999.

82. WTO, "Labelling," www.wto.org/english/tratop_e/envir_e/labelling_e.htm.

83. For additional information about the Forest Stewardship Council, see www.fsc.org.

84. For more information, see the Marine Stewardship Council's website: www.msc.org.

85. Food and Agriculture Organization of the United Nations (FAO), *State of World Fisheries and Aquaculture 2012* (Rome: FAO, 2012), 68.

86. Since 1994, labeling and related issues have been discussed in the WTO's Committee on Trade and Environment, the Committee on Technical Barriers to Trade (TBT), and the Committee on Sanitary and Phytosanitary Measures, as well as during two triennial reviews of the TBT agreement, at various informal WTO symposia, in external conferences attended by WTO Secretariat staff, and in dispute-settlement panels and appellate bodies. See also WTO, "Labelling."

87. Marie Wilkie, "Tuna Labeling and the WTO: How Safe Is 'Dolphin-Safe'?" *BIORES* 6, no. 2 (June–July 2012), 16–19, ictsd.org/downloads/bioresreview/biores6-2.pdf.

88. WTO, Committee on Trade and Environment, *Report of the Meeting Held on 14 November 2011*, WT/CTE/M/53, January 27, 2012.

89. See WTO, Committee on Trade and Environment, *Environmental Benefits of Removing Trade Restrictions and Distortions: Note by the Secretariat* (Geneva: WTO, 1997); Gareth Porter, *Fisheries Subsidies, Overfishing and Trade* (Geneva: UNEP, 1998); IMF, *Energy Subsidy Reform: Lessons and Implications* (Washington, DC: IMF, 2013).

90. U. Rashid Sumaila, Ahmed Khan, et al., "A Bottom-Up Re-Estimation of Global Fisheries Subsidies," *Journal of Bioeconomics* 12 (2010): 201–225.

91. ICTSD, "Trade Leaders Call for Fisheries Subsidies Reform on World Oceans Day," *Bridges Weekly Trade News Digest* 13, no. 21 (June 10, 2009), ictsd.net/i/news/bridgesweekly/48339.

92. ICTSD and IISD, "Trade and Environment."

93. UNEP, *Fisheries Subsidies: A Critical Issue for Trade and Sustainable Development at the WTO: An Introductory Guide* (Geneva: UNEP, 2008), 4–5.

94. WTO, "Ministerial Declaration," WT/MIN(05)/DEC, Annex D, December 22, 2005, www.wto.org/english/theWTO_e/minist_e/min05_e/final_text_e.pdf.

95. WTO Negotiating Group on Rules, "Draft Consolidated Chair Texts of the AD and SCM Agreements," Tn/Rl/W/213, Annex VIII, WTO, November 30, 2007, www.wto.org/english/news_e/news07_e/rules_nov07_e.doc.

96. ICTSD, "Trade Leaders Call for Fisheries Subsidies Reform."

97. WTO, "Eliminating Trade Barriers on Environmental Goods and Services," accessed December 24, 2012, www.wto.org/english/tratop_e/envir_e/envir_neg_serv_e.htm.

98. OECD, "Opening Markets for Environmental Goods and Services," September 2005, www.oecd.org/dataoecd/63/15/35415839.pdf.

99. UNEP, the International Trade Centre (ITC) and the ICTSD, "Trade and Environment Briefings: Trade in Environmental Goods," *Policy Brief* 6, June 2012, ictsd.org/downloads/2012/06/trade-in-environmental-goods.pdf.

100. ICTSD, "Liberalization of Trade in Environmental Goods for Climate Change Mitigation: The Sustainable Development Context," paper prepared for the Seminar on Trade and Climate Change, Copenhagen, Denmark, June 18–20, 2008, www.gmfus.org/doc/economics/GMF-EGS.pdf.

101. World Bank, *International Trade and Climate Change* (Washington, DC: World Bank, 2007). For additional information on trade and climate change, see Peter Wooders, *Greenhouse Gas Emission Impacts of Liberalising Trade in Environmental Goods and Services* (Winnipeg: IISD, 2009), www.iisd.org/pdf/2009/bali_2_copenhagen_egs.pdf.

102. Sachs and Reid, "Investments Toward Sustainable Development," 1002.

103. This paragraph has been adapted from Pamela S. Chasek, "Sustainable Development."

Chapter 7—The Future of Global Environmental Politics

1. United Nations Environment Programme (UNEP), *GEO 5: Global Environmental Outlook: Environment for the Future We Want* (Nairobi: UNEP, 2012).

2. Pamela S. Chasek and Lynn Wagner, "An Insider's Guide to Multilateral Environmental Negotiations Since the Earth Summit," in *The Roads from Rio: Lessons Learned from Twenty Years of Multilateral Environmental Negotiations*, ed. Pamela S. Chasek and Lynn Wagner (New York: RFF, 2012), 1–2.

3. Maurice Strong, "Opening Statement to the Rio Summit (3 June 1992)," www.mauricestrong.net/index.php/opening-statement6.

4. Pamela S. Chasek, Lynn Wagner, and Peter Doran, "Lessons Learned on the Roads from Rio," in Chasek and Wagner, *The Roads from Rio*, 253.

5. Ibid.

6. Neil Carter, *The Politics of the Environment: Ideas, Activism, Policy*, 2nd ed. (Cambridge: Cambridge University Press, 2007), 272–273. For additional views on this argument, see Jagdish Bhagwati, *In Defense of Globalization* (Oxford: Oxford University Press, 2004); and Jennifer Clapp and Peter Dauvergne, *Paths to a Green World: The Political Economy of the Global Environment* (Cambridge, MA: MIT Press, 2005).

7. Carter, *The Politics of the Environment*, 273; and Ronnie D. Lipschutz, *Global Environmental Politics: Power, Perspectives, and Practice* (Washington, DC: Congressional Quarterly Press, 2004), 121.

8. Carter, *The Politics of the Environment*, 273; and Arthur Mol, *Globalization and Environmental Reform* (Cambridge, MA: MIT Press, 2003), 71–72, 126.

9. Adil Najam, David Runnalls, and Mark Halle, *Environment and Globalization: Five Propositions* (Winnipeg: IISD, 2007), 6–7, www.iisd.org/pdf/2007/trade_environment_globalization.pdf.

10. For more on this concept, see Arturo Escobar, "Construction Nature: Elements for a Post-Structuralist Political Ecology," *Futures* 28, no. 4 (1996): 325–343.

11. Chasek, Wagner, and Doran, "Lessons Learned on the Roads from Rio," 257.

12. Najam, Runnalls, and Halle, *Environment and Globalization*.

13. Ibid.

14. Lars-Göran Engfeldt, *From Stockholm to Johannesburg and Beyond* (Stockholm: Government Offices of Sweden, 2009).

15. Andrew Deutz, "Rio+20: What Does Success Look Like in the Post-Copenhagen Era?" *Guardian* (London), June 19, 2012.

16. Ibid.

17. Ibid.

18. Ibid.

19. For examples, see IISD's coverage of side events at Rio+20, 2012, www.iisd.ca/uncsd/rio20/enbots.

20. Chasek, Wagner, and Doran, "Lessons Learned on the Roads from Rio," 256.

21. As discussed in Chapter 3, HFCs were developed as a substitute for ozone-depleting CFCs. Widely used around the world, HFCs do not deplete stratospheric ozone but are powerful greenhouse gases.

22. Chasek, Wagner, and Doran, "Lessons Learned on the Roads from Rio," 259–260.

23. Richard Gardner, "The Role of the UN in Environmental Problems," in *World Eco-Crisis*, ed. David A. Kay and Eugene Skolnikoff (Madison: University of Wisconsin Press, 1972).

24. Pamela S. Chasek, *Earth Negotiations: Analyzing Thirty Years of Environmental Diplomacy* (Tokyo: United Nations University Press, 2001), 1–2.

25. Frank Biermann, "Reforming Global Environmental Governance: The Case for a United Nations Environment Organisation (UNEO)," Stakeholder Forum SDG2012 Paper, February 2012, www.ieg.earthsystemgovernance.org/sites/default/files/files/publications/Biermann_Reforming%20GEG%20The%20case%20for%20a%20UNEO.pdf.

26. Jacques Chirac, "Paris Call for Action," speech, Paris, February 6, 2007, www.ens-newswire.com/ens/feb2007/2007–02–06-inschi.html.

27. See "Environmental Governance," United Nations General Assembly Sixty-First Session, 2007, www.un.org/ga/president/61/follow-up/environmentalgovernance.shtml; "Environmental

Governance," United Nations General Assembly Sixty-Second Session, 2008, www.un.org/ga/president/62/issues/environmentalgovernance.shtml; "Environmental Governance," United Nations General Assembly Sixty-Third Session, 2009, www.un.org/ga/president/63/issues/environmentalgovernance.shtml.

28. Najam, Runnalls, and Halle, *Environment and Globalization*, 32. See also Adil Najam, Mihaela Papa, and Nadaa Taiyab, *Global Environmental Governance: A Reform Agenda* (Winnipeg: IISD, 2006).

29. James Gustave Speth, "Beyond Reform," *Our Planet* (February 2007): 16, www.unep.org/pdf/OurPlanet/OP_Feb07_GC24_en.pdf. For more on the World Environmental Organization proposal, see Daniel Esty, "The Case for a Global Environmental Organization," in *Managing the World Economy: Fifty Years After Bretton Woods*, ed. P. Kenen (Washington, DC: Institute for International Economics, 2004), 287–307; Frank Biermann, "The Rationale for a World Environment Organization," in *A World Environmental Organization: Solution or Threat for Effective Environmental Governance*, ed. Frank Biermann and Steffen Bauer (Aldershot, UK: Ashgate, 2005), 117–144.

30. A specialized agency is an autonomous organization linked to the UN through a special agreement, such as the Food and Agriculture Organization, the International Atomic Energy Agency, and the International Labor Organization, among others.

31. United Nations, *Report of the United Nations Conference on Sustainable Development* A/CONF.216/16 (New York: United Nations, 2012), 18.

32. United Nations, "The Future We Want," document A/66/L.56, July 24, 2012, www.uncsd2012.org/thefuturewewant.html. See paragraphs 87–90.

33. In December 2012, the UN General Assembly adopted resolution 67/213 implementing the recommendations from Rio+20. The first universal session of the UNEP Governing Council was held in February 2013.

34. "Summary of the United Nations Conference on Sustainable Development: 13–22 June 2012," *Earth Negotiations Bulletin* 27, no. 51 (June 25, 2012): 20, www.iisd.ca/download/pdf/enb2751e.pdf.

35. "Summary of the Nineteenth Session of the Commission on Sustainable Development: 2–14 May 2011," *Earth Negotiations Bulletin* 5, no. 304 (May 16, 2011): 13, www.iisd.ca/download/pdf/enb05304e.pdf.

36. United Nations, *Report of the United Nations Conference on Sustainable Development*, 16.

37. "Summary of the United Nations Conference on Sustainable Development."

38. Massoumeh Ebtekar, "Market Messengers," *Our Planet* (February 2007): 15, www.unep.org/pdf/OurPlanet/OP_Feb07_GC24_en.pdf.

39. Ministry of Foreign Affairs, Republic of Colombia, "Rio+20: Sustainable Development Goals (SDGs): A Proposal from the Governments of Colombia and Guatemala," 2012, www.uncsd2012.org/content/documents/colombiasdgs.pdf.

40. Ibid.

41. United Nations, *Report of the United Nations Conference on Sustainable Development*, 46–47.

42. For more information on the High-Level Panel, see www.post2015hlp.org. For more information on the UN System Task Team, see www.un.org/en/development/desa/policy/untaskteam_undf/index.shtml.

43. UN System Task Team on the Post-2015 Development Agenda, *Realizing the Future We Want for All: Report to the Secretary-General* (New York: United Nations, 2012), i.

44. United Nations, *Report of the United Nations Conference on Sustainable Development*, 47.

45. UN System Task Team on the Post-2015 Development Agenda, *Realizing the Future*, i.

46. Jason Hickel, "The World Bank and the Development Delusion," *Al Jazeera*, September 27, 2012.

47. International Institute for Applied Systems Analysis, "Nature Climate Change: Action by 2020 Key for Limiting Climate Change," press release, December 16, 2012, www.eurekalert .org/pub_releases/2012–12/iifa-ncc121312.php. See also Joeri Rogelj et al., "2020 Emissions Levels Required to Limit Warming to Below 2°C," *Nature Climate Change* 2012.

48. See, for example, David Adam, "ExxonMobil Continuing to Fund Climate Sceptic Groups, Records Show," *Guardian* (London), July 1, 2009; Union of Concerned Scientists (UCS), *A Climate of Corporate Control* (Cambridge, MA: UCS, 2012).

49. Carter, *The Politics of the Environment*, 268.

Index